JERICHO BEACH

and the
West Coast Flying Boat Stations

JERICHO BEACH

and the

West Coast Flying Boat Stations

by Christopher Weicht

JERICHO BEACH and the West Coast Flying Boat Stations

by Christopher Weicht

Cover painting: Michael Dean

Interior design and production: Pilot Press Ltd.

Christopher Weicht
Box 85
Chemainus, BC
V0R 1K0

Canadian Cataloguing in Publication Data

Weicht, Christopher, 1935-
Jericho Beach and the West Coast flying boat stations

Includes bibliographical references and index
ISBN 0-9681158-0-2

1. Canada. RCAF Station (Jericho Beach, B.C.) – History. 2. Aeronautics, Military – British Columbia – History. 3. Air bases – British Columbia – Pacific Coast – History. I. Title.
UG635.C22J47 1997 358.4'131'0971 C97-910030-5

First Printing, February, 1997
Second Printing, September, 1997

In 1995 the author, Chris Weicht, commissioned Michael Dean to create an original watercolour for the cover of Jericho Beach and the West Coast Flying Boat Stations. Dean based his work on a National Archives of Canada photograph (PA 133584) which depicts Curtiss HS-2L, G-CYGA, on the slipway at Jericho Beach on January 6, 1925.
The original watercolour is now part of the British Columbia Aviation Heritage Collection initiated by West Coast Aviator Magazine and generously sponsored by corporations and individuals from within the British Columbia aviation community. A collection of twelve paintings, destined to become a permanent display in the gallery area of Vancouver International Terminal, will be a visual reminder of our rich British Columbia aviation heritage.

The author gratefully acknowledges the support received from the Air Force Heritage Fund, Air Command Headquarters Westwin, Manitoba.

Printed and bound in Canada by Morriss Printing Company Ltd. Victoria, B.C.

JERICHO BEACH

and the West Coast Flying Boat Stations

ACKNOWLEDGMENTS

It has taken over two years to bring this publication to fruition. Had I known the complexities of the project, I may have had serious doubts about my ability to complete the task. But, once started, it became something I could not leave alone and I found myself engulfed in a quest to record this important period of British Columbia's aviation history. However, the main source of continued motivation came from the former airmen and airwomen of all ranks and positions who contacted me with pictures and stories of a period in their lives, half a century past, that I suspect was a highly memorable time for all of them.

To each of you: those letters and phone calls fired me with your irresistible enthusiasm and put life into the book. I am grateful for your support, for trusting me with your memories and your photographs. Now, knowing something about you, and what you accomplished, I salute your valour and take courage from your personal dignity, your humour and your allegiance to "Per Ardua Ad Astra":

Robert Baribeault, Harry Bryant, Paddy Burke (via son Brian Burke), W.O. Cameron, Thomas Colbeck, Ted Coombes, Bill Coulter, Alex Crombie, Thomas Furlong, Harry Galbraith, William Fawcett Hill, Rusty Hopper, W.N. Hoye, Jack Hunter, McGregor Knight, Guy LaRamée, Cy Luce, Jack McMahon, Louis McPhee, Lock Madill, George Maude, J.H.Palmer (via son Tom and daughter, Dot), Arthur Parry, Art Perry, Bill Penny, Allan Sinclair, Eric Stofer, Rev.G.E.Taylor, Evelyn Timpe, George Williamson.

I appreciate the extra help given to me by several of the airmen who were there: George Williamson, who was still flying commercially until the 1980s, filled in many gaps for me; George Maude, who was in the RCAF Marine Squadron, was a goldmine of information on the era and gave me unrestricted access to his carefully organized personal "archives"; Ted Coombes and Harry Bryant gave generously of their time and allowed me to conduct tape recorded interviews.

This book owes its physical existence to great teamwork: Jack Schofield, Editor of West Coast Aviator Magazine, a ready and reliable resource of encouragement and assistance for the project, which reached a printable state due to the pre-press expertise and patience of the magazine's producer, Danielle Letourneau and Karen Dietz, my sister-in-law, whose sharp eye for inconsistency and error was a major contribution to the final edit of the manuscript. However, without the partnership of my wife, Christine, there would be no book to involve anyone in. She has worked with me throughout the entire project, transcribing my hieroglyphic handwriting, editing the material and assisting me to shape the book.

ACKNOWLEDGMENTS

Next, I want to thank Lieutenant-Colonel Paul Crober, C.D., Chief of Staff Land Forces Western Area, and former Commanding Officer of Vancouver Detachment CFB Chilliwack. He moved mountains to make this project a reality, and arranged for me to spend ten days in Ottawa at the Directorate of History DND, where (then Senior Research Officer) Dr. Carl Christie's ever-diminishing staff was most helpful. And Tim Dube, Military Archivist at the National Archives of Canada, also deserves a vote of thanks for his staff's assistance. These knowledgeable people are the "roadmap into the vault" and without their efforts I would have had a very frustrating time tracking down information.

The Director of the National Aviation Museum in Ottawa, Fred Short, gave his encouragement to the project and arranged an introduction to Major Bill March, Senior Staff Officer, Air Force Heritage and History at Air Command Headquarters in Westwin, Manitoba. The assistance and all-round enthusiastic support I have received from Major March has been instrumental in the successful completion of this project.

Many others have contributed to the undertaking and also deserve thanks:

The excellent photo reproduction work by the staff of 19 Wing Photographic Unit, CFB Comox, Sgt H. Fraser, Cpl M. Tsagatakis, Cpl J.Manard, Cpl D. McIntyre;

Major Scott McLain, CFB Masset lent me his station's records of the RCAF presence in the Queen Charlotte Islands during World War Two;

Jerry Vernon, a tireless, very helpful, and extremely knowledgeable aviation historian, always answered his phone - even when he knew it was me;

The curator of the Comox Air Force Museum, Corky Hanson, and his wife Shirley;

Prince Rupert Archivist Barb Sheppard;

Carl Vincent allowed me to use material from his excellent work on the Blackburn Shark aircraft;

Well-known BC artist Michael Dean, who lives in Ladysmith, created a superb rendition of an HS-2L at Jericho Beach for the cover of the book;

Paddy Gardner provided information on the RCAF Deltas and gave permission to use his line drawings;

Authors Eric Stofer and his brother Ken, were very generous with their information and photographs;

The project really got off the ground due to the support of Airman Fred Warrant, my Stepdad, and another former Airman, Laurie Winters, who came up with a generous solution to our computer and printer problems;

Ingwald Wikene, a former Jericho airman now with the BC Museum of Flight and Transportation;

Steve King, a good friend, and a fellow pilot, donated his time to take current aerial photographs of what is left at Jericho Beach in late 1996;

and both Christine and I owe thanks to our friend, Maureen Wilson, whose computer skills have come to our rescue on several occasions - from the chaos of my handwritten lists, she created order in the Appendix.

Please, read on and enjoy the fruit of our labour.

Chris

ABBREVIATIONS

ABC-22	Joint Canadian-United States Defence Plan No. 2, 1941
AC	Army Cooperation Squadron
a/c	aircraft
AC1	Aircraftman First Class
AC2	Aircraftman Second Class
A/C	Air Commodore
ACAS	Assistant Chief of Air Staff
A/C/M	Air Chief Marshal
ADC	Aircraft Detection Corps
ADJ	Adjutant
AFC	Air Force Cross
AFHQ	Air Force Headquarters (RCAF)
A/M	Air Marshal
AOC	air officer commanding
A/S	anti-submarine
ASR	Air Sea Rescue
ASW	anti-submarine warfare
A/V/M	Air Vice-Marshal
AWOL	absent without leave
BCATP	British Commonwealth Air Training Program
BR	Bomber Reconnaissance Squadron (anti-submarine)
BCRD	British Columbia Reconnaissance Detachment
CAC	Coast Artillery Squadron
CAF	Canadian Air Force (1920-1924)
CAFA	Canadian Air Force Association
CAS	chief of the air staff
Cat "A"	catagory aircraft accident: a write off
Cat "B"	catagory aircraft accident: major, repairable at depot
Cat "C"	catagory aircraft accident: major, repairable at Unit
Cat "D"	catagory aircraft accident: minor, repairable at Unit
CFRC	Canadian Forces Recruiting Centre
CFS	Canadian Forces Station
CFTSD	Canadian Forces Technical Service Detachment
CGS	chief of the general staff (Canadian Army)
CMU	Construction and Maintenance Unit
CinC	commander in chief
CO	commanding officer
Col	Colonel
Com	communcations
Cpl	Corporal
CV	Canadian Vickers
CWAC	Canadian Womens Army Corps
CWC	Cabinet War Committee (Canada)
DAS	Director of Air Staff
DCAS	Deputy Chief of the Air Staff
DCGAO	Directorate of Civil Government Air Operations
DET	Detachment
DF	direction finding
DFC	Distinguished Flying Cross
DFM	Distinguished Flying Medal
DM	deputy minister
DND	Department of National Defence
DOT	Department of Transportation
DR	dead reckoning
DRO	Daily Routine Orders
DSO	Distinguished Service Order
EAC	Eastern Air Command (RCAF)
EFTS	Elementary Flying Training School
Eng	engineer
ETA	estimated time of arrival
F	Fighter Squadron
FB	Flying Boat Squadron
FE	Flight Engineer
F/L	Flight Lieutenant
F/O	Flying Officer
F/Sgt	Flight Sergeant
FTS	Flying Training School
G/C	Group Captain
GMT	Greenwich Mean Time
GP	General Purpose Squadron
GR	General Reconnaissance Squadron
GVRD	Greater Vancouver Regional District
HF	high frequency
HF/DF	high frequency direction finding
HMS	His Majesty's Ship
HMCS	His Majesty's Canadian Ship
HWE	Home War Establishment
ICAO	International Civil Aviation Organization
IG	inspector general
JAG	judge advocate general
JCS	Joint Chiefs of Staff (United States)
LAC	Leading Aircraftman
LCol	Lieutenant-Colonel
LFWA	Land Force Western Area
Lt	Lieutenant
Maj	Major
MARPAC	Maritime Pacific Command
MC	Military Cross
MD	Military District
MO	medical officer
MED	medical
MP	Member of Parliament
MT	motor transport
MTB	motor torpedo boat
NAC	National Archives of Canada
Nav	Navigator
NCO	Non-Commissioned Officer
NDHQ	National Defence Headquarters, Ottawa
NORAD	North American Air Defence Command
NPF	Non-Permanent Force (RCAF)

ABBREVIATIONS

NRC	National Research Council
NWAC	North West Air Command
OBE	Order of the British Empire
obs	observer
OC	officer commanding
OIC	officer in charge
OTS	Operational Training Squadron
OTU	Operational Training Unit
PAC	Public Archives Canada
PC	order-in-council
PDSIU	Pacific Detachment Special Investigative Unit
PF	Permanent Force
PJBD	Canada-United States Permanent Joint Board On Defence
P/O	Pilot Officer
QM	Quarter Master
QMG	Quarter Master General
RAF	Royal Air Force
RCAF	Royal Canadian Air Force
RCCS	Royal Canadian Corps of Signals
RCMP	Royal Canadian Mounted Police
RCN	Royal Canadian Navy
RCNAS	Royal Canadian Naval Air Service
RDF	radar direction finding
RFC	Royal Flying Corps
RN	Royal Navy
RNAF	Royal Norwegian Air Force
RNAS	Royal Naval Air Service
RNNAF	Royal Norwegian Naval Air Force
RO	radio officer or radio operator
SAO	senior air officer
SAR	Search and Rescue
SASO	senior air staff officer
SFTS	Service Flying Training School
Sgt	Sergeant
Standard Pilot	Pilot with incomplete training assigned to guard duty, etc
S/L	Squadron Leader
SOS	struck off strength
Sqn	Squadron
SSgt	Staff Sergeant
TB	Torpedo Bomber Squadron
TOS	taken on strength
u/s	unserviceable
u/s a/c	unserviceable aircraft
USAAC	United States Army Air Corps
USN	United States Navy
USS	United States Ship
USSR	Union of Soviet Socialist Republics
VAN DET	Vancouver Detachment Canadian Forces Base Chilliwack
WAC	Western Air Command (RCAF)
WAG	wireless air gunner/wireless operator
W/C	Wing Commander
W/D	Women's Division
W01	Warrant Officer First Class
W02	Warrant Officer Second Class
W/T	wireless telegraphy
YMCA	Young Men's Christian Association
Z	Greenwich Mean Time (Zulu time)

PHOTO CREDITS

BCMFT	British Columbia Museum of Flight & Transportation, Langley, BC
Baribeault	Robert Baribeault, Trois Rivieres, Quebec
Burke	Brian Burke, Atlin, BC
CFB Comox Rowe Library	Geoffrey A. Rowe Library, Comox, BC
Colbeck	Thomas Colbeck, Burnaby, BC
Coombes	Ted Coombes, Salt Spring Island, BC
Coulter	Bill Coulter, Summerland, BC
Crombie	Alex Crombie, Trail, BC
DND	Department of National Defence, via Air Command Heritage & History, Westwin, Manitoba
D/Hist	Directorate of History, DND, Ottawa
Driscoll	Robert Driscoll, Comox, BC
Ellis	via Frank H. Ellis
Furlong	Thomas Furlong, Vancouver, BC
Galbraith	Harry Galbraith, Moncton, NB
Gilbert	via Walter E. Gilbert
Hunter	Jack Hunter, Thornhill, Ontario
Knight	McGregor Easson Knight, Honolulu, Hawaii
LaRamée	Guy LaRamée, Inverness, NS
Lord	Fred M. Lord, via Bruce Lord, Vancouver, BC
McPhee	Louis McPhee, Sidney, BC
Madill	Lock Madill, White Rock, BC
Masset	Canadian Forces Station, Masset, Queen Charlotte Islands, BC
Maude	George Maude, Sidney, BC
NAC	National Archives of Canada, Ottawa, Ontario
PRA	Prince Rupert City & Regional Archives
Palmer	Tom Palmer, Victoria, BC
Parry	Art Parry, Islington, Ontario
Schofield	Jack Schofield, Sidney, BC
Stofer	Eric Stofer, Victoria, BC
Taylor	Reverend G.E. Taylor, Pender Island, BC
VPL	Vancouver Public Library, Vancouver, BC
White	Elwood White, Shawnigan Lake, BC

TABLE OF CONTENTS

FOREWORD

The history of Canadian military aviation is rich with topics which have yet to be explored. One of these areas which "begged" for further study was the role played by the Air Force on Canada's west coast during the inter-war period. Fortunately, Chris Weicht, with the publication of "Jericho Beach and the West Coast Flying Stations", has filled in this gap in Air Force history.

Concentrating primarily on the history of the Air Station at Jericho Beach, the author explores the unique circumstances that drove flying boat operations on the west coast. He chronicles the activities conducted by the fledgling Canadian Air Force, and, after 1 April 1924, the permanent Royal Canadian Air Force. The picture he weaves is one where a handful of men, in a few outdated and underpowered machines, establish a legacy of perseverance, ingenuity and dedication undertaking missions which would not be out of place in today's headlines. Among the first in the world to fly such missions as fisheries, forestry and anti-narcotic patrols, these individuals provided peace-time support for Canada while still maintaining a military capability that would prove invaluable during the Second World War. In effect, they "paved the way" for the multi-role service which our Air Force is expected to provide for the nation into the 21st century.

Chris Weicht traces the story of the west coast flying boat stations through peace and war, bringing to life an exciting part of our history. It is, however, much more than a history of places; it also deals with the aircraft, the pilots who flew them and the men and women who supported these operations. As such, the book will be of interest to those with a desire to delve deeper into this aspect of our Canadian aviation heritage.

October, 1996

A.M. DeQuetteville
Lieutenant-General
Commander
Air Command

PREFACE: GENESIS

My attachment to Jericho Beach began in my early teens. I joined 531 Squadron Royal Canadian Air Cadets at New Westminster, and, in company with a number of other "sprogs" of assorted sizes and shapes, I was dispatched to RCAF Jericho Beach to be issued a uniform. Ill-fitting though it was, once that uniform was buttoned up over my awkward length I was a new man, purpose-filled, patriotic, and proud.

A few years later I enlisted in the RCAF Reserve unit and was able to visit the hallowed Air Force halls at Jericho Beach on many occasions. I had little interest then in the history of this venerable establishment, but the impressions were tucked away in the recesses of my young mind for a later rediscovery.

Many, many years later I took a position as the Chief Pilot and Operations Manager for a company that was in the process of developing a Native-owned airline, and the job required a temporary move up the west coast to Bella Bella. On the Shearwater side of Denny Island I discovered intriguing evidence of wartime activity.

The mouldering, decrepit, and in most cases, abandoned buildings of an RCAF Flying Boat Station piqued my curiosity. The one remaining hangar had been "pre-empted" by a local shipyard as a dry repair facility; the massive concrete slipway provided a handy means to launch and retrieve customers' boats. A second concrete ramp was always in use by visiting amphibious aircraft: Grumman Goose, Cessna 206, De Havilland Beaver, and a small logging company operated a dryland log-sort on the large concrete pad at the top of the ramp. The airmen's barracks, in a very poor state of repair, was used occasionally by transients, but the base hospital building was well maintained and served as a schoolhouse for the local children.

I also kept coming across intact sections of what I determined must have been a narrow, corrugated roadway made out of wooden boards. At one time it must have tracked uninterrupted through the seemingly endless knarled and stunted cedar growth, crossing the muskeg-like floor of the forested island to end at an abandoned BC Packers fish cannery. Here I found another group of buildings and elevated docks; obviously in their last stages of practical use in this sodden west coast climate.

Very few of the local residents had any detailed knowledge of the bits and pieces of history decaying around them, and even fewer had any interest in the story that these "artifacts" had to tell. The entire image of an almost forgotten history was presided over by the watchful eye of the Raven.

That winter in Bella Bella the fading echo of something that I as yet did not fully understand prompted me to begin a journal in which I recorded what I saw, and what I felt. Engrossed in my self-appointed record-keeping, I shortened the length of the long, stormy evenings and gradually developed an uncanny sense of kinship with the men who had been stationed on this remote island almost forty-five years before.

Late in 1994 a newspaper article prophesying the closure of the last vestiges of a military presence at Jericho Beach rekindled my interest in the former Air Station. I contacted the Commanding Officer at the Army facility at Jericho, Major Paul Crowber, CD, who was enthusiastic about my suggestion of a written history of the Vancouver Station and offered any assistance, short of funding, that he and his staff could provide.

PREFACE: GENESIS

Through the LEGION and the AIRFORCE magazines I addressed an appeal to airmen who had been stationed at Jericho Beach Air Station, as well as to the airmen who had manned the RCAF Flying Boat Stations on the west coast; I needed their help in my quest to record this period of aviation history. The results were phenomenal. A number of the former airmen telephoned to talk about the time they had spent with Flying Boats on British Columbia's west coast. Letters arrived from across Canada and the United States, and even Hawaii, containing hundreds of precious photographs, mementoes, and wonderful anecdotal stories. For most of these men it was a "time of a lifetime" and their memories infused the drab palette of recorded history with living colour, and reinstated the human element in the historical data I was gathering.

Viewed in isolation, every event is historical data, but when the data is arranged in sequence and connected by an examination of cause and effect it becomes history; as traceable as footprints in wet cement; the stuff we should carefully analyze, applying the conclusions wisely to plan our future. Recent Federal government decisions regarding the downsizing of Canada's military forces lead me to believe that we have not done our history homework. Once again we are caught up in the old economy-driven mania that supports the irrational theory that destruction creates efficiency.

Seventy-five years, and billions of taxpayers' dollars, have gone into building the valuable resource of our military forces: an established strength of proud and productive men and women whose wealth of experience cannot easily be replaced. In British Columbia we have already lost a big chunk of this investment, and we are about to lose more with the departure of Land Forces personnel who are being displaced as, one by one, the remaining buildings at Jericho Beach are razed. Once the "battle for Jericho" is over and development of the land, in whatever form, is complete, the "footprints" of the past will be totally obliterated.

Ironic? I doubt Major MacLaurin, Air Commodore MacLeod or Air Vice-Marshal Godfrey would see it that way.

Two years ago, when I began researching the history of Jericho Beach and the West Coast Flying Boat Stations, I discovered the unswerving focus and enthusiasm of the early British Columbian Air Force pioneers and the Officers and Airmen who joined them in peacetime and war. Manning the Flying Boat Stations, I found a large group of tenacious, loyal Canadians who carried on, under difficult conditions, doing the job that needed to be done.

I can only hope that the "life and times" that I have attempted to record in this book meet the hopes and expectations of the men who lived them.

Chris Weicht - November, 1996

1921 DND

The Changing Face of Jericho Beach

1924 DND

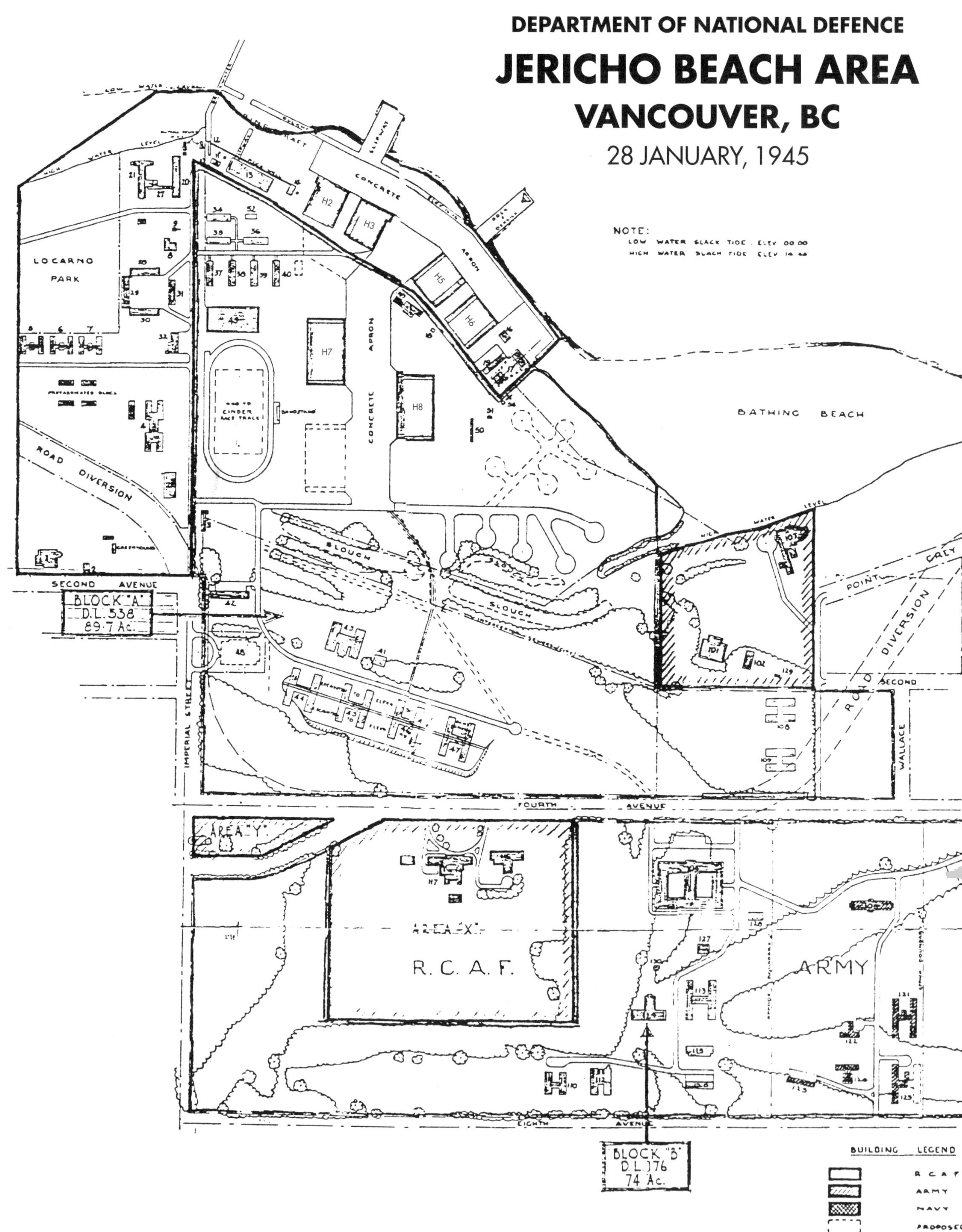
DEPARTMENT OF NATIONAL DEFENCE
JERICHO BEACH AREA
VANCOUVER, BC
28 JANUARY, 1945
NOTE:
LOW WATER SLACK TIDE . ELEV 00.00
HIGH WATER SLACK TIDE . ELEV 14.44
LOCARNO PARK
CONCRETE
APRON
SLIPWAY
H2
H3
H5
H6
H7
H8
CINDER RACE TRACK
BANDSTAND
CONCRETE APRON
BATHING BEACH
ROAD DIVERSION
SLOUGH
SECOND AVENUE
BLOCK "A"
D.L. 538
89.7 Ac.
IMPERIAL STREET
POINT GREY
ROAD DIVERSION
SECOND
WALLACE
FOURTH AVENUE
AREA "Y"
AREA "X"
R. C. A. F.
ARMY
EIGHTH AVENUE
BLOCK "B"
D.L. 176
74 Ac.
BUILDING LEGEND
R.C.A.F.
ARMY
NAVY
PROPOSED

R.C.A.F. STATION & No. 3 R.D.
LEGEND

H2	HANGAR	
H3	HANGAR	
H5	HANGAR	
H6	HANGAR	
H7	DOUBLE SEAPLANE HANGAR	
H8	DOUBLE SEAPLANE HANGAR	
1	OFFICERS MESS	W.A.C.
2	GARAGE	
3	GUARD ROOM & POST OFFICE	W.A.C.
4	N.C.O.'s QUARTERS	
5	W.D. QUARTERS	W.A.C.
6	W.D. QUARTERS	W.A.C.
7	W.C. CANTEEN	W.A.C.
8	SECURITY GUARD	
9	SEWAGE PUMP HOUSE	(CITY)
10	SENTRY	
11	MAGAZINES	
12	MARINE STORES	
13	STORES & MARINE BUILDING	
14	GASOLINE STORAGE & PUMP HOUSE	
15		
16	ENGINE TEST HOUSE	
17	25 YD RANGE	
18	PHOTOGRAPHIC BUILDING	
19	W&B MAINTENANCE (WAS GARAGE S32-25)S-32-43	
20	HOSPITAL (SEE #27) (WAS HEADQUARTERS & OPER)	
21	HOSPITAL (SEE #27) (WAS SICK QUARTERS)	
22	RECREATION HALL	
23		
24		
25	CENTRAL HEATING PLANT	
26		
27	ADDITION TO HOSPITAL (SEE #20 & 21)	
28	GARAGE	
29	GARAGE	
30	GARAGE	
31	WORKSHOP (REV. DWG. NO J.B. 22-4-91)	
32	FIRE HALL	
33		
34	CLOTHING STORE	
35	AIRSCREW REPAIR	
36	WELDING SHOP	
37	W/T REPAIR	
38	ARMAMENT	
39	ENGINE REPAIR	
40	ENGINE REPAIR	
41	CENTRAL HEATING PLANT	
42	ADMINSTRATION BUILDING	
43	O.R. MESS	(720)
44	W.D. QUARTERS	
45	O.R. QUARTERS	(380)
46	O.R. QUARTERS	(380)
47	O.R. QUARTERS	(380)
48	RECREATION HALL	
49	STORES BUILDING	
50	COAL STORAGE COMPOUND	
51	INCINERATOR	
52	BATTERY CHARGING ROOM	
53	PIGEON LOFT	
54	GUN PROOFING RANGE	

JOINT SERVICES HEADQUARTERS
LEGEND

101	OPERATIONS BUILDING	
102	W/T BUILDINGS	
103	NAVY OPERATIONS ADMINISTRATION	
104	R.C.A.F. OPERATIONS ADMINISTRATION	
105	ARMY OPERATIONS ADMINISTRATION	
106		
107	OFFICERS MESS	
108	OFFICERS QUARTERS	(88)
109	OFFICERS QUARTERS	(88)
110	N.C.O.'s QUARTERS	(96)
111		
112	N.C.O.'s MESS	(150)
113	O.R. QUARTERS	(304)
114	O.R. MESS	(350)
115	O.R. CANTEEN	
116	W.D. MESS	(350)
117	W.D. QUARTERS	
118		
119		
120	GARAGE (R.C.A.F.) (8 BAY & WORKSHOP)	
121	N.C.O.'s QUARTERS	(57)
122	N.C.O.'s MESS	(50)
123	O.R. QUARTERS	(152)
124	O.R. MESS	(150)
125	GARAGE (ARMY) (8 BAY & WORKSHOP)	
126	GARAGE (NAVY) (8 BAY & WORKSHOP)	
127	BOILER HOUSE	
128	CAMOUFLAGE BUILDING	
129	GENERATOR HOUSE	
130	INCINERATOR	

1943 DND

1943 DND

1944 DND

RCAF NCOs barracks (now youth hostel). Weicht Collection

Officers' Mess, RCAF Jericho Beach (former Spencer Estate). 1956. Weicht Collection

Former RCAF recreation hall. Weicht Collection

Front door, former Officers' Mess. Weicht Collection

1996 Weicht Collection

JERRY'S COVE - The Historical Setting

1792: In the month of June a group of Native Indians are gathering berries at the mouth of a fresh-water creek that empties into a crescent-shaped cove. They watch in amazement as, slowly and gracefully, like large clouds, several sailing ships float into the bay. The ships drop anchor, and strange men row ashore in long boats to take fresh water from the creek.

One of the ships is the Royal Navy vessel HMS Discovery, under the command of Captain George Vancouver. Vancouver is impressed with the giant trees that crowd to the shoreline of this glorious natural harbour, which he names English Bay. And he is pleased to find that here the Native people are not as openly hostile as some of the other tribes he has encountered in his voyage of discovery in the new world.

The Native people do not think their world is "new"; many of their own people have gone before them, and their brave deeds are recounted from one generation to the next. They are Musqueam Indians, and they are the first known human inhabitants of the English Bay area.

1859: The Royal Navy survey vessel, the HMS Plumper, under the command of Captain G.M. Richards and Second Master D. Pender, chart the waters of English Bay and Burrard Inlet and make the first diagram of the coastline, showing the shape of the bay, the Inlet, and Vancouver Harbour. On the south shore of English Bay, near the mouth of a fresh-water creek, they survey a large tract of 155 acres and claim it as an Admiralty Reserve. Except for the occasional use of the creek to replenish the fresh water supply on board some of their ships, the Royal Navy never use the site.

1860: Land laws are established giving settlers the right, by pre-emption, to lay claim to the tracts of land they are occupying. The unsurveyed boundaries of each claim are guarded jealously by each pre-emptor. After several years, conflicts arise over the exact location of the boundaries between neighbouring properties.

John Morton pre-empts land that is destined to become the west end of the future city of Vancouver. According to his neighbour, Robert Burnaby, Morton's claim is encroaching on the boundaries of Burnaby's claim, and Morton seeks the professional advice of Judge Mathew Baillie Begbie. Begbie tells Morton to ignore Burnaby's complaints, and the dispute escalates. A precise survey is needed in order to avoid a "Hatfield vs MacCoy" situation.

1863: Colonel R.C. Moody instructs the Royal Engineers to conduct a survey of Burrard Inlet to report on all recent pre-emptions and record property boundaries. The dispute between Burnaby and Morton is settled peaceably. The area now known as Stanley Park is recorded as a Military Reserve, and a Naval Reserve is officially recorded on English Bay on land now known as Jericho. The survey also shows a number of interesting local landmarks; Siwash Rock is marked as "large rock about 30 feet high", and the Capilano River is identified as "a large river".

JERRY'S COVE: The Historical Setting

1864: Jeremiah Roger, an enterprising logger with no knowledge of the Royal Navy or interest in knowing about its land claim, enters into a relationship with the Hastings Mill Company in False Creek and begins a profitable business logging the 155 acre Naval Reserve. He calls his operation Jerry And Company and his logging site is well known locally as Jerry's Cove. The fellows over at the mill refer to him as old "Jerry-Co".

1877: additional lots surrounding the original Naval Reserve on English Bay are registered as a Military Reserve and appear on a map entitled "Portion of New Westminster District, 1877". The Crown, in the right of British Columbia, holds title to these government reserves.

1890: Dr. D. Bell-Irving, G.A. Hanky, T.S.C. Sanders, H. Hulbert, MacIver Campbell and other prominent Vancouver citizens decide to build a Country Club on the outskirts of their flourishing city. They choose the site on English Bay known as Jerry's Cove and arrange a lease from the Crown. It is decided to carry on local tradition and name the new venture the Jericho Golf and Country Club. The sand-constructed fairways and greens stand up to four years of sea-side play before a particularly wild storm sweeps them away.

1899: Five years after the storm the Club returns, determined to conquer the elements by building a dyke to protect their investment. They rebuild a 9 hole golf course, and continue to develop their playground: tennis, badminton and squash courts, and bowling and croquet lawns. By 1920 the Club has an elegant clubhouse and a well-designed 18 hole golf course.

1919: To the dismay of the Country Club membership, The Air Board selects the Naval Reserve property on English Bay to build a west coast Air Station.This property is connected to, and surrounded by, the land occupied by the Country Club. Many Club members say "there goes the neighbourhood" and try to block Air Board efforts to obtain use of the property.

1920: A Provincial grant authorizes the Air Board's use of lot L5098 Group (1) New Westminster - a strip of shore property 200 feet by 1200 feet: "for the use of the Canadian Air Board so long as required and used for the purpose of the said board only"; construction of the Jericho Beach Air Station is underway.

1996: The Musqueam Native Band would like their land back.

JERICHO BEACH

and the West Coast Flying Boat Stations

SIC ITUR AD ASTRA

"This Is The Way To The Stars"

chapter one

"THROUGH ADVERSITY TO THE STARS"

The establishment of Jericho Beach Air Station at Vancouver in 1920 brought official endorsement to an aviation presence in British Columbia, a presence represented by a complement of only three officer pilots and twenty-five men in technical and administrative capacities. This small but dedicated and industrious group of Airmen pursued their dream of a Canadian Air Force, nurturing it from Air Board to RCAF, and passing on their legacy to present day Airmen.

Pioneers

But, to begin at the beginning, interest in aviation in Canada developed slowly. It was not until 1909 that the first official flight in Canada took place at Baddeck, Nova Scotia. On February 23, John McCurdy left the frozen surface of Bras d'Or Lake in a pioneer machine built in 1908 by the Aerial Experiment Association, an association founded by Dr. Alexander Graham Bell. McCurdy flew the SILVER DART on a steady course above the Lake for over half a mile, recording the first heavier-than-air flight in Canada. Aviation history later officially recognized McCurdy's achievement as "the first controlled flight of an airplane by a British subject at any point in the British Commonwealth".

FEDERATION AERONAUTIQUE INTERNATIONALE

AERO CLUB OF AMERICA

No. 110

The above-named Club, recognized by the Federation Aeronautique Internationale, as the governing authority for the United States of America, certifies that

W. M. Stark

born 2 day of Nov 1884

having fulfilled all the conditions required by the Federation Aeronautique Internationale, is hereby licensed as Aviator.

Dated April 10 1912

V. President.

Secretary.

Signature of Licensee: W M Stark

Aviator certificate No. 110 issued to W.M. (Billy) Stark, April 10, 1912. via Frank H. Ellis.

Five years later, at the outbreak of World War I, Canada had only two licensed pilots: John A.D. McCurdy from eastern Canada, and William (Billy) M. Stark in the west. McCurdy held Aviation Pilot certificate number 18, issued to him by the Aero Club of America on October 5, 1910. The mechanically inclined Stark decided to take up flying in 1911, and became the proud owner of certificate number 110 on April 10, 1912. Although he earned his flying certificate four years after McCurdy, Stark soon began to make significant contributions to flying in British Columbia.

The Curtiss Aviation School, operating at North Island near San Diego, California, accepted Billy Stark's application for flight training. Early in 1912 he began instruction under Glenn Curtiss, who was impressed with his new student's grasp of the principles of flight. Stark's mechanical ability certainly gave him a keener understanding of the aircraft, but his natural talent for flying quickly led to a successful flight examination, and graduation on March 22, 1912. Billy immediately purchased a 75 h.p. Curtiss Biplane for $5,500 and shipped it home with him to Vancouver.

The exciting sport of exhibition flying had caught Stark's attention and the twenty-eight year old aviator wasted no time in assembling the biplane and launching his career. On April 20, 1912, Stark was ready for his first exhibition which he held on the outskirts of Vancouver at Minoru Park race track on Lulu Island. The large crowd that made its way out to the race track was rewarded with breath-taking stunts which had never been seen on the west coast before.

Four days later, on April 24, James Hewitt, the sports editor of the Vancouver Daily Province, settled himself on a make-shift seat on the wing of Stark's biplane, took a firm hold on the struts, and accompanied Stark on an eight minute flight. It was the first time in western Canada that two people had flown in one plane. When Stark completed the circuit, his wife was waiting to take Hewitt's

top; Billy Stark takes Vancouver Province sports editor James Hewitt for flight, April 24, 1912. via Frank H. Ellis.

above; Mrs. Olive Stark became Canada's first woman air passenger, April 24, 1912. via Frank H. Ellis.

below; Stark's Curtiss mounted on a single pontoon by Vancouver's VanDyke & Sons ship builders. via Frank H. Ellis.

place. Her six-minute flight also made aviation history: Olive Stark became the first woman in Canada to go aloft as a passenger.

In the summer of 1914 Billy Stark's fascination with flying "boats" earned him another western Canadian aviation "first". Stark commissioned a large pontoon from the Vancouver boat builders, Van Dyke & Sons, and his good friend William McMullen, one of Canada's first aircraft builders, worked with Stark to mount the Curtiss on the single float. On June 14, 1914, Stark, in his converted Curtiss, circled Stanley Park and thrilled bathers at English Bay by deftly setting the craft down on the water close to the shore. That summer afternoon the pontooned Curtiss, the first of its kind to be developed in western Canada, introduced Vancouver to the hydroplane.

Hopeful Aviators "Sign Up"

When England declared war on Germany on August 14, 1914, Canada was the first country to come to the mother country's aid. However, the Dominion of Canada lacked organized air power, military or civil, and the regular army had diminished to 3,000 officers and men plus an active militia of 47,000. Recruiting posts sprang up overnight and "signing up" consumed every young man's thoughts. Those who wanted to go overseas as pilots had no choice but to enlist in the regular Canadian military forces and hope to be among the fortunate chosen to be transferred for training to either the Royal Naval Air Service or the Royal Flying Corps.

By 1915 the RFC and the RNAS required that Canadians who wished to serve with them would only be considered for a commission if they could produce a certificate of flight training from the Royal Aero Club of Great Britain or the American Aero Club. The Canadian government, while acknowledging the need for a national flight training program, was not prepared to undertake the necessary financial responsibility. As an interim measure, the government agreed to pay selected pilots' training expenses and transportation overseas, on the understanding that the young men would join either the Royal Flying Corps or the Royal Naval Air Service.

Two private flying schools opened in Canada in 1915 to train flyers for war service: the Curtiss Aviation School near Toronto, and a Vancouver flying school located on Lulu Island. As word of government sponsorship spread, the schools were inundated with applications. The Curtiss "Flying" School began training in May 1915 with a carefully selected group of thirteen students. In a very short time the first ten graduates found themselves overseas as war pilots and the envy of hundreds of other aspiring pilots for whom flying school was not an option.

The Curtiss Aviation School was parented by the recently established Curtiss Aeroplanes & Motors Limited, a Canadian branch of the American based Curtiss Company. The Toronto plant, and Canada's first flying school, were under the able management of eastern aviation pioneer John McCurdy. One hundred and twenty-nine pilots graduated during the school's period of operation: May 1915 to December 1916.

On the west coast, in the summer of 1915, the enterprising Billy Stark inspired a group of Vancouver businessmen to attend a meeting to discuss the possibility of forming an aviation school that would train pilots for the Royal Flying Corps and the Royal Naval Air Service. From that meeting, the Aero Club of British Columbia was formed. Funds were provided by 27 supporters who contributed $100.00 each, and, in a gesture of corporate support, Imperial Oil Limited donated 200 gallons of gasoline and 20 gallons of oil.

As soon as funding allowed, the Club purchased Stark's Curtiss biplane and hired the airman as an instructor. Flight training began at the Minoru Park race track but Stark moved the operation to a field in near-by Steveston to gain a larger space for taxiing practice. After careful preparation of the ground, a hangar was constructed and training recommenced at the new Terra Nova Field.

H.O. Bell-Irving Senior, a founding director of the Aero Club of British Columbia, and one of the flying school's staunchest supporters, warned his fellow Club members that, in view of the Club's "shoestring" budget, one accident could spell the demise of their operation. As a successful business man he was keenly aware that relying on unpredictable donations would not sustain their venture.

In September 1915 Bell-Irving was able to take advantage of a visit to Vancouver by Canada's Governor General, Earl Connaught, and his Military Secretary, Lieutenant Colonel Stanton. Bell-Irving joined their train at Sicamous, and, while travelling into Vancouver, he discussed the flying school's potential and its future. This meeting, while it resulted in Bell-Irving being appointed as the unofficial Royal Flying Corps recruiting officer in British Columbia, did not produce any financial "wellsprings".

Just before the weather deteriorated at the end of November, the School's first two students took their flight examinations from Lieutenant Colonel C.J. Burke of the RFC. Not long after that, boggy field conditions prompted Stark to move the Curtiss to the Hoffar Brothers boat yard on Burrard Inlet. The Hoffar Brothers converted the aircraft to a seaplane, and, when the weather permitted, Stark continued training. It was during one of these training sessions that Bell-Irving's worst fears materialized.

On a dull, grey December day the aircraft struck a sodden, partially submerged log that hung in the murky water directly in the taxiing path of the Curtiss. Stark and his pupil took an unscheduled swim and the biplane was badly crippled. It was the end of training for the year, and possibly for the foreseeable future unless the Club's financial situation improved. At this juncture, Stark wisely severed his working relationship with the flying school.

The fortune of the Aero Club, and its neophyte military pilots, was near rock bottom. The financial plight of the students, still hopeful of graduating, was brought to the attention of the Commanding Officer of the 58th Heavy Battery of the 15th Field Brigade of the Royal Canadian Artillery. In December 1915 he agreed to take the flight students on strength, which gave the students pay and allowances to tide them over until the Aero Club straightened out its affairs. They were issued standard uniforms, with the exception of a small bronze badge which they wore on each lapel. Raised on the surface of the badge was a vertical propeller and a horizontal wing surrounded with the inscription 'THE BRITISH COLUMBIA AVIATION SCHOOL'.

The Tractor Biplane supplied to the B.C. Aviation School by the Hamilton Aero Manufacturing Company. via Frank H. Ellis.

The new name for the Aero Club's endeavour resulted from a complete reorganization. In an effort to generate more funds, the school was advertised as a non-profit, patriotic venture to train pilots for the Great War. Vancouver citizens were encouraged to purchase stocks, the money to go toward financing new aircraft on order from T.F. Hamilton, operator of premises on Vancouver's 4th Avenue as a branch of his Seattle, Washington based Hamilton Aero Manufacturing Company.

The difficulty of relying on donations to fund a project of this size, coupled with a second aircraft accident, sealed the fate of the Vancouver flying school. By the end of

1916 it had ceased operation. Well-schooled in ground instruction, but without officially graduating, the 15 charter pupils all moved on to serve with distinction in a branch of His Majesty's Services. In fact, over 22,000 Canadians served with the RFC, the RNAS and the RAF during World War I and 1,500 of these men lost their lives in the conflict.

It was not until 1917 that the Royal Flying Corps created its own training school in Canada. Aerodromes were established at Camp Borden and at Leaside, each of which accommodated a Wing. The British found the severe eastern winter made flight training very difficult, and Major Knight and Major McPherson of the Royal Engineers were sent to British Columbia to select two potential training sites for the RFC in western Canada. The engineers chose a 304 acre site at Ladner, and another 276 acres near Steveston on Lulu Island.

The Imperial Government representative, Lt. Col. C.G. Hoare, dispatched to inspect the properties, undervalued the "British Columbia idea", labelling it "a make-shift arrangement". In his correspondence with Brigadier General Charlton, Hoare was unintentionally patronizing in his disparaging remarks:

> *"British Columbia, on the whole, is bad for flying. If it were not for the necessity of having one Wing where climatic conditions are not so severe in Winter, and also for the necessity of stimulating interest in aviation in the West, I should not recommend having a Wing in British Columbia at all."*

Reluctantly, Hoare purchased the land, but shortly after construction began both sites were abandoned. The United States had entered the war, and the American and Canadian governments negotiated a reciprocal agreement that gave the RFC access to pilot training facilities in the United States. Arrangements were made to continue winter training at a location near the American city of Fort Worth, Texas.

Aviation after Armistice

When the Armistice was signed on November 11, 1918, the Canadian government was still putting off a decision to form a permanent peacetime Air Force; Canada offered its returning Airmen little hope for a career in aviation. As the Airmen came home to rebuild their lives, many of them simply went back to their former occupations and considered themselves fortunate to have survived their time in uniform. But a dedicated few had acquired a love of flight that inspired them to create ways of remaining in aviation. Many in this group were responsible for the birth, and the survival, of the Royal Canadian Air Force, and it is to these men that aviation in Canada owes its existence.

Even though the British Army Council suggested in 1915 that the Dominions organize their own air units to serve in the RFC, no action was taken until November 1918 when two Canadian squadrons were formed in England. By the time organization was underway the Armistice was signed. Similarly, the Royal Canadian Naval Air Service was formed late in the war in response to the need for anti-submarine patrols in the North Atlantic shipping lanes out of Halifax, Nova Scotia. Again the War ended just as operations began and the service was disbanded on December 5, 1918. The last member of the RCNAS was Major Claire C. MacLaurin, who remained on strength until December 10, 1919. As the sole member of the service, MacLaurin kept himself busy on inspection tours of Canada's only RCNAS air stations, at Dartmouth and Sydney, in Nova Scotia.

The Canadian government's decision to disband its two British-based Canadian Air Force Squadrons, and the Canadian Naval Air Service at home, indicated that there was no immediate future for military or civil aviation in this country. For those who lobbied in favour of forming a separate Canadian Air Force and a national aviation policy, the situation was more deeply frustrating given that aviation was not an item of any importance on Prime Minister Sir Robert Borden's agenda. His attention was occupied by international affairs, which took him out of the country for long periods of time. Without cohesive direction, his Cabinet floundered, and Parliament gave little support to aviation. Complicating the matter further, very few members of Parliament knew anything at all about the subject. In fact, Borden received the reports of the British Civil Aerial Transportation Committee in May, 1918, but did not act on them.

The Paris Peace Conference in 1919 pointed out the need for domestic legislation to guide national aeronautical development. The International Commission on Aerial Navigation convened in Paris to begin the process of arranging an international regulation system - a system that provided the framework for Canadian flying regulations which were adopted in 1920.

Before the war, flying was not regulated and was, in Canada, informally supervised by Canadian affiliates of the Federation Aeronautique International. In 1914, in response to the War Measures Act, barnstorming and stunt flying on the popular flying exhibition circuit, disappeared and all other flying activity was severely curtailed. Now the war was over, and the country was flooded with demobilized airmen eager to continue flying. And there were hundreds of war surplus Curtiss Canucks that could be had for a song. With no regulations governing the purchase - cash up front and no questions asked - many of the machines were snapped up by eager Canadian flyers.

Barnstorming and stunt flying resurfaced as an overnight sensation. The public still turned out in droves to see an aviator show off his prowess in the air, and gladly parted with their hard-earned money to show their appreciation of his often reckless courage. On many occasions stunt flyers were guilty of pushing their luck, and for many of them, judging by the escalating accident reports, their luck was running out. Mounting concern for the pilots' safety aloft, as well as concern for the safety of the citizens below them, increased pressure on the government to legislate aviation safety standards.

The accident rate increased at an alarming rate, yet the government had no idea how to regulate the persistent aviators, who made it very clear that they were going to continue to fly. In the meantime, the Aero Club of Canada announced, in February 1919, that the Royal Aero Club of England had authorized them to control aviation within the entire Dominion of Canada. The Canadian Club recognized the need for some form of control, but were overwhelmed by the magnitude of the mandate so grandly assigned to them by their parent club.

The Canadian directors fired off a letter of appeal to Cabinet in which they strongly urged the government to enact legislation to govern the country's flying activities. While they waited for the government to act, the Canadian Aero Club began issuing "aviator certificates" to returning officers of the Royal Air Force, and to anyone else who could pass the required flying test.

Sir Willoughby Gwatkin, the Chief of General Staff for the Department of Militia and Defence, summarized the government's lack of action:

> *"Everybody's business is nobody's business. Nearly every Department of State is concerned, but no one Department is charged with aviation."*

In order to fill this vacuum of responsibility, Gwatkin drafted an order-in-council in February 1919, proposing that the Department of Militia and Defence resume its wartime control of aviation and be permitted to establish an air board to supervise all aspects of aviation. Cabinet turned down his submission. It seemed that Gwatkin was marching a step ahead of the parade.

A year earlier Gwatkin spoke in favour of forming a Canadian Air Force after the War was over. He specifically commented on the need to form a separate identity for such a Canadian Flying Corps, and pointed out that it must be more that just another unit of the Militia. His long-sighted vision for the future of aviation in Canada encompassed a multitude of commercial uses that would assist the peacetime development of a strong Canadian economy.

Now, in early 1919, Gwatkin found that his outspoken views were endorsed by several well-placed public servants in both the federal and the provincial government: the Deputy Minister of Mines and Resources had considered using flying boats to transport geologists to remote locations; the forest industry supported the use of aircraft for fire detection and patrol; Geodetic Surveyors were interested in the benefits of aerial photography for mapping projects; and the International Boundary surveyors saw easier access to unsurveyed territory. The possibilities generated a lot of enthusiasm, but were not connected by a unified effort - aviation needed a champion.

Not one champion, but a forceful duo took up the cause of peacetime aviation: J.A. Wilson and Major Claire C. MacLaurin, two officials of the Department of Naval Service. MacLaurin, a 1915 graduate of the the Curtiss Flying School in Toronto, had served in the Royal Naval Air Service on coastal patrols in England. Still in wartime service, MacLaurin was appointed as a staff officer, first in Washington, and then Ottawa. It was here that he met Wilson, who had joined the Department of Naval Service in 1910, advancing to the position of assistant deputy minister. Both men served on the departmental committee which organized the Canadian Naval Air Service. Their individual wartime experiences brought them together in strong support of the unlimited uses of the aircraft, especially in the economic development of Canada's vast hinterland.

Wilson and MacLaurin each prepared several submissions to the government arguing in favour of a centralized, federally controlled air service, and they lobbied extensively within government circles. It may have been their membership in the established bureaucracy that gave their views additional weight, but their influence had a significant impact on the future of aviation in Canada.

From Air Board to Air Force

In March 1919, Wilson was asked to prepare legislation for Cabinet's consideration. Without hesitation, Wilson had a draft ready in two days. His submission included establishing an Air Board to take responsibility for forming and implementing general aviation policy and providing advice to the government on air defense. The last clause was unacceptable to the military service chiefs and the draft was modified to allow Air Board cooperation with the armed forces until the matter of a national defense policy was settled.

On April 29, 1919, after a lengthy and heated debate, Parliament passed its first postwar aviation bill: the Air Board Act. The Act, based on Wilson's draft, placed responsibility for aviation in the hands of a seven-member Air Board appointed by Cabinet, under Arthur Sifton as chairman and Colonel O.M. Biggar as vice-chairman. Wilson accepted the position of secretary, and two board positions were filled by representatives of the Militia and the Naval Services. Parliament's action gave Canada the distinction of being the first nation to enact legislative control over the whole realm of flight.

In theory, the responsibilities given to the Air Board were straightforward: to regulate aviation, construct air bases, manage aircraft and equipment, and regulate and operate air services. Using the British Air Ministry as a model, a division of authority created five main branches: Air Force; Civil Operations Branch; Licensing Branch for the control of Civil Aviation; Engineering and Equipment Branch; and an Administrative Branch for correspondence and finance.

The Air Board held its first meeting on the 25th of June, 1919. The pressing matter of a gift of surplus aircraft, offered by Great Britain at the beginning of the month, spurred the board to a decisive organization of their internal structure. After quickly putting their house in order, Air Board members immediately turned their attention to sorting out the confusion that now surrounded Great Britain's offer of a donation of surplus landplanes, seaplanes and flying boats. Differing political interpretations of the criteria for accepting the aircraft, and a lack of clear communication on the part of everyone involved, had already placed the "gift" in danger of disappearing in a bureaucratic stalemate.

The Canadian Overseas Ministry had initiated a selection of combat machines and trainers, based on the misconception that the British government would withdraw its offer if the aircraft were not used to develop a Canadian Air Force. By the time Biggar and Wilson became personally involved on behalf of the Air Board, the Canadian Ministry had broken off communication with the British Air Ministry pending a statement from the Air Board that the aircraft would be used for military purposes. Although the Air Board desperately wanted to secure usable aircraft and equipment, its main focus was on flying boats and seaplanes, aircraft which their civil operations branch could put to work without delay.

The miscommunication continued for four months after the Imperial offer had been made. Finally the impediment, caused by "two nations separated by a common language", was removed by Sir Hugh Trenchard, the British Chief of Air Staff, who made it quite clear that his Ministry encouraged both Military and Civil Air Services, and had never suggested that the donated aircraft be used exclusively by the Military. Biggar quickly contacted Trenchard to confirm that the newly formed Air Board intended, in the immediate future, to champion some type of Canadian air force. The seasoned diplomat then requested permission to resume negotiations for aircraft.

More than one hundred aircraft were crated up and shipped to Canada, with eleven Felixtowe F-3s, two Curtiss H-16s and a single Fairey III C seaplane earmarked for use by the Air Board's Civil Operations Branch. The entire donation had a value of over five million dollars. In addition to British generosity, the United States Navy donated twelve Curtiss HS-2L flying boats that had operated in Nova Scotia on convoy patrols during the War. Many Air Board members predicted that if the machines came, an air force wouldn't be far behind.

At the Air Board's November meeting Colonel Biggar, true to his word, brought forward the issue of supporting the formation of a Canadian Air Force as a non-permanent force. His proposal outlined an air militia that would be administered by unpaid Air Force Associations in each province. These Associations would recommend ex-officers of the Great War for reserve commissions and select officers for short-term refresher courses. The Board's employees in the civil operations branch would also receive officer status in the new Canadian Air Force. The Air Board ratified their vice-chairman's recommendations and asked him to approach Cabinet with their sanctioned proposal.

Biggar prepared a clear and concise presentation which he delivered to Cabinet in February 1920: the CAF would be an essentially non-permanent force with a very small nucleus of permanent force personnel responsible only for Air Force training.

Fully aware of the government's funding limitations, Biggar emphasized that in peacetime an air force would make better use of its men and equipment than any of the other services. This argument, and other skillfully presented discussion, persuaded the government to approve the formation of the Canadian Air Force. However, Cabinet chose to use the unsubstantial terms of Section 5 of the Air Board Act to authorize the employment of officers and men, an action which created a non-permanent status for employees, in a non-permanent militia.

A weak start for a national air force was strengthened by the appointment of Major General Sir Willoughby Gwatkin as Inspector General of the new CAF. The position of Air Officer Commanding was accepted by Lieutenant-Colonel A.K. Tylee, and in May CAF Headquarters opened in the Air Board offices in Ottawa. A staff of five Airmen worked with Tylee over the summer to prepare regulations for governing the new CAF, and once again the Royal Air Force acted as a guide.

In June 1920, CAF general policy formation and overall administration was placed in the hands of a Canadian Air Force Association with Headquarters in Ottawa. Provincial branches, operated by a volunteer executive, were responsible for recruiting and selecting officers and airmen for the reservist training program.

The former RAF flying training base at Camp Borden, Ontario, was an ideal location for the CAF training centre; this was the only station directly under the control of the CAF. An arrangement was made at the beginning of January 1920, to reopen the base to prepare for the arrival of the first shipment of aircraft from England. Captain G.O. Johnson was appointed Station Superintendent and he and his crew faced the formidable task of unpacking and assembling all the aircraft during the long, cold months ahead. By March the crew had one of the Avro trainers ready for its flight test. The assembly continued at a steady pace and, as each machine was completed, Johnson took personal responsibility for the test flight. In addition, he supervised the work crews who were getting the rest of the camp ready for its first season as a Canadian Air Force ground and flight training centre.

At the beginning of June 1920, administrative staff and instructors began to arrive at Camp Borden. In August, Wing Commander J.S. Scott, Controller of Civil Aviation for the Air Board, and former head of the Certificate Branch, was the first "part-time" CAF candidate to finish the course. By the end of the year over 700 hours of flying time had been logged and 197 veteran officers and airmen had taken the course.

In spite of positive reports from Camp Borden, there were CAF and Air Force Association members who were disillusioned with the results. These men hoped to build a future for aviation in Canada and they questioned how aviation could progress if no new pilots were trained. The pay inequality between the civil and the military aviation branches, and the lack of continuity created by the constant turnover of underpaid non-permanent CAF staff, were two issues of concern created by the Air Board's operation of two aviation branches. It was increasingly obvious that the overall organization had some serious flaws.

Nevertheless, the confusion did not halt progress for the Air Board's Directorate of Flying Operations. Under the direction of Superintendent Lt. Col. R. Leckie, civil air stations were established in four Provinces: Rockcliffe in Ottawa; Roberval, Quebec; Morley, Alberta; and Vancouver, British Columbia. These stations were Civil Operation Stations operated by civil servants; personnel were appointed by the Civil Service Commission and were given leave from their duties to attend Camp Borden and receive CAF training.

Early air photo and layout of Jericho Beach Air Station. DND PL143834

JERICHO BEACH AIR STATION: 1920

In the fall of 1919, Major C. MacLaurin, Major A.G. Lincoln, Captain G.O. Johnson, and Captain J.W. Hobbs were commissioned by Air Board Headquarters in Ottawa to personally research and then submit recommendations for the location of Air Board Flying Stations in various regions of the country. Captain Hobbs visited the west coast of British Columbia. In meetings with officials of the Provincial government, and with western representatives of Federal government departments, Hobbs determined that a Vancouver Air Station would be of national service and would be well-supported.

The Government of British Columbia granted, free of charge, a plot of land on English Bay adjacent to the Jericho Golf and Country Club. Far from being a site best suited as an embarkation point for amphibious aircraft, the Air Board's decision to build the Vancouver Air Station at Jericho Beach was highly motivated by the fact that the property could be obtained through bureaucratic channels at no cost.

Major Claire C. MacLaurin was appointed by the Air Board as the Station's first Superintendent. Early in 1920 he arrived in Vancouver to carry out the responsi-

Site preparation at Jericho Beach, 1920. DND PL 1438445

bility of building an Air Station from the ground up. A carefully chosen group of twelve Airmen, who considered themselves the "charter" Station members, began to report for duty in the following months. MacLaurin found office space in the old Vancouver Post Office and opened a temporary headquarters, then quickly moved on to the next order of business, manpower. Twelve good men was a start, but they had a big job ahead of them. He employed six more men, and now every member of the staff willingly pitched in alongside MacLaurin to build their fledgling Flying Boat Station.

In the spring and early summer of 1920 MacLaurin and his crew prepared the station site on the beachfront at the end of Point Grey Road. Seagull tracks were obliterated by the little Cletrac tractor that industriously cleared the beach of drift-logs. Air pilot Navigator MacLeod was assigned a rotation on the Cletrac, shoving the sand aside to prepare a foundation for a large cement apron and the construction of a wooden-planked slipway that disappeared beyond the water's edge. Next to the slipway an oblong floathouse was attached to the end of a new dock that stretched out into the waters of English Bay.

Behind the apron, and parallel to the shoreline, a large wooden framework went up, walled with huge sections of canvas. Curtains of canvas, with an intricate system of guy ropes and pulleys, hung from two massive beams that stretched across the front of what was now recognizable as a hangar. While a second of these Bessineau-type hangars was being erected, another crew quickly put together a group of temporary frame buildings to house the administrative offices.

Although MacLaurin and his staff worked liked Trojans, the construction of the Station took longer than everyone had anticipated. The Jericho Country Club had enjoyed sole leasehold proprietorship of the entire property since 1890 and deeply resented the Provincial government's sudden introduction of "new neighbours" on a piece of what they considered to be their land. There was also a problem with what MacLaurin referred to as "underhanded propaganda" being circulated by the Air Services Association. Their openly hostile attitude created an additional hardship for MacLaurin, and eventually eliminated the hope of operating a 1920 flying season.

MacLaurin's physical bearing added credibility to his calm and diplomatic approach to sorting out these difficulties. His restraint was admirable in view of the frustration he revealed in a letter to the Air Board on June 20, 1920:

> *"They (the Air Service Association) gave me considerable trouble in connection with the Board of Enquiry and of course have been abusing the Air Board and following a destructive policy right along. However, I feel that their efforts are guided by a few hare-brained fanatics and their principles are so 'rotten' that their organization will either fall to pieces in the very near future or undergo a complete change."*

While MacLaurin dealt with politics and public relations, the temporary facilities at the Station had progressed sufficiently to allow Air Mechanic Harold Davenport and the fourteen other Station mechanics to assemble aircraft in the Bessineau hangars. From the group of four HS-

top; HS-2Ls at Jericho Beach. DND PL 143823
above; G-CYBA, Jericho's first HS-2L being launched. DND PL143813

2L Flying Boats donated by the United States Navy, the mechanics had G-CYBA ready for a test flight in September 1920. A twin-engine Felixtowe F-3, G-CYDI, an aircraft from the British donation, had also been shipped to the station. All the machines were assembled and in operation by the summer of 1921.

Air Mechanic Harold Davenport recalled that there were 18 people involved in the first phase of operations at Jericho Beach. The Station's two young Air Pilot Navigators, Earl MacLeod, and William (Bill) Templeton, both went on to fashion long and distinguished careers out of their love of flying. Earl MacLeod rose to Air Commodore, and Bill Templeton spent twenty successful years as the Manager of the Vancouver Airport.

Air mechanics at Jericho Beach, 1921. (left to right) Clark, Dickie, Davenport, Slemmons, Corp. DND

Twenty other ranks manned the Station in its first year of operation, and a well-known Vancouver girl, Miss Edith Henley, efficiently organized the administration office and took care of the secretarial duties.

Davenport	Harold	Mechanic
Ballentine	Gordon	Mechanic
Hines	Howard	Equipment Section-Head
Cressy	Ted	Mechanic
Moffat	Kenneth	Wireless Section-Head
Duncan	Clarence J.	Air Photography Section-Head
Coupland	Robert	Shop Foreman
Hartridge	A.C.	Mechanic
Bell	Harry	Mechanic
Corp	Frank R.	Mechanic
Hill	Tommy	Mechanic
Slemmons		Mechanic
Walker	Alf	Mechanic
Nicholson	John	Mechanic
Terry	Norman	Mechanic
Dickie	Alex	Civilian Head Pigeon Loft
Tall	Bill	Mechanic
Gear	Bill	Mechanic
Clark	F.M.	Mechanic

Four aircraft, courtesy of the United States Navy, were transported to Vancouver by train:

Curtiss	HS-2L G-CYBA *the first aircraft assembled*
Curtiss	HS-2L G-CYBB
Curtiss	HS-2L G-CYDX *the first aircraft to complete a trip to Prince Rupert*
Curtiss	HS-2L G-CYEA *Crashed at Point Grey on September 11, 1922 killing Major MacLaurin*
Felixtowe	F-3 G-CYDI *Withdrawn from service by 1923*

Felixtowe F-3, G-CYDI at Jericho Beach.
Vancouver Public Library via Elwood White

The HS-2L had an empty weight of 4,300 pounds, which made it slow and cumbersome and hard on fuel even without a payload. Nevertheless, with its wooden hull and double-layered, mahogany-planked bottom, the aircraft was well chosen in view of the punishment it took from rough seas and novice pilots during its service-life on the west coast of Canada. The large F-3 Flying Boat didn't stand up as well as the HS-2Ls did. Continual maintenance put it in disfavour because of its potential drain on the Station's shoestring budget: YDI was struck off strength at the end of 1923. But in truth, neither aircraft had been designed with the geography of the interior of British Columbia in mind; and the HS-2L with a ceiling of 9,200 feet was used in regions of the province where mountain peaks rise to 10,000 feet, leaving little room for error.

MacLaurin took each machine for its test flight when assembly was completed, as he did on September 22, 1920 in G-CYBA. Once he was sure of YBA's airworthiness, he directed his full attention to unfolding his business plan, a sequence of events that would promote the Air Station and prove the versatility of its aircraft.

MacLaurin flew G-CYBA to Victoria to introduce British Columbia's Premier Oliver to the HS-2L. In a meeting with the Premier, MacLaurin concentrated on forming a relationship between his Air Station and the Provincial government. He pointed out the aircraft's potential to increase the efficiency and the productivity of many government projects, an obvious translation into money saved, which piqued the interest of Premier Oliver.

At the end of September 1920, Superintendent MacLaurin took YBA on a second flight that gained more favourable attention for the work that could be accomplished by his Airmen and their aircraft. He took a government entomologist to the vicinity of Stave Lake, which was believed to be the source of a large mosquito infestation affecting the Fraser Valley. The entomologist was excited about the ease of access into this remote area, and the advances that could now be made by the ground patrols based on his aerial over-view.

In October 1920 Jericho Beach happened to be in the right place at the right time to benefit from national attention directed at the west coast on the completion of a dramatic trans-Canada flight - the first and the last major exercise undertaken by the Canadian Air Force. Cross-country airmail, airfreight or passenger flight service was a tantalizing possibility. Therefore, in the summer of 1920, the Air Board prepared to test the feasibility of coast to coast flight.

During the previous summer a Curtiss JN-4 Canuck, owned by the British Columbia Branch of the Aerial League of Canada and flown by Captain E. C. Hoy, D.F.C., crossed the Rocky Mountain range, claiming a triumph over the greatest obstacle to trans-Canada flight. The JN-4, took off at 4:13 AM on August 7, 1919 from Minoru Park on Lulu Island. Flying eastward, Hoy crossed the Rocky Mountains and landed at Lethbridge, Alberta, at 6:22 on the evening of the same day.

On October 7, 1920, the Air Board commenced the first leg of its trans-Canada flight. The flight drew a lot of publicity as it proceeded westward with Wing Commander Leckie and Squadron Leader Hobbs, at first in a Fairey Seaplane, but forced by storm-damage to continue in an HS-2L. After a three-day battle with the weather, they landed at Selkirk, Manitoba, which triggered the next leg of the journey flown by Air Commodore A.K. Tylee and F/L J.B. Home-Hay in a De Havilland DH-9. Engine trouble caused an unscheduled landing at Regina but they were able to continue in another DH-9 to meet F/L G.A. Thompson in Calgary to complete the last leg of the journey. By October 13 the two aircraft, plagued by bad weather, had managed to cross the Rocky Mountains and land at Revelstoke. They waited out the storm for a day before continuing on October 15, but the weather closed in again at Merritt where they impatiently waited another day. On October 17 at 11:00 AM, they finally arrived at Vancouver. Weather, the reigning master of the sky, and not the Rocky Mountains, had asserted itself as the greatest obstacle in coast to coast air travel.

After conferring with Major MacLaurin, who had originated the idea of a trans-Canada flight, Tylee and Thompson decided to continue the flight on to Victoria using an HS-2L from Jericho Beach. They departed in the afternoon of October 20, but after flying for two and a half hours they were forced to land at Port Townsend, Washington, due to heavy fog in the Victoria area. An hour later they set out again, but had to put down at Friday Harbor in

YBA on C.P.R. flatcar enroute to Shuswap Lake, October 28, 1920.
DND PL143820

the American San Juan Islands. Some small mechanical difficulties interfered with a take-off before dusk and the men stayed overnight, making a fresh start the next morning. They made the half hour flight to Esquimalt without further incident and landed amid scoffs and gibes from the local press because of their extended route. MacLaurin travelled to Victoria by boat and flew the station's HS-2L safely back to Jericho Beach that same afternoon.

Major MacLaurin used G-CYBA on another promotional venture on October 28, when he had the aircraft shipped by rail to Carney's Landing on the Shuswap Lake near

Air Board and Forestry personnel at Kamloops, November 1920. P/O Clarence J. Duncan, air photographer (2nd from left); Maj. Clarence (Claire) C. MacLaurin, station Superintendent (3rd from left). DND PM82-174

Sicamous, British Columbia. In company with mechanic A.C. Hartridge, photographer C.J. Duncan, and Forestry Officer R. Cameron, MacLaurin made a series of flights as far west as Kamloops, taking photographs of timber limits for the forestry department. At the conclusion of the successful exercise, MacLaurin loaded the machine back onto a flat-car for the return trip to Jericho Beach. The next month, MacLaurin flew YBA on an extended demonstration flight to the Okanagan Valley. As he had planned, the exploits of the Air Station and its HS-2L continued to gain public attention, and people on the west coast were becoming aware of the new potential at Jericho Beach.

In retrospect, the Superintendent might have viewed the hectic months of organizing the temporary base as the easiest part of his new job. The next item on his agenda was an even greater challenge: to convince the key people in the provincial and federal government agencies to negotiate the contracts which would allow his Air Station to generate some revenue.

P/O MacLeod, P/O Templeton and the other charter members at Jericho Beach had ably assisted their Superintendent to build the Station and market the practical application of their aircraft, but now it was up to MacLaurin to deal with the politicians and the bureaucrats.

To fulfill this part of his plan, MacLaurin approached various government departments to solicit contracts for flying services. He had two things working in his favour: an inherent business sense, gained by growing up in the family's lumber business; and valuable experience in the art of political persuasion, hard-won by his participation in setting up the Air Board. MacLaurin now applied every means at his disposal to establish an economic base for the Jericho Beach Air Station - many individual dreams of a career in aviation rested on his success.

The government of British Columbia had paid a portion of the construction costs of the Jericho Beach Air Station, but they had done so with obvious reluctance. Premier Oliver continued to be very vocal in his criticism of federal government expenditures on civil aviation, particularly with respect to using aircraft on forestry patrols. However, the lumbermen in British Columbia had great expectations that these federally sponsored experiments would benefit their enterprise. In the government's heated debate with the forest industry, MacLaurin saw a job that would put his Air Station on the map. Confident that one season would make converts out of the most skeptical critics, including the Premier, he proposed that Jericho Beach operate a trial season of forest patrols.

Air Stations Gain A Foothold: 1920

At the end of 1920 the Air Board's Director of Flying Operations, Wing Commander Robert Leckie, and his group of capable station superintendents and their Airmen, had made significant strides in organizing the four air stations. Every airman knew that success rested on his station's ability to prove its economic viability to the government masters. Failure to do so meant facing the withdrawal of the meagre financial support from their own provincial government, and from the government in Ottawa, a government which was, at best, skeptical of their enterprise. At the close of the 1920 flying season, these veteran pilots had flown their obsolete World War One aircraft for 2,200 hours on behalf of the various civil service agencies of the country.

To help them assess the first year of operation, the Air Board called an interdepartmental meeting in November. The response was excellent. Representatives attended from thirteen departments and agencies ranging from the Surveyor General, Commissioner of the RCMP, Superintendents of Indian Agencies, and the Dominion Park Commission. Without exception these senior civil servants endorsed the use of Air Board aircraft and supported their expanded use in the following season.

In its report to government the Air Board stressed the high degree of confidence with which its members approached the second year of civil operations. Across the country, 1921 brought Air Board pilots a growing list of projects for nine federal departments and three provinces: British Columbia, Ontario and Quebec. But, in spite of glowing reports from department officials, many ministers continued to criticize the Air Board's operation.

JERICHO BEACH: 1921

In British Columbia, criticism centred on the expense involved in a total commitment to aviation. However, MacLaurin's efforts, and the constant pressure from the lumbermen and a few influential people within the Forestry Department, were at least partially responsible for the Provincial government revising its attitude. Early in 1921 the government allocated twenty thousand dollars for exploration and reconnaissance of British Columbia's forests, and Jericho Beach was awarded a trial season of forestry patrols. That spring and summer, Airmen flying the Station's HS-2L Flying Boats proved beyond doubt that their aircraft could help save the forests from fire and disease.

The Vancouver District Provincial Forestry Supervisor happened to be a former Camp Borden RAF Flying Instructor, Major Leonard Andrews. Andrews supported MacLaurin's belief in the aircraft as a valuable asset in peacetime, and, throughout 1921, he utilized the services of the Jericho Beach Airmen in a large number of projects for his department: general reconnaissance patrols, aerial photography assignments, forestry patrols, and the transportation of fire fighters and equipment. By the end of the year contracts with the Department of Lands and Forestry were fast becoming the Station's "bread and butter".

Major MacLaurin had spent considerable time selling his station's capabilities, and now a few other government departments were waking up to the potential at Jericho Beach. The Station's HS-2Ls and their crews were called on to assist in a varied schedule of flying activity for a number of both provincial and federal agencies. Critics still existed, but they temporarily complied with the voices of reason which suggested that you couldn't say something didn't work until it had been tried. Therefore, as the Air Board report predicted, 1921 turned into quite a busy year for the Vancouver Air Station.

The Collector of Customs at Vancouver, Colonel A.B. Carey, was delighted when the aerial escorts provided for ships inbound from the Orient began to have a dampening effect on narcotic trafficking on the west coast. The surveillance patrols allowed customs officers to spot any suspicious debris dropped over the side of a ship as it approached the Vancouver harbour. Officials could then give chase to the smuggler's speed boat as it swooped in, accompanied by a cloud of seagulls, to pick up the floating package. Colonel Carey informed MacLaurin that the aircraft patrols were causing a drug shortage as far

HS-2L G-CYDX at Steveston, B.C. on fishing fleet inspection. NAC C22738

down the coast as Seattle; the shortage caused the price to go up and this was creating havoc in the local trafficking trade.

The government Geodetic Survey contracted the Jericho HS-2Ls to help determine the best sites for locating a series of triangulation stations across the high mountain ranges of southern British Columbia. Once the sites were chosen, the aircraft transported the working parties and their supplies to the closest body of water. Mr. Fred Lambert, who was in charge of installation, estimated that with the assistance of aircraft he and his crew had completed in one season work that otherwise would have taken ten years to accomplish.

1921 continued to unfold as a "trail blazing" adventure for the aviators at Jericho Beach. Proof of the unlimited uses of an aircraft evoked serious consideration in boardrooms around the lower mainland and, as a result, project followed project. All of these proposals used an aircraft for the first time, which meant that the Airmen often tested their flying skill and called on their mechanical wizardry in order to bring back satisfactory results in the outdated HS-2Ls.

Aerial photography, which was causing quite a sensation, began an ongoing map project that was assigned to all the Air Stations across Canada. Jericho Beach received an Eastman Camera specifically designed for vertical photography. Modifications were made to the hull of one of the Station's HS-2Ls to accommodate the large piece of equipment, and the cockpit was enlarged to make room for the camera operator. Pilot Officer MacLeod and Air Photographer "Dunc" Duncan made several important photo-flights for the Vancouver Harbour Board. The two airmen pioneered the process of aerial panoramic photography on the west coast and in so doing they found it necessary to apply the principle of "creative borrowing" to make sure that their results were completely satisfactory.

Earl MacLeod recorded the incident in his paper, 'Early Flying In British Columbia':

> *"Because economy was an important consideration at that time, we were allowed sufficient film to provide only a five percent overlap, instead of a sixty percent overlap that came to be considered essential for good results in later operations for air mapping.*
>
> *In our case, rough air and side-wind, or 'drift', unfortunately adversely affected our very demanding precision flying on one of our runs. When we pieced together the photographs for the mosaic we discovered a small gap in the centre of Stanley Park. Our reputations at stake, we transferred a few trees from one of the prints of the Seymour Creek area to fill the gap satisfactorily."*

MacLeod and Duncan also photographed Chadsey Lake, at the top of Sumas Mountain in the Fraser Valley. These preliminary photos for the Sumas Lake Reclamation Dyking Project led to more work in aerial panoramic photography in the spring of 1922.

Jericho HS-2L intercepts passenger vessel inbound to Vancouver.
CFB Comox Rowe Library

In 1921 the Fisheries Department also began their long association with aircraft. Through Major MacLaurin's discussions with Major J.A. Motherwell, the Inspector of Fisheries at Vancouver, the Department used the HS-2Ls in a variety of research projects which included transporting fish fry to previously inaccessible lakes and streams in aid of a project to restock the watersheds. And Motherwell's fisheries officers found that aerial surveillance of the fishing grounds greatly increased their ability to enforce fishing regulations and control poaching.

So far, with the determined efforts of Superintendent MacLaurin, the west coast Air Station was managing to pay its own way. MacLaurin had exceeded even his own expectations for securing work for the Airmen, but, being the pragmatic business man that he was, he never lost sight of fiscal responsibility; he watched cash flow and expenditures like a hawk. Everyone associated with the daily routine at Jericho Beach lived and breathed MacLaurin's "Economy of Operation". Even the carrier pigeons in the Station Pigeon Loft served his exacting cost-accounting system.

When the Station site was under construction, MacLaurin had a pigeon loft installed close to one of the Bessineau hangars. The carrier pigeons were used for communication from aircraft to base in order to save the weight-load of a wireless operator and the heavy wireless equipment. Air Pilot Navigator MacLeod gratefully discovered that the pigeons could also "save your bacon". Engine trouble forced him to land at an isolated spot about fifty miles west of the Station. He determined that a faulty magneto was causing the problem and released a young female pigeon with his SOS message. In a very short time a second HS-2L arrived with a replacement magneto.

Without exception, the year-end reports from each government department noted that where air service was used there was a marked increase in efficiency and productivity. What could better demonstrate the advantages of using the aircraft.

MacKenzie King and his Liberals: 1921-1922

In Ottawa most of the criticism directed at the Air Board came across the floor of the House of Commons from the Liberal opposition. 1921 was an election year, and economy in government was the principal plank in the Liberal platform. CAF Inspector General Gwatkin voiced his concern about the future of the Canadian Air Force should there be a change in government. Gwatkin quietly expressed a fear that a budget-cutting Liberal government might try to bring the CAF under the authority of a Militia Council.

General Gwatkin had always displayed unfailing devotion to the concept of an independent Canadian Air Force administered as a third service, and he upheld these beliefs throughout the unsettled years of Air Board and CAF organization. But Canada had a poor track record where military air services were concerned. Within a period of less than 6 years Canadian governments had created and then extinguished three military air services: first, in 1914, the Canadian Aviation Corps; then the two-Squadron Canadian Air Force in England in 1918; and then the Royal Canadian Naval Air Service had been disbanded in 1919. Gwatkin strongly suspected that the process would be repeated again under a Liberal administration.

The Canadian voters supported Mackenzie King and his austerity program and the Liberal government took its position in Ottawa in December 1921. The Finance Minister's budget announcement early in 1922 revealed that the Air Board allotment was reduced to $1,000,000.00 for the year, but funding for civil air operations was increased. In the spirit of "robbing Peter to pay Paul", government agencies or departments received a budget increase to cover the cost of their air services. The Air Stations were instructed to bill each department individually for the hours of air time they used. Under the same heading of reduced government spending, the CAF Camp Borden Refresher Course was also cancelled.

Not long after the new administration had dealt these substantial blows to the dream of a National Air Force, the Prime Minister ordered a hard line taken to tighten up the organizational structure of the country's defence forces. George Graham, the recently appointed Minister of National Defence, responded by introducing a proposal to consolidate the Navy, the Army, the Militia, and the Air Board under the authority of a Department of National Defence.

The Prime Minister's unyielding position on government spending left no room for negotiation. Gwatkin and the other Air Board members were not surprised when, in March 1922, Graham's National Defence Act encountered little debate in the House of Commons. The Act had the weighty endorsement of Major-General James MacBrien, the Chief of General Staff; Eugene Fiset, the Deputy Minister of the Department of Militia and Defence; and Sir Arthur Currie, the Inspector-General of the Militia. Effective January 1, 1923 the new Department of National Defence would be responsible for all defence matters, eliminating the authority of the Air Board. The legislation ignored civil aviation, and created an amalgamation which placed the Canadian Air Force in danger of extinction - a dismal forecast for the future of aviation in Canada.

Earlier in 1922, the British government was teetering on the brink of eliminating its Air Ministry and altering the status of the RAF. Graham and MacBrien, adamant in their belief that Canada should follow the Imperial example, intended to incorporate the CAF as a Corps of the Active Militia. However, this action would reduce the Air Force to a support-arm of the Army and the Navy, an unacceptable position for those who had worked so hard to establish a distinct identity for the CAF.

Prior to their last curtain call, a delegation of Air Board members met with Graham in one last attempt to preserve the CAF as a separate force. The delegation had the substantial support of Inspector-General Gwatkin, who openly expressed his concern for the future of the Air Force and stressed the important role it should play in the development of aviation in Canada. Representatives of the Army and the Navy presented the Defence Minister with their own list of concerns, but in spite of the evidence of discontent in all quarters, the consolidation proceeded. MacBrian ordered his militia staff to begin a reorganization of the CAF as a component of the Department of National Defence.

Gwatkin stood firm in his conviction that the Air Force must retain a role as a third service; the Inspector-General was not a man who quietly stepped aside in a difficult situation. He carefully monitored the government's progress with the sharp perception of a seasoned diplomat. His vigilance was rewarded when he learned that the British government had decided to leave its Air Ministry intact. Gwatkin instantly recognized a precedent of major importance that would uphold his argument on behalf of the CAF. He immediately notified MacBrien of Great Britain's decision.

The Chief of General Staff and other senior officials reluctantly confirmed their commitment that Canada's military structure would follow Great Britain's lead: the CAF would be aligned with the RAF. In a statement issued early in 1923, MacBrien acknowledged that he had altered his original plan for the CAF: *"It is a separate service, and when its expansion so warrants its administration will conform to the other services of the Department."* Every CAF supporter took the opening phrase of this vague statement as the small ray of hope they had been looking for.

above; Jericho airmen pose with HS-2L. DND PL143812
right; Jericho pilot in flying gear. DND PL143814

Regardless of the uncertain political climate, the Airmen at the Air Stations ignored the whispering winds of change and dedicated their energy and enthusiasm to getting on with the job at hand. The 1922 flying season turned out to be an even greater success than the previous season.

JERICHO BEACH: 1922

The amazing plan to install a pumping station to drain Sumas Lake and reclaim over 10,000 acres of fertile Fraser Valley farmland was in the second year of research and development. Jericho Beach aircraft were recalled in the spring of 1922 and MacLeod and Duncan returned to complete the aerial photography project. They took off from Jericho Beach in HS-2L G-CYDX on the morning of April 13, carrying enough supplies for the week-long assignment. To take advantage of early morning light and a forecast of good weather, the Airmen were billeted at the Empress Hotel in nearby Chilliwack. Each day they laboured above the swollen lake taking hundreds of photographs detailing the physical features of the surrounding terrain. Each evening they returned to Chilliwack at last light and tethered YDX to a tree on the bank of the Fraser River at Chilliwack Lower Landing at the foot of Wellington Street, about a mile from the hotel.

MacLeod's next assignment took him from sea-level to 10,000 feet above the forests of British Columbia in a series of flights for the Federal Department of Agriculture. White Pine Blister Rust threatened to destroy large stands of timber all across North America and a cooperative research project was attempting to control the spread of airborne Rust spores. The Department issued several HS-2L pilots with disinfected, sealed test tubes coated on the inside with a thin coating of vaseline. At varying heights, up to 10,000 feet, the pilots unsealed a tube and held it in the air-flow. By this method researchers found that spores were trapped at every level and a site-specific means of control would have to be developed. One of the enterprising pilots, tired of fighting wind velocity while holding the small tubes over his head, managed to fix his tubes to one of the vertical struts, but experienced great difficulty maintaining level flight while he stretched out to unseal each tube. Perhaps it was just as well that no one kept an accurate cost accounting regarding the number of tubes used during the project.

The exceptionally dry summer of 1922 created hazardous conditions in the forests, forcing the Provincial Forestry Department to order all logging operations shut down. The urgency of the situation required spreading the word to each bush operator and logging camp. Radio

Felixtowe G-CYDI flies by Jericho boat house outbound on patrol. Vancouver Public Library via Elwood White

communication was not reliable so forestry officials visited MacLaurin at Jericho Beach to contract the services of the HS-2Ls.

At the beginning of July, Lt. Earl MacLeod and two forestry officials operated out of Alert Bay for three days delivering closure notices to every camp between the Queen Charlotte Sound - Rivers Inlet district, south to Campbell River, Drury Inlet, Carriden Bay, Neepah Lagoon, Nimmo Bay, Sullivan Bay, Greenway Sound, Moore Bay, Scott Cove, and Nimpkish Lake. The camps were remote and difficult to find under normal conditions, but now the air was filled with a milky, smoke-haze and navigation was tricky, even for the forestry men who knew the area well.

During the week that followed, the coastal inlets became choked with the smoke of forest fires, reducing visibility close to zero. MacLaurin and his pilots were now flying as long as there was daylight in an attempt to spot new fires and map their locations. On one flight alone they reported 12 new fires.

Maj. Clarence MacLaurin's fatal crash at Point Grey, September 11, 1922. CFB Comox Rowe Library

On July 28, one of the HS-2L pilots spotted a fire at Buttle Lake on Vancouver Island. The pilot reported to base and his coordinates were mapped out, identifying the remote area around Twenty Mile Point as the exact location of the fire. An immediate request went out to Jericho Beach. MacLaurin responded by bringing in G-CYDI, the Felixstowe Flying Boat, with Lt. MacLeod as his second pilot.

The F-3 took off carrying a load of 4,895 pounds, which included a portable firepump engine, 1,200 feet of fire hose, tools, tents, and provisions for the six firefighters also on board. After the men and their equipment were unloaded, MacLaurin immediately returned to pick up additional firefighters and equipment from Campbell River and Comox and deliver them to the scene of the fire.

The F-3 saved forest service firefighters two full days of ground travel, hacking out a 14 mile trail through the bush in order to reach the site of a fire which would by then be raging out of control. The dedicated efforts of the Jericho Beach Airmen received high praise from forestry officials, and as the season progressed there were numerous occasions when the Airmen flew above and beyond the regular call of duty. At the end of the season the Forestry Department expressed its gratitude by recording that the value of timber saved was incalculable and far outweighed any expense incurred in the use of aircraft.

As the demands on the Jericho Beach Air Station grew, the strain took its toll on the Station's aircraft as well as its Airmen. The lack of adequate funding on a national level restricted the Civil Operations Branch in their plan to provide the Air Stations with better equipment than the old HS-2Ls and F-3s. Fortunately, all the air stations had attracted excellent machinists, fitters and carpenters and these men were the backbone of the operation. Somehow, they used a combination of skill and an empathy with the machines under their care to nurse the ageing aircraft through each season.

However, on September 11, 1922, HS-2L, G-CYEA, ended the flying season with a tragic finality. Major MacLaurin took off from Jericho Beach Air Station in YEA on a flight along the Fraser River to the Sumas Lake Reclamation project where Lt. MacLeod was waiting for his

Rescuers attempt to save occupants of HS-2L YEA after Maj. MacLaurin's crash. Only Air Mechanic A.C. Hartridge survived. CFB Comox Rowe Library.

arrival. Station mechanic A.C. Hartridge was with MacLaurin, and they carried a passenger, John Duncan, the engineer in charge of the dyking project. Shortly after take-off Hartridge advised MacLaurin that the radiator was boiling and, moments later, as MacLaurin initiated a return for landing, Hartridge noticed a gasoline leak across the engine manifold. MacLaurin immediately cut off the engine ignition and fuel supply to prevent a fire. Base personnel watched in stunned horror as YEA plunged into a steep descent. The aircraft failed to recover and struck the water in a near-vertical dive with such force that it broke the back of the aircraft.

Pilots F/L Tom Cowley and F/L Elmer Fullarton, and the shop foreman, Robert Coupland, took off in a second HS-2L and flew to the crashsite. They could see that a boat had already arrived at the site, but the water was too shallow to allow them to land their aircraft and they had to return to the Air Station. Hartridge and Duncan, both seriously injured, were taken to the hospital but Major MacLaurin was not in the aircraft.

Meanwhile Lt. MacLeod waited patiently by Sumas Lake at the appointed place. He was well-acquainted with the eccentricities of the HS-2L, but after several hours he became quite concerned. As soon as he received word of the tragedy he made his way to the crash site as quickly as possible, travelling in from the Fraser Valley on the B.C. Electric Railway.

Jericho CAF Honour Guard present arms, 1923. DND PMR792L

MacLaurin's body was still missing. MacLeod joined the sombre search party, staying out all night, along with Norman de Graves of the Customs Department, combing the beach and the tidal waters offshore from Point Grey. Just before sunrise the following day they found MacLaurin's body, and later in the day they heard that John Duncan had not survived the crash. The funeral service was held at Christ Church Cathedral in downtown Vancouver on September 14, 1922. MacLeod, accompanied by "Dunc" Duncan and Charley Plant, circled overhead in G-CYEB in a last tribute to their Station Superintendent, a man who had earned the love and respect of all the members of Jericho Beach Air Station.

Throughout his career, MacLaurin's straightforward approach and his unshakeable belief in the future of aviation had won many converts, and even those who didn't share his point of view admired him. From the west coast to the east coast of the country, the news of Major Claire MacLaurin's death shocked and saddened a great many Canadians.

At Jericho Beach the loss of their Superintendent was deeply felt by the Airmen, but, in honour of the work he had begun with such energy and zeal, the Station's activities carried on without interruption. The new Station Superintendent, S/L E.A. Godfrey, arrived on October 18, 1922. His command at Jericho Beach spanned the next several years of transition as the Air Force moved from CAF to RCAF. And Godfrey was there at the dawn of flight service offered by private enterprise. Godfrey, also committed to developing the use of aircraft for the economic benefit of the country, used his position at the Air Station to encourage these young companies in their fight for survival.

Ottawa Adopts The Imperial Pattern: 1923-1924

At the beginning of 1923 individual Members of Parliament were confronted by a growing number of civil department heads who gave irrefutable evidence of the value of civil air operations in the exploration and conservation of the country's resources. The bold initiatives taken by the Air Station Superintendents and their pilots were paying off.

This was the kind of attention that the CAF needed. But, while it served to strengthen the position of a national civil aviation service, it also clearly demonstrated the symbiotic relationship between the two branches of the Air Board: a civil operation dependent upon air force pilots and their aircraft. Even though the importance of civil operations had been brought into focus, the hard-won identity of the Canadian Air Force still remained in jeopardy.

In the spring of 1922, in a move to cement the sovereignty of the CAF, Major General Gwatkin had renewed the Air Board's request for permission to use the "Royal" prefix. Gwatkin backed his submission with the statement that: *"as a firmly established force the CAF should be granted the privilege accorded the Navy and permanent units of the militia"*. He also correctly reasoned that a "Royal" Canadian Air Force, with close ties to the Royal Air Force, would strengthen the case for a separate and permanent air force. His request proceeded through the Chief of General Staff, an Army General - the Air Force did not have complete autonomy until just before World War II.

As Sir Willoughby Gwatkin prepared to retire at the end of 1922 and return to his native England, he felt confident that he had done his utmost to secure a position for a permanent Canadian Air Force. He had served as a member of the Air Board and then as Inspector General of the CAF during a frustrating period in National aviation history. Gwatkin was a dynamic soldier with a passion for military aviation, but he confessed to have little use for Canadian politics and even less use for its politicians.

It is highly likely that the Air Force would have remained an adjunct of the Canadian Army had it not been for the persistent political and personal pressure applied by Gwatkin and other key Air Board members. But the foothold that aviation had gained since the inception of the CAF was a direct result of the vision, strength of character and single-minded purpose of a small force of airmen. They developed a professional air service in spite of financial restraints that offered no incentive to enlist in the CAF in the first place, nor to remain in service after training. The lack of funds severely restricted any plan to upgrade machines and equipment, and hampered the ongoing maintenance of the eclectic fleet of existing aircraft.

Meanwhile, the "Royal" application moved swiftly through formal application in January 1923, to "King's approval" in February. The Department of National Defence officially recorded His Majesty's notification of approval on March 12, 1923, and a year later, on April 1, 1924, the Royal Canadian Air Force was formally announced.

Further evidence of a renewed identity for the RCAF came with a change in uniform. CAF officers and airmen who had survived the process of amalgamation now exchanged their silver buttoned, navy blue uniform for the light blue uniform of the RAF. The RAF ensign had been adopted by the CAF in November 1921, another building block in the security of the Canadian Air Force arranged by Gwatkin, and then in April 1923, adoption of the stirring RAF motto "Per Ardua ad Astra": "Through Adversity to the Stars", completed the Imperial pattern.

With the demise of the Air Board, the confusing duality of Civil Operations staff, who were part civil servant and part commissioned officer, disappeared. All flying was Air Force flying, although fully two-thirds of RCAF operations were still at the request of other government departments. This was in keeping with a directive, issued in mid-1924, which outlined the RCAF mandate: "to carry on with Air Force training; to maintain a nucleus around which a military Air Force could grow, if required; and to conduct flying operations for other government departments."

Up until the date of change, Civil Government Air Operations and Civil Aviation had been controlled by the Air Board's Directorate of Flying Operations. Under the umbrella of the Department of National Defence and reporting to the Deputy Minister of National Defence, the reorganized Air Force now had four branches: the RCAF continued as the military branch of the air service, reporting to the Chief of Staff; the Civil Government Air Operations was separated from the RCAF and placed under its own director; the Controller of Civil Aviation was responsible for creating and operating airways and other related matters; and the Aeronautical Engineering Division serviced the other three directorates. The first Controller of Civil Aviation was none other than J.A. Wilson, who had been with Major C. MacLaurin in the RCNAS in 1918.

JERICHO BEACH: 1923 - 1924

P/O MacLeod, S/L Earl Godfrey, P/O Cowley, Jericho 1923.
DND PMR79-288

Close attention was still being paid to the economic viability of the Air Station. In response to another Liberal Government reduction in the Air Force budget, Jericho Beach continued to search for ways to increase its role in "civil flying for other government departments". As the 1924 flying season approached, Station Superintendent Godfrey was pleased to renew a contract with the Department of Marine and Fisheries.

Earlier, at the end of the 1922 fishery patrol season, the government realized that existing patrol methods were ineffective. A growing concern centred on the Prince Rupert district, the largest fishing area on the British Columbia coast. Regulation enforcement in the district had always been a challenge, but reports indicated that the situation was getting out of control. Fishery officials decided to test the use of aircraft to curb the flagrant violations.

The Prince Rupert patrol area extended from the Alaskan boundary southward to Cape Caution. Between these two points there were thousands of miles of coastline and intricate waterways, and the fishery patrol boats found it almost impossible to cover the area completely. An aircraft covered a much greater area in far less time, and gave the inspectors a broader scope of vision from their elevated vantage point. The sudden approach of an aircraft introduced an element of surprise that in itself acted as a deterrent to even the most blatent offenders.

The 1923 fishery patrol season opened with a temporary base set up in Seal Cove at the north end of the city of Prince Rupert. Flying Officer Earl MacLeod and crewmen Harold Davenport and Harry Bell operated HS-2L, G-CYDX, in a busy two and a half months of inspections and patrols. They found that many of the fishing boats were committing more than one infraction, and that most of the boats were illegally using long-nets; fishermen found it difficult to resist the temptation of attaching their emergency short-net called a "Handy Billy" and extending the legal length of their nets.

Many of the Fishery Supervisors and Patrolmen flew with MacLeod on the daily patrols, including D.S. Cameron, G.B. Taylor and a Mr. Collison, who MacLeod listed as "a pioneer on the coast, and son of an early missionary." On flights with no accompanying inspector, one of MacLeod's Aircrew remained on board an offending boat until the authorities arrived to lay charges. Later in the season MacLeod and his crew members were appointed as fisheries inspectors with the power to issue summonses for all infractions.

In mid-September 1923, as the salmon migration moved south into the Vancouver Island and Fraser River waters, the small Prince Rupert detachment returned to Jericho Beach and continued their patrol duties from the Vancouver Station. In addition to these regular checks for illegal fishing practices, Fishery officers also used the aircraft from Jericho Beach to monitor the movement of their patrol boats and to keep in closer touch with their officers, who often worked at widely separated points in their districts.

Although it was an old wartime type, the HS-2L was, in many ways, well-suited for this sort of work. Thanks to its rugged construction and proven seaworthiness, it stood up to rougher use and heavier seas than most other seaplane-types of the period. Its aerodynamic qualities were slightly out of date, but it gave yeoman service under hard conditions. Now the Liberty engines were beginning to show their age; spares were inadequate, and as a result engine trouble caused more than a few forced landings which interfered with the efficiency of the service. Flying Officer MacLeod had good reason to be grateful that his fitter had nimble fingers and an innovative nature - on several occasions Corporal Davenport's mechanical improvisations repaired the crippled HS-2L and got them out of a tight spot.

At the end of the 1923 season, Fisheries Inspector Mr. Adam Mackie was very impressed with the results of MacLeod's work. In his report, Mackie claimed the trial patrol season a resounding success and enthusiastically supported RCAF Flying Boat patrols for the next season. However, Mackie's glowing appraisal was not unanimously accepted within the Department of Marine and Fisheries. There were one or two other inspectors who felt that the time-worn HS-2L was unreliable.

In spite of the critics, the 1924 Fishery Patrol program was expanded. Earl MacLeod, now a Flight Lieutenant, was again selected as Officer in Charge of the seasonal Prince Rupert detachment at Seal Cove. He arrived in HS-2L, G-CYBB, on July 17, and was joined by F/O Alan Hull flying HS-2L, G-CYEB. Their crewmen were Cpl Harold Davenport and LAC Norman Terry. An existing boathouse at the edge of the cove was once again used as a workshop for maintenance and as a base for refuelling the aircraft.

From July 17 to September 21, MacLeod, Hull and their crews actively and effectively patrolled the Prince Rupert area in the HS-2Ls, logging a total of 81 flights. The flights were made during the weekends when fishing was banned - one HS-2L patrolled over the Naas and Skeena River areas in the north, while the second HS-2L covered the southern area, flying either from Swanson Bay or Bella Bella. On a single weekend patrol, one of the HS-2Ls logged 920 miles in 14 hours and 57 minutes, made 23 landings, and took 115 photographs between Friday morning and Sunday evening. A patrol to the Queen Charlotte Islands, a forty minute flight, completed a trip that would have required at least 15 hours by motor boat.

With fog, rain, and uncertain weather as persistent all-season obstacles, flying the HS-2Ls on the northern coast of British Columbia was not an easy job. Better facilities were needed to handle emergency repairs during the long and arduous patrols over the bleak and uninhabited coast and inland waterways.

At the beginning of the season, to partially bridge the communications gap, the two Flying Boats were equipped for W.T.(Radio) communication with Seal Cove. A detachment from the Royal Canadian Corps of Signals travelled to Prince Rupert by boat to set up temporary wireless facilities at the base. The three-man detachment was under the command of Lieutenant Christopher Sanford, with Sergeant Anderson, and B. Megilla, a sixteen year old "boy-soldier" who later rose to Brigadier General in the Canadian Army.

Unfortunately, it was late in the season by the time the base equipment was ready for use and the deteriorating weather frustrated its use. Fog and cloud often lay so close to the water that the aircraft had to fly "on the deck", making it impossible to lower the wireless aerial. In good flying conditions, however, they did have successful communication by both radio-telephone and morse code.

The change-over to full military status on April 1, 1924 had taken place very smoothly at Jericho Beach. The Station now operated under the jurisdiction of the District Officer Commanding, Military District Number 11 at Esquimalt, on Vancouver Island, and, because of the distance from RCAF Headquarters in Ottawa, the Air Station developed a closer relationship with that Army Headquarters than otherwise would have been the case.

In an overview of his years in the Air Force, Earl MacLeod summarized the cooperation received from the Esquimalt Headquarters:

> *"Our medical and engineering services were now supplied by the Army. Our Army Medical Service became keenly interested in, and developed, an outstanding specialized Aviation Medical Service. The Army Engineers played an important role in the expansion of our Base facilities, and in the establishment, later, of RCAF bases on the west coast, and of airports. An Army Drill Instructor was added to our strength - we became proud of our participation on many Ceremonial occasions."*

The following personnel were on strength at RCAF Station Vancouver, Jericho Beach on April 1, 1924:

S/L	A.E.	Godfrey	Commanding Officer
F/L	E.L.	MacLeod	
F/O	A.H.	Hull	
P/O	C.J.	Duncan	Photographer
P/O	F.B.	Gillespie	Stores
F/Sgt	R.W.	Coupland	Carpenter
LAC	E.C.	Tennant	Storekeeper
Sgt	F.R.	Corp	Carpenter
Sgt	G.	Gorrill	Fitter
Sgt	J.	MacAslan	Clerk
Cpl	H.O.	Bell	Machinist
Cpl	H.E.	Davenport	Fitter
Cpl	A.	Dickie	Carpenter/Boat Builder
LAC	F.M.	Clark	Clerk
LAC	W.	Gear	Fitter
LAC	N.C.	Terry	Fitter
LAC	W.A.	Wilson	Carpenter
LAC	F.	Young	Carpenter
AC1	A.S.	Coburn	Carpenter
AC1	J.R.	Johnson	Carpenter
AC2	A.D.	Campbell	Driver
AC2	E.	Huggard	Aircraft Hand
AC2	W.S.	Tall	Aircraft Hand
AC2	G.B.	Taylor	Standard
LAC	E.	Aldersley	Clerk
AC2	I.H.	O'Neil	Clerk
AC2	H.J.	Winney	Standard

RCAF status promoted Jericho Beach Air Station into a new position of responsibility as the only Permanent Force Unit serving in Vancouver. On a Provincial level,

Jericho's permanent hangars, 1924. DND PMR73-843

the Airmen proudly took their place in all activities involving the other Permanent Forces of the Army and the Navy, and they were also called on to assist with training programs and other initiatives of the numerous Non-Permanent Militia Units in the lower mainland.

HS-2L G-CYGA January 6, 1925 at Jericho Beach. NAC PA133584

JERICHO BEACH: 1925 - 1936

On April 1, 1925 the first of the RCAF operations squadrons, Number 1 Operations Squadron, was formed at Jericho Beach. Additional duties were assigned to the Squadron, which included carrying out combined training operations in artillery observation and W.T.(Radio) communications with both the Army and the Navy. Along with the increased responsibilities, the Squadron fulfilled the seasonal forestry and fishery contracts for 1925. Aircrews logged 45 hours on forestry reconnaissance patrols alone.

During the winter all officers and airmen at Jericho Beach took a winter training program to bring the Air Force members up to operational standards. Physical training and drill instruction sharpened their military stance and such courses as Air Force Law and Discipline, Airmanship, Aeronautical Engineering, Interior Economy and Air Pilotage broadened their general Air Force knowledge.

A new program, initiated that year, earned the Station recognition as the RCAF's Seaplane Training Base. Hopeful of receiving a commission into the RCAF, graduates and under-graduates from universities across Canada arrived at Jericho Beach to learn the complexities of operating seaplanes and flying boats. The training program made use of one of the Station's four HS-2Ls and its one and only Vickers Viking. The Viking, however, demonstrated poor characteristics in the water, and was withdrawn from use at the end of the year's flying. F/L Earl MacLeod's first student was C. Roy Sleman, who rose through the ranks to become an Air Marshal in the RCAF.

Flying Officer Albert Carter visited Jericho Beach in April to give the Airmen their first parachute course. Following the introductory training, the "live" jumps were conducted at Lulu Island. The following month S/L Godfrey was appointed to RCAF Headquarters in Ottawa and S/L J.H. "Tuddy" Tudhope took over command of the Station on May 19, 1925.

July arrived and it was "business as usual" for F/L MacLeod and F/O Hull as they flew north in their HS-2Ls, G-CYGA and G-CYBU, to begin the summer's fishery patrol season in Prince Rupert. A third HS-2L, G-CYGM, and F/O A.L. "Laurie" Morfee, an Air Photographer fresh from pilot training at Camp Borden, joined the detachment. MacLeod's records also show a fourth pilot who increased the officer ranks to four: *"Flight Lieutenant F.J.Mawdesley, an Observer, RCAF, who had also recently obtained his wings as a pilot, joined our detachment to be converted to seaplanes, and to become familiar with the special kind of operations that we were doing."*

F/L MacLeod settled his detachment at a new base-site at Casey Cove, across the harbour from the city of Prince Rupert, on Digby Island, the future location of the Prince Rupert Airport. The season was exceptionally busy. Out of a total of 560 flying hours completed during the year by Jericho Beach Air Station, the Prince Rupert detachment claimed 296 hours, while seaplane conversion and naval cooperation training accounted for 176.5 hours.

At the end of the Prince Rupert fishing season an HS-2L, under the command of F/L MacLeod, was assigned to follow the migrating salmon south. Forty-two hours were flown from a temporary sub-base located at Bamfield on the west coast of Vancouver Island where dense smoke from forest fires in the area merged with the thick, coastal fog to create very hazardous flying conditions. MacLeod included a description of the patrol in a 1972 paper, "In Retrospect":

> *"On September 30th, 1925, with Claire Tennant as my crewman, I flew, in G-CYGN, to Quathiaski Cove, based for a few days at Winter Harbour, and later at Bamfield Cable Station, to continue the patrol of the south-bound salmon migration on the west coast of Vancouver Island.*
>
> *On October 14 we experienced a complete engine breakdown not far from the Carmanah Lighthouse, at a point marked on our chart as 'the Graveyard of the Pacific'. The visibility was quite bad but the sea, fortunately, was quite calm. We found ourselves slowly but relentlessly drifting toward shore*

with the increasingly thunderous and somewhat terrifying sound of ocean waves pounding on forbidding-looking breakers and cliffs, and with no boat in sight.

After a long time a small fishing boat came into our view and passed near to us. The lone Japanese fisherman onboard continued on his way and out of our sight with a completely impassive expression on his face, notwithstanding our shouted requests to be towed to safety as he passed, and the offer of a hundred dollar bill, that I happened to have in my purse, waved in the air to tempt him. He no doubt was hastening to his fishing area and was reluctant to spare precious time away from that activity.

However, he must have changed his mind about helping us, and very shortly we were more than delighted when he came back into view. He towed us to Port Renfrew on Port San Juan Bay, a small community with a pier, but badly exposed to prevalent southeasterly gales in late fall and winter.

In Port Renfrew, with the help of Mr. George Nicholson, Proprietor of an important service in the community - the beer parlour and hotel - we were able to hire two rum runners, who were operating out of Port Renfrew to points across Juan de Fuca Strait. They towed us to Esquimalt Harbour with their scarred Columbia River-type fishing boat. This entailed a night-time stopover at Cherrington Lighthouse, with our plane tied to a piling.

We were welcomed by the Lighthouse Keeper and his family, whose members we felt we already knew as we had exchanged hand-waves many times when we had flown past. We were extended the hospitality of sharing family meals, and two of the children doubled up with other members of the family in order that we could use their room. At the RCN pier at Esquimalt we were able to remove the old engine and to install a new one shipped to us from Jericho Beach. We were able to fly on October 20th, under still foggy conditions, to our Vancouver Base at Jericho Beach."

By the end of the 1925 season, the HS-2Ls were on their last legs as serviceable aircraft for the demanding patrols. The cost involved in maintaining the seasonal program, particularly in the Prince Rupert district, put a severe strain on the Air Force budget and replacing the worn-out

HS-2Ls YEB and YDX in hangar at Jericho. DND PMR82-175

machines was out of the question. An ironic situation existed: the Air Stations now had lots of work, but no aircraft to work with; five years of building a successful peacetime air service had used up their aircraft.

A temporary solution to the dilemma came about in 1926 when Air Force funding was again targeted for a decrease. The government wasn't the only one to resort to major cut-backs in a time of economic restraint. After a period of budget reevaluation, RCAF Headquarters notified the Department of Marine and Fisheries that it would have to abandon the northern British Columbia fishery patrols. The Department did not offer any financial assistance to support the operation, and, even though Provincial Members of Parliament strongly contested the issue in the House of Commons, the RCAF decision stood.

On July 1, 1927 administrational responsibility for the Jericho Beach Air Station was transferred to the non-military Directorate of Civil Government Air Operations, a branch of the Department of National Defence. Instigated by political interests, the DCGAO was formed to administer and control all air operations other than military. However, Jericho Beach continued to be staffed by RCAF personnel who were not attached to this new bureau, therefore the military designation of Jericho Beach lapsed effective on the date of transfer.

The Air Station remained as the RCAF's specialist seaplane conversion and flying boat training centre and, throughout 1927 and 1928, pilots were assigned from Camp Borden in Ontario to Jericho Beach for seaplane conversion. Among a group who arrived in 1927 were F/O E.J.(Paddy) Burke, F/O F.M. Carter, F/O L.H. Weedon, F/O J.C. Uhlman, and F/O Stan R. McMillan. In 1929, after retiring from the service, McMillan and a fellow pilot completed a flight of exploration from Winnipeg, Manitoba to north of the Arctic Circle, earning them the honour of being the first airmen to penetrate the Barren Lands in winter. Paddy Burke, who also became involved in northern flying expeditions, sadly perished in 1930 after making a precautionary landing on a river in northern British Columbia. Stan McMillan participated in the salvage of his friend's Junkers F-13 the following year.

In 1929 fifty-one RCAF pilots and four civilians received conversion courses at the Jericho Beach seaplane training centre. With its Vickers Vedette flying boats and a single DH-60 Gipsy Moth seaplane, the Station recorded an impressive 2065 hours of flying time.

During this period, civil flying operations still occupied an important position in the daily routine at Jericho Beach. Geodetic surveys were added to the regular patrols for Customs and Immigration, but the Station received an increasing number of aerial mapping projects. To sustain the viability of the expanding mapping program, a detachment was established at Shawnigan Lake on Vancouver Island with F/L L.H. "Laurie" Phinney in charge. Phinney was later moved to Forbes Landing on Lower Campbell Lake.

F/L C.R. Dunlap was in charge of a detachment that carried out a mapping project on the Queen Charlotte Islands. Dunlap later rose to the position of Air Marshal, and, prior to the unification of Canada's armed services, he was the last officer to hold the position of Chief of Air Staff, relinquishing this post to become the NORAD Deputy Commander. A third Vancouver "mapping" detachment was located at Summit Lake north of Prince George, British Columbia with F/L A.L. Morfee placed in charge.

An interesting deviation from the regular seasonal flying occurred during 1931. Aircrews from Jericho Beach were assigned to accompany the seal migration to the pupping area in the north Pacific. The Canadian and American governments had agreed to suppress seal hunting in Canadian waters, and, as a result, RCAF aircraft joined forces with the HMCS Vancouver to protect the fur bearing seals from illegal hunting parties.

top; F/O Paddy Burke in Avro at Jericho Seaplane course, 1928. B. Burke Collection

2nd from top; F/O Paddy Burke and F/O F.M. Carter in front of Jericho adminstration building, 1928. DND PMR72-709

3rd from top; 1928 course graduate F/O Stan McMillan stands in cockpit of Stranraer. authors collection via S. McMillan

bottom; F/O Weedon and F/O J.C. Uhlman on graduation from 1928 Jericho Seaplane course. DND PMR72-710

In early January 1931, a number of promising young airmen from RCAF stations across Canada were selected to receive flight training at Camp Borden, Ontario. This group included Norv "Molly" Small, George Desbiens, Harry Bryant, and John "Jack" Hunter.

Jack Hunter listed the Senior Officers at Camp Borden at that time as: W/C G.M. Croil, Commanding Officer, and F/L George Howsam, Adjutant. The Flight Commanders were S/L "Bun" Shearer, S/L "Black Mike" McEwan, and S/L George Brookes, and some of the other officers were E.E.Middleton, "Wib" Van Vliet, Dave Harding, "Soup" Campbell, "Bull" Riddell and O'Brien-Saint.

After graduation and Wings Parade, Hunter, along with the rest of the group, was posted to RCAF Station Jericho Beach for seaplane training. The conversion course took six weeks, but at the end of their training the Airmen got caught in one of the Air Force's periodic "zero expenditure" time frames. No money came through to transfer them back east, which left the group in Vancouver until May 23 of the following year.

Airman Hunter recalls that no one regarded this turn of events as a particular hardship. During their stay at the Jericho Beach Air Station the Airmen were assigned to an interesting variety of operations: Fisheries patrols; Narcotic and Immigration patrols, which were still escorting ships coming into the Vancouver harbour from the Orient; and an unforgettable

Jack Hunter after early training flight in Avro 504 at RCAF Borden, 1931. Jack Hunter Collection

introduction to members of the feathered flight department from the Station's Pigeon Loft. By the time a posting home was issued, the Airmen had survived a series of west coast "adventures in flight" which remained a vivid memory for Jack Hunter:

"Our Commanding Officer at Jericho was S/L Earl MacLeod with F/L A. deNiverville as Adjutant:

Instructors were F/Ls deNiverville, Bennett, Holmes and Mawdesley. We trained on Gipsy Moths on floats, Vedettes, Vancouvers, and the sole Consolidated Courier. We also had the one and only Vickers Vista, a tiny single-seat flying boat that was used only for taxiing practice.

One time I was assigned to a special patrol up the west coast of Vancouver Island, when a schooner was spotted off the coast of Washington. It was apparently carrying a number of Chinese, who planned on landing illegally in some secluded cove along the US coastline. The coast Guard tailed them for several days and then passed the word to our Immigration people when the schooner entered Canadian waters. We were asked to help by setting up a patrol to search out the coves and inlets on the west coast of the Island.

It was getting late in the fall and the weather in that area was certainly not the best. We were given a Vancouver for the job and searched as best we could, up the coast from Esquimalt to Barkley Sound through rain and fog patches. A Destroyer of the RCN was standing by there with our fuel. We pulled up to her stern and made fast with a bow and two wing lines while I remained on the aircraft to assist in the refuelling.

A sudden squall came down the mountains and the Destroyer started to drag anchor; this was no place for the skipper, so he took off, with us in tow. I was in the cockpit at the time, and the wind was so strong that on easing back on the control column I could get airborne behind the destroyer. We were in tow from shortly after noon until nine that night and finally found shelter at Port Renfrew. I was soaked to the skin by that time and so cold I had to have assistance in getting aboard the ship. Down in the wardroom, a full glass of Navy Rum helped to stop my shaking but didn't help too much in trying to mount a Navy hammock, my bed for the night.

We often went out on fisheries patrol to check on the amount of net being used by fishermen in Howe Sound and up the Straits of Georgia. I remember one day landing beside a Japanese fisherman who was using about twice the legal footage limit. I signalled him to approach the aircraft and he started up and charged at me full bore. I pulled a Very pistol out of my map case and let one fly at him. The Very light bounced off his deck and you never saw a boat go into reverse as fast in your life - he didn't want any part of that. I copied down his boat license number and turned it in to the Fisheries people for further action."

Sgts Jack D. Hunter and Harry Bryant at Jericho Beach, 1931. Jack Hunter Collection

The Vedettes and Vancouvers had no wireless equipment so a violation report often took many hours to reach the appropriate authorities. However, on occasion, the innovative use of the Station's carrier pigeons brought the pilot's message "home". Jericho Beach continued to stock the pigeon loft and the pilots were often instructed to take along a wicker basket of birds to release from the aircraft during the flight. This served a duel purpose: the pigeons got some exercise, and it gave both pilot and pigeon some practice in "air mail" communication. The pigeons, usually nesting females, anxiously waited for their basket to open and then made a speedy return directly to their loft. But on one practice outing, Airman Hunter had a basket of unenthusiastic flyers:

"I released the birds at Esquimalt and they seemed reluctant to leave the aircraft, in fact, I had to shoo them away two or three times before they climbed, circled and disappeared from view behind the mountains.

When I got back to Jericho, our CO, S/L Earl MacLeod, was pacing the beach waiting for me to taxi the Vedette to shore. I sensed that there was something wrong but didn't know what I was in for. I no sooner beached the aircraft than MacLeod said, 'You didn't release the pigeons, did you, Sergeant?' 'Oh my, my, my!' was all I could say. It turned out that these particular birds had been sent over from the King's loft in Britain and were for breeding purposes only - they had never flown in this country. We waited around all the rest of that day, but they never did come home."

Pigeon loft, Jericho Beach. DND PL143818

During 1931 Jericho Beach was staffed by four officers and thirty-five airmen under the acting command of S/L Earl MacLeod. MacLeod was succeeded on December 28, 1931 by S/L A.B. (Bun) Shearer.

In 1932 the effects of the economic depression took a drastic toll on the RCAF. The government slashed Appropriations, forcing a reduction in strength on a national level. Out of 177 officers only 78 remained, and the number of airmen on strength dropped from 729 down to 100. A further 110 civilian employees also found themselves out of work. Most of the aircrew released were engaged in civil operations, and the officers held non-permanent commissions. Two Sergeant pilots who were released had been members of the Air Force since 1923. In all, 65 pilots were released from the RCAF and all air photography ceased except for map making.

One positive note in the year was the return of service designations that had lapsed since 1927. Number 1 (Operations) Squadron was the first RCAF unit to receive its designation. It was formed as No. 4 (FB) Flying Boat Squadron at Jericho Beach on February 17, 1933 and W/C A. B. Shearer was assigned as the Commanding Officer.

Although responsibility for the drastic reduction in RCAF personnel during 1932 rested entirely with the Bennett government, the same administration initiated an increase in flying activity during 1934 and 1935. Five new, non-permanent squadrons were recruited, including one in Vancouver in 1934, and the first purchase of aircraft since 1931 was approved. Included in the purchase were 5 Canadian Vickers Vancouver Flying Boats, numbers 902 to 906, which all eventually served at Jericho Beach. Many of the other "new" aircraft were refurbished, obsolete RAF machines, but the RCAF viewed them as a step in a positive direction.

Earl MacLeod, a founding pilot of the Jericho Beach Air Station and without question its longest serving staff member, was promoted to the rank of Squadron Leader on April 1, 1934. Effective November 30, 1935, he was appointed Air Staff Officer at Military District No. 11 at Victoria. S/L MacLeod gave the following explanation of his duties as a RCAF Liaison Officer;

"In 1935 a decision was made, because of increasing need for cooperation on the west coast between the RCAF, Army, and RCN, to have an RCAF Liaison

S/L Earl MacLeod prepares to fly Lord and Lady Tweedsmuir from Intata Lake to Bella Coola in a Fairchild 71, August, 1937. via Walter E. Gilbert

Officer at MD 11 Headquarters, Esquimalt. I received that appointment and assisted the District Officer Commanding, an Army Officer, in air matters. By that time non-permanent RCAF Squadrons had been organized in the Province and their administration came directly under the District Officer commanding MD 11 Victoria.

In August of 1937 while I was serving as RCAF Liaison Officer at MD 11 Esquimalt, I was detailed from Ottawa to take charge of a detachment of 4 aircraft to supply air transportation for a very special occasion - a fortnight's outing in which the planes would be used in the newly established Tweedsmuir Park - an event that was hosted by the B.C. Government. The guests of honour were to be the Governor General, Lord Tweedsmuir and Lady Tweedsmuir and members of the party accompanying them. The B.C. Government had established a splendid wilderness camp on Intata Lake at Susan Point. Our four planes at Intata Lake (Fairchild 71s) were flown by myself, and Captains Ted Dobbin of Vancouver, Charlie Elliot of North Vancouver and F/L F.J. Mawdesley of the RCAF.

On instruction from Vancouver in connection with the selection of coastal RCAF bases, Mawdesley and I flew our Fairchilds to Prince Rupert on August 27, 1937 thence to Alert Bay on August 30, and returned to Jericho Beach on August 31 before I returned to my liaison duties at Esquimalt."

Number 4 Squadron personnel at Jericho Beach, mid-1930:

S/L	A.B. Shearer *CO No. 4 (FB) Squadron Jericho Beach February 17, 1933 - November 4, 1936; posted Ottawa November 4, 1936. Later to become a Wing Commander.*
F/O	J.H. Ferguson *February 1932 to November 1934*
F/L	M. Costello *May 1932 to September 1934*
F/L	A.L. Johnson *January 1933 to April 1937*
F/L	J.L. Plant *November 1934 to May 1936*
F/L	C.B. Turner *October 1934 to January 1939*
F/L	Harold Pearce *Joined No. 4 Squadron as a Corporal Photographer May 1934, and left as an Officer in Aug. 1939*
F/L	F.J. Mawdesley *May 1935 to February 1939; as S/L was CO of No. 4 Squadron October 21, 1939 to March 11, 1940*
S/L	L.F. Stevenson *February 1936 to 1939; Air Commodore Stevenson: later became an Air Vice Marshal, returning to the west coast as Air Officer Commanding Western Air Command at Command Headquarters Jericho Beach.*

F/Sgt. H.J. Winney and Sgt. N.E. (Molly) Small were also active members of the Squadron. And, in July 1936, P/O N.B. Petersen, P/O W.E. Kennedy, and F/O E.H. Evans were posted to No. 4 Squadron.

The personnel of No. 4 (FB) Squadron began training in 1935 in Coastal Reconnaissance duties according to the schedule for ground and aircrew training laid down by the Royal Air Force. As new aircraft and equipment for ground instructional purposes were received, the scope of training increased, and Army cooperation exercises were carried out with units in Military District No. 11.

Shortly after joining the Squadron in April 1936, S/L Stevenson, in company with F/Sgt. Winney, left Jericho Beach on a survey flight of the Queen Charlotte Islands. The Airmen were assigned to report on potential locations for airfields and flying boat stations in preparation for the defence of the west coast of Canada in the event of war.

Throughout the next three years survey flights along the pacific coast became a major activity of the Squadron. As the certainty of a war and the fear of a Japanese invasion of the west coast grew, Stevenson, Mawdesley, and others attached to the British Columbia Reconnaissance Detachment made the final selection for the construction of five west coast Flying Boat Stations.

The following form is a reproduction of the original DAILY DIARY prepared by S/L F.J. Mawdesley during a tour of duty at Alliford Bay six days before Canada entered the war September 10, 1939.

SECRET

R.C.A.F.R. 65

THIS FORM IS TO BE USED IN ACCORDANCE WITH PARAGRAPHS 1931 and 1932r K.R. & O. FOR THE R.C.A.F. AND AIR FORCE ADMINISTRATIVE ORDER A.39/1.

REFERENCE TO APPENDICES

DAILY DIARY OF
(unit or formation) Alliford Bay Detachment, RCAF

PLACE	DATE	TIME	SUMMARY OF EVENTS
Alliford Bay	4.9.39		Alliford Bay Detachment arrived at Alliford Bay at approximately 1730 hours. Stranraer 912 flew over at 1700 hours. Baggage and freight moved into storehouse. Personnel unable to move into quarters allotted due to lack of heat, water, light and bedding. Now temporarily accommodated in construction camp bunkhouse. Stranraer arrived at approximately 2000 hours. refuelled. remaining overnight. Guard duties assumed and guard mounted at 2000 hours.
Alliford Bay	5.9.39		Unpacking and straightening up of equipment and quarters. Stranraer 912 departed at noon. C.G.S. Nitinat arrived at approximately 1700 hours. Radio equipment assembled and schedules attempted without success. Guard duties as per operation order No. 2-39
Alliford Bay	6.9.39		Straightening up and checking of stores carried out. Contact with Bella Bella by radio made. Radiogram sent through Dead Tree wireless station to Vancouver Air Station. Men employed cutting wood for fuel for the stoves. Gasoline delivered from Skidegate by motor launch "Qualis". Guard duties as per operation order. Guard duties and other essential duties leave but one man available for fatigues; unsatisfactory.
Alliford Bay	7.9.39		Commenced construction of walk from bunkhouse to tarmac over rough and boggy ground. Cutting fuel for the stoves. M.S. Imperial docked at approximately 1730 hours. Supply of gasoline and diesel oil delivered. All radio messages passed through Bella Bella Station. RCAF Station contacted direct by radio during the late evening. Guard duties as per schedule.
Alliford Bay	8.9.39		Weather observations. Attempts being made to contact Vancouver Air Station by radio every hour. M.S. Imperial departed at 1500 hours. Nightly radio schedule arranged with Vancouver Station. Three schedules daily with Bella Bella. Guard duties as per schedule.
Alliford Bay	9.9.39		Weather observations. Guard duties as per schedule. Routine work.

F.J. Mawdesley Sqn. Ldr.
OC No. 4 (BR) Squadron

1

2

3

4

5

6

1. *Felixtowe and three HS-2Ls between Bessineau hangars at Jericho Beach, 1921.* DND PL143836
2. *Cletrac tractor moving engine at Jericho, 1921.* DND PL143825
3. *Reassembly of YBA at Carney's Landing on Shuswap Lake.* DND PL143830
4. *YBA being launched into Shuswap Lake.* DND PMR82-173
5. *YBA arrives back at Jericho on Kelly truck after Sicamous survey.* DND PL143821
6. *Felixtowe YDI at rest on Nootka Sound, 1922.* Fred M. Lord c/o Bruce S. Lord

7

8

9

10

11

7. *Air mechanics prepare to beach Felixtowe YDI after it returns to Jericho.* DND PL143827

8. *Tom Cowley (left) and Earl MacLeod (right) pose with Earl Godfrey in front of HS-2L.* DND

9. *S/L E. Godfrey(left) and WO M. Graham enroute from Ottawa to Jericho in FC-2, September, 1928.* DND

10. *Airmen drill in front of Jericho Headquarters building, 1923.* DND PMR79270

11. *HS-2L G-CYGM crashes near Klemtu, 1924.* CFB Comox Rowe Library

12

13

THE FOREST WATCHER

Over lake and pine-clad forest,
Over river flashing by,
Sails the white-winged forest watcher,
Softly in a cloud-swept sky.

Softly drones the distant engine,
Over virgin timberland,
Speaking peace unto the forest,
Where the mighty giants stand.

Onward then o'er tracts scarce charted,
Over cataracts asweep,
Over mountain, plain and valley,
Over glades that lie asleep,

Far into the western twilight,
Flashing wings against the sun,
Hums the softening song of engine,
Throbbing until day is done.

F/L F.V. Heakes, RCAF, 1928

14

15

16

12. *Fairchild FC-2W over Nimkish Lake, Vancouver Island. (G-CYXN).* CFB Comox Rowe Library
13. *Two Vedettes at Harrison Lake, BC. Flown from Jericho Beach by Sergeant pilots Harry Bryant and Jack Hunter.* Jack Hunter Collection
14. *Vickers Varuna at Shirleys Bay, BC.* PAC HC843
15. *Sgt. Molly Small.* Jack Hunter Collection
16. *Sgt. Jack Hunter and Sgt. George (Beans) Desbiens.* Jack Hunter Collection

17

18

19

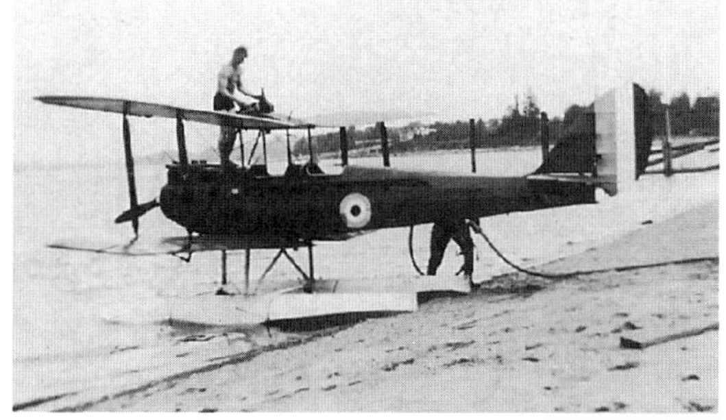

20

21

22

23

24

17. *Vedette near Sidney, BC, 1929.* Jack Hunter Collection
18. *Airman Lock Madill in flying gear with DH-60 at Jericho, 1929.* Madill Collection
19. *DH-60 Moth (RCAF #104) being fuelled at Jericho Beach, May 23, 1929 by Lock Madill.* Madill Collection
20. *Vickers Viking G-CAEB at Jericho Beach, 1931.* Madill Collection
21. *Three Moths and Vedette next to slipway at Jericho Beach, May 23, 1929.* Madill Collection
22. *An unusual aircraft at Jericho Beach during 1930. A Fairey IIIF MKIVGP on loan from the RAF for evaluation.* Madill Collection
23. *Vedette FY-F of No. 4(BR) Squadron Jericho Beach, Spring 1940.* DND 77-156
24. *Consolidated Courier #24 on single float as used at Jericho, 1930.* BCMFT (DND)

chapter two

PRELUDE TO WAR

Vancouver #906 over Vancouver Lions Peaks. Coombes Collection

The dawn of 1936 brought a climate of change, not only to Canada, but also to the entire civilized world. The Conservative government of R.B. Bennett was defeated in October 1935. Early in February 1936 the Liberal government of William Lyon MacKenzie King opened its first session of parliament with the Prime Minister leading the House in mourning for King George V. The Versailles peace settlement also died in 1936 as a result of Mussolini's refusal to recognize the economic sanctions placed against Italy by the League of Nations: sanctions imposed after Mussolini's troops ruthlessly conquered Ethopia in the fall of 1935. The League of Nations remained powerless in enforcing its authority, and Adolf Hitler's National Socialist regime quickly seized the opportunity to march into a demilitarized Rhineland in the spring of 1936.

By midsummer of the same year Spain provided Hitler, Mussolini, and Stalin with a bloody manoeuvring ground upon which to test their developing military might. Japan, an ally in the First World War, also abandoned the League of Nations and delivered a proclamation of her ambitions for empire; the Japanese march into Manchuria in 1931 was a forerunner of this mounting ambition.

Vedette #803 beaching at Jericho Beach. Madill Collection

On the eve of his retirement in 1935, the Canadian Chief of General Staff Major General A.G.L. McNaughton, wrote a paper clearly stating the realities of defense in Canada. He reviewed the breakdown of international order: the departure of Japan from the League of Nations, the rise of Hitler, and Germany's withdrawal from the League. Chastising the Canadian government for its failure to provide even a minimum standard of national defense, his report revealed that air force strength had diminished, between 1932 and 1935, to below thirty percent of the agreed minimums. MacNaughton was also gravely concerned that the proposed partition of Europe into an armed alliance was strongly reminiscent of 1914.

McNaughton fully realized the responsibility he had assumed by excluding from his paper any recommendations for the Land Forces. He believed that a strong Air Force organization was the most urgent requirement: an essential element in the defence of the Pacific Coast. In McNaughton's view it was vital for the Canadian Air Force to be able to respond immediately and decisively to

No. 4 (BR) airman poses in front of Jericho barracks. Driscoll Collection

any attempt by the enemy to establish submarine or aircraft bases within an effective radius of action. He argued that the most probable contingency seemed to be Canada's defence of her neutrality in a war in which the United States might be engaged with a Trans-Pacific Power. In this event Canada would remain friendly with her American neighbour, and liabilities might be restricted to ensuring that the Japanese respected the Rules of Neutrality prescribed by the Treaty of 1872.

McNaughton could not have been clearer in his criticism:

> *"The requirements for Forces sufficient to discharge our obligations for the maintenance of our neutrality in the West are neither extensive nor very costly and it seems to me that by their absence we are taking a risk to our future wholly disproportionate to the interests we have at stake."*

He emphatically stressed that Canada's defence establishment's main emphasis was to protect Canadian neutrality, and to protect the country's coasts, ports and sea routes.

The United States Congressional Committee voiced a warning that paralleled McNaughton's evaluation. They concluded that it was entirely possible for a belligerent to attack the United States using a Canadian base, and that Canada was not in a position to defend itself. They reasoned that if a nation hostile to the United States was to overfly Canada, or utilize Canada's bases in order to mount an attack, this action would force the United States to take steps to defend Canada. The Canadian Department of External Affairs obtained a copy of the United States Congressional hearing and submitted it to the Canadian Military for comment. Their reply was sympathetic to the United States military viewpoint, stating that the United States was obligated to contemplate measures to protect itself from an attack, not by Canada, but via Canada.

An editorial in the Ottawa Evening Citizen sent out

The first RCAF Blackburn-built Shark II #503 at Trenton, 1936. Driscoll Collection

Fairchild FC-2 G-CYXN with Vedette at Forbes Landing. DND/PA 62982 via CFB Comox Rowe Library

another clear message to MacKenzie's government. It pointed out that the United States had to look after its own interests - if Canada was not doing its share it was because the government had virtually disbanded the Royal Canadian Air Force. The writer suggested that if Canada continued to ignore its defence responsibilities the pretense of nationhood must be abandoned. These warnings made slight impact on MacKenzie King's Liberal government. They had a huge majority of 174 Members of Parliament; a large segment of this majority believed that no military commitment should be made in advance of its need, and that every question should be judged upon its merits by Parliament. There were just 40 Conservatives, the smallest number since Confederation, but they represented established ways, solid wealth and big business. Among their strongholds were the Victoria and Vancouver South ridings.

Ian MacKenzie, Canada's new Defence Minister, painted a glowing picture of the RCAF while carefully emphasizing Canada's neutrality as the prime requisite. The aviation estimates which the Defence Minister presented to the House in May 1936, called for an appropriation of $5,801,100 - an increase of almost $1,500,000 over the previous year. There were, as usual, three items: the RCAF was to receive $4,130,000 (an increase of $1,000,000); civil government air operations would receive $408,300 (a decrease of $16,700); and civil aviation would receive $1,262, 800 (an increase of $514,900).

The debate on the RCAF item consisted almost entirely of an exchange between Mr. H.C.Green, the Conservative member for Vancouver South, and the Defence Minister. Mr Green opened the discussion by asking whether any steps had been taken to develop air defences along the Canadian coast: the first time such a question had been asked in the House of Commons. The Minister replied that this was one of the first problems before the Department, as it had been for several years. Following plans put in place by his predecessor for a study of coastal defence - particularly in B.C. - Mr. MacKenzie pointed out that the budget increases would provide for more accommodation at Vancouver's Jericho Beach Air Station. The air defences would be increased from time to time, as funds became available, with the ultimate plan being a considerable increase in the air forces on the Pacific coast. The Minister disclosed his feeling that air and naval expansion should move ahead concurrently, but he admitted that this was being done in a very modest way; however, he noted that they were proceeding as fast as the economic resources at present would permit.

While commending the Defence Minister for the increase in the appropriation, Mr. Green pressed for information about the cost of establishing a complete program of air defence on the Pacific coast. Mr. Mackenzie said the answer to that question would depend entirely upon how far the government in power would go in a policy of expansion, and also upon the technical advice of the officers responsible for the command of an air force sufficient to look after the defence of the Dominion. MacKenzie referred to the budget increase as an indication that the government was alive to the situation, but added that he

top; No 4(GR) Squadron air gunners at Jericho Beach, December 14th, 1938. left to right Sgt. Bendall, Cpl. McLean, Cpl. Whalen, Cpl. Wilcock, Cpl. Smithers, Sgt. Randall. CFB Comox Rowe Library

above; Front Lewis gun on Vickers Vancouver. January 31st, 1936. NAC 133581

personally thought an even greater increase was necessary.

Despite the acknowledgement from both sides of the House regarding the importance of air defence, most of the money was used for new ground services, equipment and maintenance, and only three new aircraft (Blackburn Sharks) were actually purchased.

On the British Columbia coast, the Jericho Beach Air Station found itself poised on the edge of a political hornet's nest. It was a time of transition from peacetime activity to making preparations for an unrest that no one could accurately predict. However, one thing was clear: the defence capabilities of the military presence on the west coast were being questioned, and both military and political leaders wanted to display the best of what they had to offer.

Until 1936 Jericho Beach Air Station was the only RCAF station on the west coast of British Columbia. It was the headquarters for all Air Force activity on the Pacific coast. From their location at Vancouver's English Bay, detachments continued their mapping projects and seasonal forestry, fishery, and customs patrols on behalf of various government agencies. For nearly 15 years the RCAF had served the needs of communities on the rugged British Columbia coast and throughout isolated areas in the interior of the Province.

As a precursor to the drastic changes that would evolve over the next few years, No. 4 (FB) Flying Boat Squadron, at Jericho Beach Air Station, received orders to begin surveying the coast of British Columbia to identify potential land and seaplane bases. In October 1936 the Squadron Commanding Officer Wing Commander A.B. Shearer and Sergeant N.E. Small, flying Fairchild seaplanes, left Jericho Beach in the company of Royal Canadian Navy vessel HMCS Vancouver. Sites visited on their inspection tour included: Ucluelet and Coal Harbour on the west coast of Vancouver Island, Bella Bella, Alliford Bay in the Queen Charlotte Islands, and Seal Cove at Prince Rupert.

Shearer was promoted after his return to Jericho Beach in November and he turned the command of the Squadron over to Wing Commander A. L. Cuffe. On November 18, 1936, Senior Air Officer Air Commodore G.M. Croil, advised

Northrop Delta on floats (RCAF #676). Maude Collection

W/C Cuffe that his unit would soon be called upon to prepare an extended survey of all possible sites for land and sea aircraft bases along the British Columbia coast. The following month a reconnaissance party, under the command of F/L F.J. Mawdesley, went to Patricia Bay on Vancouver Island to make the initial preparations to establish an air base. This same group completed surveys of Sproat Lake and Forbes Landing on central Vancouver Island, and Alert Bay. The survey party, officially referred to as the British Columbia Reconnaissance Detachment, operated one Fairchild and a Vancouver Flying Boat on these expeditions.

Preparation for the defence of Canada's west coast became an increasingly urgent matter, and, in light of the growing concern over Japan's intentions, earlier warnings took on greater significance. From a defence standpoint, the rugged, often inaccessible west coast was now viewed as a liability instead of an asset. The possibility that Canada would become the front line of attack, and a probable invasion point, could no longer be ignored.

Jericho Beach Air Station, under Wing Commander Cuffe's command, quickly assumed a tighter military stance. Considerable energy went into recruiting in the Vancouver area, and the enlisted recruits were immediately sent to Camp Borden and to Trenton for training.

Air Vice-Marshal Croil, the RCAF's first Chief of Air Staff. CFB Comox Rowe Library

Jericho's Vickers Vancouver Flying Boats were fitted with Lewis guns and bomb racks, and the men received new-armament training courses. An explosive storage area was established, and RCAF meteorological detachments were set up at Bella Bella and Prince Rupert.

A detachment from No. 6 (TB) Torpedo Bomber Squadron arrived from Trenton with Two Northrop Deltas on floats, flown by F/O H.M. Carscallen, and Sgt. R.I. Thomas. The detachment carried out photographic operations on the west coast before returning to Ottawa in November 1937. The flurry of activity at Jericho Beach accelerated during the year with initiatives on the part of Station personnel greatly assisting the sense of a developing defensive air force.

RCAF "Scow" at Bella Bella, summer 1939. Galbraith Collection

Number 4 (FB) Squadron continued their surveying duties throughout 1937, as well as participating in army cooperation exercises with coastal defence batteries. During August, three Vickers Vancouver Flying Boats arrived at Bella Bella to establish a meteorological reporting station, and later that year Squadron Leader Mawdesley was assigned temporary duty at Prince Rupert with one of Jericho's Fairchilds. Number 4 (FB) Squadron completed 735 hours during the period 1936 - 1937, and 750 hours in 1938. The Squadron was second only to No. 2 Squadron at Trenton, Ontario in its volume of flying activity.

Additional personnel at Jericho Beach in 1937 were:

F/O R.C. Ripley, January 1937 to April 1938;

F/L J.G.W. Weston, an RAF exchange officer, January 1937 to March 1937;

F/L R.C.F. Luke, April 1937 to September 1938;

F/L W.P.G. Pretty, an R.A.F. exchange officer, May 1937 to November 1938;

F/L W.I. Riddell, November 1937 to May 1938;

F/O H.B. Jasper, December 1937 to March 1939.

On March 18, 1937, Wing Commander Cuffe sent a report to Air Commodore Croil advising that the No. 4 (FB) Squadron Reconnaissance Detachment was at Alert Bay and proposed to move to Bella Bella on April 5th. Subject to Croil's approval, they planned to locate a scow seaplane tender at Bella Bella. The scow would house three facilities: an aircraft refuelling base, a weather reporting station, and a wireless communication facility. In his report, W/C Cuffe recommended that permanent detachments be stationed at Prince Rupert, Alliford Bay, and Quatsino Sound in order to report weather conditions. The Air Commodore approved Cuffe's report but did not immediately act on the Wing Commander's recommendations.

In January of 1938, Major General E.C. Ashton, McNaughton's successor as Canadian Chief of General Staff, visited his American counterpart in Washington. Lieutenant Colonel M.A.Pope, Secretary of the United States Joint Staff Committee, repeated the American government's concern regarding Canada's ability to remain aloof in the event of hostility between the United States and Japan. He pointed out that the United States would probably ride roughshod over Canada and use her facilities as needed. Lack of confidence in their northern neighbour's ability to defend her neutrality, and the threat this created to the defence of the United States, forced the Americans to make an offer: the United States Army would, on Canada's agreement, extend its area of responsibility to include the Canadian coastline from Alaska to the 49th Parallel. They also offered to provide both mobile artillery and aircraft providing there were suitable landing areas.

As its responsibilities for Canada's national defence increased, the RCAF again began to question its subordinate status to the Army, a situation that had existed since the Air Force was incorporated into the Department of National Defence in 1922. In 1935, Air Commodore Croil had recommended a full scale revision of the administrative and the command structure of the RCAF.

In the fall of 1937, Croil again campaigned for the cause of Air Force independence and the need to decentralize control through regional air commands. He pointed out that the British Columbia Reconnaissance Detachment on the west coast had been, for the last year or more, determining base sites: they had no local coordinating authority to provide direction, nor was there any RCAF headquarters to command either the permanent or the non-permanent units stationed in British Columbia.

The permanent unit stationed at Jericho Beach, No. 4 (FB) Flying Boat Squadron, reported to Air Force Headquarters in Ottawa for training, employment, and technical maintenance, while it reported to the Officer Commanding No. 11 (MD) Military District Army, in Victoria, for administration. The non-permanent unit No. 111 (CAC) Coast Artillery Cooperation Squadron was entirely under the jurisdiction of the Officer Commanding Military District No.ll in Victoria for all matters.

The deputy Minister and the Minister of National Defence agreed with Croil, and machinery was set into motion to create an RCAF Western Air Command. On March 15, 1938, Western Air Command was finally authorized and, effective April 15, Group Captain G.O. Johnson, Commanding Officer of RCAF Station Vancouver (Jericho Beach), assumed command. As of August 1, this command included all RCAF units on the British Columbia coast.

Wing parade No. 3 (RD) practice for King's visit. WO T. Livingstone left, F/L W. Van Vliet centre, WO J.H. Palmer right. Palmer Collection

In the July 1938 edition of the Canadian Defence Quarterly, Colonel H.F.G. Letson, E.D., reiterated the importance of the move toward greater command efficiency:

> *"We must have an adequate air force for air purposes of reconnaissance and for direct action against enemy naval and air forces. To fortify every possible landing place on this endless coast line of B.C. would involve a prohibitive expenditure of money and manpower, and would be in contradiction to that axiom of war, namely economy of forces."*

Effective January 1, No. 4 Squadron received redesignation as a General Reconnaissance Squadron. During 1938 the Squadron continued its coastal survey duties with detachments at Prince Rupert and Bella Bella. They also participated in photographic activity in conjunction with a detachment of No. 6 (TB) Squadron's two Deltas which were again on the Pacific coast attached to Jericho Beach.

On February 23, 1938, Wing Commander A.C. Cuffe handed over command of No. 4 (GR) Squadron to S/L Earl MacLeod who, eight months later, was posted to command Station Vancouver (Jericho Beach) and promoted to Wing Commander. S/L W.I. Riddell was given command of No. 4 (GR) Squadron as Jericho Beach Air Station prepared for expansion. Number 6 (TB) Squadron, at Trenton Ontario, received notice of their transfer to the west coast. An advance party arrived in Vancouver in October, followed on November 1 by the balance of the Squadron with its five Blackburn Shark IIs tied down on flat cars. The Squadron, led by S/L A.H. Hull, had two other officers: F/L Springall and F/O Doyle; two NCO pilots, WO Horner and F/S Ready; and 51 airmen. The Squadron completed its move by November 6 and groups of airmen were immediately dispatched to the Boeing Aircraft Company plant, on Georgia Street in downtown Vancouver, for instructional courses on the Shark aircraft.

top, Shark #507 dropping torpedo in English Bay, 1939. DND D/HIST
above, Stranraer #915 (FY-B) at Jericho Beach. DND D/HIST

On January 3, 1939, S/L A.J. Ashton assumed command of No. 4 (GR) Squadron, and S/L Riddell was posted to Trenton. No. 4 and No. 6 Squadrons were issued gas masks and given instruction on the Lewis guns installed earlier on the Vickers Vancouver Flying Boats. The Squadrons also received training in the operation of camera guns, and trap shooting. In January three sergeant pilots joined No. 6 (TB) Squadron: E.R. Austin, R.R.B. Hoodspith, and R.H. Mervin. In March Pilot Officers J. Ewart and R.F. Gibb were transferred to the Squadron

Sharks 519, 520 undergoing final assembly after delivery from Boeing Plant to Jericho Beach. Palmer Collection

along with exchange officer F/O C.F. Herington, who replaced S/L Springall after Springall returned to the RAF.

On February 16, a detachment from Jericho Beach No. 4 (GR) Squadron left for Kennedy Lake, near Ucluelet. They were assigned one Vickers Vancouver Flying Boat to patrol Barkley sound and to complete a five week survey of the area in connection with the future development of a base at Ucluelet. No. 4 Squadron's stated war duty was to make a seaward reconnaissance of the Barkley Sound area, and to this end the Squadron was eventually stationed at Ucluelet.

Tentative sites for Direction Finding stations were selected at Ucluelet, Coal Harbour, and Alliford Bay, and detachments from both No. 4 and No. 6 Squadrons started regular patrols of the entire coast. The RCMP vessel MacDonald was stationed at Ucluelet to provide security and communications for aircraft refuelling there.

Squadron members who remained at the Jericho Beach Station continued their training on Lewis guns and camera guns. The pilots took a link trainer course as well as formation flying instruction, followed in the spring of 1939 by a torpedo course. During April 1939, No.6 (TB) Squadron started to receive its first Shark III's, which were being assembled at Jericho Beach. This enabled the unit to increase their formation flying training and torpedo bombing practice. The arrival of King George VI and Queen Elizabeth, in the spring of 1939, provided a welcome break from training. A formation of five Sharks from the No. 6 (TB) Squadron, and three Vickers Vancouver Flying Boats attached to No. 4 (GR) Squadron, escorted the King and Queen on their return trip to Victoria, B.C.

On October 31, 1939, No. 6 Squadron was officially redesignated as a bomber reconnaissance squadron and commenced regular patrols of shipping in the Gulf of Georgia. The Squadron was placed on stand-by as a striking force, and two Shark IIs were detached and sent to RCAF Station Ucluelet: Shark #503 flown by W/C Allan H. Hull and crewed by Sgt. Middleton and A.C. Galt; Shark #501 piloted by Sgt. Austin, and crewed by Cpl. Haddon

RCAF Jericho Beach Annual Inspection, 1931. S/L Earl MacLeod commanding, seated 4th from left. Lock Madill Collection

and Cpl. Gill.

Number 6 (BR) Squadron led a very lonely existence, living in primitive conditions at the partially completed station at Ucluelet. Some personnel had difficulty with the drinking water which gave them a type of cedar poisoning that developed into uncomfortable hives. A further hardship was created by the necessity of mooring the Squadron's Sharks at the end of Ucuelet's inlet. Station personnel were required to do guard duty in row boats - a most unpleasant duty during long, wet and foggy nights. During their nine month stay the detachment saw little of military interest on its patrols. The two Sharks and their crews represented the vanguard of personnel at Ucluelet until May 1, 1940, when No. 4 (BR) Squadron's Stranraers, Sharks, and a Fairchild seaplane arrived to take over operations.

With Canada's declaration of war against Germany on September 10, 1939, the activity at Jericho Beach Air Station increased tenfold. A detachment from No. 4 (GR) Squadron was dispatched to Alliford Bay in the Queen Charlotte Islands to establish communications and take weather observations. On September 12, the first war time coastal patrol was dispatched in Stranraer #912 flown by S/L Mawdesley, who had temporarily been reassigned to Jericho Beach because of the hostilities. Mawdesley had ferried #912 to Jericho Beach from eastern Canada in July of 1939 with S/L Ashton serving as co-pilot.

On October 31, 1939, the Squadron's status changed to No. 4 (BR) Bomber Reconnaissance, and S/L F.J. Mawdesley assumed command of the Squadron. They were re-equipped with No. 5 Squadron's Stranraers which, as the aircraft became available, were ferried out to Jericho Beach from eastern Canada. As soon as this was accomplished, No. 4's Vancouver Flying Boats were relegated to the Seaplane Training School at Jericho Beach.

Sergeant Pilot Grant McConnell participated in the Stranraer transfer from the east coast. Attached to No. 5 Squadron, he was in command of Stranraer #918 which he ferried from Dartmouth, Nova Scotia in company with Stranraer #922. On the final segment of their journey the

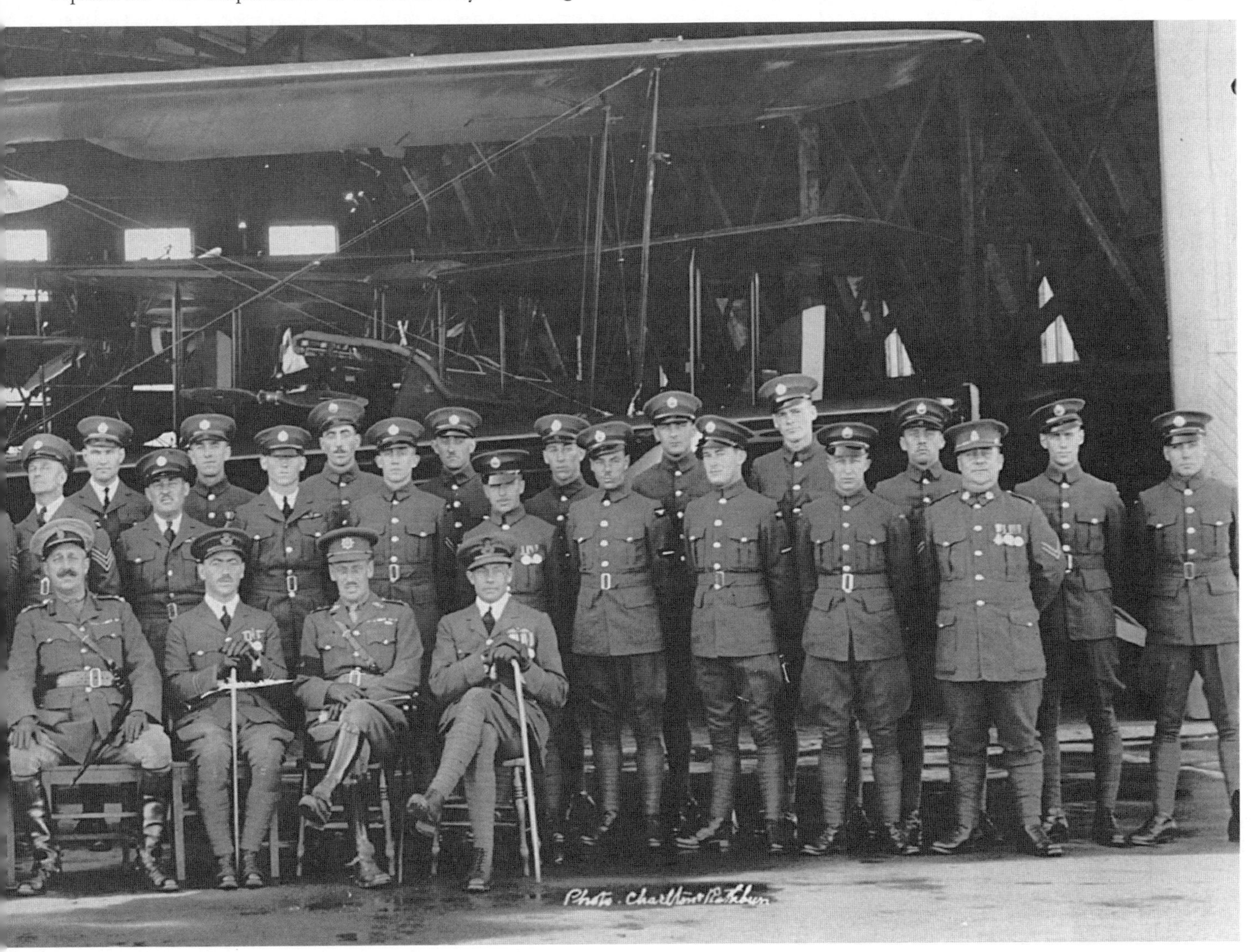

two aircraft were weathered in at Nelson, British Columbia for several days. When they finally arrived in Penticton they found a third No.5 Squadron Stranraer, #946, tied up to the dock in preparation for a departure to Jericho Beach.

The following morning Sgt. J.F. Bliss, the pilot of #946, left Penticton with five airmen on board. They set course for Vancouver but were engulfed in deteriorating weather conditions. Sgt. Bliss and his crew were not seen again, and the aircraft was listed as missing - it was not found until 1947 when its wreckage was discovered at the headwaters of the Indian River, south east of Squamish, British Columbia.

The balance of No. 4 and No. 6 (BR) Squadron personnel remained at Jericho Beach Air Station. Number 6 (BR) Squadron continued to receive the new Shark IIIs as they were completed at the Boeing Aircraft plant. On September 5, 1939, five Sharks were taking off from English Bay on a patrol when #515 hit a heavy swell and crashed. Shark #514 hit the same swell, momentarily became airborne and, after porpoising, it also crashed. Both aircraft quickly sank, although the crews sustained only slight injury. Again, on October 15, further problems were experienced as Shark #516 also crashed on take off. The pilot of Shark #514, RAF exchange officer F/O Herington, earned the title of "Crasher" after he demolished his second Shark, #507. A third Shark, Blackburn-built #526 in service on the east coast as a target tug, also suffered at the hands of the "Crasher". F/O Herington, who had been transferred to No. 10 Squadron at Dartmouth, Nova Scotia, managed to run #526 into the crash truck. In November of 1940, the Shark III was shipped back to No. 3 Repair Depot at Jericho Beach, and, after repairs were completed, it was taken on strength with No. 7 (BR) Squadron at Prince Rupert. Two years later F/O G.A. Doolittle managed to permanently write off the ill-fated aircraft in a glassy water landing at Seal Cove.

By April of 1940, No. 6 (BR) Squadron had received all of its allotment of Sharks, and training was complete. On April 6 the Squadron received warning notice of the move to their permanent war station at Alliford Bay in the Queen Charlotte Islands. Five of the No. 6 (BR) Squadron Sharks, (numbers 501, 503, 506, 545, and 546) were turned over to No. 4 (BR) Squadron for that Squadron's move to their wartime station at Ucluelet. Shark II, #502, stayed behind for service in eastern Canada where it was used as a bombing and gunnery trainer until early May, 1940; the aircraft was then assigned to Western Air Command and ferried across Canada. Number 502's pilot set a record for the cross-country flight: he took close to two months to make the journey, apparently barnstorming his way across the prairies, putting on exhibitions along the way to earn sufficient travelling funds. After leaving Lethbridge, Alberta, he tried his hand at soaring, taking advantage of the thermals present in the foothills and in the Rockies themselves. Eventually #502 arrived intact at Jericho Beach and was taken on strength with No. 3 Repair Depot on June 25, 1940.

With the relocation of Western Air Command to Victoria on November 25, 1939, and the departure of No. 4 and No. 6 (BR) Squadrons to their wartime operational stations in the spring of the following year, the emphasis at Jericho Beach was to again change. The flying boat school continued to train pilots in the complexities of waterborne operations prior to the pilots being posted to their operational units. No. 3 (RD) Repair Depot undertook the responsibility for major repair and maintenance work on all of the aircraft assigned to the flying boat squadrons on the coast of British Columbia.

Jericho Beach Air Station hosted a seemingly endless stream of young men from across Canada who were assigned to the station in preparation for their reassignment to Ucluelet, Alliford Bay, Prince Rupert, Coal Harbour, and Bella Bella. The airmen were quick to seize the opportunity to take in the bright lights of Vancouver before heading off to the remote and rugged environment of the coastal flying boat stations.

A large proportion of the young men who passed through the Jericho Beach Air Station were barely out of high school - "We were really just kids, but we didn't know it at the time," recalls one former airman from Nova Scotia. Regardless of where the men came from, the experiences and the friends who shared those experiences have created a common bond in memories that have lasted for a lifetime.

1

3

2

4

6

5

7

1&2 *Vedette #803 beaching at Jericho Beach.* Madill Collection

3. *Vancouver #906 on ramp at Jericho Beach.* Madill Collection

4. *Jericho Beach hangars looking north; 1938.* Galbraith Collection

5. *No.4 (FB) fitters and riggers service a homebuilt Corben Baby Ace on floats.* CFB Comox Rowe Library

6. *Shark #525 at Slipway, Jericho Beach, May 1939.* CFB Comox Rowe Library

7. *Vickers Vancouver #906 nears Point Atkinson on patrol from Jericho Beach, September 1939.* Coombes Collection

8

10

9

11

13

12

14

8. *Vancouver at Jericho Beach receiving Lewis gun installation.* CFB Comox Rowe Library
9. *Vancouver being equipped with Lewis gun at Jericho Beach.* CFB Comox Rowe Library
10. *Jericho Beach, 1939 from corner of Trimble and Belmont.* Galbraith Collection
11. *Wing parade No. 3 (RD) practice for King's visit, Jericho 1939. (Note: officer with busby at front).* Palmer Collection
12. *Wing parade 3(RD) Section Jericho Beach, 1939.* Palmer Collection
13. *Wing parade present arms - Jericho Beach, 1939.* Palmer Collection
14. *Shark II #505 taxiing at Trenton, 1937.* Galbraith Collection

15

16

17

19

18

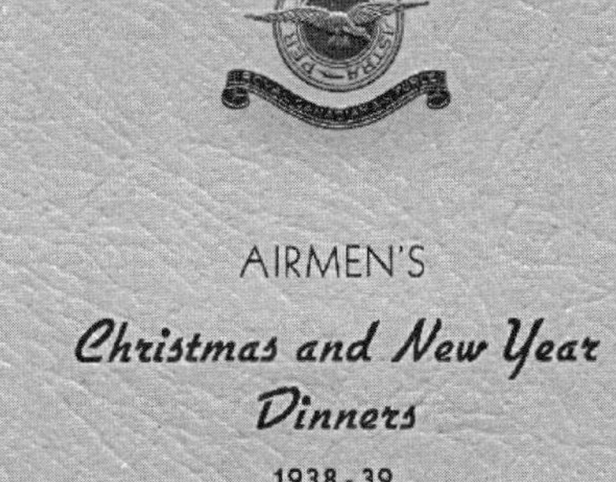

AIRMEN'S

Christmas and New Year Dinners

1938 - 39

HELD AT

JERICHO BEACH, VANCOUVER, B.C.

13.00 Hours

December 25th, 1938

January 1st, 1939

20

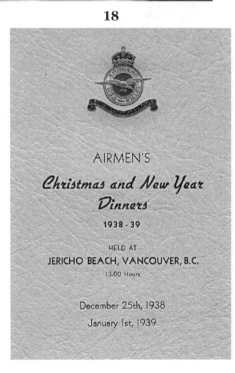

15. *Fairchild's XN and XQ at Forbes Landing on Campbell Lake.* CFB Comox Rowe Library
16. *Jericho Beach RCAF Station looking west, March 3, 1943.* CFB Comox Rowe Library
17. *Vickers Vancouver #906 taxiing in English Bay Vancouver.* CFB Comox Rowe Library
18. *Airmen's Mess dinner, Christmas 1938.* Galbraith Collection & Coombes Collection
19. *#906 undergoing refit at Jericho Beach.* CFB Comox Rowe Library
20. *No. 4 (BR) airman poses on ramp at Jericho Beach, early 1930s.* Driscoll Collection

chapter three

A LEGACY OF COMMAND: The Formation of Western Air Command

Early in 1935, in response to the disturbing evidence that a second world war was inevitable, senior RCAF officers began to examine the role the Air Force would play in the defence of Canada. The officers agreed that before an effective defence plan could be drawn up, the RCAF must gain control of its own service. The time had come to press the Department of National Defence to create a centralized RCAF organization which could act as a separate entity. The first step was crucial: the current system of Air Force administration had to be restructured.

Under the present "chain of command" the Senior Air Officer,Air Commodore G.M. Croil, was responsible for the RCAF, and he in turn was responsible to the Chief of the General Staff, who was an Army Officer. At this transfer point, the RCAF administrative system branched off into a complex maze of overlapping areas of dual-service responsibility. Croil was determined to rectify this "diverse method of administration", which he labelled as "the greatest objection to the present system".

In August 1935, Major General E.C. Ashton, the Chief of General Staff, received a lengthy memorandum from A/C Croil which clearly traced the convoluted paths of command and summarized the situation in plain language:

> *"The present system requires the issuing and observing of different regulations and instructions governing the same subject matter. As can be appreciated, such an arrangement is not conducive to efficiency. A study of the problems likely to arise on mobilization for war further emphasizes the need for some clearly defined and uniform system of control in peace, to permit rapid mobilization and training of the Air Force for war."*

Croil also briefly outlined two proposals that laid out well-developed solutions to the problems his memorandum described; a succinct evaluation followed each of the methods he presented. His final remarks underscored the urgency shared by all his senior officers:

> *"It is recommended that the suggestions contained above be given consideration at the earliest possible moment, and an endeavour made to arrive at a solution of the present unsatisfactory system of administration of the Air Force, to permit it to operate at its maximum efficiency in peace and to permit the drafting of adequate and workable mobilization instructions."*

There was no official response from the Chief of the General Staff. However, unofficial declarations of support for an independent Air Force came from Canada's new Minister of Defence, Ian MacKenzie, and the Deputy Minister, Lieutenant-Colonel L.R LaFleche. Croil was relieved that at least the politicians acknowledged that the time for change had come. Now it was a question of waiting, remaining alert to every nuance, taking advantage of every opportunity to exert effective political pressure.

Deputy Minister LaFleche put his avowed support into action in mid-1936 when he suggested that the senior air officer of the RCAF be elevated from an associate member to full membership on the Canadian Defence Council. The Chief of the Naval Staff agreed with LaFleche, but the Chief of General Staff objected to the appointment. LaFleche asked Croil for his opinion, giving the Senior Air Officer another opportunity to repeat what he had been saying with conviction for the past several years: that the RCAF held a position as the third important component in a balanced national defence plan and should be treated as an equal partner.

Major-General Ashton's resolve was slowly being eroded by Croil's methodical appeals and now it was apparent that others had taken up the Air Force "cause". In July 1936 the Defence Council overruled Ashton's objections, and Croil, as Senior Air Officer, was given a seat on the

Council. This was the first tangible sign that the Air Force was gaining ground in its move toward recognition as Canada's third service.

Early in 1937 Defence Minister Ian MacKenzie received a recommendation from the Army, Navy, and Air Force Chiefs of Staff that the three individual services should be directly responsible to Canada's Minister of Defence. The amendment was supported without enthusiasm by a weary Chief of General Staff, but again no further action was taken. MacKenzie, Ashton, and the Department of National Defence were taking direct hits from a nervous Canadian public asking questions about their country's security, and the heightened international tension also had United States military leaders pounding on their door exerting pressure for Canada's participation in a defence plan for the Pacific and the Atlantic coastlines.

In the meantime A/C Croil authorized S/L Mawdesley, 3 other officers and 13 Airmen to be detached from RCAF Station Jericho Beach to conduct a survey for potential defence sites along the coast of British Columbia. The survey carried out by the British Columbia Reconnaissance Detachment was the first step in the strategic plan to prepare a defence of the west coast. The information collected by Mawdesley and his survey party laid the foundation for construction of five west coast RCAF Flying Boat Stations. Plans were also underway to establish one permanent force unit and five other non-permanent force units to assist in coastal defence. The need for an Air Force Command Headquarters at Vancouver to coordinate the burgeoning Air Force presence in the west was acute.

It was nearly the end of 1937; Croil's first proposal for administrative reorganization of the RCAF had lain dormant for almost two years. Croil updated his 1935 memorandum, and, on November 3, 1937, he put the new document in the hands of the Deputy Minister for immediate consideration by the Minister of Defence.

CONFIDENTIAL D.M.

Co-ordination of the Command of Air Force Units for the Defence of the Pacific Coast

1. Although the defence problem of the Pacific Coast is one in which the air force is a predominant partner, it alone of the three services within the department lacks any co-ordinating authority over its units in this area.
2. The present complex system of control and administration, which in view of the lack of any other machinery has had to be accepted, has proved to be most impracticable. As a result, the preparation and execution of plans for defence have not been given the attention they warrant; furthermore, the present expansion of the air force in this area will add considerably to an already very unsatisfactory state of affairs. The diverse systems of control and administration of the air force throughout the country was pointed out in my memorandum of August 27, 1935, file 866-1-38 and a solution offered.
3. Briefly, the present system applied to the air force units at present in British Columbia is as follows: The Military District Headquarters in Victoria is held directly responsible for the control and administration of all activities of the Non-Permanent squadron in Vancouver. District Headquarters is further held responsible for matters of discipline, pay, medical and engineering services pertaining to the Permanent squadron in Vancouver, but not for its technical maintenance, training or employment, the responsibility for which lies with the staff of RCAF Headquarters of National Defence Headquarters, (Ottawa).

   There exists, therefore, the unique situation of two units of the same service, intended for the defence of the coast and located in the same place, administered and controlled under two entirely different systems, which is clearly illogical and not conducive to efficiency or economy.
4. At the present time the difficulties involved in the supervision of training, maintenance, employment and in the annual inspection of squadrons to ascertain their efficiency falls on the staff at RCAF Headquarters, Ottawa. This staff is neither large enough nor sufficiently well acquainted with local conditions or details of the problems involved to cope with the situation at so great a distance, and visits to these units are usually confined to one inspection trip yearly by the Senior Air Officer which has to be of such short duration that the time available is entirely inadequate for the purpose. This situation, under present conditions, will be considerably magnified when the following additional units, all intended for employment in coast defence duties, are located in the west:

1 Torpedo Bomber Squadron, Vancouver (P.F.)
1 Repair Depot (including a Torpedo Section) Vancouver (P.F.)
1 Small Magazine Staff, Kamloops (P.F.)
1 Fighter Squadron, Calgary (P.F.)
1 Equipment Depot, Calgary, (P.F.)
1 Fighter Squadron, Calgary (N.P.F.)

5. Bearing in mind the extensive responsibilities of the air force in the preparation and execution of plans for the maintenance of neutrality and operations in war on the Pacific Coast, the necessity for the co-ordination of all air force activities under an air force commander is evident if any progress is to be made in such vital matters.

   I cannot, therefore, too strongly stress the necessity for the organization of an Air Force Formation Command Headquarters at Vancouver at the earliest possible date. The Air Force Commander would be responsible for all matters pertaining to operations, training, discipline, personnel, development and supply. These responsibilities would not include medical services, pay services or supply of rations. These matters, for the time being, could remain the responsibility, as they now are, of the Officer Commanding the Military District in which Staff units are located. The organization of a Formation Command Staff would automatically eliminate the necessity for the four Air Staff Officers and their clerical staffs, either presently located or shortly to be posted to Military Districts 11 and 13.

6. I request that the subject of this memorandum be placed before the Honourable the Minister at the earliest possible moment for his favourable consideration.

(Sd) G.M. Croil, Air Commodore,
Senior Air Officer

This time the Minister of Defence took action as early as December 22, 1937 when he approved "Pacific Coast Development", with "further expansion to be considered", and forwarded Croil's document early in January to the Chief of General Staff.

As A/C Croil pointed out, the Air Force was the "predominant partner" in the Pacific defence plan. Coastal geography restricted a quick response by land or sea, but weather was the only severe restriction to air reconnaissance. Aircraft could cover a far greater range in an immediate response to an invasion of Canadian territory from the Pacific. Therefore, even before the RCAF received full autonomy from the Army in November 1938, a General Order, issued on March 1, formed Western Air Command at Vancouver British Columbia.

Group Captain G.O. Johnson, who reported directly to the Chief of the Air Staff in Ottawa, took command at Headquarters established in the Federal Post Office in Vancouver. His responsibility included all of the RCAF units in British Columbia, Alberta, Saskatchewan and Manitoba. Johnson was promoted to Air Commodore; A/C Croil, who had been promoted to Air Vice-Marshal, was appointed Chief of the Air Staff in December 1938.

On July 30, 1938 the organization of Western Air Command was as follows:

PERMANENT FORCE
Command Headquarters Vancouver
RCAF Station Headquarters Vancouver
No. 3 Repair Depot
No. 4 (General Reconnaissance) Squadron
No. 9 (General Reconnaissance) Squadron
No. 21 (Magazine) Detachment, Kamloops
No. 111 PF Detachment, Sea Island
No. 113 PF Detachment, Calgary

NON-PERMANENT FORCE
No. 111 (CAC) Squadron, Sea Island
No. 113 (F) Squadron, Calgary
RCAF Headquarters Order No. 343, issued 31/10/38 announced:
The following units are allocated to the Western Air Command effective dates shown:

PERMANENT
No. 2 Equipment Depot, Winnipeg, Manitoba
No. 112 PF Detachment, Winnipeg, Manitoba
No. 120 PF Detachment, Regina, Saskatchewan
effective 15/10/38
No. 3 (Bomber) Squadron, Calgary, Alberta:
effective 18/10/38
No. 6 (Torpedo Bomber) Squadron, Vancouver, BC,
effective 25/10/38

NON-PERMANENT
No. 112 (Army Co-op) Squadron, Winnipeg, Manitoba
No. 120 (Bomber) Squadron, Regina, Sask.
effective 15/10/38

A/V/M Croil had little time to reflect on his part in securing autonomy for the RCAF, the assured status as a third service that had been so dear to Gwatkin's heart almost twenty years earlier. Emotionally, politically, historically, there had been a victory, but, turning to face the military task that now lay ahead, there were no spoils for the victor. Croil had an enormous job ahead of him, little money to do it with, and even less time to do it in.

As he had demonstrated in the past, Croil was a clear-headed analyst. He drew up a list of all the problems involved in implementing a plan for the air defence of Canada, arranged them in order of importance, and distilled two salient facts on which he hung Canada's ability to man, train, and equip an effective defence force: future RCAF budget allotments must be greatly increased, and immediate steps must be taken to reduce delay by producing Air Force equipment in Canada.

In the fall of 1936, the tri-services Joint Staff Committee concluded that a minimum of 23 Service Squadrons were mandatory in order to effect an air defence of Canada. The Chief of the Air Staff pointed out that now, under the current budget restrictions, the RCAF would be lucky if they could man and equip more than five Permanent Force Squadrons, and even partially train and equip twelve Non-Permanent Squadrons. In the RCAF at this time there were only 150 officers and less than 1,000 airmen, and half of these men were reservists. Canada's Air power consisted of 31 aircraft that were, at best, obsolescent. It was fortunate that the enemy was occupied elsewhere early in 1939.

When war broke out in September 1939 there were only two permanent units at Western Air Command in Vancouver: No. 4 (GR) Squadron, with one Stranraer and two Vancouver Flying Boats, and No. 6 (TB) Squadron with five Blackburn Sharks. Western Air Command had, on paper, three non-permanent, or ancillary squadrons, but only one of these Squadrons, 111 Coast Artillery Co-Operation Squadron, was equipped with an aircraft - an out-of-date Avro 626 trainer.

To carry out the west coast defence plan, the Joint Services Committee Pacific Coast divided the 1,000 mile long British Columbia coast into five defensive areas, which Western Air Command was expected to patrol with 8 aircraft, 2 of which, the Vickers Vancouvers, were hardly allowed out of sight of the maintenance facility at Jericho Beach.

In order to effectively service the five patrol areas, Western Air Command was responsible for constructing Air Stations in each defensive area. The identified sites for RCAF Flying Boat Stations, and aerodromes at Tofino, Port Hardy and Patricia Bay, were based on the recommendations of the British Columbia Reconnaissance Detachment. The actual construction work fell to the Works and Building Section and civilian construction companies working under contract.

An almost embarrassing shortage of equipment necessary to proceed with assigned defence duties was not limited to the Air Force. The Army repeatedly appealed to A/C Johnson at Western Air Command Headquarters for aircraft assistance to the Coast Artillery Co-operation Units. The only aircraft on strength, 111 Squadron's Avro 626, was not capable of effective participation in spotting exercises. The best solution Johnson could come up with was that the RCAF should take over the operation of Ginger Coot Airways, which operated radio equipped float aircraft out of Vancouver. He made this recommendation to Air Force Headquarters in Ottawa, but in response A/V/M Croil issued 111 Squadron with an Armstrong Whitworth Atlas and directed everyone to get on with the job as best they could.

In November 1939 Western Air Command moved to Victoria to allow a closer liaison between the RCAF, Military District No. 11, and Naval Headquarters at Esquimalt. Command Headquarters settled into the Belmont Building with A/C Earl Godfrey now in command, and plans proceeded on the construction of RCAF Station Alliford Bay. Preparations were made to begin construction at the Prince Rupert Station, and Ucluelet, Bella Bella and Coal Harbour followed early in 1940.

One year of warfare had settled Canada in a slightly complacent role as a "coast guard" under "Big Brother" Uncle Sam's watchful eye. The situation was perceived differently on the west coast, where defence preparations revolved around Japan's threat to invade the Pacific coast of North America. The people in British Columbia were in a state of growing uneasiness over the apparent lack of serious concern in Ottawa, and their fears were not pacified by repeated warnings from American military leaders who pointed out the extreme risk of an unprotected coastline.

In May 1940, with very little public fanfare, Western Air Command ordered No. 4 and No. 6 Bomber Reconnaissance Squadrons to their partially complete wartime stations at Ucluelet and Alliford Bay, No. 111 Coastal Artillery Co-operation Squadron completed a move to Patricia Bay, and No. 13 Operational Training Squadron was formed at Sea Island, Vancouver. And the general public might have been relieved to hear that the RCAF Marine Squadron had accumulated a small but reliable fleet of marine craft, and, with little public acknowledgment, they made a valiant contribution in support of the Squadrons of Western Air Command.

The rapid expansion of the RCAF, accelerated by the nation-wide mobilization of Airmen, led MacKenzie King to create a position for an Associate Minister of National Defence for Air. In May 1940, Major C.G. Power was appointed to the position. A "personality gap" was evident between Power and Croil, and, after a blunt but honest evaluation of his working relationship with the Chief of the Air Staff, Power asked Croil to resign. A man of Croil's status could not be left sitting around with nothing to do, so another position was created and A/V/M Croil became the Inspector General of the RCAF.

On November 29, 1941 Western Air Command was instructed by the new Chief of the Air Staff, Air Vice-Marshal L.S.Breadner, to provide the closest possible collaboration with both the Canadian Army and the Navy, and with the American west coast defence establishments. Acting under these orders, A/C Godfrey prepared to attend a combined western defence meeting organized by Lieutenant General John DeWitt, the commander of the American Western Defence Command. However, Admiral Yamamoto's carrier force attacked Pearl Harbor on December 7, 1941 before the meeting could take place.

January 1, 1942, Air Commodore L.F. Stevenson arrived at Western Air Command Headquarters to take over command from A/C Godfrey who was posted as Deputy Inspector General for western Canada at Air Force Headquarters in Ottawa

Japan's violent assault on Pearl Harbor and the losses incurred by the United States Navy altered, very suddenly, the position of Western Air Command as a "backup" force on a "when necessary" basis for their powerful American neighbour. All RCAF Squadrons were ordered to a No. 1 Alert status and Bomber Reconnaissance Squadrons No. 9, No. 120, and No. 7 were immediately dispatched to man their wartime Stations at Bella Bella, Coal Harbour, and Prince Rupert. British Columbia was in the front line of attack and Western Air Command was responsible for holding the first line of defence.

In the early spring of 1942 the Vancouver Sun newspaper, apparently in an attempt to strengthen public demands for reinforcements for the defence of the west coast, ran an article that accused Ottawa of failing to grasp the implications of Japan's war strategy. A second series of articles later in the month charged that the Department of National Defence lacked any resemblance of front line aircraft and was totally unprepared to withstand a determined Japanese attack; the Sharks and the Stranraers were condemned as far too obsolete and worn-out to be of any use, and, in zealous overstatement of his case, the newspaper reporter threw the "military men" into the same category of decrepit anachronisms.

It is possible that reporters had heard some of the stories that were circulating around Vancouver about the antiquated Flying Boats. One of these rumours reported that No. 7 (BR) Squadron at Prince Rupert had received orders that in the event of an attack they were to fly their Sharks to Lake Lakelse near Terrace and disburse the aircraft along the lakeshore. And Airmen loved to refer to the Stranraers as "whistling bird cages", a flying centre-section of the Lions Gate Bridge, and worse, and joked about patrols flying backwards in a high wind.

The Vancouver Sun was charged with violations under the Defence Act of Canada and fined three hundred dollars, but the newspaper articles had fired the people of British Columbia with new courage to voice their concern, now bordering on paranoia, which shook military circles in Ottawa. The Minister of National Defence, Colonel J.L. Ralston, and senior officers of the three Services got out to Vancouver as quickly as they could. They intended to defuse the situation with a series of inspection tours followed by several terse and carefully worded statements issued to the press which would reassure the general population.

In the end the citizens were not so easily placated. The Joint Service Committee Pacific Coast was forced to commit to an *"allocation of sufficient force to provide reasonable insurance against all predictable scales of attack and, at the same time, to satisfy public opinion."* This translated into an acceleration of the construction already underway on airfields at Tofino and Port Hardy to support Flying Boat operations at Ucluelet and Coal Harbour, development of land bases in strategic areas throughout the province, and some general improvements in equipment and other supplies at all the established RCAF coastal stations.

The Deputy Chief of the Air Staff, Air Vice-Marshal G.O. Johnson, visited Western Air Command Headquarters at the end of March 1942 to conduct his own evaluation of the situation. His report to Air Force Headquarters in Ottawa illuminated a surprising vulnerability on the American west coast, especially in view of the pre-war statements made by the United States Congressional Committee about being "forced to take steps to defend Canada" in the event that Japanese forces attempted to invade the United States through Canada. By comparison, Canada was in a better position to defend its coastline than the United States was, and out-dated though they were, the RCAF Flying Boats were making a show in the defence of the west coast.

Johnson found an excellent spirit of cooperation between Western Air Command forces and their American counterparts, but inter-service jealousy between United States Navy and United States Army Air Force personnel hampered a maximum effect from their cooperative operations. He cited the example of inshore patrols by the United States Army 4th Bombardment Unit at McChord Field in Washington State which were only moving out to a 50 mile limit from shore. The patrol aircraft were capable of a much greater distance but were restricted to the 50 mile limit unless specifically requested by the United States Navy. The Navy was responsible for seaward reconnaissance in that area but only had four PBY Catalinas to do the job. Instead of solving the internal problem, they were requesting cooperation from Western Air Command for RCAF patrols to supplement their operations. Patrols from No. 4 (BR) Squadron at RCAF Station Ucluelet were ordered to patrol an area south of the border to a point off shore from Hoquiam, Washington. Western Air Command had enough strife to contend with in its own area of command without taking on the Americans' problems.

By mid-1942 the responsibilities of Western Air Command extended over a considerable number of Squadrons using both flying boat and land aircraft. Command Headquarters in Victoria found effective communication was becoming increasingly difficult, particularly in the case of some of the more remote squadrons. The frustration was felt on both ends; the lack of land lines, and the occasional breakdown of wireless communication caused by atmospherics caused units in the northern sector of the command area to feel isolated from Headquarters.

In order to form a coefficient force in the northern portion of the province, an order was given to establish a north-sector Group Headquarters at Prince Rupert. On the west coast of North America, the port of Prince Rupert was the main transfer point for supplies, equipment, and personnel moving to theatres of operation on the Pacific coast. As of April 6, 1942 Western Air Command was responsible for the coordination of operations with the United States Army and Navy forces, and close communication was vital.

Effective June 16, 1942 No. 4 Group Headquarters was established at Prince Rupert under the command of Group Captain R.C. Gordon, who was also Commanding Officer of RCAF Station Prince Rupert. S/L G.S. Austin was appointed Senior Air Staff Officer, F/L T.B. Jones, Administrative Officer, and F/O G.E. Devereau, Adjutant. G/C Gordon quickly established a liaison with the Army and the Navy units at Prince Rupert and organized a war room where joint-service personnel tracked the movements of all ships and aircraft, including any movement of enemy forces.

Number 4 Group was responsible for the operational control of all RCAF units on the Pacific coast between the Alaskan border and a line drawn through Cranstown Point, and Triangle Island in the Scott Islands; which gave Group Headquarters jurisdiction over No. 6 (BR) at Alliford Bay, No. 9 (BR) at Bella Bella, and No. 7 (BR) at Prince Rupert.

One of the major concerns of No. 4 Group was finding a suitable site to construct an aerodrome capable of accommodating a fighter squadron. National security demanded that an aerodrome be located within a 50 mile radius. The closest aerodromes were approximately 70 miles away: one at Annette Island at the southern tip of the Alaskan Panhandle, and the second one at Terrace, British Columbia - a similar distance, but located in mountainous terrain.

There was no "suitable" site anywhere near Prince Rupert; any of the strategic locations would require extensive blasting, logging and excavating. After a thorough search of the area, the site with the least disadvantages was chosen: Metlakatla, approximately five miles northwest of Prince Rupert on Tsimpsean Peninsula. A preliminary cost estimate for the project came in at over five million dollars, which effectively put the aerodrome on hold. To solve the problem of providing fighter protection for Prince Rupert a temporary air strip (weighing 1,968 3/4 tons) was purchased from the United States. A Pierced Plank Portable Steel Mat Runway was laid down on the beach south east of Entry Point, near Masset Village at the north end of the Queen Charlotte Islands.

Group Captain R.H. Foss replaced G/C Gordon as Commanding Officer of No. 4 Group on June 12, 1943. Foss remained in command until the unit was disbanded on April 1, 1944.

Western Air Command Headquarters moved back to Jericho Beach on January 1, 1943. Joint Service Headquarters were also set up at Jericho Beach to allow closer cooperation between all three of Canada's armed services. Each Service was headquartered in a building adjoining the other two Services.

While Headquarters prepared for the move, and during the period of resettling in Vancouver, No. 2 Group was formed at Victoria as a temporary expedient to ensure uninterrupted operational command. For a little over a year No. 2 Group operated at Belmont House in Victoria under the command of Air Commodore Earl MacLeod with W/C R.C. Mair as Senior Air Staff Officer, and Camp

Commandant F/L H.S. Morton. Staff members included: Acting Squadron Officer I.R.S. Hutchins, Womens Division Officer; P/O R.E. Brook, Personal Assistant to the A.O.C.; F/O R. Curtis, Equipment Officer, F/L J.N. Ballinger, Armament Officer; P/O W.S. Pearce, Photographic Officer; F/L G.S. Rothwell, Medical Officer; F/L F. Henry, Intelligence Officer; F/O G.W.C. McKay, Signal Officer. No. 2 Group was disbanded on March 15, 1944.

By August 18, 1943 all Japanese invaders had been evicted from the Aleutian Islands and the state of emergency that had existed moved away from the coast of British Columbia. The sole Japanese presence at this time was the fire balloons launched against North American from Japan, constituting more of a curiosity than a threat. From this point on Western Air Command steadily decreased in size.

Air Vice-Marshal Shearer visited Jericho Beach Headquarters late in 1943 and carried out an inspection of the British Columbia RCAF Stations in preparation for the disbandment of all unnecessary units on the west coast. After his inspection tour, Shearer announced the order in which Squadrons would be disbanded. In March 1944 disbandment proceedings began and were continued, until Western Air Command became a shadow of its former self. Its focus then changed from defence matters and refocused on training and transportation.

The history of Western Air Command reveals a story of an organization with a humble beginning forced by the shadow of war to quickly evolve into a complex system of command. In March 1938, when Command Headquarters opened in the Federal Post Office Building in Vancouver it faced the responsibility of developing a complete system of air defence for one of the most difficult parts of the Dominion of Canada to defend.

Apart from a small settled area in the southwest corner of the Province, British Columbia was still in a "pioneer" stage of development. The telephone system was in its infancy and communication relied heavily on rail transportation: the Pacific Great Eastern line from Squamish to Quesnel and the Canadian National Rail line between Jasper and Prince Rupert. There was an effective coastal steamship service that connected scattered pockets of "bush folk" who had filtered up the coast, but once Western Air Command started to prepare for the formation of the western defence squadrons, any move away from the lower mainland reduced the officers and men to "bushing it".

However, the constant struggle with rugged terrain, foul weather, lack of funds, and unsuitable equipment did not deter the Officers in command, nor the Airmen under their command, from following their avowed purpose, "to be of service, in peace or in war, to their country."

RCAF Jericho Beach looking south from 3,500 feet, June 4, 1944. CFB Comox Rowe Library

WESTERN AIR COMMAND HEADQUARTERS:

During World War Two, 16 operational squadrons passed under the administration of Western Air Command Headquarters:

No. 4 Squadron	No. 14 Squadron	No. 132 Squadron	No. 160 Squadron
No. 6 Squadron	No. 111 Squadron	No. 133 Squadron	No. 163 Squadron
No. 7 Squadron	No. 119 Squadron	No. 135 Squadron	No. 165 Squadron
No. 9 Squadron	No. 120 Squadron	No. 147 Squadron	No. 166 Squadron
No. 13 Squadron			

Other units in the Vancouver area during the war that also fell under the authority of Western Air Command were:

No. 8 Elementary Flying Training School:
opened at Sea Island on 22 July 1940, operated by Vancouver Flying Training Company Limited under RCAF supervision; moved to 18 EFTS at Boundary Bay on 19 December 1941 to make Sea Island aerodrome available for emergency operations; disbanded there on 2 January 1942.

No. 18 Elementary Flying Training School:
Formed at Boundary Bay on 10 April 1941, operated by Boundary Bay Flying Training School Limited under RCAF supervision; a double capacity school - the largest formed to that date; officially opened by Prime Minister King on 2 July 1941; in the December 1941 emergency it was first proposed to relocate the School in Saskatchewan but No. 18 was disbanded on 25 May, 1942 to vacate Boundary Bay for home War squadrons.

No. 24 Elementary Flying Training School:
opened at Abbotsford on March 29, 1943 and operated by the Vancouver Flying Training School Limited; under the supervision of the RCAF; disbanded in September 1944 to make Abbotsford available to No. 5 Operational Training Unit for their force training program.

No. 3 Operational Training Unit:
Jericho Beach and at Patricia Bay, November 1942 - August 1945

No. 5 Operational Training Unit:
at Boundary Bay, April 1944 - October 1945, also at Abbotsford August 1944 - October 1945

No. 6 Operational Training Unit:
at Patricia Bay August 1941, moved to Comox May 1944

Radio Mechanics Detachment:
at University of British Columbia, 30 May 1941 - February 1943

No. 6 (U of BC) Squadron, UATC:
at University of British Columbia, 20 August 1943 - 31 December 1944

No. 4 Pre-Aircrew Educational Detachment:
at University of British Columbia, 1 February 1943 - 14 August 1944

No. 8 Release Centre
at Vancouver, 1 January 1945 - 31 July 1946

No. 3 Repair Depot:
at Vancouver in 1937, closed October 1945

No. 13 Aeronautical Inspection District:
originated as No. 13 Technical Detachment in 1938, redesignated No. 13 AID in August 1942, inactivated February 1947.

No. 22 Sub-Repair Depot:
at Sea Island, October 1944 - November 1945

No. 8 Radio Detachment:
at Sea Island, August 1942 - September 1946

No. 9 Construction and Maintenance Unit:
moved to Vancouver from Ucluelet, July 1942; disbanded 31 March 1947.

No. 7 Reserve Equipment Maintenance Unit
at Vancouver, November 1945 - March 1946

WAC Marine Squadron
at Vancouver, November 1943 - October 1946; then moved to Patricia Bay

No. 2 Supply Depot
No. 2 Supply Depot has perhaps the longest continuous history of service of any unit in the RCAF. Formed as No. 2 Aircraft Depot at Winnipeg, late 1936; renamed No. 2 Equipment Depot and remained there until 8 March 1940; moved to Calgary on 1 November 1940; and to Vancouver on 1 August 1942; remained there throughout the war as equipment depot for Western Air Command. In May 1948 it was redesignated No. 2 Supply depot.

The Command of Western Air Command was held by A/V/M F.V. Heakes from June 10, 1944 to February 13, 1946 when A/V/M J.C. Plant assumed command until March 1, 1947 when Western Air Command was disbanded.

Wing Commander Harry Bryant, the last Commanding Officer of Jericho Beach Air Station, recalled that by December 1945 there were no operational aircraft at Jericho Beach, but personnel of No. 3 (RD) were repairing damaged aircraft where possible, or reducing unrepairable aircraft to scrap. Number 3 (RD) was also compiling an inventory of aircraft parts and scrap for potential disposal by the Crown Assets Disposal Corporation. After the inventory was completed, and equipment removed for sale, Jericho Beach was reduced to a care and maintenance facility.

The Air Station closed on March 1, 1947 and W/C Bryant was posted as Camp Commandant, North West Air Command at Edmonton, Alberta. With the closure of RCAF Station Jericho Beach the remaining RCAF establishments were:

No. 12 Group Headquarters on 4th Avenue (Jericho Beach), Vancouver
No. 2 Supply Depot, Kitsilano, Vancouver
No. 13 Technical Services Section
No. 121 Communications Flight, Sea Island
No. 123 Rescue Unit, Sea Island

RCAF Recruiting Unit
No. 442 (Reserve) Squadron, Sea Island
No. 9442 Squadron Support Unit and (Reserve)

University Flight, Sea Island
No. 4000 Reserve Medical Unit
No. 2442 Aircraft Control and Warning Unit (Reserve)
No. 1 Air Cadet Wing and four Air Cadet Squadrons: Numbers 57, 59, 111, and 135

chapter four

WEST COAST FLYING BOAT STATIONS

RCAF Station Ucluelet

RCAF Station Alliford Bay

RCAF Station Prince Rupert

RCAF Station Coal Harbour

RCAF Station Bella Bella

NUMBER 4 (BR) SQUADRON
RCAF STATION
UCLUELET

STATION ESTABLISHED: MAY 01, 1940

STATION CLOSED: OCTOBER 15, 1944

STATION NEWSPAPER: WESTERN FLIGHT

EDITOR: FLT/LT DUNN (PADRE)

STATION MOTTO: WE DELIVER

SQUADRON MOTTO: TIKEH KLAP MESACHEE TILLIKUM

RCAF STATION UCLUELET

RCAF Ucluelet looking west. CFB Comox Rowe Library

Ucluelet Harbour on the southwest side of Vancouver Island was one of the sites investigated by Wing Commander A.E. Shearer and his No. 4 (GR) Squadron reconnaissance detachment. At the conclusion of his inspection tour in October 1936, W/C Shearer highly recommended the naturally protected haven on the Pacific side of Barkley Sound as a location for a west coast Flying Boat station. His report concluded that from Ucluelet there was unrestricted access to a patrol area extending seaward, as well as proximity to the Washington State Olympic Peninsula, an area that would be included in future Canadian maritime patrol responsibilities.

The possibility of a Japanese invasion made the protection of Barkley Sound a prime consideration in the defence scheme of the west coast. Through Barkley Sound into the Alberni Canal the city of Port Alberni and its harbour at the head of the Canal were vulnerable to attack. The enemy would then have direct access to the Straits of Georgia, placing them on the city of Vancouver's doorstep in a position of power that no one wanted to contemplate. The War Plan for the defence of the west coast called for an RCAF Flying Boat Station at Ucluelet. But until the threat of a Japanese invasion came closer to a reality, daily patrols carried out by a small detachment of No. 6 (BR) Squadron personnel provided sufficient security.

Prior to war being declared on September 10, 1939, Number 4 (BR) Squadron was based at the Jericho Beach Air Station where crews received flight training and armament practice. The Squadron operated a mixed assortment of obsolete aircraft: one Canadian Vickers Vedette, two Canadian Vickers Vancouvers, one Fairchild 71, two Supermarine Stranraers and, in April of 1940, three Shark IIs and two Shark IIIs were taken on strength. The Squadron received the order that it would move to its wartime station at Ucluelet on May 1, 1940. This gave them a scant two weeks to familiarize themselves with the Sharks, and it is to the credit of these men that No. 4 (BR) Squadron

top; No. 6 (BR) Detachment at Ucluelet. NAC 141360
above; Fairchild 71, XQ over Port Alberni. CFB Comox Rowe Library

had the distinction of being the only Squadron in the RCAF who did not write off any Sharks.

The "Barkley Detachment" arrived at Ucluelet in their five recently acquired Sharks, two Stranraers, and a Fairchild seaplane, and took over patrol operations from No 6 (BR) Squadron. At the same time, the Coast Construction Company moved its men and equipment onto the site,

No. 1 hangar and machine shop October 15, 1940, RCAF Ucluelet. Stofer Collection

and the construction of RCAF Station Ucluelet was underway. When the detachment was not on a fisheries patrol or out on regular patrols of the important Barkley Sound area the men continued training and operational exercises. Meanwhile construction continued around them, and the number of personnel at the Station increased in proportion to buildings completed to accommodate them.

During 1941 construction progressed rapidly. The Officer commanding the Squadron and the Detachment was S/L C.M.G. Farrell, who had 352 men under his command at the end of August: 16 officers, 259 airmen, one officer of the Veterans Guard and 76 other ranks.

Wives were permitted to accompany Number 4 (BR) Squadron personnel, with the provision that the men provide and maintain their own accommodations - no easy matter in that tiny, remote settlement. There were no roads that connected the community with the rest of the outside world. Families travelling into the area found themselves involved in a coastal marathon: first a ferry from Vancouver to Nanaimo, then a bus to Port Alberni, and finally a 5 hour journey by steamer down the Alberni Canal to Ucluelet. Only the very determined took up permanent residence.

Japanese Village from RCAF Station Ucluelet. McGregor Knight Collection

On December 4, 1941 the Squadron aircraft were assigned to anti-submarine patrols in the Bamfield search area: a precaution which prepared the Squadron for the active war status that followed a few days later. On December 7, 1941 radio reports were received that the Japanese had attacked Pearl Harbor. Later that same evening a message from the Chief of Staff notified all RCAF units that a state of war existed between Canada and Japan - tragic proof that the worst fears for the safety of the west coast of North America were real. RCAF Station Ucluelet was positioned to stand guard over the crucial Barkley Sound against an enemy that had shown itself to be stealthy and ruthless.

Immediate results of Japan's aggression were felt by all the Japanese nationals operating fishing boats in the area. Using the Station at Ucluelet as temporary headquarters, Lieutenant G.B. McKenzie of the Royal Canadian Navy Volunteer Reserve carried out his orders to seize all Japanese-owned fishing boats. The Station also became a temporary base for personnel from the Royal Canadian Corps of Signals, and two members of the B.C. Provincial Police Force while they completed another security precaution to monitor the activities of the Japanese Canadians. Their orders were to remove all telephones in use by Japanese residents in Ucluelet and the surrounding area.

Tension on the Station increased as security measures were tightened: all personnel were ordered to carry respirators and steel helmets while on duty, and a complete blackout was strictly enforced. Mystery and secrecy surrounded the presence of 33 officers and men of the US Navel Air Force who arrived aboard the USS Teal and two United States PBYs. The men were attached to the station for rations and quarters for one week before quietly returning to Seattle on December 17. They were involved in preliminary work in regard to a secret aircraft direction finding project; however security remained intact, and even the Station Diary shows no record of the men's activities.

A United States Army R.D.F. detachment of 50 officers and men

Stranraers FY-A, FY-J, FY-B over Ucluelet. McGregor Knight Collection

arrived in February 1942. They set up an early warning device (radar) at nearby Spring Cove and gave operating instructions to their Canadian counterparts at the Ucluelet Station. The detachment departed four months later leaving well-trained personnel from Ucluelet in charge.

The Stranraer patrols continued throughout December of 1941, and the frequency and duration of each patrol became an endurance test for the inexperienced crews and their obsolete aircraft. The Station's first fatal air accident occurred on December 30, 1941. Stranraer #928 lost power from both engines shortly after take-off and crashed into the forest about a half mile south of the Station. Pilot, F/O R.J. Gray, Second Pilot, Sgt. M.N. McKay, Navigator, P/O A.C. Scruton, and Air Mechanic, Cpl. W.J. Zenkie were killed. The other four crew members, Sgt. Rogas, Cpl. Atkinson, Sgt. Davies and Sgt. Gordon, survived with minor injuries.

Number 4 (BR) Squadron's assigned patrol area extended south to a point close to Hoquiam, Washington - about 50 miles north of the Washington/Oregon state border. Early in 1942 a Stranraer crew, carrying out a regular patrol off the Washington coast, saw a large fleet of what appeared to be United States warships. At first the crew could not believe their eyes, and immediately used their ALDIS lamp to ask the vessels to identify themselves. The response came using the correct code of the day, followed a few moments later by another signal ordering the Stranraer crew not to breech radio silence. Salvaged from Pearl Harbor, the fleet of US Navy battle wagons were now limping or being towed back to the US Navy's shipyards at Bremerton, near Seattle, Washington. The patrol returned to Ucluelet, and during debriefing the Pilot Officer described the unusual convoy they had flown over. He was sent first to Jericho Beach and then to Air Force Headquarters in Ottawa to report on what he had witnessed.

Another unusual sighting was reported by a Stranraer patrol February 3, 1942. The crew spotted the Cunard Liner Queen Elizabeth on its way to the Canadian Naval Base dry dock at Esquimalt, just outside of Victoria, British Columbia. Esquimalt was the only dry dock in the British Commonwealth on the Pacific after the fall of Singapore.

On February 13, 1942 S/L Farrell turned the command of RCAF Station Ucluelet over to W/C R.G. Mair. The Station now had a strength of 445 personnel: 11 officers and 434 airmen. A note in the Station Diary on March 19, 1942, records that the SS Maquinna completed the evacuation of Japanese residents from the area adjacent to the Station. This action came only one month after a Valentine's Day dance in the Airmens Mess. A photograph captured a smiling young Japanese woman enjoying the party with a group of her friends.

Day after day, throughout May of 1942, patrols from Ucluelet reported sightings of American Naval craft and

Valentine's Day Dance, February 1942. Ucluelet Community Hall. McGregor Knight Collection

transports enroute to the Aleutians. The American military, nervous about the growing interest the Japanese were showing in Alaska and the Aleutian Islands, were sending in reinforcements as quickly as possible. The United States would not be taken by surprise again. When the Japanese planes attacked Dutch Harbor in the Aleutians on June 3, 1942, the Americans were waiting for them. The alarm reverberated up and down the entire coast: blackout regulations were enforced, all passes and leaves were cancelled, and every station was ordered to stand ready to revert to Number 1 Alert at a moment's notice. RCAF Station Ucluelet suddenly lost the dull similarity of one day to the next. The threat of invasion could not be taken lightly: there was a war after all.

On June 7, the Japanese issued a second jolt to complacency and brought the war even closer to home for Station personnel. The Squadron received a report that an American ship had been torpedoed by a Japanese submarine - the first torpedo incident on Canada's west coast. At 04:50 an aircraft took off from Ucluelet to search for survivors. At 05:31 the crew spotted a life raft and fired off green flares to direct an R.C.N. Corvette, on a search grid about 10 miles away, to the scene to pick up the survivors. This event reinforced the important position the Station held in the protection and security of a vulnerable coastline.

Sightings of Japanese submarines were increasing, and the uncertainty of what the enemy's next move might be was making everybody jumpy. Then, like a deadly jack-in-the-box, a Japanese I-Class sub surfaced off Estevan Point. In the early evening of June 20, 1942 the Government Signal Station reported that it was being shelled by a Japanese submarine. The shelling continued for about a half hour but little serious damage was done. Estevan Point, 60 miles north of Ucluelet, was a little too close for a few of the Coast Construction employees. They downed tools and returned to Vancouver.

On June 23 a submarine surfaced in Esperanza Inlet. The sighting was reported by Noah Paul, a local Indian. Every half-submerged log had become an object for close scrutiny, but a pattern was emerging of a growing concentration of enemy submarines in the area. Patrols from Ucluelet also noticed the number of Russian freighters they encountered. The Russians were shipping lend-lease equipment offered to them by the United States to strengthen Russia's war effort against Germany. It was more than luck that allowed these large ships safe passage through the sub-infested waters of the west coast. The Japanese High Command was anxious to ensure that Russia had no reason to enter the war against them in the Pacific.

S/L K.F. Macdonald, Officer Commanding No. 4 (BR) was posted to Air Force Headquarters in July 1942 and was replaced by F/L E.W. Beardmore.

On August 23, 1942 Stranraer #951, on a No. 120 (BR) Squadron patrol out of Coal Harbour, reported that an inflight mechanical problem was forcing them to ditch the aircraft. The radio operator gave their position at 49.30 north, 130.30 west, 100 miles at sea. The last radio contact with the Flying Boat confirmed that they were safely on the water and needed a ride home. A rescue flight located the downed aircraft, but rough seas made it impossible to pick up the crew. A second aircraft circled over them throughout the night, but by early dawn there was no sign of the men or their aircraft. For the next two days No. 4 (BR) Squadron Stranraers and marine craft participated in an intensive search, but #951 and her crew were never found: the Pilot, F/Sgt. E.T. Cox, and his crew of seven all perished.

Sharp eyes in a variety of locations near RCAF Station Ucluelet continued to spot and report sightings of enemy submarines: a sub was seen near Cape Flattery; on October 15 another one was sighted near Nootka Light; two more were spotted on November 3 - one around Amphitrite Point, and the other one well out to sea; on November 20, Ucluelet patrols joined five Stranraers from Patricia Bay in a search for a reported Japanese aircraft carrier; on December 11 the lighthouse keeper at Kains Point saw a periscope a mile off shore but poor weather conditions prevented a search being ordered.

RCAF Ucluelet looking east, 1942. McGregor Knight Collection

On December 16, 1942 Wing Commander Mair handed over command of RCAF Ucluelet to S/L J.N.McNee, former Officer Commanding No. 9 (BR) Squadron Bella Bella.

Each sighting of anything out of the ordinary, and every report of a possible enemy submarine - no matter how vague or improbable the descriptions seemed - was immediately investigated. It was difficult for the men to maintain enthusiasm for these long and often tedious flights searching for an enemy they heard rumours about, but seldom saw.

An unusual report came in late in the evening of February 6, 1943. This time more than one or two people simultaneously reported a flame rising into the air from a point due west of the Station and approximately five miles out to sea. The high speed motor launch Malecite was ordered out to investigate and came across an American fishing boat whose captain confirmed that a flare had gone up in the area. At first light a search patrol took off from Ucluelet to spend many hours in a fruitless search.

Two RCAF Tofino-based Harvards created the next stir of excitement. They sighted an enemy submarine near their base on March 10, but one of the pilots had to return to base to notify RCAF Station Uclulet because the Harvards did not have radio equipment - by the time No. 4 (BR) Stranraers came on the scene the submarine had submerged. Another search for a Japanese submarine took place on March 14 at Pachina Point. And the following month Ucluelet dispatched an aircraft in response to a report by a US Naval vessel that it had made positive contact with a submarine in the Straits of Juan de Fuca. In both cases the enemy slipped beneath the surface and avoided detection.

On June 4, 1943 S/L McNee was posted to Western Air Command, and S/L E.N. Beardmore took temporary command of RCAF Station Ucluelet until W/C H.J. Winney, OBE, was posted from Alliford Bay on June 25 to take command. In September S/L R.H.Lowry assumed command of No. 4(BR) Squadron when S/L Beardmore was also posted to Western Air Command Headquarters.

above; M-234 RCAF crash boat "Montagnais" at Ucluelet. Stofer Collection
top; No 4 (BR) aircrew board Canso, RCAF Ucluelet. Crombie Collection
below; Catalina #FP294 moored at RCAF Ucluelet. Schofield Collection

As of November 30, 1943 the station had 20 officers, 125 NCOs, and 148 airmen; Number 4 (BR) Squadron complement was 41 officers, 87 NCOs and 109 airmen, with 5 Canso As and one Stranraer attached. The Canso A was a step in the right direction - away from the antiquated "Whistling Birdcage" as the Stranraer was often jokingly referred to. Then, in January of 1944, three Catalina Flying Boats were ferried from eastern Canada by No. 4(BR) Squadron air crews.

The Cansos got a lot of use in search and rescue operations in the early months of 1944. In January Canso 11016 was searching for a Bolingbroke from Tofino when the crew spotted an oil slick and an overturned H-type dinghy. They directed the rescue launch to the spot but no survivors were found. On February 7, a Hurricane from Tofino ditched at sea and a No. 4 (BR) Squadron Canso located the pilot and directed his rescue. The next day another Hurricane ditched after take-off from Tofino, and again a No. 4 Squadron Canso located the site, but when the rescue launch arrived the pilot was dead.

In a lighter vein, crew member Norman Beaton recounted a training incident that involved No. 4 (BR) Squadron's last remaining Stranraer. The following is condensed from ON A WING AND A PRAYER:

"I arrived at Ucluelet RCAF Station in early February, 1944. The station was isolated, accessible only by air or water. My first flight in an aircraft at Ucluelet is, for some unknown reason, not recorded in my log book. I distinctly remember the old Stranraer flying boat; two wings, two engines, a hull, then a couple of miles of wire to bind it all together. The engines were radials of ancient British manufacture; seven cylinders with a wooden propeller. These engines were started by what was called an inertia starter. On the right hand side of each engine was a metal crank, about a foot and a half long. This is where the inertia bit came in. The engineer wearing a Mae West scrambled out the top rear of the hull, then up on the wing. Once

Stranraer #912 (FY-A) on ramp at RCAF Ucluelet. McGregor Knight Collection

on the wing a trapeze act was required. He threaded his way between various bracing wires to reach a streamlined strut about two feet from the engine. Then opening a small door in the nacelle, a long attached crank was exposed. The crank was unfolded then turned with great pushing, pulling, straining and colourful expletives. Somewhere in the bowels of this pre-historic monster was a heavy inertia wheel attached to a clutch. Outside these entrails was the crank. Once the crank was turned at an appropriate speed, a distant hum was heard. The pilot yanked a cable connected to the clutch - the engine then did or did not start. In the latter case, start cranking again complete with aforementioned physical and vocal encouragement. I was the new boy, fresh from a course in aeronautical engineering on Sherbrooke Street in Montreal. In general my knowledge was that a boat floated, an airplane had engines and wings. Put the two together and presto there was a flying boat. That was roughly a Stranraer, if you threw in a couple of miles of wire. My immediate superior that day was a flight engineer named Starrett, a man of few words. My pilot was F/O Bobby Davis, a young blonde-haired, blue-eyed affable American a few years my junior. Out in the bay, tethered to a buoy, was the flying boat. Bobby Davis, the co-pilot, the radio operator, the engineer and I entered the dinghy. Emblazoned on its bow was the name 'Bugger U.' The water was calm with hardly a ripple, which was in our favour due to the fact that our little boat with its cargo barely had four inches of freeboard.....Once safely aboard the old, leaky, cramped hull, Bobby sat in the left pilot's seat."

Sergeant Starret then ordered Beaton, *"to get up front, open the hatch and unsnap this tub from the buoy."* Opening the front hatch revealed the buoy about 10 feet away with the snaphooks at the far end. While Beaton puzzled just exactly how he was supposed to undo the snaphook, Starrett gave him further instructions, *"I will start the port engine. When I do you pull the rope. When you get up to the buoy, unsnap the mooring rope and stow it aboard. Then close the hatch."*

The port engine started and Beaton watched Starrett stow the crank, then head for the hull to walk across to the starboard engine. Beaton stowed the mooring rope, then closed the hatch and returned to stand behind Davis. The rpm and oil pressure dials told them that both engines were now running. F/O Davis instructed Beaton to locate Sgt. Starrett. They were on the step doing about 60 miles an hour before a complete search for the Sergeant revealed that he was not in the boat. The assumption was that he had fallen off the wing into the water. Beaton rushed back to the rear entrance and looked out.

The aircraft was now in full flight, climbing 50 feet above the water at 70 miles an hour, but there was the Sergeant sitting on the starboard wing, his arms and legs embracing the main strut in a grip of iron, his pale hair as straight back as a ruler, his head down, eyes shut. F/O Davis immediately put the aircraft into a shallow turn to port with Starrett on the top side, held on almost against his will by the force of the turn.

They landed quickly but safely on the surface of the water. Starrett had not moved:

"His glazed eyes opened half way and his head lifted just a little. His fair hair was now limp and very fluffy

- air dried. Bobby and the co-pilot climbed over to Starrett. His arms and legs were almost in a state of rigor mortis about the strut. Still the Sergeant sat there. Then he raised his head. He understood that this was real, that he was still alive and that there would be at least one more tomorrow for him, that was if he didn't kill the rest of the crew."

After considerable persuasion they got Starrett pried loose and back to the cabin. F/O Davis demanded to know what in God's name he had been doing out there and Starrett, sufficiently recovered to speak, pointed out that Davis was supposed to retard the starboard engine after starting. Davis had not done that and the petrified Starrett had come in on a wing and a prayer.

In Eric Stofer's book - R.C.A.F.STATION UCLUELET (RECOLLECTIONS) - Stofer, a former aero-engine mechanic at Ucluelet, gives a memorable description of a Stranraer, serviced and ready for duty:

"General practice, when launching a Stranraer was to tow the aircraft, bow-first, down the launching ramp, using the shop-mule; with that high and ponderous monstrosity, the heavier tractor connected by cable to the aircraft's stern."

This particular three a.m. launching had run into a small snag: the shop-mule was unserviceable. A minor detail to Corporal Harvey Herron - *"To heck with the shop mule!"* he cried. *"We can launch this birdcage without it, eh Sarge?"* To which Sgt. Jackson conceded it was possible - providing they were careful. Corporal Herron went into action, shouting instructions to Stofer, Rankin, and Waters to hook the tractor cable to the Stranraer's bow and stand by with their chocks.

"Herron's intention; tow the aircraft to the very edge of the launching ramp, block both wheels with the chocks, disconnect the tractor, drive back around the aircraft, reconnect the cable to the Stranraer's stern, remove the chocks, then slowly reverse the tractor, to allow the big aircraft to roll down into the water as usual. Easy. Or so it seemed at the time."

From there on, Stofer said, very little went right. The Corporal did not hear the cries to "hold it!" when he and Waters got their chocks in place. The rolling Stranraer wouldn't stop. It knocked the chocks askew and gathered momentum. There was just enough time to unhook the cable and jump clear - somehow Herron managed to drive that lumbering old tractor into the clear.

Aircrew board Canso #9802 in heavy rain for night patrol. Crombie Collection

"Unfettered, the Stranraer shot past him. Like a freed white swan, it tore down that ramp, and headed for the water. And gliding in, it floated gracefully away from shore - beaching gear and all. 'Beautiful!' Sgt. Jackson cried. 'Ruddy beautiful! Maybe we should launch 'em that way all the time.... Get Marine Section over here with a dinghy, on the double, and get a line on that thing, before it drifts off to China or some other friggin' place!'"

Late in the evening of March 4, 1944 Group Headquarters ordered a night search in response to a reported enemy submarine sighting. S/L Lowry took off at 01:00 hours, remaining airborne until 10:30 hours with negative results. Submarine sightings were becoming less frequent but when one was reported it was dealt with swiftly and seriously. The last recorded submarine sighting was reported by a fisherman on Zayas Island, near Prince Rupert. Canso 9771 and 9801 were dispatched to assist in the search but after a week no sign of any submarine activity was evident and the aircraft returned to Ucluelet.

The revised Defence of Canada Plan, 1944-1945, signaled the beginning of the end for the RCAF Stations on the west coast. The document stated that it was now possible to reduce the number of stations on the west coast, which would also include a reduction in air coverage of the sea approaches. The last four months of activity at the Station were reported in excerpts from the Station Diary:

11 May, 1944: an explosion took place in the armament section. Cpl. MacKay died as a result of injuries: 3 others were injured. The explosion was caused by a bomb going off, a result of the fuse being stripped.

03 June: S/L Beardmore turned over command of the station to W/C R.I. Thomas.

09 June: Canso 11019 crashed at Ucluelet and exploded on landing. Only the Navigator, F/O C.M. Amos, survived.

29 June: an escape exercise was held - one crew of 4(BR) attempted to "escape" after a supposed landing in enemy territory.

15 July: After a stay of nearly four years, the Coast Construction Company departed Ucluelet. Construction on the station was finally completed.

August: the wives of personnel living in the vicinity were given a six-day Anti-Gas Course. In the last day of the course they were put through the Gas Chamber.

19 August: Western Air Command issued Secret Operation Order No. 33 authorizing the movement of No. 4 (BR) Squadron from Ucluelet to Tofino on 24 August, 1944. This movement was necessitated by the intention of Air Force Headquarters to bring RCAF Station Ucluelet to a care and maintenance basis.

W/C R.I. Thomas turned over command of the Station to S/L R.A. Gilmour on September 5, 1944. S/L R.W. McRae followed S/L Lowry as Squadron Commanding Officer and remained the CO until the Squadron was disbanded. Number 4 (BR) Squadron remained at Tofino with its Canso A aircraft until August 7, 1945. Its last mission was a patrol on July 31 in Canso A 11016 which returned early due to poor weather conditions.

Station personnel were very proud of the Command Efficiency Award presented to them by Western Air Command on May 24, 1944. The Squadron won this award again the following September. The Squadron had also designed its own unit crest to commemorate the long history of their Squadron's service on the Pacific Coast. The figure of an eagle, copied from a Nootka ceremonial drum, represented the Pacific coast, and had an added significance for a Squadron so recently engaged in anti-submarine work - in the mythology of the Pacific Coast Indians the eagle represented the mortal enemy of the whale. "Tikeh Klap Mesachee Tillikum", the motto, translated from the old Chinook jargon, meant "Seek the Enemy."

The Squadron, under the command of S/L R.W. McRae, was stood down and disbanded at Tofino on August 7, 1945.

1

2

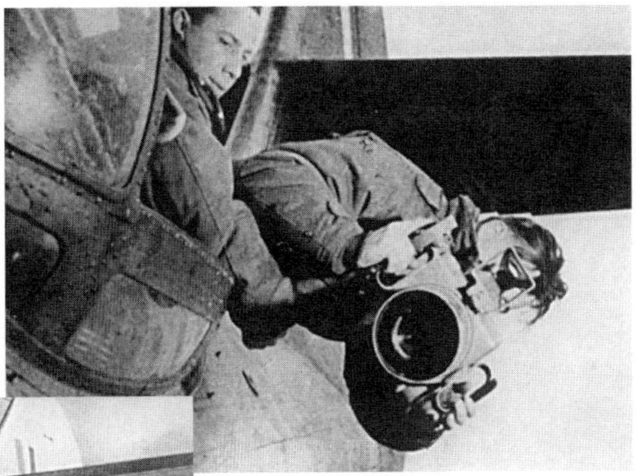

3

4

5

6

7

1. *No. 4 Canso airgunner awaits the enemy - RCAF Ucluelet.* Crombie Collection
2. *Photographer at left blister of Canso.* Crombie Collection
3. *Airgunners load armament for Canso patrol, Ucluelet.* Crombie Collection
4. *Canso #9771 crew boards for patrol from Ucluelet.* Crombie Collection
5. *Sergeants' barracks Ucluelet, February 1942.* Stofer Collection
6. *Sergeants Jeff North and McGregor Knight, Ucluelet, June 1942.* McGregor Knight Collection
7. *Aircrew work party, Ucluelet 1943.* McGregor Knight Collection

8. *No. 1 hangar and launching ramp RCAF Ucluelet, 1940.* Stofer Collection

9. *Shark dropping torpedo at Ucluelet.* McGregor Knight Collection

10. *Airmen's Mess RCAF Ucluelet, November 1940.* Stofer Collection

11. *Ucluelet area looking east, 500 ft.* CFB Comox Rowe Library

12. *Japanese Village from Ucluelet Village.* McGregor Knight Collection

13. *No. 4 (BR) Canso landing at RCAF Ucluelet.* Schofield Collection

14. *Workshop and No. 1 hangar, October 1940, RCAF Ucluelet.* McGregor Knight Collection

15

16

17

18

15. *Sergeants' Mess, RCAF Ucluelet.* McGregor Knight Collection
16. *Interior of airmen's barracks, RCAF Ucluelet, 1940.* Stofer Collection
17. *No. 4 (BR) Squadron aircrew hit bright lights of Vancouver on 72 hour leave.* McGregor Knight Collection
18. *Airmen "whooping it up" RCAF Ucluelet, 1941.* Stofer Collection

NUMBER 6 (BR) SQUADRON

RCAF STATION

ALLIFORD BAY

STATION ESTABLISHED: MAY 13, 1940

STATION CLOSED: JULY 25, 1945

STATION NEWSPAPER: DOG WATCH

RCAF STATION ALLIFORD BAY

An RCAF Flying Boat Station in the Queen Charlotte Islands, Canada's most westerly body of land, was of prime importance in the defence plan for the west coast. In 1937 the reconnaissance detachment recommended locating an RCAF Station on the south shore of Skidegate Inlet, at Alliford Bay - one of few areas in the Charlottes that combined natural protection and strategic location. Orders were given in 1938 to begin construction on RCAF Station Alliford Bay, and from 1940 until 1944, Number 6 (BR) Squadron operated from this remote station. The airmen dealt with the effects of living in such total isolation with good humour and hard work, and the station developed a reputation for maintaining a consistently high morale.

Number 6 (TB) Torpedo Bomber Squadron, was the second permanent force unit stationed at Jericho Beach. The Squadron had arrived from RCAF Station Trenton late in October 1938, and at the outbreak of war in 1939, their Squadron designation was changed to (BR) Bomber Reconnaissance. This reflected the new role they were about to play in countering the threat of a silent enemy - the Japanese submarine.

The Squadron had five pilots on strength: Commanding Officer S/L A.H. Hull, S/L E.A. Springall, F/O M.G.Doyle, WO2 Horner, F/S Ready; and three sergeant pilots under instruction: A/Sgt. Austin, A/Sgt. Hoodspith, and A/Sgt. Morris. These men joined fellow airmen from No. 4 (BR) Squadron in gunnery, bombing and flight training programmes to prepare them for duty at their wartime stations. When the aircrews were not training they took part in daily patrols of the Gulf of Georgia to identify ships and report on their movements. S/L Hull initiated patrols from Gabriola Island south to Pender Island, and down the west coast of Vancouver Island from Ucluelet to the Straits of Juan de Fuca. On September 12, 1939 all aircraft were ordered to stand by as a striking force. Patrols immediately ceased, with orders to carry on only if a definite object was reported. This policy remained in effect

above; Officers' Mess and Army Guard barracks. Baribeault Collection
top; Barracks: RCAF Station Alliford Bay, 1940. Galbraith Collection

until the spring of 1940.

During the first year of the war most of the RCAF Shark aircraft were serving with No. 6 (BR) Squadron on the Pacific coast. The Boeing-built Sharks were assembled in a hangar at Jericho Beach, and as one airman remembers, "We kept crashing them just about as fast as they could turn them out." The Shark crews - a pilot, a rigger or fitter, and a wireless operator carried out gunnery exercises and practiced dropping dummy torpedoes to familiarize themselves with the idiosyncrasies of their aircraft. Under the energetic and efficient command of S/L Hull the Squadron achieved a very high standard of proficiency. By the end of February 1940 the Squadron had reached its maximum strength of fifteen Sharks. S/L Hull was promoted to Wing Commander and posted to Western Air Command Headquarters in Victoria, and S/L Wray assumed command of the Squadron.

While the RCAF slowly and methodically prepared for the defence of the west coast, the war in Europe accelerated. Germany invaded Norway, and on April 10, 1940 No. 6 (BR) Squadron received orders to "bomb up" two Sharks, #517 and #524, and "stand ready" to intercept Norwegian ships in the ports of Vancouver and Chemainus. Pilots were ordered to drop their bombs in front of the ships if the Norwegians attempted to clear port and head to sea: however, the Norwegians remained calm until the situation was clarified, and no action was necessary.

The Squadron received orders on April 27, 1940 that it would move to its war station at RCAF Alliford Bay. The

Canadian Scottish vs RCAF at Alliford Bay. Colbeck Collection

Squadron's Shark aircraft were waiting for take-off on the morning of May 13. Wireless operator Harry Galbraith was flying with F/L Mike Doyle, who was to lead the flight of Sharks up the coast to their new home. Galbraith recalls that:

> *"we didn't even get away from the buoy to which we were moored because the first two aircraft that took off crashed shortly after take-off. We tried again the next day and this time everything went okay, and we had an uneventful flight to our new home."*

The majority of the Station personnel were transported on the navy vessel HMCS Sans Peur, and the remainder arrived by coastal steamer.

The station site at Alliford Bay had been carved out of

Shark #518 mooring at Alliford Bay, 1940. Baribeault Collection the dense forest that claimed the rocky terrain down to the edge of the ocean. The challenge of bringing in construction equipment and material to this isolated bay had been compounded by the Queen Charlotte's wild and unpredictable weather. Now the Squadron found themselves a long way from anywhere at a station that was far from complete. The pier, the hangar, and some of the equipment buildings were in a half-finished state, but enough housing was complete to allow the Squadron to sleep under a solid roof - a luxury fully appreciated by those members of No. 6 (BR) Squadron who, in the fall of 1939, were detached on coastal patrol duty out of Ucluelet and had lived in a makeshift assortment of canvas tents.

Under the command of S/L Wray, effectively assisted by his adjutant F/L A.H. Cocking, Squadron personnel were divided into work parties - more frequently referred to as "Bull Gangs" - and the men took over the hard work of completing their station. All ranks wielded an axe or a shovel. Working side by side they built a sea wall, set up technical equipment, and carried out all the mundane, small jobs that were necessary to get the station fully operational. Strong friendships were forged and a spirit of cooperation developed amongst the men which sustained a high morale in spite of the fact that Alliford Bay was the most isolated of all the RCAF coastal Flying Boat Stations.

Forty-eight hour passes were never issued - the "outside" was too far away and too inaccessible. Adding to the loneliness, the men's wives were not allowed to live on the base. The closest pocket of civilization was a Haida Indian village across Skidegate Inlet. An airman with a highly developed sense of humour dubbed the station an "Eveless Eden", and the nickname was aptly represented by a memento in the Officers' Mess. Behind the bar reposed a pith helmet of the type used in a bygone era in Egypt or the Middle East. Under the helmet was the inscription *"The Second Most Useless Thing In Alliford Bay."* Two years later, a young flying officer established an exception to this general ruling. The Station Diary records that: *"With Station Padre F/L F.A. Springborn officiating, F/O P.A. Vatcher and Miss Margaret Craig were married in the Officers' Mess, 14 June 1942."*

Recreation programmes and an entertainment schedule was the responsibility of a Y.M.C.A. representative who was posted to the Station. Some of the profit from the Canteen went to buy sports equipment, and from these small beginnings the men organized a basketball team that quickly earned respect on the "local circuit." Air Frame mechanic Tom Colbeck remembers his teammate George Siborne, a member of the Account Section, as *"one hell of a basketball player, a really aggressive and talented player."* They were playing the Haida Native team and the coach told Colbeck to go in and substitute for Siborne. As Siborne passed him, Colbeck hissed - *"who's your check?"* and Siborne shot back - *"the black-haired one."* Out on the floor and ready for action, Colbeck suddenly realized that they all had black hair. A quick look at Siborne: *"he was on the sidelines busting a gut laughing."* However, the team's record shows that they played serious basketball, winning 10 straight games

High tide: RCAF Station Alliford Bay, supply boat in foreground.
Baribeault Collection

against the Canadian Scottish Army on base, the Haida team, and the team from RCAF Station Prince Rupert.

After several months of concentrated effort the "Bull Gangs" were making progress, and an organized Station was taking shape. This meant that flying patrols could begin on a limited basis. On May 30, 1940 Shark #524, with F/L Gill and crew, completed the Squadron's first operational patrol. But an unexpected event occurred in the following month that sent the "Bull Gangs" into frantic, dawn-to-dark construction on the Station's defence systems.

On June 21, Western Air Command ordered the Station to establish a 24 hour watch. Half an hour later a second signal ordered them to go to full alert: all ground defences were manned, and aircraft and crews were standing by; guards were doubled, and a complete blackout was ordered - all the necessary precautions were taken to prevent a surprise attack. The next day the Sharks went up on patrols over Graham and Moresby Islands while the rest of the men filled sand bags to reinforce the defence positions, and construction crews rushed to finish the machine gun emplacements. Nothing happened - Western Air Command cancelled the alert as suddenly as it had called it, but the importance of being able to stand ready at a moment's notice was taken very seriously. The fever pitch of activity continued until the Station's defence systems were complete.

Four days later ground defence for the station was in

Farewell dinner for statlion Adjutant: F/L Huggett, 1942. Colbeck Collection

the capable hands of a contingent of Irish Fusiliers. Lieutenant Brown and 72 other ranks, under the command of Major Cannon, arrived on the naval vessel HMCS Sans Peur. The Fusiliers knew their job. During the night of July 7, an RCN vessel entered Skidegate Inlet without giving the Daily Recognition Signal, and it was immediately fired upon. Following this incident all surface craft were careful to comply with the order to identify themselves by flashing the Daily Recognition Signal.

A cryptic description of the weather was entered into the Station Diary on July 13, 1940: *"This is the 8th day in the past 63 that it has not rained."* Regardless of the weather the Station had gradually settled into the regulated order of daily routines. The odd, unexpected departure from normal duties kept Station life interesting. On one occasion, three Sharks were ordered to the Rose Harbour whaling station to conduct a search for secret radio equipment. The raid did not discover anything, but the officers and other ranks who attended, and the managers of the whaling station, all enjoyed the diversion.

The Station's Sharks were a valuable resource to the civilians living in small, detached communities scattered around the islands of the Queen Charlottes. No matter what the situation was, RCAF Station Alliford Bay always did everything they possibly could to help out. Emergency calls were frequent when the logging season was in full swing, and the Sharks went out on many mercy flights to deliver injured loggers to the hospital at Prince Rupert. Fishermen in distress knew they had a chance of survival when they heard the roar of the Shark's engine overhead. Not every call was an emergency: the B.C. Police requested to be flown to the mouth of a river where a fisherman was known to be engaged in illegal fishing. Repeated attempts by the police had failed to catch the man in the act, but as the Shark taxied up to the fishing boat the man, eager to break up his day with a little conversation, waved at them in friendly recognition - until the officer "popped" up.

The Shark was rugged and strong. In a crash its hull would take an incredible amount of punishment, and there were many aircrews who owed their life to this strength. The love/hate relationship between pilots and Sharks was softened by a general feeling of confidence inspired by the aircraft's excellent manoeuvrability, reliable engine, and first-class groundcrew maintenance. There were only two problems: starting, and landing, but once airborne there wasn't a pilot on record who didn't agree that the Shark was a pleasure to fly.

The notoriously bad landing characteristics of the Shark were exaggerated in glassy water landings, which caused the Squadron's first flying accident on July 19, 1940. Shark #525 was making a fast landing in calm air on the mirror-smooth surface of the bay. Just as the Shark skimmed the surface the float tips dug in and #525 overturned. The aircraft was a total write-off but the crew managed to escape without serious injury. The second accident occurred eight days later, but three Squadron members on a dive-bombing exercise in Shark #517 were not as fortunate.

The Shark was designed with dive-bombing capabilities, therefore this practice was a standard part of operational training. On July 27, 1940 the use of Sharks in dive bombing practice ended with tragic finality. A No. 6 (BR) wireless air gunner flew as crew in #517 while different pilots practiced dive-bombing a small island, and he recorded the events that took the lives of his fellow airmen:

> *"Each pilot had his own flying characteristics. F/L Ready had the gentlest dive and F/O Halpenny, a former bush pilot, the roughest. In one of F/O*

Halpenny's dives he threw the plane into a 45 degree dive nearly throwing me out. I had to jam my feet into stowage holes and grab the sides of the plane.....As the dive settled down I relaxed and was nearly thrown out a second time as Halpenny threw the plane into a vertical dive so as not to overshoot the target.....Then the pull out began. I was sitting on a little seat and I was pressed down so hard it felt as though my stomach was flowing out onto my lap. Little did I know how close to death I was until the next day. The next day (27 July, 1940) I was putting on my parachute harness to go up with F/O Halpenny again....As I was getting ready my signals officer, F/O Al Simpson, tapped me on the shoulder and said he was going up instead, and Richardson was going along for the ride. I took off my harness and went about my business. Suddenly someone yelled out and I looked towards the bay and there was a great flame where the plane plunged in and I saw part of the plane still in the air. It looked like an aileron rolling and spiralling down."

Airmen's quarters: Alliford Bay, 1940. Baribeault Collection

As Shark #517 had started to pull out of a full power vertical dive, the horrified observers saw the upper wing twist and break up, and the aircraft crash into the sea. The three Squadron members on board were the first airmen to lose their lives in a crash of an RCAF Shark.

Sharks #519 and #521 were immediately flown to No. 3 Repair Depot Vancouver where an inspection of the upper wing revealed rib buckling and main spar movement. The remainder of Alliford Bay's Sharks were ferried to Vancouver for modification, leaving No. 6 (BR) Squadron with one aircraft on strength - a single Norseman utility aircraft. The decision to attach two-foot strengthening sections to the upper wing spars at the points where the interplane struts were joined to them, was time-consuming. The wing had to be stripped, which meant a great deal of stitching, doping and fabric work. Despite No. 3 (RD) personnel working three shifts and an unusual amount of overtime, it was months before all the Sharks were completed. The strengthened sections prevented any recurrence of the upper wing weakness, but never again were RCAF Sharks used as dive-bombers.

S/L L.E. Wray was posted to Patricia Bay as Commanding Officer on November 6, 1940, and F/L M.G. Doyle was promoted to Squadron Leader and assumed command of No. 6 (BR) Squadron. The Squadron adjutant, F/L Cocking was posted to the Repair Depot at Calgary on December 7, and his position was filled by F/O G.E. Huggett.

Effective January 1, 1941 a Western Air Command policy came into effect whereby Alliford Bay and other isolated locations would exchange personnel after 6 months in isolation. This policy was greeted with enthusiasm and resulted in a positive injection into the Station's morale. Forty-seven airmen from Alliford Bay were exchanged with Vancouver and Patricia Bay, followed in February by a further twenty-three.

On February 19, 3 officers and 75 men of the Rocky Mountain Rangers arrived to relieve the Irish Fusiliers in the defence of the station. They were in turn relieved 5 months later by Lt. Mollison, Lt. Lees and 56 men of the 2nd Battalion, Canadian Scottish.

The Squadron training officers made good use of regular training programmes to boost energy and raise morale. Bombing and gunnery exercises continued, but the men were also exposed to a wide range of information through training lectures. An intense schedule was drawn up with lectures given on armament and anti-gas procedures, maintenance and repair of W/T sets, aircraft engine maintenance, as well as reconnaissance procedure and enemy intelligence. Each section was responsible for setting out a schedule of training for its personnel.

The arrival of the auxiliary cruiser HMCS Prince Henry, on the 30th of July 1941, provided the Squadron officers with an opportunity to add a little variety to the training schedule. The cruiser was anchored in the bay for two days, and during that time the officers organized a cooperative operational exercise. Several of the Naval Officers were taken on flights over their ship to give them an idea of the type of target they presented to enemy aircraft. When the ship left the harbour two days later, the Squadron staged an interception, and aircrews carried out practice air attacks. Several more interceptions and attacks were made when the Prince Henry was in the vicinity again on August 18.

Training had prepared the airmen to defend their station and their patrol area against the enemy - many wished for the same confidence in their equipment. The RCAF Squadrons on the west coast had gone into the war under less than desirable conditions. The aircraft acquired by the Department of National Defence were out-dated at best - they were, in fact, obsolete. Although aircrews had found the Supermarine Stranraers to be a very seaworthy flying boat its range was considerably less than the Catalina and Canso's range. But for reasons of economy the Canadian government had purchased the Stranraer, and the same could be said for the Blackburn Shark. If the Shark had been used in serious defence of Western Canada it would not have done well against aircraft such as the Japanese Mitsibushi Zero, or its float counterpart the Rufe. The best that could be said for the Stranraer and Shark was that they were there, and both aircrew and groundcrew did a magnificent job of doing their best with what they had.

The Japanese attack on Pearl Harbor December 7, 1941, brought orders from Western Air Command to adopt No. 1 Alert procedures. Blackouts were enforced in the whole area, including Queen Charlotte City and the Indian village at Skidegate. Station personnel reacted swiftly: aircrews went on immediate standby, and maintenance crews worked all night to ensure that every plane was ready for service; aircraft patrols were intensified, the station defences were manned, and surprise drills were called to test the men's efficiency in dealing with a gas attack. The Squadron's one Stranraer, which had been taken on strength in October, was on patrol throughout the next day, while the Sharks waited patiently - all bombed up but no where to go.

Operating an effective front line of coastal defence relied heavily on the ability of No. 6 (BR) Squadron air patrols to track the enemy's movements far in advance of the coastline: the demands of the situation had moved beyond the capabilities of the faithful Shark. They flew on their last operational patrol for No. 6 (BR) Squadron on December 9, 1941. A formation of five Sharks flew over the Station in a final salute, and two days later the Squadron watched with mixed feelings as five Sharks were ferried out to No. 7 (BR) Squadron at Prince Rupert. There was a slight touch of irony in the release of Shark #550, which followed the other Sharks to Prince Rupert a short time later. It seemed appropriate that the last Boeing-built Shark was the last Shark to be taken off strength.

A group of airmen, posted to RCAF Station Alliford Bay that December, arrived just in time to see the last Shark transferred out. LAC Harry Tate, posted in from No. 12 SFTS Squadron in Brandon, Manitoba, recorded his first impression of Alliford Bay and the Station:

> *"The bay and surrounding area look beautiful after the Prairies - the bay is open on one end and surrounded by low, heavily wooded mountains on three sides. The camp is built among the tall trees. There are two large hangars and a single slipway at the inside end. The mess hall, barracks and Officers' Mess are about a quarter of a mile*

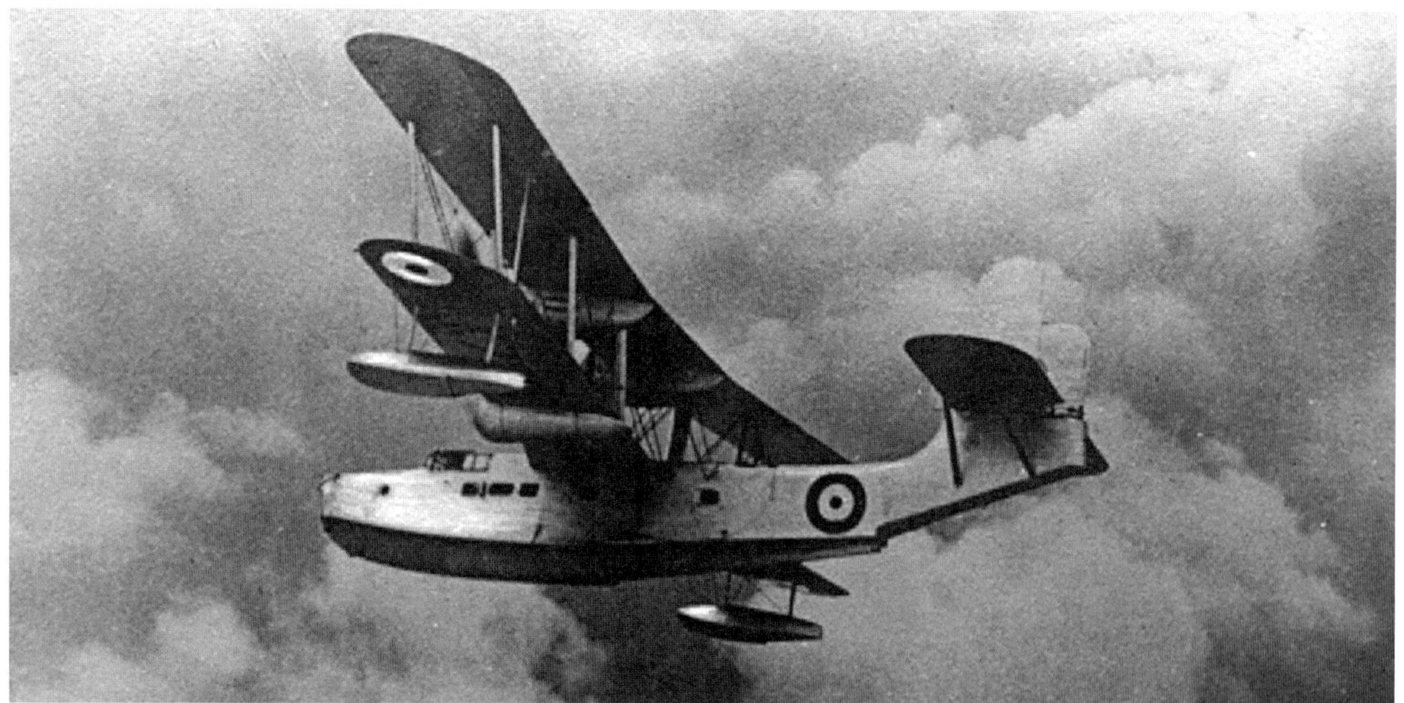

Stranraer in flight over Queen Charlotte Islands, 1940. Colbeck Collection *east on the south shore. The loading ramp for the supply boats is practically in line with the airmens' mess.....There are some compensations in Alliford because of being isolated - the food is excellent as we have the best flight sergeant cook on the west coast. The officers are glad to get orderly officer duty as that is the only time they get really good meals."*

Tate, an aero engine mechanic, was assigned to aircraft maintenance and got caught up in the excitement of the arrival of Stranraer Flying Boats which replaced the Sharks. Air frame mechanic Tom Colbeck also remembered some excitement involving a Stranraer that ushered 1941 out with a bang.

On New Year's Eve, the aero engine mechanic in the bunk above Colbeck got a call to go down to the hangar and fix the engine on Stranraer #922. The crew had been trying to get fireproof lights to replace the coleman-type lanterns used for working on the planes at night, but there was no sign of them so far. Colbeck said:

"So, my bunk air engine mechanic was draining gas out of the engine, and the riggers were fixing a patch on the wing below - BOY! did we have fire works that night - New Year's Eve and all. The ammunition was exploding, the old aircraft burning - and the Crashboat over in Charlotte City trying to get provisions. By the time they had a line on her, the aircraft was starting to be a sub and slowly sank."

In the first 6 months of 1942, postings and promotions occurred in rapid succession: Squadron Adjutant F/L Huggett was posted to Patricia Bay on January 31, and P/O W.A. Murrey assumed his position; A Station Headquarters was established in February under the command of S/L B.N. Harrop who had replaced S/L Doyle as Squadron Commanding Officer late in August 1941; F/L W.M. Emery was assigned officer commanding No. 6 (BR) Squadron. Adding to the new faces at the Station, the Edmonton Fusiliers arrived on March 3 to replace the Canadian Scottish detachment on aerodrome defence duties. On April 1, 1942 F/L Emery was posted to Pat Bay, and S/L H.J. Winney, OBE arrived to take command of the Squadron.

S/L Winney had a reputation for being the Squadron's finest flying boat pilot. Groundcrews could always tell when Winney was flying the aircraft - "you would see the approach and the rear part of the hull would just gently begin to ripple the water and then spread it out." The CO's skill as a pilot, his quiet, sincere manner and natural friendliness gained him the respect and loyalty of his officers and men.

At the end of June 1942 W/C Harrop received a posting to Western Air Command, and a farewell dinner was held in the Officers' Mess. Squadron CO, S/L Harry Winney, was assigned as Officer Commanding the Station,

above; Leaving Alliford Bay for Coal Harbour, April 1944, (left to right) LACs Alex Crombie, Willis, Butt, Brown. Crombie Collection
top; Canso #11099 at Alliford Bay, 1944. Crombie Collection

and F/L A.C. Neale took temporary command of No. 6 (BR) Squadron, until S/L G.C. Upson assumed command on August 25. On that date S/L Winney's position as Station Commander was made permanent, and two months later he was promoted to Wing Commander. Postings and promotions were an accepted part of the system, but later that fall an announcement from Western Air Command had a major impact on the entire Squadron.

On October 11, 1942 Western Air Command ordered the posting on exchange of NCOs and airmen who had been at the station for more than 12 months - this affected over 80 men. Some of them were anxious to be closer to their families in southern British Columbia, and some were restless, and eager for a change, but all of them felt a sense of regret as they left Alliford Bay. It was another reminder that, in spite of their isolation, in spite of the weather and all the other hardships they had gone through, they would miss the close friends and spirit of comradeship that set RCAF Station Alliford Bay slightly apart from the other Stations.

Station life resumed its normal pace - which lasted less than a month. On November 16, acting on orders from Western Air Command, No.6 (BR) Squadron moved to Bella Bella and No. 9 (BR) Squadron moved from Bella Bella to Alliford Bay. The purpose of the exercise was to "practice active mobility, in case of an emergency." Number 6 (BR) Squadron returned to Alliford Bay on December 3, and began preparations for the third Christmas at the Station.

On December 13, S/L Upson was posted to No. 4 Group Headquarters at Prince Rupert, and S/L V.A. Margetts assumed command of No. 6 (BR) Squadron.

1943 began tragically with the loss of Stranraer #935 and its crew. On February 14, while on a training flight, the Stranraer crashed in Skidegate Channel between Maude and Lina Islands. P/O D.S. MacLennan, P/O L.G. Thompson, P/O F.W. McConkey, Accounts Officer C.T. Fields, Sgt. J.O. Gilmour, and Cpl. J.P.Spraling were all killed. Squadron members sent out to investigate the crash site found a lot of debris and a large number of dead fish floating all over the area. From the evidence they concluded that the aircraft's four depth charges had exploded on impact.

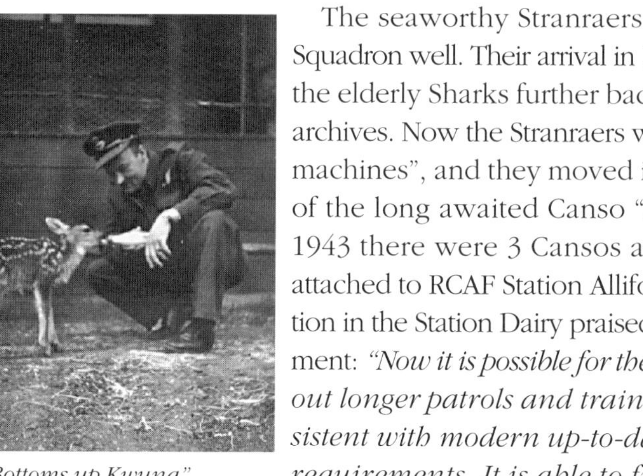
"Bottoms up Kwuna".
McGregor Knight Collection

Any accident involving loss of life understandably lowered the Squadron spirit. But it was at times like this that the airmen talked about the many episodes where they had skirted death with a twist of fate and quick thinking on the part of a fellow airman. Tate, now a Corporal, recounted one of these episodes:

> *"One of the hazards of flying in the nose or tail turret in rough air was the possibility that you might lose the aircraft during a downdraft and find yourself 2000 feet above the sea without even the proverbial paddle. One day I was on another test flight and one of my air gunner friends went out to the tail turret to relax, put up the gun and have a smoke. In the front and rear turret there was a "G-string" attached to the floor that was to be clipped to your parachute harness to prevent you going overboard in rough air. Benny proceeded out to the tail and had been there for a while when the air became exceedingly rough. The radio operator and I wondered how he was making out. I couldn't see his legs so went back to investigate. It's lucky I did since Benny had not hooked up the G-string and he went out, but grabbed the gun. He was hanging onto the gun, head down, with only water below him a couple of thousand feet away. I tried to pull him in but was unable to with the slipstream, so I left him, got the RO, and between us we yanked Benny back in the aircraft."*

The seaworthy Stranraers had served the Squadron well. Their arrival in 1941 had pushed the elderly Sharks further back into the dusty archives. Now the Stranraers were the "ancient machines", and they moved into the shadow of the long awaited Canso "A". By July 10, 1943 there were 3 Cansos and 3 Stranraers attached to RCAF Station Alliford Bay. A notation in the Station Dairy praised the new equipment: *"Now it is possible for the station to carry out longer patrols and training that is consistent with modern up-to-date operational requirements. It is able to fulfill its service responsibility now that it has proper equipment."* However, many of the airmen voiced a different feeling: *"The Stranraer was a real rugged airplane it could be landed and taken off on open ocean if the swells were reasonable. It was much more seaworthy than the Canso and the Catalina and could absorb considerably more punishment without staving in the hull."* Another airman held the opinion that: *"The Stranraer was the best biplane boat built and we all loved her,"* - and, *"There was something about a Stranraer that you couldn't resist. I never felt the same way about the Canso."*

S/L L.A. Harling was now temporary Officer Commanding the Squadron, and his position was made permanent in September 1943. S/L C.C. Austin had been assigned to succeed W/C Winney, OBE as Commanding Officer of the Station. W/C Winney was posted to Ucluelet in May, and before his departure the Officers' and the Sergeants' Mess each made a presentation to him.

In July 1943 Alex Crombie was posted to Alliford Bay after being at Pat Bay for a short period. One of the first jobs he was given, along with other riggers and fitters, was to get one of the last Stranraers airworthy enough to fly to Jericho Beach. By March 1944 No. 6 (BR) Squadron had 7 Catalina flying boats, 2 Canso "A"s and only 1 Stranraer.

Catalina and Canso crews continued a rigorous schedule of bombing and gunnery practice, and during some of the exercises the misfiring of machine guns caused more damage to the aircraft than the enemy ever got around to doing. Twice Crombie recalls a Catalina landing and the air gunners scrambling out of the Blisters and up on the port side wing. *"They had shot one or two 50 calibre holes in the starboard float and they were trying to keep it out of the water until we could beach it."* Another time startled ground crew members moved quickly aside as a Canso came roaring up the ramp. *"This time,"* Crombie said, *"they'd put the 50 calibre machine gun in the storage position and for some reason it fired and put a hole in the hull."* Practising with live ammunition had its disadvantages, and a couple of incidents involving depth charges and Cansos gave everyone a few anxious moments. The aircrew ran a Canso up on the tarmac and the depth charges fell off the wings; and once during a maintenance inspection in the hangar someone hit the wrong switch and down came the depth charges. Crombie summed it up - *"Thank God for safety rings!"*

Air and ground crew of No. 7 (BR) Squadron with Canso at Alliford Bay, 1944.
McGregor Knight Collection

On April 21, 1944 No. 6 (BR) Squadron received orders to begin a move to Coal Harbour on Holberg Inlet on the north end of Vancouver Island. The move was completed on April 23rd.

Corporal Harry Tate wrote the final word on RCAF Station Alliford Bay: *"Alliford Bay was a terrific place - we had the best food, the best CO - Harry Winney - and the best morale on the coast. AND we flew more hours."* But the narrative would not be complete without mentioning the station deer.

The deer, a species peculiar to the Queen Charlotte Islands, were very small, weighing about 90 pounds on the hoof. They were docile little creatures who roamed freely wherever they wished because they had no predators on the islands. They had no fear of the airmen and gradually developed an idle curiosity in the station. With a straight face, airmen from Alliford Bay tell of having to chase the deer off the rifle range before target practice could begin.

Over time, there were several deer who became very friendly and were "adopted" as station pets. The airmen called the deer Kwuna, and gave it the full privileges of the station, including the Officers' and the Sergeants' Mess. On invitation, or simply because the door had been left open, Kwuna would wander in, searching for one of its favourite titbits - cigarette butts. Next to that, it was passionately fond of licking the leather coverings of the armchairs. The deer became an integral part of station life and was incorporated into the official Station crest.

As No. 6 (BR) Squadron completed their move to Coal Harbour, No. 7 (BR) Squadron, under the command of S/L R. Dobson, moved to RCAF Station Alliford Bay. During their year at the Station the Squadron aircrews set several records.

On June 14, 1944 a fisherman sighted a submarine in Dixon Entrance, just off Zayas Island, 50 miles north-west of Prince Rupert. S/L Dobson launched four patrols. A target was detected with anti-submarine equipment but due to the heavy fog the crew was unable to establish visual contact for an attack. Again, on June 24, S/L Dobson was in command of a Canso that completed a night patrol of 20 hours and 40 minutes - the longest patrol in Western Air Command records.

On June 27, 1944 S/L Dobson was posted to Western Air Command and was replaced as Commanding Officer by S/L A.C. Neale. On July 26, W/C J.W. McNee succeeded W/C Austin as Station Commanding Officer.

Number 7 (BR) Squadron completed its last mission on July 14, 1945. F/O Craddock and crew flew Canso A 11070 from Alliford Bay on an anti-submarine patrol. The Squadron was disbanded at Alliford Bay on July 25, 1945 and the Station was reduced to care and maintenance basis.

1

3

2

4

5

6

7

1. *Shark #525 after crash at Alliford Bay, July 19, 1940.* CFB Comox Rowe Library
2. *Remains of Shark #525.* CFB Comox Rowe Library
3. *Grumman Goose #524 at Alliford Bay, 1940.* Baribeault Collection
4. *Airmen's barracks, low tide, 1940.* Baribeault Collection
5. *Blackburn Sharks on ramp at Alliford Bay, 1940. #522 in foreground.* Baribeault Collection
6. *Supply ship, 1940.* Galbraith Collection
7. *Transmitter shack, Alliford Bay, 1940.* Galbraith Collection

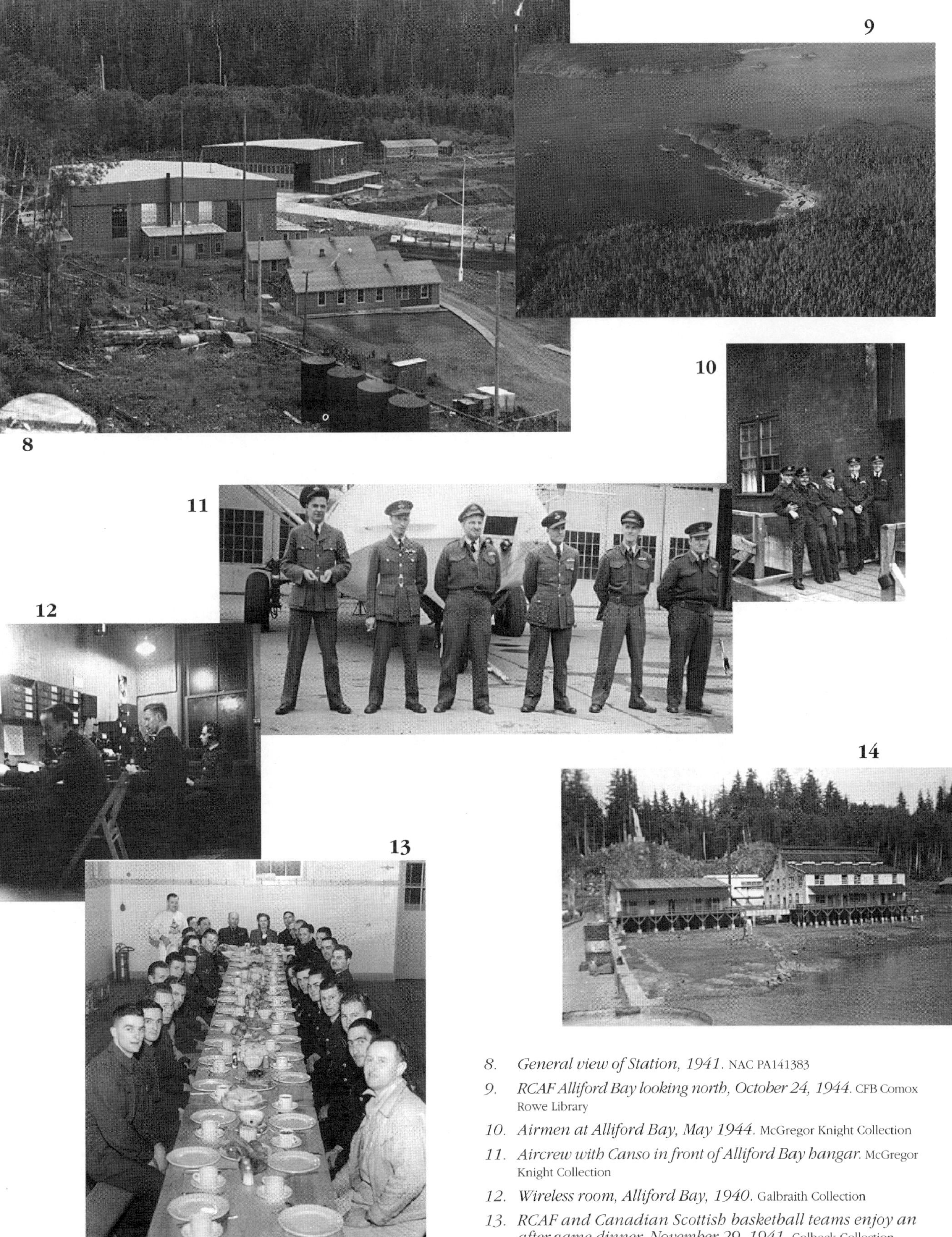

8. *General view of Station, 1941.* NAC PA141383
9. *RCAF Alliford Bay looking north, October 24, 1944.* CFB Comox Rowe Library
10. *Airmen at Alliford Bay, May 1944.* McGregor Knight Collection
11. *Aircrew with Canso in front of Alliford Bay hangar.* McGregor Knight Collection
12. *Wireless room, Alliford Bay, 1940.* Galbraith Collection
13. *RCAF and Canadian Scottish basketball teams enjoy an after game dinner. November 29, 1941.* Colbeck Collection
14. *Airmen and Officers' quarters, 1940.* Galbraith Collection

15

16

17

18

19

15. *Kwuna in Officers' Mess, October 1942.* CFS Masset

16. *Sharks on beach, Alliford Bay.* CFS Masset

17. *LAC Baribeault dressed in S/L Wray's Uniform.* Baribeault Collection

18. *Shark at Rose Harbour Whaling Station.* CFS Masset

19. *Cheers for departing Commanding Officer, S/L Mike Doyle.* CFB Comox Rowe Library

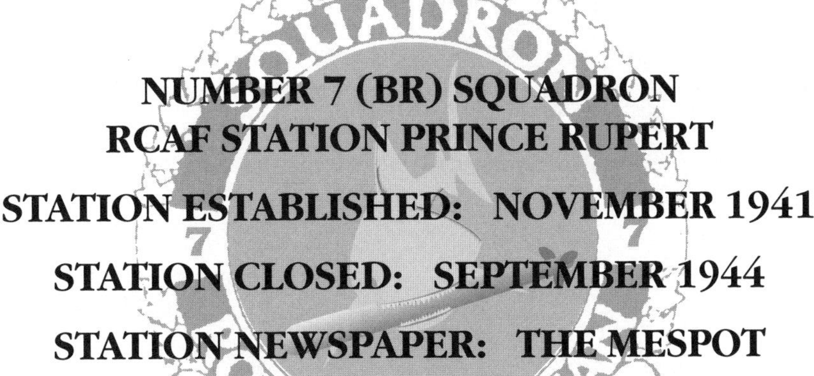

NUMBER 7 (BR) SQUADRON
RCAF STATION PRINCE RUPERT

STATION ESTABLISHED: NOVEMBER 1941

STATION CLOSED: SEPTEMBER 1944

STATION NEWSPAPER: THE MESPOT

RCAF STATION PRINCE RUPERT

RCAF Prince Rupert looking west, May 14, 1943. CFB Comox Rowe Library

In the early 1920's Jericho Beach Air Station accepted the challenge of flying coastal fishery patrols within the vast boundaries of the Prince Rupert fishing district. Major Earl Godfrey, and crewmembers Harold Davenport and Harry Bell, were detached from Jericho Beach Air Station. Davenport and Bell formed the first RCAF detachment stationed on the rugged coast of British Columbia. Flying Curtiss HS-2L, G-CYDX, the three airmen left Jericho Beach in the early morning of July 23, 1923. The Curtiss arrived at Prince Rupert before dark, having made two refuelling stops, one at Alert Bay and the second at Bella Bella. It was the first time an aircraft had flown the length of the British Columbia coast.

F/L Earl MacLeod was placed in charge of the small detachment. He chose to locate his temporary seaplane base at Seal Cove - a sheltered lagoon at the north end of the city of Prince Rupert. For 15 years detachments operated seasonal fishery patrols from this "temporary" base until, in 1937, the British Columbia Reconnaissance Detachment identified Prince Rupert as a key location for an RCAF Flying Boat Station. Seal Cove was the logical choice for the construction of the station.

The Canadian military agreed with the United States government that Prince Rupert would be a prime target in a Japanese invasion of the west coast of North America. Geographic location had dictated the city's rapid growth as a major centre of industry and transportation: it was already an established deep sea port with a growing and important ship-building industry; it was the main port of call for the coastal steamers that provided a life-line to northern communities in British Columbia and Alaska; and it was the railhead of the Canadian National Railway. But the shadow of Japan's threat to "march into this continent enroute to the White House" gave Prince Rupert a new, strategic importance. The city was a natural guard post at the mouth of the Skeena River; a coastal waterway leading into the heart of the province.

The Canadian Navy, Army, and Air Force converged on Prince Rupert: the Navy protected the entrances to the harbour from infiltration by enemy submarine or surface craft; the Army set up a strong defence of anti-aircraft guns and heavy artillery; and the RCAF was charged with the responsibility of patrolling the seaward approaches, protecting the shipping lanes, and acting as a striking force to prevent an enemy invasion. Events were moving fast and the construction of a Flying Boat Station at Prince Rupert became an immediate priority.

The challenge of preparing the physical site so that building could begin was one thing all the coastal RCAF stations had in common. Blasting began at Seal Cove in December 1939, and small mountains were levelled and removed. At the end of September 1940 the land had been cleared and the grading was almost complete, but only a few buildings were underway. However, enough progress had been made to warrant posting a security guard, and on September 24, F/L M.G. Doyle, F/O S.C. Leary, F/S Pomers and Cpl. Brooks arrived from Alliford Bay. The security detachment was completed the following day by 45 "Standard Pilots" posted in from Brandon, Manitoba.

In the remaining four months of 1940, heavy blasting created enough space for the building contractors to move ahead with their work. By the beginning of November a transmitter had been installed and the signal station was in operation, and by December construction was well underway on all the station buildings. One station member quipped that the explosions and flying rock made him feel he was on active duty in the centre of a warzone. A year later construction was complete, with the exception of finishing work on three buildings: the recreation hall, the link trainer building, and the Works and Building headquarters.

The wartime Station for No. 7 (BR) Squadron was ready. On December 1, 1941 Western Air Command issued the order that re-formed No. 7 (GP) General Purpose Squadron as a (BR) Bomber Reconnaissance unit at Prince Rupert, effective December 8, 1941. The preceding day Japan launched their devastating attack on Pearl Harbor, and the United States was at war with Japan. The Station was ordered to put number 2 Alert procedures in place, and a complete blackout was enforced. Station personnel who were living off the Station were ordered to return, and all leaves were cancelled. An odd situation existed for the next three days - No. 7 (BR) Squadron operated a coastal Flying Boat Station without any aircraft.

On December 11, the promised Sharks arrived. They were ferried in from Alliford Bay by F/O Barney McLeod, P/O E. Kenny, P/O F.N. Dale, Sgt. Thomas, and Sgt. Avent. The following day three more Sharks transferred in from Ucluelet. The Sharks #518, 519, 523, 524, 526, 545, 547 and 549 were taken on strength, and F/L R.H. Morris was appointed temporary Officer Commanding both No. 7 (BR) Squadron, and RCAF Station Prince Rupert.

Time had become a critical factor in preparing for operational duty. The airmen worked long hours over the next several days to get the Operations Room organized and arrange the flight patrol schedule. On December 15, 1941, the Squadron was fully operational and took over its stated responsibility of patrolling the seaward approaches to Prince Rupert. Four Sharks carried out the Squadron's first operational anti-submarine patrols - Sharks #523 and #545 in the morning, and #547 and #549 in the afternoon.

The increase in the Squadron's activity, as well as the business of operating a busy Station, meant an increase in Station personnel. Squadron Adjutant F/O T.D.H. Hodgins reported for duty just before Christmas, and by the first of January 1942 the Station had a strength of 13 Officers, 69 NCOs and 237 other ranks.

F/O George A. Doolittle joined No. 7 (BR) Squadron that December and soloed in one of the Sharks a month later. He developed a feeling of respect for the Sharks that was definitely not shared by everyone. His remark that, *"No one who has ever flown the Shark will forget it,"* was always greeted by vigorous head-nodding and a chorus of *"AND YOU CAN SAY THAT AGAIN!"* Doolittle carried on to explain that he thought the Shark was *"a tricky little beast at its worst, but a sturdy little work horse too, and one not likely to let you down. I have known a few pilots who went out of their way to avoid the little gal; I am happy to say I was not one of them."*

Completed hangar at Seal Cove. P.R. Archives

Number 7 (BR) Squadron was the last operational Shark Squadron, therefore most of the surviving Sharks ended up with the Squadron at RCAF Station Prince Rupert: 14 Shark IIIs, and 2 Shark IIs. The two Shark IIs were converted into target tugs, and training exercises were organized in cooperation with the coast artillery and the navy units stationed at the entrance to Prince Rupert harbour. Squadron aircrews did their best to give the gunners at Point Barrett Fort realistic practice. The mock attacks enhanced the spirit of friendly competition that existed between the aircrews and the "ground pounders", but one Shark attack produced more "enhancement" than the aircrews had intended. To add interest and the element of surprise, the Shark crews dropped one-pound flour bombs on the gunners. Shortly after the drop it started to rain, turning the flour into an oozy, sticky paste which took the army gunners weeks to remove.

The Squadron worked their Sharks IIIs hard day after day for nearly two years, sending up three or four patrols each day, seven days a week. The continual flights during daylight hours left the groundcrews to work their miracles through the night, and their skill and ingenuity squeezed every ounce of life out of the aged aircraft. The bomb-laiden Sharks patrolled two at a time: one patrolled south of the station, and the other patrolled to the north. The usual south patrol went out to Langara Island at the extreme northwestern tip of the Queen Charlotte Islands, flew seaward for about 10 minutes, then flew north for about 8 minutes before reversing the outbound track and returning to base. The north patrol followed along the headlands of the Alaskan islands out to Forrester Island, and then flew south for about 10 minutes before also reversing its track, and heading back to Prince Rupert.

The aircrews spent long, monotonous hours scanning the surface of the ocean for unusual activity. The major coastal shipping routes were not in the Squadron's patrol area, but occasionally they spotted small fishing boats. These were all carefully investigated. From the air they might appear to be innocent fishing craft but reports were circulating that the clever Japanese had found a way to disguise their submarines.

Each Shark was armed with bombs or depth charges and the crews were ready to take action if the situation required - but often the day's only battle was with the weather. High wind, heavy rain, and dense fog harassed the Squadron patrols year round, and on many occasions patrols fought their way back to the Station through extremely hazardous conditions. However, weather never caused the loss of a Shark at RCAF Station Prince Rupert.

The newly formed Squadron was shaken by its first fatality on January 4, 1942. Returning from a routine patrol, Shark #518 crashed and burned about 12 miles northwest of Prince Rupert, on Finlayson Island, near Big Bay. Pilot F/O Barny McLeod, and Sgt. E.E. Cormier, were killed. Crew member Sgt. Trevor Collins managed to parachute to safety. F/L Norris and a detail proceeded by crash boat to the scene and remained out overnight, returning the next day with the bodies of their fellow airmen.

The patrol, heading in to Rupert from the north, had just passed Dundas Island when they spotted Shark #550 at a lower altitude, returning to Rupert from the south. With the idea of having some fun, F/O McLeod turned slightly on an intercepting course, put the nose down to increase speed, and gradually gained on the second

HMCS Courtney retrieves wreckage of one float of Shark #524, June 20, 1942. P.R. Archives

Shark. Now moving faster and still unseen by the crew of #550, McLeod flew #518 underneath and intended to pull up well in front of the other aircraft but he had made a grave error in judging their relative speeds. There was no time to get out of the way. Shark #550 struck #518's rudder - #518 pitched forward and headed down. Collins was in the rear cockpit on one of the fold-down seats attached to the sidewall. He hadn't hooked the safety clip on his parachute harness and was thrown violently off his seat. In his fight to get himself upright, he managed to grab a chest pack parachute and got one clip hooked up just as he fell out of the aircraft. Somehow, through his sheer terror, he managed to attach the second clip before he pulled the rip cord. Collins landed about 300 yards from the burning aircraft.

Wreckage of Shark #518 on Finlayson Island, January 4, 1942. P.R. Archives

The Squadron suffered its second fatal accident five months later, on June 20, 1942. F/S H.E. Phillips, flying Shark #524, moved in behind another Shark, hit that aircraft's slipstream at too low an altitude to effect a recovery, and crashed off Metlakatla Island. Phillips, and F/S H. Baum were killed, and the only trace of #524 was a single float picked up by the Minesweeper HMCS Courtenay.

Just before dawn on a morning early in February 1942, a small Japanese seaplane was reported over the city of Prince Rupert. Sightings were reported by a night watchman in the Naval shipyard, two Canadian Army security guards, and a B.C Provincial Policeman. The aircraft, a submarine-launched Yokosuka E-14Y1 (Glen), circled the Prince Rupert harbour and Seal Cove Air Force Station before slipping away through the half-light, moving northward in the direction of Work Channel. Number 7 (BR) Squadron scrambled a Shark but an hour elapsed before F/O Pete Gault and his crew were airborne. Later in the day a Native woman reported that she saw a black "stick" moving along in the water north of Port Simpson. Sightings in the same day, of an airplane and a possible periscope, served to remind everyone that the enemy was watching.

Guard House at RCAF Prince Rupert. P.R. Archives

Wing Commander R.C. Gordon was now in command of the Station, and on April 1, S/L J.E. Jellison assumed command of the Squadron. Early in the spring, RCAF Station Prince Rupert received notice of a visit from the Deputy Inspector General, A/C A.E. Godfrey. On April 12, 1942, the Station looked sharp and all personnel stood ready for inspection. When the Station Diarist recorded the events of the day he mentioned that during the inspection:

"a PBY Canso flew over and quite a few heads and necks started to turn about. A/C Godfrey apparently appreciated the moment and, after a few kind words, dismissed us just as the machine started to climb up the slipway. This machine, the first of its kind many of us had seen, was a beauty. It appears that the officers on board noticed us drawn up on the apron in our best drill manners and thought we had turned out to greet them. They were quite worried, as they had not brought their best clothes, and were greatly relieved when they found out it was somebody else we were dressed up for."

On May 16, 1942 F/L H.E. Jones reported as Senior Intelligence Officer. He had been an observer in the RFC and the RAF during World War I, and delighted in giving vivid accounts of his adventures. The Station Newspaper "Mespot" published some of his stories, which made good

Presentation at 7 (BR) Officers' Mess July 1942 on the retirement of F/O Griffin; extreme right, Geo. Doolitlle; 3rd from right, Bill Coulter; 4th from right, S/L Brooks; 5th from right F/O Griffin; 6th from right, W/C Austin; 7th from right, G/C Gordon. Coulter Collection

reading on long, dull evenings.

At this time the Station was notified that a group headquarters would temporarily operate from RCAF Station Prince Rupert. Plans were ready for the construction of No. 4 Group Headquarters on a site southeast of the city of Prince Rupert, and it was expected that the buildings would be complete by December, 1942. Two major concerns prompted Western Air Command Headquarters in Victoria to decentralize control of the isolated northern Flying Boat Stations: atmospheric conditions often made wireless communications difficult and the landline telephone system was unreliable - occasionally communication failed altogether; it was also necessary to maintain close cooperation with the United States forces in Alaska, therefore a direct liaison between the northern Services was essential. Number 4 Group Headquarters assumed operational control of the northern British Columbia coastal RCAF units on June 16, 1942. The Station Commanding Officer G/C R.C. Gordon, was posted from the Prince Rupert Station to command No. 4 Group, and F/L Jones was also posted from Prince Rupert, to become Group Intelligence Officer.

ARRANGE FOR
A SPECIAL PARTY
PHONE 233
Blue Wings
Cabaret

During June S/L L.H. "Doc" Brooks took command of RCAF Station Prince Rupert. The Squadron Commanding Officer, S/L Jellison, was posted to Western Air Command as Controller, and F/L Morris was reappointed Officer Commanding No. 7 (BR) Squadron - Morris received a promotion to Squadron Leader on August 1, 1942.

Prince Rupert fish packing plant in foreground and RCAF Station at Seal Cove beyond, looking east. Winter 1946. P.R. Archives

P/O Bill Coulter Wireless Air Gunner poses with Shark at Prince Rupert. Coulter Collection

The organized daily routine of the Squadron had much in common with the other coastal Flying Boat Squadrons, but there was one significant difference. No. 7 (BR) Squadron's location at Seal Cove gave the airmen easy access to the city of Prince Rupert and all the amenities of a large city. The Blue Wings Cafe and Cabaret was a popular local "hot spot" where the waitresses were fondly referred to as "Cuddle Bunnies". Instead of spending their money, some of the airmen chose to work on their days off. The local cold storage fish plants, and the contractor building the new Rupert to Terrace highway benefited from Station personnel eager to supplement their Air Force pay.

By August 1942 the Station strength had increased to 20 officers and 436 airmen - the count did not include the personnel of No. 4 Group Headquarters, nor did it include the constant flow of airmen in transition to or from Alliford Bay and Annette Island in Alaska. These men used the Station like a rest stop and aptly nicknamed the overcrowded airmen's and officers' barracks "The Seal Cove Hotel."

Wireless Air Gunner P/O Bill Coulter, had been with No. 7 (BR) Squadron since March. His first operational flight was with F/O Doolittle in Shark #546. Coulter flew 45 sorties before he left 7 (BR) Squadron on September 16, 1942 to begin pilot training. Two weeks before his departure he took off in Shark #526 on his last patrol - it seemed fitting that F/O Doolittle was again in command.

The morning was clear, without a cloud in the sky. The picture-perfect reflection on the surface of the bay washed apart as #526 plowed through the water, reached the step and lifted off. A few minutes later total stillness had been restored. At 07:30 on this beautiful September morning P/O Coulter had no inkling that it would also be the last patrol for #526.

> *"The patrol was without incident until we returned to base three hours later. On attempting to land under glassy-water conditions the pilot misjudged his height above the water and the floats nosed in causing the tail assembly to move sharply upward and the propeller to hit the water. This caused the propeller tips to be bent about ninety degrees. The pilot pulled the stick fully back and we climbed to about 100 feet rolled over to the left and dropped like a stone into the drink.*
>
> *The left wing caved in and water rushed into the rear cockpit where the observer and I were located. I was knocked onto my back to the floor of the cockpit and as the water rushed in I was able to get to my feet and I just dove headfirst out of the plane into the water.*
>
> *Once in the water I looked back and saw the pilot had got out of the front cockpit and was standing on the fuselage. He released the dinghy which inflated and dropped into the water.*
>
> *I then returned to the aircraft and looked into the back cockpit and saw that the observer was still there. Fortunately the plane remained afloat and I was able to assist him out of the fuselage and into the water. He had banged his face on the bulkhead and was bleeding from the mouth and nose. His were the only apparent injuries. We then managed to scramble into the dinghy and await the rescue boat."*

The timely arrival of a fishing boat saved the poor old Shark from sinking to the bottom of the bay, but because of the damage to its port wing and the loss of its floats, #526 was written off. Station Commanding Officer W/C "Doc" Brooks was keenly aware of the Sharks' poor landing characteristics, as well as its other less threatening imperfections. The CO told Doolittle that he would earn a recommendation for the Air Force Cross if he wrote off the other Sharks without killing anybody. It was the aircraft's unstable landing features, and not W/C Brooks' joking comment, that led to the demise of five other Sharks: 505, 506, 507, 525, and 547.

The report of an enemy submarine sighted on October 27, 1942, shot a burst of excitement through the Station. WO2 Thomas, F/S Moyles and Sgt. Fairholm, were on navigation exercises in Shark #550 when they spotted a

Remains of Shark #526 on ramp at Seal Cove, September 3, 1942. Coulter Collection

above; Shark #526, September 3, 1942, being salvaged from Prince Rupert Harbour. Coulter Collection

right; Seal Cove crane hauls wreckage of Shark #526 onto ramp, September 3, 1942. P.R. Archives submarine on the surface near Rose Point on the northwest tip of the Queen Charlotte Islands. The Japanese were also paying attention and promptly submerged in a crash dive. Thomas dropped depth charges into the swirl created by the submarine's hasty departure, but for some reason only one charge dropped. They circled, managed to release the second charge and continued to circle the area for the next twenty minutes, but saw no further evidence of the submarine. The frustration of technical malfunction had taken the edge off their excitement - now their radio wouldn't operate, and they had to return to the Station in order to raise the alarm. Number 7 (BR) Squadron Sharks were immediately scrambled, and aircraft were dispatched from Annette Island and Alliford Bay to assist in the search, but the results were negative.

S/L Morris was posted to Patricia Bay in December, and was replaced as Squadron CO by F/L P.J. Grant, who arrived from No. 5 OTU Boundary Bay. In the first month of 1943, F/L Grant and his Squadron suffered the loss of a flying officer in the crash of Shark #547.

On January 27, Pilot F/O E. Kenny, S/L W.R.C. Taylor and F/O A. Hogg had completed a routine radio frequency calibration flight and were on approach into Seal Cove. The Shark crashed on landing. On impact one of the depth charges ripped off its mounting and exploded, igniting the aircraft's fuel. All three of the crew members were severely injured but F/O Hogg's injuries were fatal, and he died eight hours after the crash.

Two months later another Shark ran into difficulty, but this time the accident occurred on take-off. WO2 Dorland with Wireless Operator F/S Cousins took off in Shark #520 to take part in an Army Co-operation flight. As the Shark broke from the water the right wing tip dipped slightly causing the float to dig in, throwing the aircraft over on its back. The Shark was towed to the crane and lifted out of the water for inspection and repairs - the crew considered themselves lucky to escape with only a startling dip in the icy bay.

The time-weary Sharks kept on giving the best they had to give and even though the groundcrews understood how to keep the "old gals" happy, the length of their service record was beginning to show. The effect of trying to run anti-submarine patrols using what were now openly referred to as historic artifacts, was also taking its toll on morale. The Sharks had been replaced in all the other Squadrons - everyone wondered if Prince Rupert's promised Cansos would ever arrive. An unsettling air of expectancy hovered over the Squadron. The arrival of Stranraer #954 in February had done little to relieve the mounting dissatisfaction with the Sharks.

Stranraer on patrol on west coast. Colbeck Collection

Stranraer #954 was taken on strength for use in transportation flights and general training. On February 27, 1943, F/L Brewaridge began to check out the pilots on the Stranraer. They were all eager to build up their boat hours and get in First Pilot's time on the aircraft. Meanwhile the Sharks carried on the stringent requirements of the daily patrols with no relief in sight.

On March 25, 1943, No. 7 (BR) Squadron dispatched their Sharks to investigate a United States Coast Guard report of a submarine at Hidden Inlet, adjacent to the Portland Canal. Aircraft from RCAF Annette Island also responded to the report, but no sighting was made. Several days later engine trouble forced a Shark patrol down at Hidden Inlet. The Station "work horse", Norseman 3531, flew the mechanics up to the inlet and F/O Van Houten was able to fly Shark #545 back to the Station.

Finally the Squadron's first Canso arrived. On April 21, Canso #9784 was taken on strength for use in carrying out transportation flights. By the end of the month the Squadron had 8 Sharks, 2 Stranraers, 1 Canso, and a Norseman.

The Squadron Commanding Officer, S/L P.J. Grant, left Prince Rupert on April 26 on a posting overseas, and S/L R. Dobson assumed command of the Squadron. W/C "Doc" Brooks, the Station Commanding Officer, was posted to Western Air Command Headquarters as Assistant Controller in the Operations Room. On May 27 W/C E.C Tennant became the new Commanding Officer of the Prince Rupert Station.

During May, almost one year after its formation, No. 4 Group Headquarters was ready for occupancy, and orders were issued to transfer to the new headquarters - an order that was equally appreciated by the airmen at RCAF Station

Prince Rupert. It meant there would be some relief to the overcrowded accommodation and general congestion that always existed at the Station. While one long-awaited event had hinged on a "move out", the second event revolved around a "move in", and the daily question still remained - when would the rest of the Cansos arrive?

On June 30 the Squadron received word that Canso #9785 was ready for transfer to Prince Rupert from Sea Island, but the transfer was delayed for a further month. By the end of July Canso #9785 and #9803 had arrived, and with 3 Cansos on strength the Squadron could now extend its patrol area and elevate the degree of its defence capabilities far beyond the scope of the Shark.

The Sharks had done yeoman's duty in their coastal crawl of the inlets and passages from Portland Canal to Principe Channel, but they were an obsolete piece of equipment limited to flying within 25 miles of the shoreline for a maximum of four hours. Shark defence patrols diminished in favour of the Stranraers and the Cansos with their longer-range capability. The arrival of additional Stranraers all but eliminated the use of the Sharks, and at the end of June 1943 the Sharks were reduced to a minor role in the Squadron's operation.

The Canso aircrews put in ten to fifteen hours on their scheduled patrols, covering wide stretches over the Pacific Ocean, through Dixon Entrance. Operating more sophisticated equipment gave Squadron morale a big boost. Now it was possible to give their maximum effort in proud fulfillment of all aspects of their service responsibilities.

On July 14 and 15, 1943, the Squadron was able to take part, for the first time, in convoy escort duties. Convoy "David" was enroute from its embarkation port of Seattle, Washington to Kiska, Alaska - one of several islands in the Aleutian chain occupied by the Japanese in June 1942. The Canadian and American troops on board were part of an assault force planned to oust the Japanese from the Aleutians and destroy their tentative toe-hold on North America. As the convoy moved into the Prince Rupert patrol area, No. 7 (BR) Squadron's Cansos patrolled overhead, keeping watch until it safely crossed into the Sitka patrol area.

The Cansos also allowed the Squadron to transport visiting "brass", and other honoured visitors, in dignified comfort and safety. On September 6 the Governor-General of Canada and his party arrived at RCAF Prince Rupert to inspect the Guard of Honour. S/L Dobson and F/L T. Benson had the privilege of flying the party to Annette Island in Canso #9784.

In the fall of 1943 the Sharks were brought out of "retirement" for a short tour of duty. On September 21, Shark #548 was given the honour of completing the last Shark patrol for No. 7 (BR) Squadron. It was #548's last flight.

After returning from patrol the crew moored #548 to a buoy and two Wireless Mechanics and two Armourers rowed out in their dinghy to do a routine maintenance check. The radio mechanics were working inside the aircraft while the armourers were in the dinghy under the wings of the aircraft. Without any warning one of the depth charges dropped from the Shark's wing. It plunged to detonation depth and blew up. The explosion capsized the aircraft - there was no chance of escape for LAC L.O. Darge and AC1 J.A. Fraser, caught under the Shark's wing. Inside the aircraft, AC1 D.A. Tite and LAC H.E. Wight narrowly escaped with their lives as the Shark sank below the surface of the bay and the second depth charge exploded. The loss of two airmen in the totally demolished aircraft turned the fairwell flight of the Sharks into a terrible tragedy. Three days later, without incident or fanfare, Shark #549 flew the final flight operation with No. 7 (BR) Squadron, an RDF calibration flight. Eventually all the stalwart Sharks were ferried to No. 3 Repair Depot at Jericho Beach for storage, or for conversion to target tugs. There were no Sharks left on Squadron strength by the end of October 1943. Aircraft on strength were: 2 Stranraers, 3 Cansos, and 1 Norseman: with two more Cansos expected.

It was a fitting end to the Sharks' service at RCAF Station Prince Rupert to have W/C "Doc" Brooks arrive in time to "write" the Sharks off strength himself. W/C Brooks had returned from Western Air Command to take command of the Station when W/C Tennant, the current CO, received a posting to Mossbank, Saskatchewan on September 26, 1943.

Warrant Officer pilot McGregor Easson Knight, who had arrived at RCAF Station Prince Rupert in August, remembers an incident that fortunately created more pleasure than it did pain. In early December 1943 Knight flew as co-pilot in one of the Squadron's Cansos which was scheduled for routine maintenance and repair by No. 3

Canso southbound along B.C. coast. D.HIST/DND

AIRCREW OF 7 (BOMBER RECONNAISSANCE) SQUADRON, RCAF PRINCE RUPERT.

from left to right - front row: F/O Doolittle, F/O Benson, F/O Stewart, S/L Morris, F/L Dale, F/O Hughes, F/O Martin
second row: F/O Davis, F/Sgt Gravelle, F/Sgt Colbeck, F/Sgt Avent, F/Sgt Morrell, F/Sgt McKenna, F/Sgt Thomas, F/Sgt Dorland, F/Sgt Fitzpatrick, F/Sgt Hankinson, F/O Rhodes.
third row: F/Sgt Campbell, F/Sgt Hawkins, F/Sgt Teague, F/Sgt Switzer, F/Sgt Elliot, F/Sgt Olsen.
Holding propeller F/Sgt Penn, F/Sgt Rainville

Sergeants' Mess Dinner, March 16, 1944 RCAF Prince Rupert. P.R. Archives

(RD) at Jericho Beach. The flight droned on smoothly until they started their descent over English Bay and found themselves caught between two converging fog banks - one from English Bay and the other rolling in from the Straits of Georgia. Knight says that, *"the fog was as thick as milk but only to about 800 feet - on top of that everything was clear."* The pilot elected to let down through the fog, and they successfully landed on the water. Knight continues:

> *"However, we landed - but Jericho was already engulfed by milk....so we put the undercarriage down and went full throttle up onto the sand at Spanish Banks (about a mile west of the Jericho Beach Air Station.) It was ebb tide and we were high and dry for over 18 hours before Station mechanics were able to free the beached Canso. Eighteen RCAF personnel from No.7 (BR) Squadron, including Don Grant, got to Vancouver early for Christmas leave."*

However, the following week Canso A #9786 was

involved in an accident which took the life of a crew member. Returning to the Prince Rupert Station from a night navigation exercise on December 19, 1943, the Canso crashed in the harbour on landing. The second pilot, P/O E.J. Fereday, was killed, but the rest of the crew managed to escape with only minor injuries.

RCAF Station Prince Rupert changed from operational to administrative status in the spring of 1944 and No. 7 (BR) Squadron prepared for orders to leave Prince Rupert. The Station was now responsible for the administration of four other Prince Rupert units and five northern B.C. units: Woodcock, Smithers, Terrace, Masset, and the Radio Detachment at Langara Island.

Effective April 18, No 7 (BR) Squadron was authorized to move to Alliford Bay in the Queen Charlotte Islands. WO McGregor Knight's log entry for April 23, 1944, reads: *"Canso #9742: self, F/O Field - A/S patrol: last Rupert patrol: landed Alliford Bay."* The Squadron Commanding Officer, S/L R. Dobson was posted to Western Air Command on June 27, 1944, and S/L A.C. Neale, on transfer from No. 4 Group Headquarters in Prince Rupert, took command of the Squadron. In three months time, on September 11, Neale was replaced by S/L T. Benson who was the Squadron's last Commanding Officer.

The final mission flown by No. 7 (BR) Squadron was an anti-submarine patrol on July 14, - Canso A 11070 from Alliford Bay with F/O Craddock and crew. The Squadron was disbanded at Alliford Bay on July 25, 1945.

above; No. 3 RD mechanics check damage on Canso, December, 1943. McGregor Knight Collection

top; Canso high and dry on beach at Spanish Banks, Vancouver, December 1943. McGregor Knight Collection

1

2

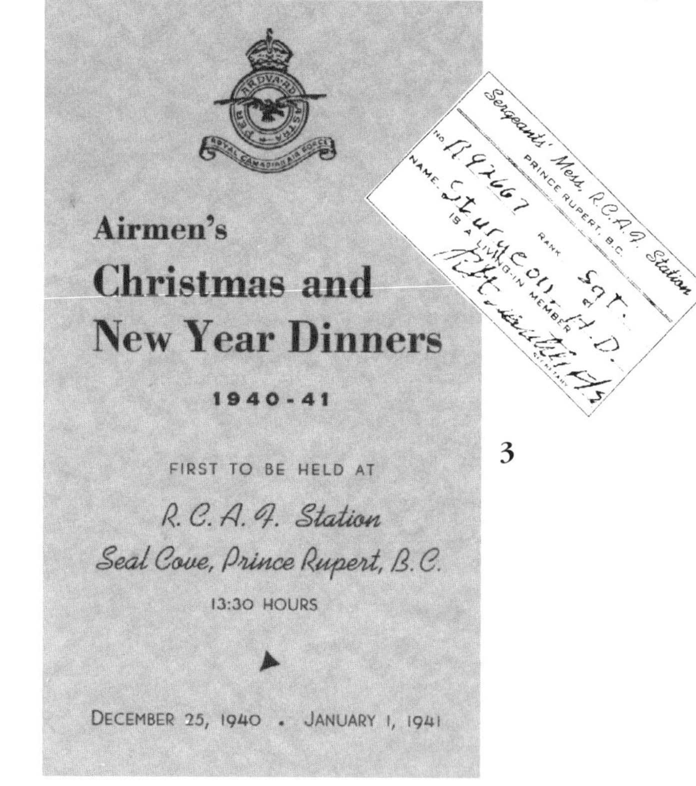

Airmen's

Christmas and

New Year Dinners

1940-41

FIRST TO BE HELD AT

R. C. A. F. Station

Seal Cove, Prince Rupert, B. C.

13:30 HOURS

DECEMBER 25, 1940 . JANUARY 1, 1941

Sergeants' Mess, R.C.A.F. Station

PRINCE RUPERT, B.C.

NO. RANK

NAME

IS A LIVING-IN MEMBER

3

4

1. *No. 7 (BR) personnel with Canso at Alliford Bay, June 1944.* P.R. Archives
2. *RCAF Prince Rupert looking north, March 1, 1944.* CFB Comox Rowe Library
3. *Airmen's Christmas and New Year's Dinner 1940-41 table card.* P.R. Archives
4. *U.S. engineering department dinner at Prince Rupert, February 1944.* P.R. Archives

NO. 120 (BR) SQUADRON

RCAF STATION

COAL HARBOUR

STATION ESTABLISHED: DECEMBER 10, 1941

STATION CLOSED: AUGUST 1945

STATION NEWSPAPER: THE SHOVEL

EDITOR IN CHIEF: P/O DAVE CROWE

RCAF STATION COAL HARBOUR

The small settlement of Coal Harbour on Holberg Inlet at the north end of Vancouver Island, was another site chosen by the B.C. Reconnaissance Detachment for the construction of an RCAF Flying Boat Station. The outbreak of hostilities in 1939 hastened the decision to build a wartime station at Coal Harbour, and construction details were given emergency priority.

The site plans moved rapidly ahead - RCAF Station Coal Harbour didn't suffer from the difficulties and delays that prolonged construction on the other coastal stations. In June 1940 Western Air Command informed Air Force Headquarters in Ottawa that construction crews were ready to begin work. They also requested permission to place an 8 man detachment on the Station to operate W/T (radio) communication and provide drivers for road and marine transport. Authorization was received, and on June 29, 1940 Cpl. Kennedy and 7 Airmen arrived at the station site. The advance party boarded for three months at the only hotel in the area - the Hole's Hotel.

Western Air Command announced its intention to open the Coal Harbour Station at the end of August 1940. Construction was already in high gear, and the airmen's quarters, administration building, two hangars and the slipway rose up out of a sea of mud and tangled debris from fallen trees - in the rush some of the stumps were not blasted out until after the buildings were completed.

By mid-August the rough but reasonably complete administration section was ready to accommodate staff. F/O E.G. Symonds was posted as Officer Commanding and personnel were selected from No. 4 and No. 6 (BR) Squadron members who had remained at Vancouver Jericho Beach due to inadequate space available at their assigned war stations of Ucluelet and Alliford Bay. The Airmen arrived at the end of August in time to meet the deadline and officially open RCAF Station Coal Harbour.

The journey to the new Station started from the CPR dock in downtown Vancouver. The airmen were excited. Full of jokes and laughter they jostled each other for a position at the rail as the Union Coastal Steamship moved away from the dock. The fun and the high jinks continued on the overnight trip up the inside passage to Port Hardy. There reality met them in the form of a dark blue, two-ton stake truck waiting in the pouring rain at the end of a small wooden wharf. The Airmen were instructed to arrange themselves and their gear in the back of the truck. The situation deteriorated as they jolted, rocked and lurched their way up an old logging road on the final twenty miles of their trip. Emerging from the gloomy, streaming forest trail into a cleared area, the Airmen caught

Log cabin in airmen's village at RCAF Coal Harbour. CFB Comox Rowe Library

their first glimpse of the Station. Airman A.J.D. Angus recorded his first, and lasting, impression:

> *"After a rough bumpy trip through the trees, an opening suddenly revealed a site containing some rather drab brownish shingled buildings, dripping wet....I can still see the two wartime hangars facing each other across a concrete area which had a slip going down into the water of the bay. A defence perimeter ran around three sides of the station, with the bay on the other side.*
>
> *The defence perimeter consisted of a massive logging operation carried out about the width of a fire-guard but nothing removed, so that it was almost impossible to cross it on foot let alone by any vehicular means."*

Tarpaper shack in village. Madill Collection

Angus also recorded the beginning of the "Air Force Village" at Coal Harbour:

> *"A few of the Station personnel brought their wives along and lived in the 'village' which consisted mainly of tarpaper shacks constructed from old packing crates and whatever lumber was available to scroungers. A few of the more enterprising found a good source of logs, and log cabins appeared in the area."*

Like RCAF Station Ucluelet, Coal Harbour welcomed the Airmen's families, with the provision that they provide their own accommodations. Many of the Airmen found themselves on the business end of an axe instead of a gun, and several unique log and frame cabins set the architectural style for the growing settlement.

Don O'Hearne was among the first group of Airmen to arrive, and he helped to build the first home - a forerunner of today's condominium - which accommodated four families. *"We built it on the waterfront just to the left of the marine dock. Mr. Hole supplied the material and we did the building."*

Log and shingle cabin at dependents' village. CFB Comox Rowe Library

The Hole family ran the general store, gas station and Post Office at Coal Harbour and had the contract to carry the mail from Port Hardy to Port Alice. They were a vital link to the outside world for the local settlers scattered over the region and a dependable port of call for fishboats. The Hole's now found themselves in the right place at the right time to appreciate the added boon to business created by the increasing number of "war-grown" customers at RCAF Station Coal Harbour. The family did everything they could to make life easier for the "boys" at Coal Harbour - but they were also astute and innovative business people ready to meet the needs of supply and demand.

The cabins built by the airmen stood on land owned by the Hole family who rented out the building sites for one dollar a year. The airmen, when they were posted off the station, sold their homes to incoming families for $250.00 to $300.00. If there were no "for sale" signs in the settlement an airman made his agreement with Mr. Hole, borrowed an axe and a shovel, and in a month or two of his spare time had a rustic home ready for his family.

On February 27, 1941, 4 officers and 76 men of the B.C. Regiment were posted to Coal Harbour to take over responsibility for the defence of the Station. The Station had a considerable number of administrative personnel, now under the command of S/L F.J. Ewart, but as yet no Squadron had been assigned and flying was limited to the transportation of men and supplies.

Months had gone by, and the long wait to begin operating a wartime flying boat station was dampening the airmen's enthusiasm. During an inspection tour of RCAF Coal Harbour on August 8, the Inspector General recognized the sag in morale and stated in his report that: *"One is impressed with the need for flying operations at this base to justify the existing number of men now there, and to raise the morale and efficiency of the Station."*

Western Air Command responded with a promise that in December a Bomber Squadron would be placed at the Station, and flying operations would commence using Stranraer aircraft. At Patricia Bay Number 120 (BR) Squadron received orders on November 21 that it was to proceed on a posting to Coal Harbour.

On December 7, 1941, four days before 120 (BR) Squadron was expected to arrive at Coal Harbour, the Station received the news of Japan's attack on Pearl Harbor. A number one Alert, which included a strict blackout of the Station and the village, was immediately ordered. J.S. Protherd described the Station's well planned preparation for a possible Japanese invasion of the harbour:

> *"Trenches were dug all along the main street; Veteran Guardmen set up machine gun posts all over the place; and all along the dock we had 250 pound bombs every 10 feet. All engines in the power house had a 250 pound bomb alongside. The scheme was that when all the station had fought a rear guard action into the woods and the wireless area was not needed any more - it would be blown. Then, and only then, the powerhouse would be blown and we could leave - if we were able."*

The Alert had totally disrupted the daily Station routine, and it was into this confusion and disarray that the Station's two-ton, dark blue stake truck deposited the first group of No. 120 (BR) Squadron members on December 10, 1941.

The Squadron was originally formed as No. 20 (Bomber) Squadron (Auxiliary) at Regina, Saskatchewan in June of 1935, and renumbered as No. 120 (B) Bomber Squadron on November 15, 1937. A call to duty was issued in September 1939, and on October 31 the Squadron was redesignated as No. 120 (BR) Bomber Reconnaissance Squadron.

On November 7, 1939, the Squadron transferred to RCAF Station Vancouver at Jericho Beach, arriving under the command of W/C R.A. Delhaye, DFC - the Squadron Commanding Officer since January 1, 1936. Barracks were provided at Jericho Beach, but the Squadron was allocated the eastern half of a Boeing hangar at Sea Island where the pilots began training exercises with fellow airmen from No. 4 (BR) Squadron.

Stranraer RS-F on ramp at Coal Harbour, 1942. Parry Collection

In May 1940 the Squadron was equipped with Northrop Delta Mk II aircraft. The first Delta, #675, was taken on strength May 7, 1940; on May 10, S/L Murray and F/O Fraser qualified as First Pilots on Delta on wheels. On May 15 Delta #670 was taken over from No. 119 Squadron. These aircraft were operated on floats and on wheels out of RCAF Station Sea Island. Delta #675, flown by F/O M.P. Fraser, completed the Squadron's first mission - a patrol for the Department of Fisheries over the Strait of Juan De Fuca, on June 30, 1940.

August 1, 1940, No. 120 (BR) Squadron, now under the command of S/L J.E. Jellison, moved to RCAF Station Patricia Bay, near Victoria on Vancouver Island. Shortly after arriving at Patricia Bay a tragic crash took the lives of five Squadron members.

Delta #670 crashed and sank in Discovery Passage, one mile south of Seymour Narrows. No trace of the crew, F/O J.J.H. Desbiens, S/L R.C. Procter, F/O Gordon, Captain Bourn, and Cpl. R.G. Brown was found, and all were presumed to have gone down with the aircraft. F/O Mahon, F/L Jacobi and Captain D'Easum (MD), flying Grumman #924, left to search the vicinity of the crash. They reported a sighting of the wreckage in about 90 feet of water - this was the first casualty recorded for No. 120 (BR) Squadron on Active Service.

S/L G.W. Jacobi took command of the Squadron from January 21, 1941, until March 29, when S/L F.J.E. Ewart succeeded him. By this time the Squadron was flying Lockheed Hudson aircraft. On November 21 No. 120 (BR) Squadron received orders to move to their wartime Station at Coal Harbour and the Hudsons were transferred to No. 13 (OT) Squadron.

Stranraer MX-C #952 moored at Coal Harbour, 1942. Parry Collection

Now the flight training program concentrated on a Conversion Course to Stranraer aircraft under the instruction of S/L Ewart and S/L Carpenter. The Squadron pilots began training on November 26 using Stranraer #923. The next day No. 120's Stranraers arrived from the factory. Stranraer #950 and #952 were taken to No. 3 (RD) at Jericho Beach for modifications to their fuel tanks, but Acceptance and Inventory Checks on Stranraer #951 were started immediately.

Squadron Commanding Officer S/L Ewart, in charge of preparing his Squadron for the impending move, was ordered to complete an inspection of RCAF Station Coal Harbour. On December 2, S/L Ewart, with F/O Palmer, F/O McKay, P/O Defieux, and P/O Crow took off in Stranraer #951 and when they returned, 25 Squadron members were given 48 hours leave. These airmen formed an advance party responsible for establishing flight operations at the Coal Harbour Station.

S/L Galloway. LaRamée Collection

December 11, 1941, the day after their arrival at the Station, the Squadron completed the first anti-submarine patrol in Stranraer #950 - also the first aircraft attached to the Squadron. The Squadron patrols covered an area from the entrance to Queen Charlotte Strait off the northern tip of Vancouver Island near Cape Scott, south to Estevan Point, flying seaward to a depth of up to 150 miles. Their slice of Pacific patrol was bounded on the north by No. 9 (BR) Squadron at Bella Bella, and to the south by No. 4 (BR) Squadron at Ucluelet, and No. 120 (BR) Squadron flight crews suffered from the same tiresome uniformity of uninterrupted ocean and monotonous drone of engines that shadowed all the coastal patrols. In the early weeks of the patrol schedule, a Stranraer crew returning from patrol spotted a group of United States Navy battle wagons heading toward Alaska. The Stranraer pilot thought that he would relieve his boredom by buzzing one of the larger cruisers. The Americans had never seen such an antiquated flying machine and incorrectly assumed that it must be Japanese. As the Stranraer approached, they opened fire. The astounded pilot uttered a few descriptive phrases and beat a hasty retreat.

After their first introduction to a Stranraer, some of the new Squadron personnel could sympathize with the Americans' point of view - as Observer Wm. Fawcett Hill discovered when he arrived at RCAF Station Coal Harbour. Hill had received his Observer Wings at Rivers, Manitoba in August, and after a very temporary assignment to 3 (RD), he was posted to No. 120 (BR) at Coal Harbour. He thought it would be great to be just outside Vancouver. But no - there is another Coal Harbour:

"It was raining when I arrived in September and I didn't see the sun again until March of the next year.

We had five or six Stranraers on line and seeing one of them for the first time on dry land in their beaching gear was an unnerving experience. They looked like a prehistoric bird (they were).

Another frightening experience occurred on my first flight in a Stranraer. As the 'new boy', I had to stand up on the lower wing to wind up the engine and get the plane started. We then taxied down the slipway, took off and circled the bay, and landed, with me still standing on the wing and clinging to the struts. I, of course, did not know the plane was not able to go in excess of eighty knots, nor did I know that they hadn't really forgotten about me out there on the wing - it was my 120 BR initiation."

Moving into the last month of 1941, the Station settled into a regular operational routine. All Station personnel participated in a strict training schedule of lectures and practice exercises to fully prepare for a successful defence against any form of enemy invasion. No. 120 (BR) Squadron organized and carried out the Stranraer patrols, groundcrews "kept 'em flying", while the administrative staff worked to keep the Station's pulse active and healthy. However, several deviations from normal punctuated the daily routine at the end of December 1941.

S/L Galloway and F/O Sutherland put on an unexpected "show" on take off in Stranraer #952 on December 22. The mishap damaged the Stranraer's port wingtip float, and left the aircraft unserviceable for a week while a new port wing was assembled and installed. On December 28, Stranraer #931 arrived from Patricia Bay under the command of W/C Mawdesley with F/O George Williamson as second pilot.

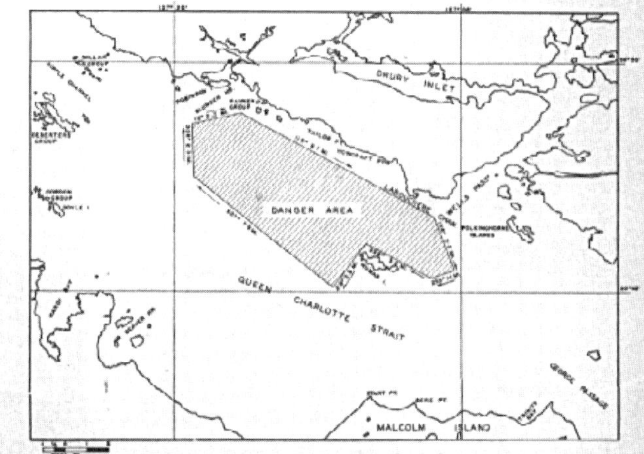

WARNING

ROYAL CANADIAN AIR FORCE

AIR FIRING RANGE

R.C.A.F. Station, Coal Harbour, B.C.

The public is hereby warned that, until further notice, AIR FIRING is liable to take place daily (Sundays included) between the hours of sunrise and sunset at the range situated in the vicinity of LABOUCHERE CHANNEL, QUEEN CHARLOTTE STRAIT, B.C., serving the above noted station.

A diagram and description of the "danger area" of this range are given below:—

Commencing at a point in Latitude N. 50°52'48", Longitude W. 127°15'12", approximately 1.5 miles south of Blunden Harbour, B.C., the boundary of the "danger area" extends over the waters of Queen Charlotte Strait 4.7 miles on a bearing of 118°; thence 2.5 miles, 158°; thence 1.1 miles, 253°; thence 3.2 miles, 298°; thence 2.1 miles, 218°; thence 7.9 miles, 307°; thence 2.3 miles, 358°; thence 2.3 miles, 078° to the point of beginning. All bearings given are true and distances are in nautical miles.

Any unauthorized person or vessel entering the "danger area" indicated and described above is liable to prosecution under the Defence of Canada Regulations.

By Order,
CHARLES G. POWER, P.C., M.C., K.C.,
Minister of National Defence for Air

CFB Comox Rowe Library

Wing Commader Mawdesley, now the postings officer at Western Air Command, Victoria, arranged to take the Coal Harbour flight in order to keep his flying hours up and to take himself away from his desk for awhile. The Stranraer brought in a group of naval ratings who had been given the unpleasant job of seizing all Japanese fish boats in the Port Hardy area. Some of these boats were taken to a storage compound on the Fraser River and others were converted for use by the Marine Section.

Early in January 1942, during bomb dropping practice, the Stranraer aircrews began testing 500 pound demolition bombs. The drops were made near the Station in Holberg Inlet, and each bomb was closely watched by the aircrew to see if it detonated or not. S/L Ewart dropped two American 500 pound demolition bombs from Stranraer #952 on January 18, reporting satisfactory results as both bombs detonated when they were released. However, this was not always the case.

The following day F/O Smith and Sgt. Foster, flying Stranraer #952, were forced to jettison their bombs as they returned to the Station. S/L Galloway, F/O Smith, and the Station Armament Officer F/O Chard, flew Stranraer #929 over the area where the bombs had been jettisoned and located the point where the bombs struck, but they couldn't be sure that both bombs had exploded. Another unexploded bomb landed in a group of inaccessible reefs near Scott Island. It was dropped from Stranraer #929 during a practice on April 8.

In the next two years the number of unexploded bombs, including the 250 pound depth charges which hung up during patrol and were jarred loose on landing, caused Airman A.J.D. Angus to speculate that the bottom of the bay must now be carpeted with bombs. In addition to this discomforting knowledge, Angus and his fellow Airmen had another reason for keeping a wary eye on the bay:

> *"The OC of the Squadron kept a .22 calibre rifle in his office which overlooked the bay, and once in a while he would shoot out his window at ducks on the bay. It was therefore not a good idea to use the roadway that ran alongside the hangar on the bay side."*

A group of like-minded Airmen decided that the personalities at the Coal Harbour Station deserved to be immortalized. In January 1942 they developed the format for a Station newspaper and christened it the 'Coal Harbour Shovel' - perhaps a reference to "digging in and getting the job done", which symbolized life on the Station, or was it an interesting twist on "digging for dirt" to keep the publication lively? Either way, the literary types involved had a highly developed appreciation for the bizarre and beautiful, ironic and idiosyncratic facets of life in general, and their fellow Airmen in particular; and the newspaper was an outlet for a rare sense of humour that was evident across the ranks and was partially responsible for maintaining high morale on the Station.

The "boys in the Kitchen" submitted a poem, published in the Volume 2, Number 2 addition of the 'Shovel', which explained their perspective on maintaining morale:

THE COOKS OF SERGEANT'S ROW

For we are the Cooks of Sergeant's Row,
We roast the meat and bake the dough,
We wash and scrub, we polish and rub,
Cut and slice; scaring hell out of mice,
The Cooks of Sergeants' Row.
Just sniff at this soup, examine that pie
You'll never beat as long as you try.
Now just taste this pudding, sample the stew,
The flavour is perfect and we're telling you

That there isn't a Mess on the whole Coast
Can serve up such a sweet smellin' roast.
Of course we're aware that Sergeants' don't care.
There'd be grumbles whatever the dish.
They make rude remarks about dead dogs and sharks
When we serve up the meat and the fish.
The soup is dismissed with 'Watinell's this'
But they know very well that life would be Hell
If the cooks all decided to go.
Though they say things about us
They'd all starve without us,
The Cooks of Sergeants' Row.

In April 1942 the Squadron recorded its first submarine sighting. Through a break in the undercast of low fog and sifting rain, a Stranraer patrol caught a glimpse of a submarine below them. The pilot circled and passed over the area at a lower altitude but crew members were unable to relocate the submarine - it had disappeared. Although the results of the sighting were negative, it added to the accumulating evidence of Japanese activity that threatened the security of the west coast of North America.

As the Station prepared to intensify defence measures, Western Air Command ordered the transfer of S/L F.S. Carpenter from Bella Bella to Coal Harbour. S/L Ewart received a posting to No. 1 Bombing and Gunnery School at Jarvis Ontario, and on May 18, 1942 S/L Carpenter replaced him as Station Commanding Officer. S/L P.B. Cox assumed command of No. 120 (BR) Squadron and immediately added his own emphasis to the defence program by initiating training in night flying.

The Station Commander, S/L Carpenter instituted the same level of efficiently organized, strictly disciplined defence training that had gained him recognition at RCAF Station Bella Bella. Personnel were divided into sections and assigned to machine gun emplacements; fire fighting, gas, and maintenance squads were assembled, and a tight training schedule was set up for the rifle and machine gun ranges. It was a tough programme. Airman Cy Luce, posted to RCAF Station Coal Harbour from the Manning Pool at Toronto, Ontario, has a clear memory of the training programme:

"We were trained like commandoes, for gas attack, with machine guns, and rifles and bayonets, and we were instructed to keep those rifles with us at all times, even when we went to eat. They were American 30-06 with a beautiful 16" bayonet - left over from the First World War - the same as our ammunition. We learned how to stick the bayonets into dummies and grunt.

We strung wires for communications around the machine gun nests which were manned by straw dummies with wooden guns that we painted black. This was done to make the camp look like we had 1500 men instead of 500. Their positions were changed at various intervals so that the (aerial) pictures the Japanese were taking would look different.

Live ammunition was fired during our sham battles and I was told that if I lifted my head more than three feet I would get it shot off. Officers were posted around the bush with rifles ready to shoot any moving object over three feet high. We also had simulated gas attacks, and had to take our gas masks off in a cloud of tear gas, then roll around the grass in pain.

We built food caches and they were hauled into the bush, for use in the event of an attack. A gallon of coal oil was kept in a red can in each office in order to destroy it for the same reason."

top; US Navy Sikorsky OS2U-1 "Kingfisher" at Coal Harbour. Parry Collection
above; US Navy Grumman J2F-1 "Duck" visits Coal Harbour. CFB Comox Rowe Library

Planned defence preparations were still being carried out to ensure that the Station could continue to function under any emergency situation that the enemy might devise. On May 28, 1942 a freighter arrived at the dock and its cargo of 2 1/2 ton circular concrete air raid shelters was unloaded. Within the next week the 32 foot converted fishboat 'Petrel' was equipped with a Lewis machine gun and mount. The boat's solid wood construction would allow it to stand up under heavy enemy gunfire. Under fire, the boat, with a gunner manning the Lewis gun, would take the aircrews safely across the bay to their aircraft.

The threat of a possible Japanese invasion was taken just as seriously outside the defence perimeter of RCAF Station Coal Harbour. The civilians in the neighbouring villages of Quatsino and Port Alice were preparing themselves for any sign of Japanese action. The Air Raid Patrol was formed and functioning, and the women of the district were taking first-aid training to help the Station medical officers and doctors care for any casualties should an invasion occur.

Military strategists anticipated that, in order to cripple and destroy major naval and shipping yards in Canada and in the United States, Japan would send forces to capture an aerodrome. This placed all the isolated RCAF Flying Boat Stations in jeopardy and created fear for the safety of the Airmen's families. The critical situation forced Western Air Command to order the evacuation of the small, handmade Air Force settlement at Coal Harbour. They did not want to see a repetition of the Japanese occupation of Hong Kong and Singapore where dependents of British Soldiers were interned and maltreated. By the summer of 1942 all families at RCAF Station Coal Harbour had been removed.

Throughout May and June the Station was an important refuelling destination for an increasing number of United States Navy Sikorsky Kingfisher and Grumman Goose aircraft enroute from Seattle to various points in Alaska. The Americans were gearing up to meet Japan's attack on the Aleutian Islands. In mid-May United States Intelligence intercepted and decoded a radioed message from the Imperial General Headquarters in Tokyo ordering their Second Mobile Force to strike the Aleutians in early June.

Canadian chiefs of staff were unaware of the details in the message - most of the information they had about the movement of Japanese forces was second-hand, or gleaned from US Navy dispatches. By the time the Canadian chiefs of staff and their counterparts in the American War Department had negotiated the role the RCAF would play in the defence of Alaska, the Japanese attack on the Aleutian Islands was underway.

The radio message received on June 4, 1942, that Japanese forces had launched air strikes from their aircraft carriers against the port of Dutch Harbor on Unalaska Island, caused a great deal of excitement at the Coal Harbour Station. A Number 2 Alert Order went into effect and machine gun posts were set up at the hangars. The posts were manned 24 hours a day by the Squadron standby crews. The other machine gun posts surrounding the Station were also manned, and one aircrew was placed on constant standby in addition to the crews on patrol.

On July 21 Air Commodore L.F. Stevenson acknowledged the fine work being done by the Station and the Squadron.

> *"It is very apparent that a high state of morale exists among the personnel as the work of the Squadron is carried out most efficiently. The serviceability of aircraft is maintained at a high peak, and patrols are completed often in the face of weather that could quite reasonably be considered unfit."*

Stevenson knew that in the face of an enemy attack, the Stranraers *"could quite reasonably be considered unfit"*. At this crucial point in the defence of the west coast No. 120 (BR) Squadron needed aircraft that could patrol further than the 150 mile limit imposed on the Stranraer. There was an indication that the Cansos would arrive soon - F/O Smith and F/O Snyder were at Eastern Air Command's Training Depot on conversion courses for the Canso; and on June 14 W02 Phillips, Sgt. Penney, Sgt. McMaster, and Sgt. Cubbage returned from Sand Point in the state of Washington, and Tongue Point Oregon, after completing their instructional courses on Consolidated aircraft.

The Japanese attack on the Aleutians didn't affect the Airmen at the Coal Harbour Station as dramatically as a signal received by the night duty wireless operator on June 21, 1942. A Japanese submarine had surfaced and Estevan Point was being shelled. The enemy action brought the war closer to "home". Three Stranraers were ordered to take off at first light, but by the time they arrived the shelling was over, and there was no sign of the Japanese submarine.

Regardless of the enemy's apparent reluctance to show itself, the aircrews continued to sharpen their response to the practice alarm signal - crews could have an aircraft in the air 15 minutes after the alarm was sounded. The daily patrols kept a vigilant watch, and every questionable movement below was investigated. However, the Stranraers were beginning to feel their age; the demands of the long patrol schedules in all kinds of weather, and the pounding they took on takeoff and landing in rough

The ill-fated Stranraer #951 moored at Coal Harbour. Parry Collection

water added to the inevitable breakdowns. Test flights to identify suspected problems were becoming more frequent, as were flights to No. 3 (RD) to deliver Stranraers that needed major repair work.

Engine trouble forced two Stranraer patrols down in rough sea in two separate incidents which happened within two months of each other. On June 25, 1942 the crew of Stranraer #952 returned with their aircraft; on August 23 the crew of Stranraer #951 did not return.

Five hours into their patrol on June 25 the failure of the port motor caused F/O Johnson and his crew to land Stranraer #952 on the water about 100 miles northwest of Coal Harbour. Minutes after receiving #952's report of its forced landing, S/L P.B. Cox and crew in Stranraer #951 took off on a search. They signaled the position of the downed aircraft to a Navy corvette and the corvette immediately headed toward those coordinates.

In the meantime F/O Johnson made the decision to taxi #952 but, after a heroic effort, heavy swells and loss of the starboard float forced him to stop. Once forward momentum dropped the Stranraer listed to starboard and threatened to capsize because of the missing float. The situation was desperately solved by moving crew members out onto the port wing. Wet, cold and precariously balanced over the stormy ocean the Airmen waited for rescue. The Navy corvette found them and took them in tow. Hours later the sodden and shivering crew, still perched on the Stranraer's port wing, gratefully arrived at RCAF Station Bella Bella. The tail of the Stranraer had received a damaging bump from the corvette and both wings were severely damaged. No. 120 (BR) Squadron aircrew members, Sgt. Beeching, Fitter, and Cpl. Brooks, Rigger, stayed at the Bella Bella Station for a month to assist with the overhaul of their aircraft.

On June 27 F/O Magor and crew took off for Bella Bella in Stranraer #951 to bring back F/O Johnson and his crew. Stranraer #951 developed engine trouble and it was necessary for everyone to stay overnight at Bella Bella. The two crews arrived at Coal Harbour in time for a practice air raid attack at 1800 hours on June 30. All the serviceable aircraft were taxied out into the bay, and Squadron personnel manned the waterfront posts and opened fire on balloons sent up over the Station.

A notation was entered in the Station Diary on July 14, that all the Station's aircraft were serviceable except for Stranraer #952 which was at Bella Bella; however, on July 20 the Diary recorded that there was complete unserviceability of all aircraft on the Station. The see-saw battle to keep the Stranraers in the air fell to the maintenance crews, who put in long hours to keep up with the myriad of breakdowns and repairs.

On August 23, 1942 Stranraer #951, with F/S E.T. Cox and a crew of seven Airmen, took off at 0920 hours on the long patrol for the day. Nine hours later, about 90 miles northwest of Cape Scott, #951 developed engine trouble and F/S Cox was forced to ditch the aircraft. The wireless operator sent out an S.O.S. giving their position and a short, cryptic message that they were down at sea and sinking. The Navy was advised, and the five remaining aircraft on the Station were immediately dispatched.

Two hours later F/O Snyder and the crew of Stranraer #952 sighted #951 - some of the #951 crew had climbed out on the wing to wave and cheer at the approaching Stranraer. The high seas made landing impossible, but the crippled aircraft's wireless operator F/S Cram, signaled that they were all relieved to be spotted and everyone was fine, with the exception of their aircraft which was taking an awful beating in the rough sea. F/O Snyder advised dispatch that they were now experiencing some engine trouble. He was ordered, if possible, to circle over the ditched aircraft until Stranraer #950 could get there to relieve them. The high speed launch, 'Malecite' M.231, which was waiting for orders in Quatsino, was dispatched to the position to pick up the crew, and all the other aircraft were ordered back to base. As total darkness closed in, it seemed that the situation was in hand.

Somewhere in their circling pattern, in the blackness beneath them, the crew of #952 lost sight of #951. Number 950 arrived and searched the area but returned to the Coal Harbour Station with negative results; the 'Malecite' also returned and reported that they had found nothing. F/O Wayave in Stranraer #909 was within sight of the search area when his aircraft also developed engine trouble and he had to turn back. He reported sighting a submarine that he thought was moving in the direction of the downed aircraft. Wayave, who was awarded the

Air Force Cross for his courageous work in trying to locate the lost aircraft, returned to the Station and took off again in one of the Stranraers fitted with long range tanks. In spite of poor weather conditions with a cloud ceiling sometimes as low as 100 feet, he circled the crash site throughout the night. As dawn came he saw no trace of #951 or his fellow Airmen. Along with the other searchers, he refused to give up hope and continued to fly long hours in the next week as the search area was expanded.

S/L Carpenter, operating out of RCAF Station Ucluelet, took personal charge of the organized search over the enlarged area. Aircraft from Coal Harbour, Bella Bella, Ucluelet, and Patricia Bay made extensive sweeps in criss-cross patrols over a large area, but the results continued to be negative. At the end of August no clue had been uncovered to explain the total disappearance of Stranraer #951 and its crew of 8 Airmen. The Japanese submarine sighted so close to the crash point also remained part of the mystery.

The Station Diary lists the following Airmen as crew of Stranraer #951:

F/S Cox, E.T.(Captain)
F/S Horn, L.A.B. (2nd Pilot)
Sgt Stuart, R.B.(Observer)
F/S Cram, M. (WAG)
Sgt Anderson, A. (WAG)
Sgt Hope, K.E. (AFM)
Sgt Oldford, L. (AEM)
Sgt Beeching, C.F. (AEM)

RCAF Station Coal Harbour lowered its Air Force Flag to half-mast in honour of its missing comrades as the Squadron and the Station struggled to resume their regular duties.

In the months that followed, every patrol that went up hoped to spot some debris that would tell #951's story. Rumours that the crew might have been washed ashore someplace, or that they had been taken prisoners by an enemy submarine, kept floating around the Station.

Apart from the reported sightings of submarines, there were other constant reminders of the presence of the Japanese: a Japanese single engine seaplane, a Yokosura E 14Yl (Glen), reportedly flew over the Station on possible reconnaissance missions, and Airman Cy Luce came by the information that a group of Japanese, who had come ashore from a submarine, were under interrogation by the Station's intelligence officers. The prisoners apparently wore business suits and carried a quantity of out-dated Canadian currency. It was rumoured that they had come ashore to assess the defence capabilities at RCAF Station Coal Harbour.

On September 15, 1942, S/L P.B. Cox received word of his posting to Western Air Command. He was succeeded as Commanding Officer of No. 120 (BR) Squadron

Christmas 1942 party at Officers' Mess. Parry Collection

This unique crest was created by Art Halpen, one of the 120 B.R. men who was stationed at Coal Harbour. The 120 Squadron aircraft at the time were carrying the highly sensitive 500 lb. bomb. Art conceived the comic idea of Pluto riding the dangerous winged bomb. Everyone agreed it was a gread idea. It was the birth of the 120 B.R. Crest.

Madill Collection

by S/L R.I. Thomas on September 24. S/L Carpenter was posted to Western Air Command and on December 9 S/L Thomas relinquished his command of the Squadron to take over as Station Commanding Officer. F/L R.J.E. Benton assumed the position of Squadron Commander, but was not officially promoted to S/L until January 1, 1943. Any disruption caused by the changeover of command was skillfully handled by F/O W.S. McDonnell who continued as Station Adjutant.

With the approach of the Christmas season, the Station Officers invited the Station Sergeants as guests at an informal evening of entertainment. On the agenda for the evening was a very special presentation to F/O J. Halpen. During the summer the Flying Officer had created a Squadron insignia - a drawing of the Walt Disney character 'Pluto' - which was placed on all aircraft directly under the Pilot's window. Walt Disney was notified of the prominent part 'Pluto' was now playing in west coast flying operations, and he sent an original drawing to the Squadron. The drawing was presented to Halpen, signed by members of 120 (BR) Squadron with many thanks for his contribution to morale.

At the beginning of the new year the Squadron received an order from Western Air Command to exchange Stations with RCAF Station Ucluelet. Western Air Command had devised an exercise that required all the Squadrons on the coast to interchange bases on a moment's notice: an exercise that gave the Squadrons practice in moving as a unit in case of emergency and prepared them to immediately carry out defence procedures from an unfamiliar base. It also broke up the long and monotonous winter routine and shook out any post-Christmas blues. On January 26, 1943 No. 120 (BR) Squadron moved to Ucluelet, and No. 4 (BR) Squadron moved to Coal Harbour. On February 8, after two weeks away from "home", each Squadron returned to its respective Station. At RCAF Station Coal Harbour a jubilant "homecoming" on a much grander scale was just a month away.

Events in the war overseas had forced Japan into a defensive position, which greatly reduced its threatened invasion of the west coast of North America. The degree of risk to the families evacuated from Coal Harbour had diminished, and they were now allowed to return to their rustic homes in the RCAF settlement. Families were reunited and the pioneer spirit was re-kindled. The close relationships in the little community continued where they had left off.

Even though the threat of invasion had been reduced, it was still considered a very real possibility, and the Station continued to function first and foremost as an operational base. Under the groundcrew's watchful eye, the Stranraers carried on the flying operations, while the Squadron waited hopefully for their Cansos to arrive. It was agreed that the Stranraers were not capable of carrying out the extensive patrols necessary to give early warning of Japanese shipping and submarine activity, however, the demand for Cansos in other theatres of war had taken priority. Finally, in the spring of 1943 the supply of Cansos increased, and they were gradually allotted to the west coast RCAF Squadrons to replace the tired Stranraers.

top; Airmen's canteen January, 1942. Parry Collection
above; Stranraer #929 at Coal Harbour. Parry Collection

The first Canso, #9753, arrived at RCAF Station Coal Harbour and, flown by P/O Freemand, took off on the daily patrol, April 6, 1943, with Stranraer #909 flown by F/O O'Hanlon. Weather conditions forced P/O Freemand to return after two hours but F/O O'Hanlon completed four and a half hours of the patrol, sighting one Liberty freighter.

Pilot Abe Freemand poses with airman Clare Parker in cockpit of Stranraer. Parry Collection

During June Western Air Command ordered the transfer of some of Coal Harbour's Stranraers to Jericho Beach, and by July 31 the Squadron had 3 Canso As on strength and only 3 Stranraers. On September 20, S/L Benton and crew returned from ferrying a Catalina on transfer from Ottawa. The Aircraft Strength report for the end of September, 1943 recorded 3 Catalinas with a total flying time of 126:55 hours.

The Cansos and Catalinas were equipped with modern anti-submarine devices which significantly increased the effectiveness and efficiency of the coastal patrols. Other methods of defence rapidly conformed to more modern methods and the Squadron's training schedule grew more specialized. Apart from conversion training to the Canso and Catalina, the pilots and aircrew took part in day and night flying and navigational exercises. New techniques in all areas of defence had to be learned and thoroughly digested: bombing, air firing, seamanship, ship recognition, signalling by Morse and Aldis Lamp, recognition signals, tactics and general war Intelligence.

The rigours of training created an accidental surprise which was particularly enjoyed by the locals. To conserve ammunition and armaments the Squadron CO issued an order that restricted bomb dropping practice flights to Thursdays each week. The residents of the RCAF village felt that the noise was agreeably offset by the abundant supply of fresh fish the explosion always produced - free for the taking.

S/L J.T. Arnold assumed command of the Squadron from S/L Benton on November 17, 1943. S/L Arnold was the Squadron's last Commanding Officer. On April 21, 1944, he authorized the final No. 120 (BR) Squadron patrol at RCAF Station Coal Harbour. F/S I.A.H. McFarlane and his crew completed the patrol in Catalina #JX 571. No. 120 (BR) Squadron was disbanded at Coal Harbour on May 1, 1944.

Number 6 (BR) Squadron relocated from Alliford Bay to Coal Harbour on April 23, 1944 under the command of S/L L.A. Harling, and the following September W/C A.C. Neale, AFC assumed command of the Squadron.

Within the last eight months of operation as a wartime station, RCAF Station Coal Harbour had the dubious honour of hosting one of Japan's new secret weapons - a Japanese Fire Balloon. In January 1945 a Station Canso forced down a balloon which settled in tangled undergrowth less than a mile inland on Rupert Inlet. *(see page 183)*

Ray Woolston, a wireless operator stationed at Coal Harbour, was a member of an eleven-man search party assembled to go in and bring the balloon out of the bush. It took the team four hours of careful manoeuvring to negotiate the short distance to the inlet, but as Woolston pointed out:

> *"Each one of us that had been in the search party were happy and a little proud that we had been given the opportunity to participate in the recovery of an almost complete specimen of a secret weapon which the Japanese were attempting to use against us."*

The Fire Balloons appeared to be a last attempt by the Japanese to wreak havoc in North America. With the end of the war in Europe and the Japanese withdrawal from the Pacific the coastal RCAF Stations began to close. On August 1, 1945, W/C Neale authorized No. 6 (BR) Squadron's last patrol, with F/O Erickson and his crew in Catalina FP290. The Squadron was disbanded at Coal Harbour on August 7, 1945.

The RCAF Station Coal Harbour Diary closed with a tribute to all Airmen, noting that each individual had carried out his duty with courage and dignity and with little of the public recognition and thanks that his responsibilities deserved:

> *"In fact, the public was peculiarly ignorant of what these Squadrons on the west coast were doing. They did not realize that the enemy was lurking beneath the vicious, stormy waves of the Pacific and was discouraged only by the constant, unremitting watch kept off our shores; the public also failed to realize that Canada's shores were kept inviolate, not because 'it can't happen here', but because Canadian youth was damned if it would."*

RCAF Station Coal Harbour was closed at the end of August 1945 and reduced to a care and maintenance basis.

1. *RCAF Coal Harbour looking south, March 27, 1945.* CFB Comox Rowe Library
2. *#950 on the rocks, rigger Bob Whitney makes repairs, 1942.* Parry Collection
3. *#950's air gunners high and dry at Quatsino Sound.* Parry Collection
4. *Pilot and air gunner of #950 catch a ride home with fishermen.* Parry Collection
5. *Fitter Fred Todd checks #950's engines after forced landing.* Parry Collection
6. *Sergeant Mick Handon poses with #950's 250 lb bomb.* Parry Collection

7

8

9

10

11

7. *Coal Harbour baseball team, 1943.* CFB Comox Rowe Library

8. *Airman Cliff Brown checks Stranraer.* Parry Collection

9. *Christmas 1943 (left to right) Squadron CWO, S/L Arnold (C.O.) and Head Cook.* Rev. G.E. Taylor Collection

10. *Airman Floogie Ried checks Strany engine.* Parry Collection

11. *Officers and Sergeants at Coal Harbour.* Rev. G.E. Taylor Collection

COAL HARBOUR: AIRMENS' POSTING LIST FROM JUNE 1944 TO AUGUST 1945

Number	Rank	Name	Posting	Province
R204976	LAC	King, A.E.	Posted WAC 11/6/44	
R118263	LAC	Johnson, H.A.	Posted 3 OTU 11/6/44	B.C.
R207387	LAC	MacDougall, R.	Posted 5 OTU 25/8/44	Que.
R192723	LAC	McKowan, W.A.	Posted 5 OTU 25/8/44	B.C.
R210601	LAC	Cousins, W.G.	Posted 5 OTU 25/8/44	B.C.
R157734	LAC	McIntosh, C.J.	Posted 5 OTU 25/8/44	B.C.
R204561	LAC	Antilla, A.A.	Discharged 15/10/44	B.C.
R192583	LAC	Paterson, B.B.	Posted Sea I. 28/11/44	
R57562	Sgt.	Stacey. H.C.	Posted Sea I. 28/11/44	B.C.
R131561	LAC	Mclure, D.R.	Posted Sea I. 28/11/44	B.C.
R65364	Cpl.	Jones, O.	Discharged 9/12/44	Ont.
R192088	LAC	Docks, R.J.	Discharged 22/5/45	Sask.
R135885	Cpl.	Lenny, L.B.	Discharged 31/5/45	Ont.
R143218	Cpl.	Wesley, V.F.	Discharged 31/5/45	B.C.
R72275	Sgt.	Doyle, E.P.	Discharged 31/5/45	Ont.
R115501	LAC	Wood, J.K.	Discharged 31/5/45	B.C.
R164426	LAC	Shields, A.H.J.	Discharged 31/5/45	
R215190	LAC	MacNutt	Posted 3 OTU 15/6/45	B.C.
R223766	LAC	Bingham, R.D.	Discharged 26/6/45	Ont.
R221523	LAC	Eamer, M.V.	Posted B.B. 5 OTU 1/7/45	B.C.
R151185	LAC	McChesney, R.D.	Posted Scoudouc N B 18/7/45	Ont.
R183151	LAC	Best, D.G.	Posted Scoudouc N B 18/7/45	N.S.
R215010	LAC	Summerfelt, G.A.	Posted Scoudouc N B 18/7/45	B.C.
R190211	LAC	Moore, H.J.	Posted Scoudouc N B 18/7/45	N.B.
R173512	LAC	Browning, E.W.	Posted Scoudouc N B 18/7/45	Ont.
K223490	LAC	Hottershead, H.E.	Posted 5 OTU 6/8/45	Ont.
R192090	LAC	Lockwood, F.E.	Posted 5 OTU 6/8/45	
R206448	LAC	Rombough, G.	Posted 5 OTU 6/8/45	Ont.
R141925	LAC	Patterson, B.H	Posted 5 OTU 6/8/45	N.S.
R224965	LAC	Shahan, M.L.	Posted 5 OTU 6/8/45	Ont.
R224954	LAC	Morrison, G.R.	Posted 5 OTU 6/8/45	Ont.

Number	Rank	Name	Posting	Province
R210716	Cpl.	Hunter, E.	Posted 5 OTU 6/8/45	B.C.
R217726	LAC	Waye, W.E.	Posted 11 BR 6/8/45	N.B.
R198813	LAC	Hobart, J.L.	Posted 11 BR 6/8/45	Alta.
R20998	LAC	Beattie, E.L.	Posted 11 BR 6/8/45	Ont.
R215063	LAC	Creer, A.G.	Posted 11 BR 6/8/45	B.C.
R252712	LAC	Pearson, W.R.	Posted 11 BR 6/8/45	B.C.
R153961	LAC	Anson, A.A.	Posted 11 BR 6/8/45	Ont.
R255505	Cpl.	Stockstad, P.	Posted 11 BR 6/8/45	B.C.
R210772	LAC	Blackmore, R.H.		B.C.
R204847	Cpl.	Bell, N.F.		B.C.
R122238	Cpl.	Cramm, F.		B.C.
R174919	LAC	Donahee, W.		N.B.
R93129	LAC	Emberly, G.I.		Ont.
R203054	LAC	Finlay, D.I.D.		Ont.
R181364	LAC	Gray, D.		B.C.
2379A	F/S	Gooding, W.G.		B.C.
R164905	LAC	Higgins, W.B.		Que.
R256891	LAC	Jenkins, G.V.		Ont.
R204513	LAC	Kotek, V.		Sask.
R177376	LAC	Lemoine, L		Que.
R220141	LAC	McGrath, F.G.		
R195942	LAC	McVeigh, E.J.		Ont.
U195539	LAC	Neuman, M.F.	Posted 18 SFTS Gim. 7/8/45	Ont.
R219331	LAC	Newbury, C.R.		Que.
4171A	Cpl.	Peppin, C.J.		Man.
R185437	LAC	Rolfe, C.P.		Que.
R204102	LAC	Ray, L.C.		Ont.
R157971	LAC	Reiz, G.C.		B.C.
R163208	LAC	Sinclair, W.		B.C.
R118262	LAC	Young, J.A.		B.C.

NUMBER 120 (BR) SQUADRON
COAL HARBOUR MONTHLY NOMINAL ROLE AS AT 23:59 HOURS 03/01/44

Establishment, Position & Rank			Name	Number	Classification Cat.	Duty Performed
UNIT HEADQUARTERS						
Officer Commanding	GL	W/C	A/S/L Arnold, J.T.	(C1442)	GL	Officer Commanding (Pilot)
Administrative General	NFL	F/O	T/F/L Douglas, R.H.	(C2041)	ADM NFL	Squadron Admin. Officer
Navigation Officer	GL	F/L	A/F/L Grigg, S.J.	(J8823)	GL	Navigation Officer (Navigator)
Engineer Aircraft	NFL	F/L	T/F/L Patterson, D.S.	(C603)	AE NFL	Engineer Officer
R.D.F. Office	NFL	F/O	T/P/O Goldman, R.	(C25324)	RAD NFL	R.D.F. Officer
SUPERNUMERARY						
	NFL		T/P/O Alexander, A.F.	(C13881)	AE NFL	Engineer Aircraft
OPERATIONAL FLIGHT						
Flight Commanders	GL	2 S/L	T/S/L Gledhill, J.W.	(C387)	GL	Pilot
Pilots General			T/F/L Bennett, R.A.	(J4424)	GL	Pilot
Pilots General	GL	8 F/L	T/F/L Reynolds, R.E.	(C1487)	GL	Pilot
			A/F/L MacFarlane, I.A.H.	(J5536)	GL	Pilot
			F/L Magor, J.F.	(J4336)	GL	Pilot
			A/F/L Morgan, R.G.	(J5124)	GL	Pilot
			T/F/O Hay, C.M.	(J9335)	GL	Pilot
			F/O Carson, V.B.	(J13313)	GL	Pilot
			T/F/O Philp J.A.	(J11812)	GL	Pilot
			T/F/O Poulain J.H.	(J11025)	GL	Pilot
Pilots General	GL	26 F/O	T/F/O Povah, J.W.B.	(J12487)	GL	Pilot
			T/F/O Spratt, W.N.	(J23042)	GL	Pilot
			T/P/O Asher, J.J.	(J27656)	GL	Pilot

Establishment, Position & Rank	Name	Number	Classification Cat.	Duty Performed
	T/P/O Boland, W.L.	(J28394)	GL	Pilot
	T/P/O Buchannon, J.E	(J28395)	GL	Pilot
	T/P/O Button, C.A.	(J27665)	GL	Pilot
	T/P/O Fairbairn, A.C	(J27662)	GL	Pilot
	T/P/O Game, D.K.	(J28577)	GL	Pilot
	T/P/O Gorse, F.W.	(J26233)	GL	Pilot
	T/P/O Harmon, L.M.	(J27622)	GL	Pilot
	T/P/O Keith, G.	(J27183)	GL	Pilot
	T/P/O Valley, M.E.	(J28161)	GL	Pilot
Navigations Officers B GL 2 F/L	T/F/O Grafton, T.D.	(J12297)	GL	Navigator (B)
	T/F/O Hughes, E.L.	(J8828)	GL	Navigator (B)
GL 16 F/O	T/F/O Rogers, J.C.	(J13779)	GL	Navigator (B)
	T/F/O Sorel, J.P.E.	(J13800)	GL	Navigator (B)
	T/P/O Amos, C.M.	(J21712)	GL	Navigator (B)
	T/P/O Crump, L.F.	(J29240)	GL	Navigator (B)
	T/P/O Lea, G.B.	(J29318)	GL	Navigator (B)
	T/P/O Park, H.	(J24565)	GL	Navigator (B)
	T/P/O Russell, J.M.	(J29398)	GL	Navigator (B)
	T/WO.I Knighton, R.A	(R78984)		Navigator (B)
Wireless Officer Operator GL 1 F/L	T/F/O Atherton, W.R.	(J13151)	GL	W.O.A.
53 F/O	T/F/O Carter, A.C.	(J12159)	GL	W.O.A.
	T/P/O Downey, J.W.	(J29906)	GL	W.O.A.G.
	T/P/O Price, T.S.	(J36016)	GL	W.O.A.G.
	T/P/O Singleton, A.B	(J29908)	GL	W.O.A.G.
	T/P/O Whidden, R.S.	(J27365)	GL	W.O.A.G.
	T/W0.2 Bain, G.	R133579		W.O.A.G.

Establishment, Position & Rank	Name	Number	Classification Cat.	Duty Performed
	T/W0.2 LePage, W.J.	R116703		W.O.A.G.
	T/F/S Day, V.G.	R141144		W.O.A.G.
	T/F/S Miller, J.D,	R121078		W.O.A.G.
	T/F/S Novis, T.T.	R146077		W.O.A.G.
	T/Sgt. Armbruster, L.W.	R189087		W.O.A.G.
	T/Sgt. Barker, R.R.	R192594		W.O.A.G.
	T/Sgt. Bergum, N.S.	R121593		W.O.A.G.
	T/Sgt. Biley, A.J.	R194335		W.O.A.G.
	T/Sgt. Boyle, J.M.A.	R195203		W.O.A.G.
	T/Sgt. Caldwell, F.F.	R176982		W.O.A.G.
	T/Sgt. Chaban, K.L.	R187170		W.O.A.G.
	T/Sgt. Clark, L.J.	R186687		W.O.A.G.
	T/Sgt. Coombs, H.G.	R187689		W.O.A.G.
	T/Sgt. Duncan, C.	R181391		W.O.A.G.
	T/Sgt. Fertich, J.M.	R149456		W.O.A.G.
	T/Sgt. Forbes, J.D.	R181351		W.O.A.G.
	T/Sgt. Keroack, A.M.	R187057		W.O.A.G.
	T/Sgt. Leslie, D.	R124708		W.O.A.G.
	T/Sgt. McGill, G.W.	R193869		W.O.A.G.
	T/Sgt. McKimm, S.C.	R186725		W.O.A.G.
	T/Sgt. Powell, L.A.	R172914		W.O.A.G.
	T/Sgt. Ross, J.	R95032		W.O.A.G.
	T/Sgt. Underwood, W.T.	R66806		W.O.A.G.
	T/Sgt. Whitehead, H.D.	R169676		W.O.A.G.
	T/Sgt. Winters, R.M.	R181197		W.O.A.G.

NUMBER 9 (BR) SQUADRON
RCAF STATION
BELLA BELLA

STATION ESTABLISHED: DECEMBER, 1941

STATION CLOSED: AUGUST, 1944

STATION NEWSPAPER: ROUNDEL

EDITOR: FLT/SGT GUY LARAMEE

STATION MOTTO: "STRAIGHT TO THE POINT"

RCAF STATION BELLA BELLA

CFB Comox Rowe Library

Bella Bella, situated on the inside ship passage approximately half-way between Vancouver and Prince Rupert, has a long history of use as an aircraft refuelling site. It was here, in July of 1923, that Canadian Air Force Squadron Leader Earl Godfrey refuelled his HS-2L enroute to Prince Rupert on Fisheries Patrol duty.

British Columbia Reconnaissance Party surveys, conducted in 1937, gained early recognition for Bella Bella as an ideal site for an RCAF flying boat station. The topography of the land offered excellent protection, particularly in the area between Denny and Campbell Islands, and the Native village was well-equipped for emergencies with the long established and well-run R.W. Large Memorial Hospital. On October 14, 1937, Wing Commander A..L. Cuffe stated in a report to Air Vice-Marshal G.M. Croil, that:

> "The Bella Bella area is well-removed from the influence of high mountains; the surrounding land is reasonably low and contains much sheltered water. It is considered to be the most suitable operating area between Queen Charlotte Sound and Prince Rupert. The facilities report is generally concurred in, but Whiskey Cove is too small for aircraft concentrations and Klik-Tso-Atli Harbour southeast of Whiskey Cove appears to be satisfactory, but requires further consideration with a view to accommodating a floating runway and finding the most suitable building site. It is submitted that the Bella Bella site could be reasonably well protected against seaborne attack without fixed defences. The narrow approach and transverse channels might be netted or mined and afford good cover for the operation of motor torpedo boats. It is also unlikely that ships would sacrifice manoeuvrability in these narrow waters while subject to attack by aircraft or motor torpedo boats."

On September 8, 1938, the recently formed Western

above, wireless room on RCAF "Scow" at Bella Bella, summer 1939. Galbraith Collection

top, RCAF seaplane tender "Scow" M-159 at Klik-Tso-Atli Harbour, summer 1939. Galbraith Collection

Air Command placed Cpl. W. Harris in charge of a detachment at Bella Bella to collect weather information. Cpl. Harris and his detachment established temporary quarters on the RCAF scow seaplane tender M159, in Klik-Tso-Atli Harbour adjacent to Denny Island. To their duties of collecting climatic information and sending weather reports to the Jericho Beach Air Station, the unit added the refuelling of aircraft enroute from Jericho Beach to Prince Rupert and Alliford Bay. Harris managed to locate a nearby freshwater lake - later named Croil Lake after Air Vice-Marshal G. M. Croil - that was suitable as a drinking water supply for the future station.

On January 1, 1939, F/O E.C.M. Sheffield was Officer in charge of the detachment, and in December he was succeeded by F/O F.F. McCulloch. During the summer of 1939, Airman Harvey Galbraith was assigned to the Bella Bella RCAF scow. Galbraith, from Moncton, New Brunswick, enlisted in the RCAF on June 28, 1937. After completing wireless operator training at Trenton, Ontario, he was assigned to No. 6 (TB) Torpedo Bomber Squadron and transferred to Jericho Beach. Galbraith was one of a crew of three airmen detached to the scow in Bella Bella: a corporal from the RCAF Marine section, who was in charge; a fitter whose main occupation was Cook; and Airman Galbraith, who was responsible for taking regular weather observations and reporting them by wireless to Jericho Beach.

Galbraith recalls that the most exciting event that summer was the unannounced arrival of a Grumman Goose, flown by F/O Larry Wray, transporting RCAF brass on an inspection trip to Prince Rupert. The predictable order of the small detachment's daily existence was temporarily shattered as they scrambled to accommodate their unexpected visitors. Advance notice of the return trip gave the RCAF Bella Bella detachment a chance to redeem themselves, and they turned out in proper dress and presented a suitable dinner for the inspection party.

Canadian Army Engineer Major Drysdale arrived in Bella Bella on June 26, 1940, and the plan for the proposed RCAF Flying Boat Station at Bella Bella was underway. In very short order, Drysdale completed a detailed study of Denny Island. Based on his survey results, he determined the location and physical layout of the new Station, and within a month work began on clearing the site. Space for the hangars, ramp and slipway were blasted out of the rocky terrain, and barges loaded with construction material began to arrive. The construction project was undertaken by the

No. 1 hangar site at Bella Bella; blasted from solid rock. LaRamée Collection

Coast Construction Company, under the supervision of engineer Val Gwyther of Western Air Command's Works and Building Department.

F/O B.N. Jones arrived in the summer of 1940 to assume command of the detachment which was still in place on the seaplane tender. During the fall a Northrop Delta on floats, enroute from Pat Bay to Alliford Bay, overnighted at the scow. The Delta, under the command of S/L Fred Ewart, with Sgt. Jack McMahone and F/O J.A. Gagnon on board, took off the next morning into low cloud and drizzle. The aircraft, climbed to 500 feet before the engine began to miss, backfired - and then silence. Faced with a sea of trees immediately below, S/L Ewart managed to drag the Delta back over the shoreline where it crashed and overturned in about seven feet of water. Fortunately there were no serious injuries, but the RCAF scow tender raced to the rescue and took the Delta crew to the R. W. Large Memorial Hospital in the village of Bella Bella.

Until May 1941 there were 12 RCAF personnel, now under the charge of Sergeant Henderson. On June 27, F/O R.G. Nichols arrived from Jericho Beach, and RCAF personnel moved into accommodations on the Station site. The days of baching in cramped quarters aboard the scow were gone, and the detachment took their meals with the construction company.

Flying Officer L.R. Chodat, the Officer Commanding the detachment in August of 1941, was very familiar with the location of his new command. In 1938, as a Corporal, Chodat had served on the Bella Bella scow, but the peace and tranquility he remembered was greatly altered by the construction progressing on the new Station. F/O Patterson was also attached to the detachment as a medical officer.

By November 1941 construction was rapidly moving ahead, and 21 buildings were now ready for use, with nine others under construction. The Heiltsuk Band in the village of Bella Bella offered a built-in work force, and, in an effort to strengthen relations with the Band, the Coast Construction Company hired many of the local natives. Vivian Wilson, one of these young men, later became a chief of the Heiltsuk Band.

At 15:30 hours on December 7, 1941, RCAF Station Bella Bella received a signal from Western Air Command advising the Station of Japan's attack on Pearl Harbor, it was followed by a second signal at 22:30 hours advising that a state of war existed between Canada and Japan. Station Officers and personnel reacted swiftly: all leave was immediately cancelled, guard posts were doubled, and members of the Veterans Guard of Canada were assigned to the posts. Machine gun posts were established at the power house, wireless station, RCAF pier, and Shearwater Island, which overlooked the Station and the flying boat ramp in Klik-Tso-Atli Harbour. The radio operators continued to receive signals regarding the war in the Pacific, but suddenly the conflict was brought closer to home: the United States now expected the Japanese to attack the west coast of North America. Immediate orders were issued for a complete blackout of the entire area, including the Indian village and the R.W. Large Hospital.

Under the very real threat of invasion, RCAF Station Bella Bella moved into the month of December 1941 with increased momentum. Lieutenant Barrington Foot assumed command of the Veterans Guard of Canada detachment from Lieutenant T.A. Dunne M.C.; engineer H.R. Silverthorne replaced Val Gwyther as construction engineer; and the first hangar was nearing completion, with a second underway. Station personnel now comprised: F/O R.E. Johnson, Adjutant; F/O F.P. Patterson, Medical Officer; F/O H.W. Green, Security Officer; and 20 security guards; bringing the Station's complement to 76.

F/L F.S. Carpenter, 1940, prior to Bella Bella posting. McPhee Collection

On December 8, S/L F.S. Carpenter arrived in Bella Bella with two Stranraers from Patricia Bay crewed by F/O H. Toye, P/O J.R. Shaw, and P/O R.J. Gordon. The group formed the advance party of No. 9 (BR) Bomber Reconnaissance Squadron assigned to RCAF Station Bella Bella as their war station. An Air Force Administrative Order, #HQ 1018-1-14 signed by Group Captain L.S. Bradner on July 30, 1938, allotted Number 9 (GR) General Reconnaissance Squadron as a permanent force unit of Jericho Beach; however, because of a lack of personnel and flying boats, the Squadron was not activated until December 9, 1941. On that date S/L Carpenter assumed command of No. 9 (BR) Squadron, and immediately commenced operational patrols with the two

Guard post above RCAF Bella Bella. LaRamée Collection

Stranraers: #949 and #936. The Stranraers took off from Bella Bella in response to a report that a Japanese submarine was sighted north of Vancouver Island in the Queen Charlotte Strait. The search was uneventful, but the sighting was real and underlined the urgency of bringing the Squadron up to full strength. Accommodation on the partially completed Station was not yet a problem; unfortunately events were now moving faster than construction, and winter weather made serious progress difficult. Several weeks later the balance of the Squadron's personnel began to arrive, and four more Stranraers were taken on strength. Just before Christmas the first contingent of Airmen disembarked from a Union Steamship into the cold and unpromising December darkness. Assembled under the stark illumination on the lighted jetty, the group was inspected by Squadron Leader Carpenter who ordered the Station Sergeant Major and his crew to complete a thorough kit search. All liquor found was emptied over the side of the jetty, taking with it any preconceived notions of a "merry" Christmas.

Flight Sergeant Guy LaRamée arrived as a Corporal with this first group of No. 9 (BR) Squadron and put in many long hours as a flight engineer for the Stranraer patrols. After a patrol returned to base, the ground crew refuelled

Union steamship vessel "Cardina" at old Bella Bella. McPhee Collection

the aircraft at the buoy from forty-five gallon drums - and still faced a pre-flight inspection of the aircraft at the crack of dawn on the following morning. F/S LaRamée had just completed one of these early morning inspections and was about to step into the motor boat to return to shore when another boat arrived, and S/L Carpenter jumped out. The Squadron Leader ordered LaRamée and a rigger, Corporal Asselin, back on board the Stranraer with the sharp command to *"Get cranking!"* - a ponderous task necessary due to the Stranies lack of a self starter. There was a slight delay because Carpenter did not notice that the master switch wasn't on, but they finally got both engines running and took off. Over the roar of the engines, Carpenter yelled at LaRamée to get the navigator and wireless operator, to which the Flight Sergeant truthfully responded, *"Not on board, Sir."* Carpenter shot back, *"Well - get me one of the air gunners!"* Again the puzzled answer was, *"No gunners on board, Sir."* Carpenter exploded in frustration - *"Who the Christ IS aboard this aircraft!"*, and took off his service hat and stomped on it. F/S LaRamée had no choice but to inform his Squadron Leader that the head count was only three. Carpenter was still barking out orders, *"Can you man the machine guns?"*... *"Yes, Sir."*... *"WELL PUT THEM ON SERGEANT!"* They flew on and on through fairly dense fog, but LaRamée still had no idea where they were going. Suddenly he heard a deafening bang, after which Carpenter cranked the Stranraer into a steep turn, and dropped all the depth charges.

Somehow S/L Carpenter found his way back through the fog, and on their return to base the angry Squadron Leader called a meeting of all aircrew members. He severely raked them over the coals for their lack of organization; this action produced looks of consternation on many sleepy faces. F/S LaRamée learned nothing conclusive about his mysterious patrol, but he firmly believed that they had responded to a Japanese submarine sighting and had been fired on by the enemy. Years later, LaRamée, an RCN Lieutenant, met Air Commodore Carpenter at Shearwater, Nova Scotia, in the station's Ward Room. LaRamée approached Carpenter and recounted the incident, but the mystery was to remain a mystery, the Air Commodore flatly denied any knowledge of the occurrence.

Stranraers continued their coastal patrols from a Station that was still far from complete. Early in 1942 a special-

Stranraer #949 on patrol from Bella Bella. LaRamée Collection ized construction party, under the supervision of F/L Aikin, arrived to build the station power house and to erect power poles for electrical and communications requirements. The first building completed at the station was the W/T (wireless) building followed by the Sergeants' Mess, NCO quarters, Airmens' Mess, Officers' Quarters and Mess, and the base hospital. Personnel at the Station increased to a complement of 27 officers and 241 airmen, plus 4 officers and 58 other ranks of the Royal Canadian Army and Veterans Guard of Canada.

Only dance held at RCAF Bella Bella, September 26, 1942. LaRamée Collection

As the Station numbers continued to grow so did the need to find suitable projects and entertainment to ease the tedium of long days and nights in this remote area far from home. As soon as the recreation hall was complete, the men organized a Station basketball team, and a competition began between the Station's team and a basketball team in the Indian village located on Campbell Island. Apart from basketball, the recreation hall added further zest to life on the Station as the first dance was painstakingly prepared for. As a solution to the serious shortage of appropriate dancing partners, a flotilla of small boats arrived, bringing lovely young ladies from Bella Bella village, Ocean Falls and Namu. The Native village of Bella Bella was off limits to the airmen, but Ocean Falls provided an interesting diversion for some of the men. Twice a week a boat travelled up to the head of Cousins Inlet to the lively company mill town. At first the airmen received a tremendous welcome and were hospitably invited to share the town's conveniences. But after a while the novelty wore off on both sides, and it became a case of - as F/S LaRamée succinctly put it - *"Too many airmen; too small a town"*

above, a "PR" visit to the Indian Village on Campell Island. LaRamée Collection
top, water safety demonstration by crew of RCAF M-266 "Takuli". LaRamée Collection

Ground transportation anywhere in the immediate area around the Bella Bella Station was difficult. The swampy surface of Denny Island was covered with knarled and stunted cedar evergreens which made even a good brisk walk next to impossible. The easiest way to travel was by small boat, but with inexperienced personnel handling small boats day and night in fog and stormy weather it was inevitable that a serious accident would occur. On January 3, 1942, AC2 I.A. Macdonald capsized his boat. He could not swim and was not wearing a life jacket, and although P/O Dewar desperately attempted to save his comrade's life, Dewar quickly became exhausted in the cold water and had to be rescued himself.

By February 1942, Station personnel numbered 455, which made the unfinished accommodations crowded to say the least, and the situation received a further complication when an outbreak of both measles and mumps required the isolation of the affected individuals. The somewhat claustrophobic feeling created by the overcrowded conditions was compounded by the physical restrictions of the Station site. Gouged out of the rocky shoreline, the site was bounded by water on one end and closed in on all sides by the awkward terrain of Denny Island.

F/O H.B. Lyon and F/O T.B. (Bert) Toye make a meal on a Stranraer. LaRamée Collection

Building the "Santa Bella Trail", as it was dubbed by the Station newsletter editor, F/S LaRamée, turned out to be a major project that kept many of the men busy for countless hours. Initially, a path of some kind was vital to get the men quickly and easily to the defense posts located on the hill above the quarters and the hangars. Once this rough network of trails was in place the project took on a new dimension. Driven by the need for diversion and exercise, the airmen began the construction of a Boardwalk from the RCAF Station to the general store and fish packing plant on the other side of the island. Material for the trail was scrounged from any source available, but the majority of the material came from packing cases. Hundreds of Station personnel have a clear memory of going back and forth to the store, or simply getting out and running up and down the boardwalk to keep in shape.

Commanding Officer No 9 (BR) S/L J. McNee. LaRamée Collection

During this time Squadron Leader Carpenter was in command of both the RCAF Station at Bella Bella, and No. 9 (BR) Squadron. He was in charge of the Air Force defence scheme at the Station, and the Station diary notes that: *"He maintained the interest of the men in this scheme and raised their work to a high peak of efficiency."* Carpenter was known as a firm disciplinarian: a leadership trait necessary to maintain order under the pressures of rapid change taking place at RCAF Station Bella Bella. On May 19, 1942, S/L Carpenter was transferred to Coal Harbour to take command of that Station, having relinquished the command of RCAF Station Bella Bella to Squadron Leader C.M.G. Farrell, DFC, in March 1942. S/L Farrell received a promotion to Wing Commander on March 17.

On May 30th, Western Air Command notified all stations that an overwhelming Japanese force was moving eastward in the North Pacific. A state of alert was declared and all leave cancelled. All personnel maintained a state of constant readiness, and blackouts were strictly enforced. At RCAF Station Bella Bella, all crews slept aboard their aircraft to ensure an instant response in the event of an emergency.Before dawn on Sunday, June 7, 1942, the Japanese landed an invasion force of 2,500 combat troops on the Aleutian Islands of Kiska and Attu. This action brought about a considerable increase in submarine activity as the Japanese high command sought to gather intelligence on American and Canadian naval activities in the Pacific northwest. Western Air Command realized the vital importance of sending out patrols that could penetrate more deeply over the Pacific and give earlier warning of the enemy's approach. Long range gasoline tanks were fitted to the Stranraers and patrols extending 400 miles from the Queen Charlotte Islands were instituted. The Stranraer patrols out of RCAF Station Bella Bella were often long and tedious, but at the beginning of each patrol the flight crews felt they had another chance to find the enemy and get a shot at him. They returned to the base tired and frustrated after another lengthy search for an elusive enemy they seldom saw - let alone got the chance to take a shot at.

On June 18, Squadron Leader J.W. McNee took command of No. 9 (BR) Squadron. Several nights later a Japanese submarine I-26 surfaced off the Lighthouse and Signal Station at Estevan Point, on the west coast of Vancouver Island. The submarine began shelling, and Lighthouse staff immediately sent out a distress signal,

above, caption for cartoon reads "DeCourcy: 'Do you think we'll make it to Rose Harbour?' Optimistic Crewman: 'Guesso, we done it before, we'll do it again!'" LaRamée Collection

top, Stranraer #937 makes a night landing on flare path. LaRamée Collection

and a full alert was raised. RCAF Stations at Ucluelet and Coal Harbour were the closest, but both Stations were unable to operate at night: Ucluelet because of harbour obstructions, and Coal Harbour because of the high terrain surrounding the Station. No. 32 Operational Training Unit (RAF) at Patricia Bay scrambled a Beaufort Bomber, but its crew managed an untimely crash on take-off which effectively blocked the runway. The only Air Force unit on the entire coast that delivered a meaningful response was No. 9 (BR) Squadron at Bella Bella.

Wing Commander Farrell ordered a station General Alert: all defence posts were manned, and a single Stranraer, #921, under the command of F/O J. Matheson, took off from Klik-Tso-Atli Harbour and set course for Estevan Point. By the time F/O Matheson arrived over Estevan Point, the shelling had ceased and the submarine was gone. Personnel on the ground heard the Stranraer circling overhead, but the inky blackness of the night sky kept it hidden from sight. After a commendable effort, #921 returned to Bella Bella, and F/O Matheson, who had never flown a flying boat at night, reached the base and landed safely at 02:00 hours.

A few Stranraer patrols ran into difficulties that, although not directly associated with the enemy, were equally as frustrating, or even as dangerous for the aircrews involved. On June 22, 1942, Stranraer #936, developed engine trouble in the last leg of a long patrol. The pilot managed to stagger back as far as the southernmost island of the Queen Charlottes. He brought the aircraft down in Rose Harbour on Kunghit Island with no injuries to the crew, but they had to remain there for a week while repairs were made to their Stranny. Rose Harbour was an active whaling station and the stench left a lot to be desired; the crew decided that in future they would be more selective of their emergency landing sites.

On July 4 Wing Commander Farrell was posted to Air Force Headquarters in Ottawa, prior to going to Edmonton as a Liaison Officer to the United States Air Force for service on the Alaska Staging Route. Squadron Leader J.W. McNee was assigned as the temporary Officer Commanding RCAF Station Bella Bella, and the busy month of July 1942 offered several additional challenges for the Squadron Leader to handle.

The Station recorded its very first Japanese submarine sighting: Stranraer #953, approaching Cape St. James on a dawn patrol early in July, sighted the submarine, but before the patrol could get close enough to drop its depth charges the submarine disappeared. This time, a Royal Canadian Navy Corvette happened to be in the area, and it was diverted to the location to continue the search. This incident served to point out the benefits of establishing and practising a policy of cooperation with the Navy.

On July 25, the United States Transport vessel A.T. Houston developed a steering malfunction and lost control, causing it to run aground in Lama Passage. RCAF Station Bella Bell immediately responded to the emergency and sent a Marine Section crash boat to the scene. Station personnel quickly found accommodation for the Houston's passengers and crew at the Native village.

On July 29, Stranraer #937 took off on the regular dawn patrol at 04:55. The sky was heavily overcast, a dense fog hung low over the sea, and as the patrol moved out over the Pacific there was no sign that conditions would improve. At 07:40 hours the pilot was forced to turn back to base. Stranraer #949 attempted to carry out the patrol at 10:00, but 15 miles beyond Goose Island the aircraft blew a cylinder on the left engine forcing the pilot, F/Sgt. Hildebrande, to also turn back. In an effort to gain altitude, Hildebrande jettisoned his extra fuel, but the weather had already forced him down to within 25 feet of the water. As he negotiated his turn, the right wing tip float struck the surface of the water and was torn off, the aircraft bounced several times before coming to a stop on the ocean swells. Their emergency signal had been acknowledged so the crew, shaken but uninjured, took to the dinghies. For the second time that day, Stranraer #937 took off from Bella Bella. In spite of the thick fog, the crew of #937 located the ditched aircraft and maintained a position directly over their comrades until a nearby Navy patrol boat arrived to rescue the downed crew and tow the aircraft back to the station.

Forward air gunner on Stranraer. LaRamée Collection

above, Whiskey Cove, "dependent's" cabin. Coombes Collection
top, No. 9 (BR) salvage crew at Rose Harbour, June 27, 1942. F/L (Fireball) Thompson at right. Sgt Max Copendale third from left. LaRamée Collection

Bad weather continued to play havoc with the operation of coastal patrols, but other aspects of Station life suffered as well. The long days of rain put the fresh water supply from Croil Lake in difficulty, and the decision was reached to drain the Lake. Once this was done there wasn't another drop of rain for the entire month of August. It was into this "dry camp" that F/O Ted Coombes found himself posted as the Station's new Armament Officer. There was sufficient water to supply the Mess for cooking purposes, but that was all. If the men wanted to wash, they washed in the sea; if they wanted to brush their teeth they used seawater or coke. When it did start to rain again in typical B.C. coast style, it took less than ten hours for the lake to once more reach overflow.

One slightly more serious difficulty that F/O Coombes immediately ran into was absence of married couples' quarters at the Station, and he discovered that the Officers were not even supposed to bring their wives with them. Some of the Officers got around this by bringing their wives up to work as nurses at the R.W. Large Hospital in the Native village. This plan developed a major flaw when hospital administrator, George Darby, refused to allow his nurses, married or otherwise, to visit the Station

- unless he escorted them. This was nonsense to both Mrs. Coombes and F/O Coombes. With the help of the men from his section, Coombes built a log cabin for his wife just above the high tide line on Whiskey Cove. It was a comfortable 20 by 25 feet, roofed with tarpaper, and came complete with an outhouse. Cabins sprang up in the vicinity like mushrooms as other Officers followed suit, and in December of 1942 the unofficial occupancy

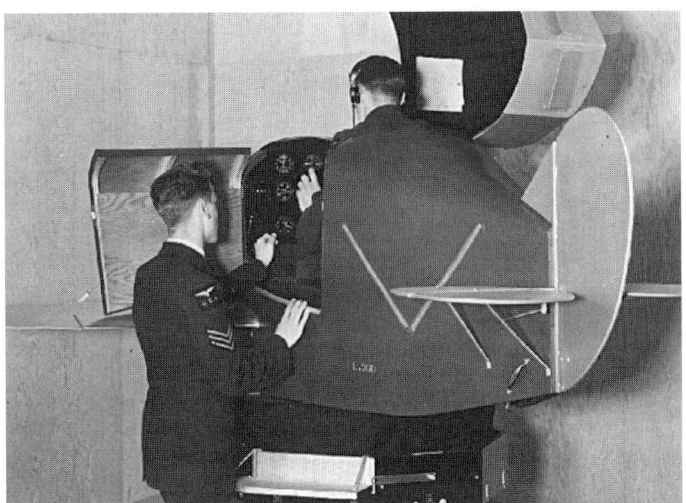

Pilots brush up on instrument flying in link trainer. LaRamée Collection

rate hovered around forty.

Squadron Leader D.E. Galloway arrived on August 13, 1942, to assume command of the Station. The following entries, recorded in the Station Diary, give a clear picture of the diligent effort and determination involved in tracking the enemy's movements on the coast of British Columbia:

> **20 August:** Stranraer #915, and a crash boat, proceeded to Calvert Island to assist in the recovery of a United States Navy Vought-Sikorsky OS2U-l Kingfisher which had crashed. The two man crew escaped injury and were brought back to the Station. W.A.C. directed the Station to salvage the aircraft. The job was completed 14 September 1942.
> Two days later a Coal Harbour aircraft sighted a submarine on a patrol, and Bella Bella joined in the search. Unfortunately, heavy fog persisted and the hunt was fruitless.
>
> **23 August:** Stranraer #951 from No. 120 (BR) Squadron at Coal Harbour was reported down on the ocean and sinking 100 miles at sea. Two aircraft from Bella Bella were dispatched to assist but failed to find the aircraft or its crew.
>
> **13 September:** It was learned that Lt. C.P. Kelly of the U.S. Army Air Corps, and son of the General Superintendent of the Pacific Mills Paper Company of Ocean Falls, had been killed recently in Hawaii. A memorial service was held 13 September in Ocean Falls as Kelly was the first young man from this town to be killed on active service. As a mark of respect to the next-of-kin, a detachment of airmen under P/O L.J. Carter was sent to represent the Station.

A sub sighting was reported in South Bentinck Arm on 4 September. A search was carried out but without result. On 25 September another report of a sighting in Fisher Channel was investigated.

All stations in Western Air Command were placed on No. 1 Alert on 4 September as a result of a signal from General Buckner, Commanding General, Alaskan Defences, to the effect that certain Japanese surface craft had left Kiska Harbor for an undetermined destination. The memory of Pearl Harbor was still fresh and the coastal units were constantly alerted to prevent being taken by surprise no matter how slim the possibility was of action with the enemy taking place.

During October and November several reports of sub sightings were received and careful searches carried out.

> **7 November:** The first representatives of the Women's Division, Squadron Officer Walker, Section Officer Cameron, Section Officer Dunbar and Dr. Charlotte Whitton, visited the station. They were on a tour of all coastal stations.
>
> **19 November:** No. 9 (BR) exchanged bases with No. 6 (BR) Alliford Bay, on an exercise designed to give practice in mobility in time of an emergency. Each squadron returned to its respective base on 2 December.
>
> **15 December:** S/L J.W. McNee was posted to Ucluelet to take command of that station and S/L P.E. Sorensen assumed command of No. 9 (BR) Squadron.

Sergeants Mess at RCAF Bella Bella. LaRamée Collection

Ocean Falls with Link Lake beyond. LaRamée Collection

24 December: F/L J.D.B. Malteson and F/L R.J. Cross were posted to Jericho Beach (a nice Christmas present) to start training on PBY-5A Cansos - a hint that the station could expect to receive some of these aircraft in the foreseeable future.

January 1943: a particularly unseasonable cold spell hit the coast causing a great deal of damage and curtailing flying.

13 March: the United States Army transport vessel "OT5590" ran aground in Lama Passage with 800 passengers on board. Civilian and Army personnel were rescued and billeted at either the RCAF Station or in homes in the Native village at Bella Bella. This sudden influx of people taxed the supplies and resources of both communities, and finally exhausted the supply of food and emergency rations had to be used until more supplies could be shipped in. By 15 March the passengers were on their way again. Before they left they contributed $115.00 to the Station Fund as a gesture of their appreciation for the welcome they received.

During the first quarter of 1943, the station strength was considerably depleted by an unusual number of postings overseas of maintenance and General Duties airmen. In very few cases were replacements available for the RCAF was increasing its commitments of overseas personnel without a proportionate increase in total strength. The training stations could not reduce their staff - training was too vitally important. Therefore it was left to the units of the Home War Defence to carry on as before but with fewer personnel. This they did.

It was not noted in the Station Diary, but about this time, Commanding Officer S/L Galloway decided that a control tower was needed on Shearwater Island. He issued an order to top a few of the tall trees and have a platform put up. When the air traffic controllers got up there to actually use the new "tower" they found the surrounding trees were too tall and completely cut off their view. The CO ordered the Armament Officer, F/O Coombes, to take some of his men up there with their machine guns and chop off the tops of the offending trees with machine gun fire.

Across the bay, the Army detachment spent most of the afternoon undercover to avoid the machine gun fire that Coombes and his men were spreading all over the place. However, Coombes felt that the Army soon had its day.

Coombes needed to pick up window glass and other material for the construction of his new cabin. To get to the packing plant and general store, he borrowed a marine section outboard and carefully stowed the supplies for the return trip. Heading back, he was amazed to find that the sentries somehow failed to recognize him, and the Army took a shot at him. Later in the evening, at the Mess, it was a great joke, with the Army types laughing like hell.

April 1943 saw the long awaited arrival of Canso A #9761, the first Canso to be allocated to the station. On April 19, S/L Galloway flew #9761 to Alliford Bay to participate in a special convoy duty escorting United States ships enroute to Alaska; he returned to Bella Bella on April 21.

On the afternoon patrol of April 22, wireless air gunner F/Sgt. Stothers, spotted a submarine ten miles off Triangle Island, the most western of the Scott Islands, on the northwest tip of Vancouver Island. The submarine crash-dived as the aircraft approached, and was not seen again. A week later another submarine was investigated near Alliford Bay but without any results.

Several changes in Station personnel during 1943, were noted in the Station Diary:

F/L R.E. Johnson, the Adjutant, was posted to Patricia Bay. Johnson had been one of the first ones here and had arrived when the station was in a mad state of construction.

S/L Sorenson was posted overseas on 19 May 1943 and was succeeded by S/L A.W. Mitchell, AFC, who had been at Ucluelet.

5 October: W/C Galloway was posted to No. 2 Group H.Q., Victoria, as Senior Air Staff Officer and was succeeded by S/L W.M. Emery.

On July 9, 1943, the Squadron received its second Canso, #9789. On a patrol July 25, her crew sighted a submarine 175 miles west of the Queen Charlotte Islands. The aircraft was at 4,000 feet and made a rapid descent through cloud to attack. When they broke out under the cloud deck at 2,000 feet, the submarine had disappeared and nothing further was seen.

The station's first fatal flying accident occurred on July 30, 1943 when Canso #9789 left Bella Bella on an extra long patrol, but ran into fog in Lama Passage and lost contact with the surface. The pilot, P/O A.J. Joseph, attempted a left turn back to the station. The aircraft, weighted down by a heavy load of fuel, was unable to climb above the fog, or to negotiate the turn in the narrow passage. Number 9789 lost altitude and crashed into the side of a mountain on Denny Island, on the east side of Lama Passage above Alarm Cove. The aircraft caught fire on impact killing the flight engineer Sgt. J.A. Cowman, and injuring the remaining 8 crew members. The Canso was totally destroyed.

In January 1944 a change of policy came into effect

Stranraer on patrol along Queen Charlotte Sound. LaRamée Collection regarding the Station's Flying Boat patrols: two long patrols 500 miles seaward were to be made daily; night patrols would be undertaken, but landings were to be made only during hours of daylight; a lighted landing area devised at Bella Bella could now only be used for emergency purposes.

There were fewer reports of submarine sightings in the area but, on March 4, the crew of Canso #11003 reported one of the closest encounters, or near encounters, with the enemy that had been experienced by any of the operational patrols in the last two years. From their position at 5,000 feet, the crew sighted a submarine on the surface. The pilot quickly sought cloud cover and rapidly descended to 2,000 feet, ready to attack. As usual, when the aircraft broke out of the undercast, the submarine had slipped below the surface. Canso #11003 remained in the area for three hours to be rewarded by the reappearance of the submarine's periscope. The jubilant aircrew attacked with depth charges and machine gun fire, however, no debris was seen and no official claim could be made.

The Coastal Construction Company finally completed the construction of RCAF Bella Bella in early April of 1944, and the company removed its personnel and equipment. Even though the completion date came just a few short months before the Station was to be disbanded, the company had finished the project under very difficult circumstances; this had been no ordinary construction project.

Wing Commander R.R. Dennis assumed command of the Station from W/C Emery, who was attached to Western Air Command on June 2, 1944. S/L Mitchell, AFC, was also posted to Western Air Command for duty on the Aircrew Assessment Board, and he was replaced, as No. 9 (BR) Squadron Commanding Officer, by S/L R.W. McRae. At the end of July 1944 the Station strength, including Army personnel, was 750.

By this time the Japanese had suffered major defeats abroad, and the threat of an invasion, particularly on the west coast of North America, had diminished. For economic reasons as well as difficulty in supplying some of the remoter stations, a decision was made to disband No. 9 (BR) Squadron. During August 1944 RCAF Station Bella Bella was reduced to a care and maintenance basis, and No. 9 (BR) Squadron was disbanded and its aircrew were transferred to other coastal units. The aircraft were flown to Alliford Bay and attached to No. 7 (BR) Squadron. By the end of August the Station strength had been reduced to 390 men.

RCAF Station Bella Bella did not have a long career but there were many things to be proud of: the Station received the first award for Command Efficiency for the quarter ending December 31, 1943; Station morale was high, and a strong feeling of comradeship developed among the men, with many friendships forged that would last a lifetime. A final entry in the Station Diary sums up the unsung heroism on the Bella Bella Station:

> *"The reports of the presence of enemy craft in our waters are investigated thoroughly and, no matter how inaccurate the report may seem to be, the squadron personnel embark on the searches with enthusiasm and keenness. The fact that the West coast stations saw little action is in part due to their unceasing vigilance. They made the waters of the Pacific adjacent to the coast a most unhealthy and unproductive locality for the enemy. Theirs was not a glamorous job. They received no applause from the people and none from the Service. They had a dirty, dangerous, monotonous job to do and they did it. That was their reward."*

Effective September 1, 1944 RCAF Station Bella Bella was disbanded.

RCAF Station Bella Bella received a short reprieve in the spring of 1945. The Station was reactivated, and in May F/L R.J. Scholes was appointed Officer Commanding the Station until June, when F/L H.G. Lyon, AFC, assumed the position of Commanding Officer. The Station operated a meteorological section as well as administering to the needs of a small emergency refuelling station at Ethalda Bay on Estevan Island, and the Radar Unit at Spider Island.

The Bella Bella Station newspaper, with Jack Rush as Editor, was also rejuvenated under the masthead "Bellascope".

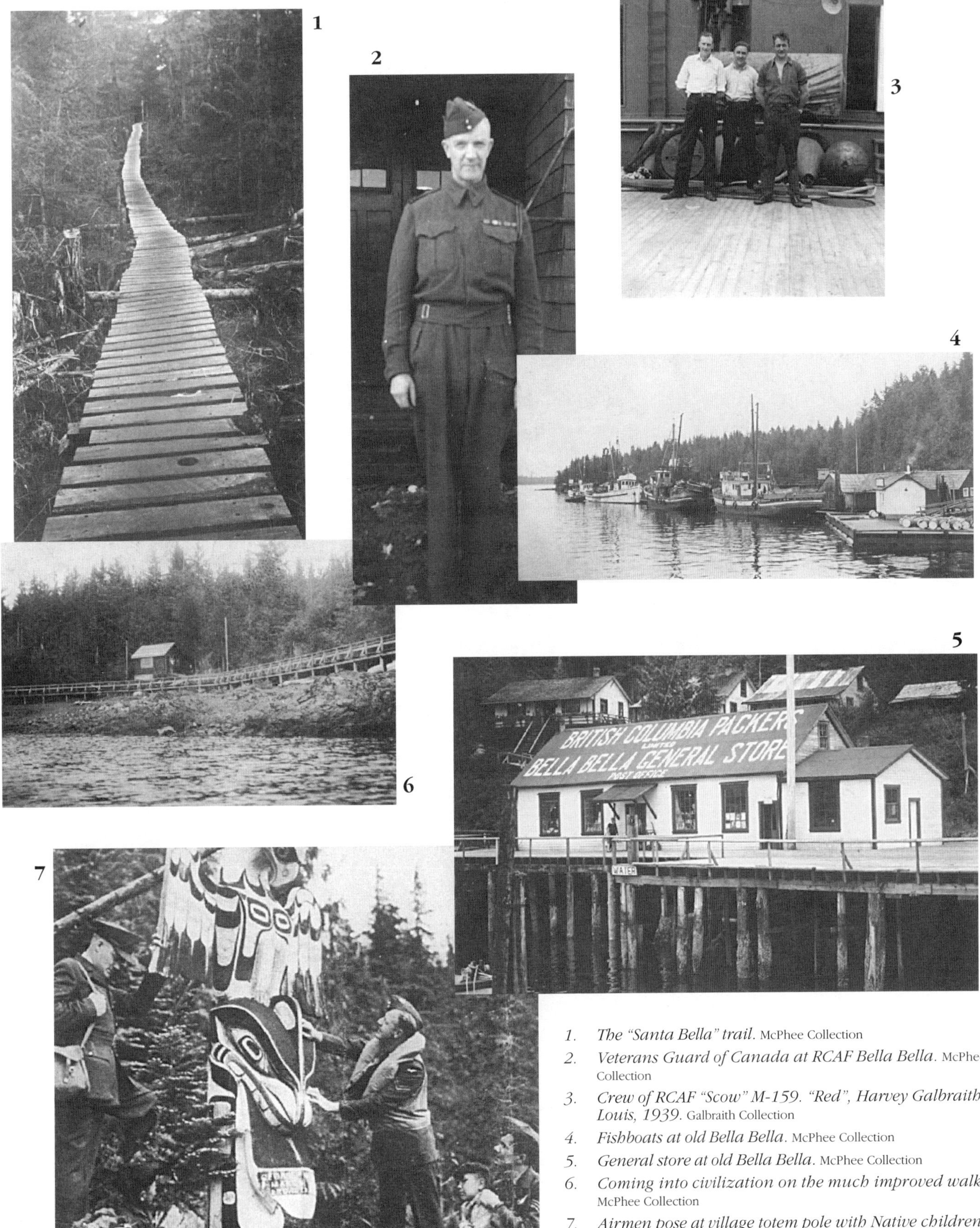

1. *The "Santa Bella" trail.* McPhee Collection
2. *Veterans Guard of Canada at RCAF Bella Bella.* McPhee Collection
3. *Crew of RCAF "Scow" M-159. "Red", Harvey Galbraith, Louis, 1939.* Galbraith Collection
4. *Fishboats at old Bella Bella.* McPhee Collection
5. *General store at old Bella Bella.* McPhee Collection
6. *Coming into civilization on the much improved walk.* McPhee Collection
7. *Airmen pose at village totem pole with Native children.* LaRamée Collection

"Weather Can't Dictate Our Movements"

THE caption of this article, though "fixed" by the Editors, is indeed appropriate of the Squadron.

This Squadron is primarily a reconnaissance squadron, and introductorily, reference must be made to the Allied Intelligence Service and its efficient compilation of information concerning the number, formation and movements of the enemies' land, sea and air forces. It is to assist in the gathering of such information, information which is vital to the successful application of our own assault forces, that the reconnaissance squadrons are put into service.

When one sees, and perhaps with wonderment, aircraft departing from this base day in and day out, with seemingly little regard for weather conditions, it must be borne in mind that negative reports concerning enemy forces are not without importance, and the element of surprise must be deprived to the enemy. It must be remembered too that naval forces are adroit at capitalizing upon weather cover, to complete movements in weather of unfavourable visibility.

Because of the nature of their duties and the tasks which confront them in carrying out those duties, an exceptionally high standard of efficiency is demanded of the personnel comprising a reconnaissance squadron. Initially, members of aircrew selected for reconnaissance squadron duties are chosen from that group of students possessing above average ability. Upon arrival at the squadron, after basic training at an Operational Training Unit, the Aircrew are further schooled in the duties of the squadron, and the type of equipment in use.

This Squadron is justly proud of its record and devotion to its purpose. To insure the maintenance of that record, a progressive course of air and ground instruction is undertaken by all members of the Squadron, instruction not only pertaining to their individual and specialized professions, but the allied trades too. (It has been said: "When Command wants a job well done, this Squadron will do it.")

S/L. J. McNEE.

S/L. J. McNee.

LaRamée Collection

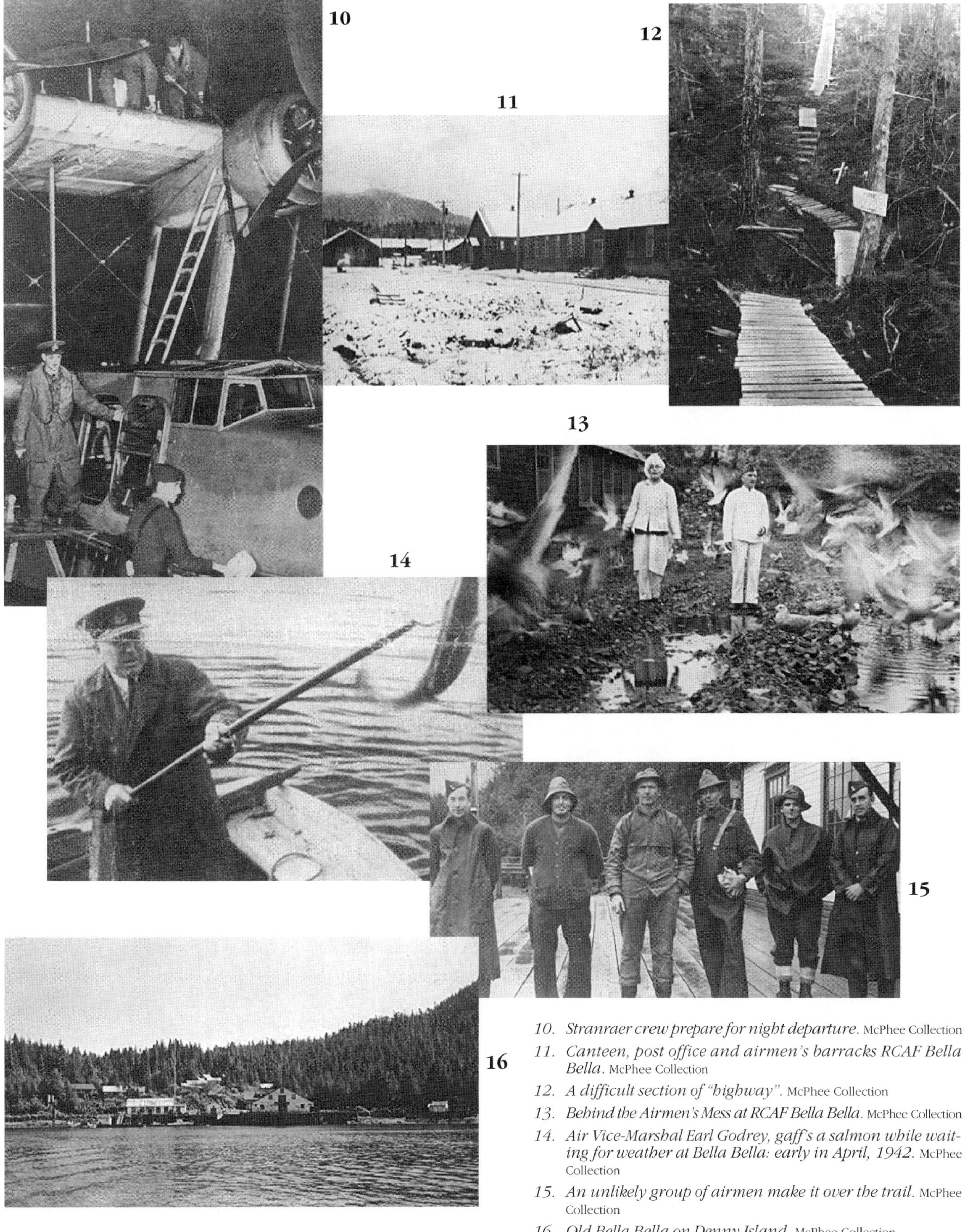

10. *Stranraer crew prepare for night departure.* McPhee Collection
11. *Canteen, post office and airmen's barracks RCAF Bella Bella.* McPhee Collection
12. *A difficult section of "highway".* McPhee Collection
13. *Behind the Airmen's Mess at RCAF Bella Bella.* McPhee Collection
14. *Air Vice-Marshal Earl Godrey, gaff's a salmon while waiting for weather at Bella Bella: early in April, 1942.* McPhee Collection
15. *An unlikely group of airmen make it over the trail.* McPhee Collection
16. *Old Bella Bella on Denny Island.* McPhee Collection

17

18

19

20

21

22

17. *Parachute section, Bella Bella.* LaRamée Collection
18. *Stores section prepare for Bella Bella defence.* LaRamée Collection
19. *Stores personnel.* LaRamée Collection
20. *Bella Bella armaments section.* LaRamée Collection
21. *Aircrews attend a briefing.* LaRamée Collection
22. *Administration office, Bella Bella.* LaRamée Collection

23

24

25

26

27

23. *Airman Louis J. McPhee on the "boardwalk".* McPhee Collection
24. *Stranraer #937 on patrol from Bella Bella.* LaRamée Collection
25. *Station personnel make elaborate preparations for dance.* LaRamée Collection
26. *No. 9 (BR) Guard of Honour are addressed by V.I.P.* LaRamée Collection
27. *Station adjutant F/O R.E. Johnson.* LaRamée Collection

chapter five

UNSUNG HEROES

Works and Bricks

The RCAF Marine Squadron

NUMBER 9 (CMU) CONSTRUCTION MAINTENANCE UNIT
"WORKS & BRICKS"

WIRELESS/TRANSMISSION PARTY FORMED:
DECEMBER 10, 1941

RE-NAMED:
NUMBER 1 (WCU) WORKS CONSTRUCTION UNIT 1942

RE-NAMED:
NUMBER 9 (CMU) CONSTRUCTION MAINTENANCE UNIT 1942

COMMANDING OFFICER 1940-1945:
W/C J.C. DUMBRILLE

NO. 9 CONSTRUCTION MAINTENANCE UNIT

Works and Bricks

Site of Masset Airport. CFS Masset

The Western Air Command Wireless Transmission (W/T) Party was formed in the summer of 1940 and established its headquarters at Ucluelet on the southwest side of Vancouver Island. From Ucluelet, the W/T Party was detached by Western Air Command to construct (W/TDF radar) Wireless Transmission and Direction Finding Stations at various locations within the command area.

In response to Canada's War Plan for the defence of the west coast, the demand for electrical installations became more pressing and the duties and responsibilities of the W/T Party gradually increased. Air Force Headquarters realized that a larger work force was necessary in order to accomplish the major construction projects that were being planned.

Temporary housing at Ucluelet. NAC 141360

On March 1, 1942 the W/T Party was redesignated as No. 1 Works Construction Unit (WCU) and took on a strength of 30 Officers and 170 Airmen under the command of S/L J.C. Dumbrille. Official headquarters were relocated to the Belmont Building in Victoria, and an equipment warehouse was installed on the Ballantyne Pier in Vancouver.

Construction of plank road to RU site. CFS Masset

At first, crews were detached to begin construction of roads and buildings at the initial W/TDF Stations, but within a few months their specialized skill was needed at radar sites throughout the province. The RCAF Flying Boat Stations and other coastal locations were now a top priority: Ucluelet, Alliford Bay, Bella Bella, Coal Harbour, Prince Rupert and the airport at Annette Island in Alaska; and other key points for radar installations were added to the list at: Kennedy Lake, Spring Cove, Amphitrite Point, Langara Island, Marble Island, Cape St.James, Spider Island, Estevan Point, Ferrier Point, Cape Scott and Port Hardy.

As the list of construction projects grew, the number of Airmen assigned to the WCU increased. At the end of June 1942 there were 3 Officers and 194 Airmen, and

Supply barge at Langara Island. CFS Masset

by the end of the following month that number had almost doubled. Many of these Airmen thought they would get off the ground in an airplane, not on a power pole or on a boat swinging through the air in a cradle harness.

The challenges faced and surmounted by the WCU can only be imagined after looking at the geographical locations of some of the radar sites, and then examining the formidable physical features of the surrounding area. The first major challenge in some cases was getting the men and their supplies and equipment onto the site. At Marble Island the best that could be done was to anchor the scow about a mile from the huge boulders that stood offshore like jagged sentinels and float the supplies ashore on large rafts. The crew, dressed in rubber overalls, would swim to shore on the incoming tide, constantly aware of the surf pounding on the treacherous rock formations.

The Unit relied heavily on RCAF marine craft, scows and coastal boats for transporting personnel, supplies and equipment, and it was essential to have an efficient, centralized dispatching system. In August 1942 a temporary Unit Headquarters was installed on part of the Terminal Dock at the Vancouver waterfront while a permanent headquarters building, works yard, dock and warehouse were constructed at Kitsilano. The Unit was installed in its final location by the end of March the following year.

The Japanese submarine campaign had the west coast poised for an attack, and in the late summer of 1942 the RCAF made a determined push to finish construction on the remaining Flying Boat Stations and the vital coastal radar emplacements. Under the direction of 10 Officers, the 414 Airmen of the CWU were stretched to their limit. Crews worked long hours, seven days a week, regardless of the weather. With a shortage of proper tools and other supplies, and not enough bush gear to go around, they accomplished the impossible - often in extremely difficult and hazardous circumstances. The escalation in construction placed heavy demands on the production of lumber and soon it too was in short supply.

As early as 1939, when the RCAF began their construction projects, small logging and sawmill operators had been an excellent source of milled lumber. However, the war effort drained their pool of local labour and production couldn't keep pace with the RCAF's requirements.

Western Air Command took over the sawmill at Telegraph Cove near Port Hardy and the WCU operated it with a work crew of 100 General Duty Airmen transferred from Brandon, Manitoba. By July 1943 the sawmill was in full production and churning out 100,000 board feet of lumber per week.

In early October of 1942, the Unit strength stood at 17 Officers, 969 Airmen and one civilian, and in mid-October there was sufficient manpower available to begin the construction of a telephone line from Williams Lake to Bella Bella. Fifty WCU Airmen under the command of a single Sergeant strung lines across the Chilcotin Plateau during a time of year when the approaching winter would test them with minus 50 degree temperatures as they worked to complete their mammoth project.

On November 9, 1942 the No. 1 Works Construction Unit (W/T) was renamed and became No. 9 Construction and Maintenance Unit - up and down the coast the Unit was generally referred to as "Works and Bricks". S/L Dumbrille remained as the Commanding Officer, and he and his staff continued their masterful job of orchestrating what looked, at times, like a three-ring circus: tracking the projects and their various stages of completion, rotating Unit personnel on their tours of duty, and arranging transportation of crews and supplies.

The redesignation caused no delay in the telephone line project which proceeded without interruption. A crew had been assigned to construct a section of the line through the bush from Ucluelet to Port Alberni. The log-

Airport site at Sandspit before construction. CFS Masset

ical quarters for the men would have been RCAF Station Ucluelet, however, the facilities at the Station were already cramped and overcrowded. The members of No. 9 CWU resolved the situation by taking up residence in tents under the trees at the perimeter of the Station. The heavy rainfalls and hurricane-force winds that whip the British Columbia coast in any season, gave these airmen many anxious nights.

In the spring and summer of 1943 the RCAF began to concentrate on constructing land-based air stations on the west coast: RCAF Stations Comox, Port Hardy, Tofino, and Sandspit were constructed by No. 9 CMU. During July the Unit set a record for the construction of a landing strip. In two weeks of solid effort and organized team work the Unit completed the construction of a perforated steel plate runway at Masset in the Queen Charlotte Islands.

On July 11, scows loaded with material and equipment and 170 Unit personnel left Prince Rupert enroute to Masset. The Airmen quickly set up their "tent town" base and got to work. Fourteen days later the first aircraft, an RCAF Dakota DC3, touched down on the new runway bringing the Air Officer Commanding Western Air Command, Air Vice-Marshal L.F. Stevenson to extend his personal congratulations on their extraordinary effort. The Chief of the Air Staff and the Minister of National Defence also sent sincere congratulations.

Without any particular fanfare, the entries in the No. 9 CMU Diary for the period of July 11 to July 25, 1943, recorded their progress as the Unit worked steadily, day by day, to complete this enormous task.

11 July 43 - Day 1: Scows of men and material moved out from Prince Rupert

12 July - Day 2: Four drafts of men totalling 170 men and camp material unloaded at Masset; two scows of steel track loaded at Seal Cove and two others loading from railroad cars; 30 cars unloaded to scows so far.

Masset Airstrip looking northeast, June 9, 1944. CFS Masset

Sandspit airport. CFS Masset

13 July - Day 3: All mechanical equipment and radio communications established at Masset; work progressing on runway.

14 July - Day 4: Work camp set up. 200 men on strength on site; 50% of log clearing completed; grading well underway; road from Minaker farm to runway now in use; Provincial Government road repaired to take heavy traffic.

15 July - Day 5: Sea too rough to move track from Rupert; large force of men engaged in repairing existing roads and bridges to take truck traffic; 800 feet of runway graded and ready for track; 90% of runway clearing completed and under grading; 240 men on site.

16 July - Day 6: Grading operations proceeding on runway, clearing nearly completed; work on roads continuing; prefabricated building started; first scow of metal track arrived at 1300 hours.

17 July - Day 7: Runway proper graded 1200 feet and ready for steel; clearing of whole runway area including 400 feet of total width was 95% complete; Government and Minaker roads ready for traffic; in preparation for exercise, a trial batch of steel was hauled to runway for instructional purposes; floors of prefabricated buildings completed.

18 July - Day 8: 400 tons of steel are now at Masset and the balance on scows at Rupert; a shortage of marine craft is noticeable but is not serious at present; it is expected that the RCAF vessels Canso and Deerleap will be available in a few days; 3,300 sq. yards of runway completed and grading is well ahead of the track laying; walls of prefab buildings are up.

19 July - Day 9: 10,000 sq. yards of runway completed and more track in transit from Rupert; weather fair, occasional showers.

20 July - Day 10: 20,000 sq. yards of runway has been completed; three scows of track arrived from Rupert; all auxiliary work well in advance of track laying.

21 July - Day 11: 31,000 sq. yards of runway completed; last scow of steel enroute from Rupert; weather showery.

22 July - Day 12: 43,000 sq. yards of runway completed; all steel at Masset; prefab building erected; other work well in hand.

23 July - Day 13: Runway No. 5 at Masset reported serviceable for 3,600 feet of length; total of 57,000sq. yards of runway has been laid and is blocked by temporary obstructions until completed.

24 July - Day 14: First aircraft landed on Masset Runway at 1700 hours; Air Vice-Marshal L.F. Stevenson, Air Officer Commanding Western Air Command, visited site.

25 July - Day 15: Routine normal. Fifty No. 9 CMU personnel to remain at the tent camp until the Army and an RCAF Detachment arrive to begin operations.

Other teams of No. 9 CMU personnel were working simultaneously on the growing number of construction projects underway, and the pressure to complete these projects required a substantial workforce. The number of personnel on strength increased to a total of 1,484 at the end of September 1943 when No. 9 CMU took over No. 1 Landlines Maintenance Unit. Although a steady increase in strength was recorded, the month by month totals fluctuated slightly as a result of the Air Force Headquarter's policy of posting "General Duties" Airmen to the Unit, which kept the hopeful aviators "gainfully employed" while they waited for a place in the British Commonwealth Training Plan course. Some of these Airmen never saw the inside of an aircraft. They remained permanently attached to No. 9 CMU for the duration of their service with the RCAF.

During April 1944 the North West Staging Route became a focus for large numbers of experienced No. 9 CMU personnel. The Airmen and their equipment were shipped from Vancouver to Dawson Creek in British Columbia, and to Calgary and Edmonton in Alberta. In spite of an increase in transfers, the west coast Construction and Maintenance Unit was the largest CMU formed during the war. In August 1944 there were 31 Officers in charge of a record number of personnel - 2,127 Airmen and 4 civilians.

By the beginning of the new year No. 9 CMU had completed all their major construction projects. The Allied successes in Europe put a halt to any further building plans, and the west coast Unit was ordered to concentrate on routine maintenance. There were still several important projects accomplished by the Landlines Section: they laid a considerable amount of submarine cable across the North and South arms of the Fraser River; they built and installed transmitter masts for the Army and Navy; and their highly developed skills with pick and shovel were put to the test in the summer of 1945 fighting forest fires in the lower mainland.

With the cessation of war with Japan in August 1945, the number of personnel reduced rapidly, and by December there were only 380 personnel on strength. These men were mainly employed in closing the stations that they had spent the last four years building.

In September of 1946 most of the Airmen had either been posted, or they had been released. A small group of 45 No. 9 CMU personnel remained in small detachments at various locations to carry out minor maintenance jobs, and one detachment was involved with runway repairs at Patricia Bay. But by early 1947 these Airmen were also being relocated, or released. Number 9 Construction and Maintenance Unit was disbanded March 31, 1947.

Number 9 CMU left a legacy and the citizens of British Columbia's west coast were among the fortunate beneficiaries. Many of the airfields constructed by the Unit were turned over to the Ministry of Transportation and form the basis for the modern public air transportation system in place today.

1

2

3

4

5

6

7

1. *Off loading barge at Langara Island.* CFS Masset
2. *DC-3 taking off at Masset, June 1944.* Furlong Collection
3. *Steel mat runway at Masset.* CFS Masset
4. *Piece of wire mat for Masset Airstrip.* CFS Masset
5. *DC-3 (Dakota) at Masset, June 1944.* Furlong Collection
6. *Supplies at Langara boat landing.* CFS Masset
7. *Clipping mat sections together.* CFS Masset

8 & 11 Unloading steel mat. CFS Masset
9 & 10 Levelling runway area. CFS Masset
12. Vehicles loaded with mats. CFS Masset
13. Cleaning brush for aircraft parking. CFS Masset
14. Bulldozers used to level airport. CFS Masset

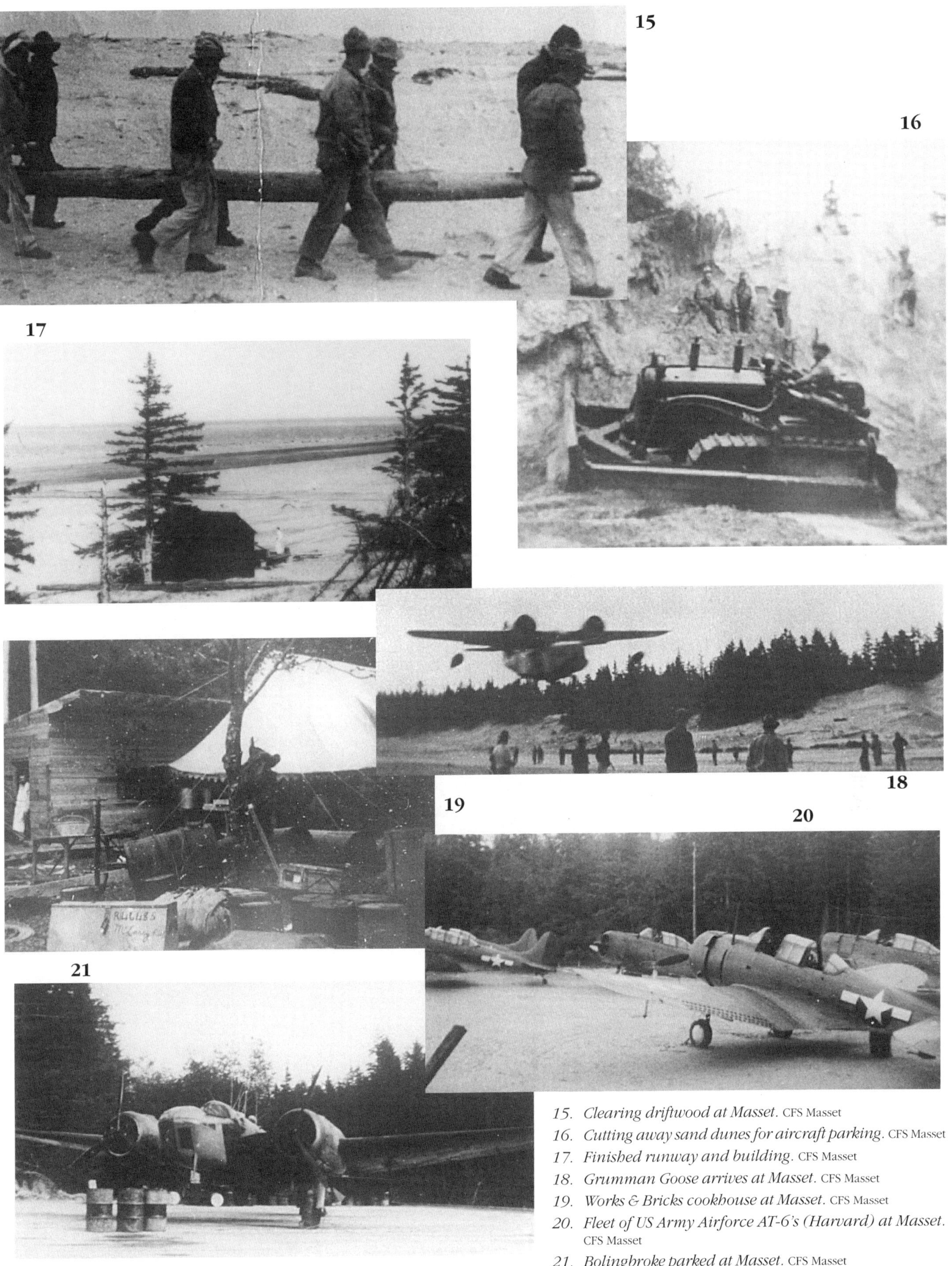

15. *Clearing driftwood at Masset.* CFS Masset
16. *Cutting away sand dunes for aircraft parking.* CFS Masset
17. *Finished runway and building.* CFS Masset
18. *Grumman Goose arrives at Masset.* CFS Masset
19. *Works & Bricks cookhouse at Masset.* CFS Masset
20. *Fleet of US Army Airforce AT-6's (Harvard) at Masset.* CFS Masset
21. *Bolingbroke parked at Masset.* CFS Masset

WESTERN AIR COMMAND
RCAF MARINE SQUADRON

SENIOR MARINE OFFICER:
S/L S.C.N. BURRIDGE

JERICHO BEACH
PATRICIA BAY
SEA ISLAND
COAL HARBOUR
UCLUELET
ALLIFORD BAY
PRINCE RUPERT
BELLA BELLA
ANNETTE ISLAND

THE RCAF MARINE SQUADRON

Western Air Command first acquired marine surface vessels for use as aircraft tenders and crash boats at RCAF Station Vancouver (Jericho Beach). The original crash boats, manufactured by Canada Power Craft of Montreal, were a 70 foot Scott-Paine design powered by two 1350 hp V-12 Packard engines. They were an impressive craft. They were considered the pride of the Marine Section, and the sight and sound of them drew admiration from all ranks. The four-inch exhaust pipes produced a deep-throated rumble that always sounded anxious to get underway. On open water the boats cruised at 35-37 knots, but under full throttle they could maintain 47 knots.

M-234 "Montagnais" near Ucluelet. Stofer Collection

Four crash boats served on the B.C. coast and were assigned Navy numbers prefixed by the letter "B" - the boats were later assigned RCAF numbers with an "M" prefix.

RCAF M-231...... Malecite (B-159)
RCAF M-232...... Takuli (B-160)
RCAF M-234...... Montagnais (B-161)
RCAF M-235...... Huron (B-162)

The boats and their crews were invaluable as a dependable, quick-response rescue team. When an aircraft was forced to ditch in the ocean the crash boat went out and towed it home; the aircrew knew they were safe as soon as they sighted the crash boat ploughing a furough toward them. During their course of service on the west coast the boats responded to many other calls for help from surface craft in distress.

On April 5, 1937 the B.C. Reconnaissance Detachment

M-159 scow seaplane tender at Bella Bella, 1937. Galbraith Collection

arrived at Bella Bella and established a "scow" seaplane tender moored in Klik-Tso-Atla Harbour. The scow, M-159, was manned by a crew of three which, by September 8, 1938, was headed by Marine Section Corporal W. Harris. The crew provided meteorological information on the area as well as acting as a refuelling base for transient aircraft.

As the pressure of war turned up the heat under Japan's despotic desires, the Airmen and the vessels of the Marine Squadrons took on an important role in preparing the defence of the west coast. The remote sites chosen by the RCAF for their Radar Stations, and most of the Flying Boat Stations, couldn't be accessed by land-based trans-

M-348 "Snow Prince" in Barkley Sound. Stofer Collection

portation. The RCAF scows and coastal boats, requisitioned tugs and fishing craft attached to the Marine Section, were the "work horses" that serviced these otherwise inaccessible locations. The small ships plied back and forth on their unscheduled runs moving construction crews, material, and heavy equipment up and down the coast of British Columbia.

Among the many vessels pressed into the service of the RCAF were: the Combat, Snow Prince, Cape Canso, Amaryllis, Dola, Jager, B.C. Star, Sekani, Midnight Sun, Deerleap, Island Mariner, General MacKenzie, Squamish, Hesquiate, and Songhees.

The RCAF Marine Section fought the west coast weather on the same level as their fellow airmen did in their Sharks and Stranraers, and also lost comrades in the unfathomable darkness of the ocean. However, unlike the Aircrews, the Marine crews could only hope that they wouldn't be confronted by the enemy. On July 23, 1943 the Marine Squadron was stunned by a tragic incident. The cause - weather, enemy action, or human error - was never satisfactorily determined.

On July 23, 1943, the M-427 B.C. Star, a 70-ton seine fishing boat in service with the RCAF, left Bella Bella enroute to the Radar Station under construction at Cape St. James in the Queen Charlotte Islands. Information regarding the movement of this type of marine vessel was classified, and all communications were coded. Lacking the necessary cypher equipment at the partially completed Station, No. 28 (RU) had no way of knowing that the supply boat was on its way. The Star and her 10 man crew were delivering a cargo of 43 tons of gravel and cement and also had six passengers on board: one RAF Airman, and five No. 9 CMU personnel assigned to the construction project.

M-427 "B.C. Star" at Bella Bella. CFB Comox Rowe Library

Ten days later a shortage of building material prompted the construction crew to radio a query about the next shipment of supplies. Only then did anyone realize that the B.C. Star was missing. An intense sea and air search covered a wide area during the next several weeks, but only three bodies were recovered, and very little wreckage was found. Evidently the Star had sunk quickly as no life boats were launched and no distress signals were sent.

Speculation and rumours circulated about the vessel being attacked by a Japanese submarine, and this information was enhanced by crewmembers aboard another RCAF Marine vessel inbound to Alliford Bay. They reported that they were listening to a Ketchikan Alaska radio station when its programme was interrupted by a strange and unidentified transmission "Star..out of bread and water..Alliford repeat message..Thank you..Good Afternoon". However, no conclusive evidence ever came to light that explained why the Star went down. Three months later, in early November, the Marine Section at RCAF Station Bella Bella experienced an "attack" which left behind ample evidence of what had transpired.

On November 5, 1943, the RCAF vessel M-449 Jager left Bella Bella in poor weather and dense fog. The crew was navigating through the narrow Gun Boat Passage when out of the gloom thundered Stranraer #915 under the command of F/O Dennis Denroche. Given the poor visibility, Denroche was flying at a very low altitude and had chosen to also "navigate" the narrow passage. There was no room for both the low flying aircraft and the Jager - something had to give way. The Jager's mast was destroyed by the Stranraers lower wing. The C.O. of 9 (BR) Squadron, S/L A.W. Mitchell, took a dim view of the incident, and F/O Denroche was court-martialled.

Like other units of the RCAF on the west coast the Marine Section saw a drastic reduction of its personnel and equipment at the end of the war.

marine craft	ser. #	call	on strength of	marine craft	ser. #	call	on strength of
Amaryllis	M-9	G3AZ	W.A.C. Marine Sqn - Vancouver	Baldpate	M-609	Y8OL	Patricia Bay
Arrow	M-537	G3AS	W.A.C. Marine Sqn - Vancouver	Blue Bill	M-1	Y8OD	Patricia Bay
Babine	M-534		W.A.C. Marine Sqn - Vancouver	Chilko	M-10	Y8OZ	Patricia Bay
Bittern	M-196	G3AH	W.A.C. Marine Sqn - Vancouver	Cormorant	M-197	Y8OB	Patricia Bay
Combat	M-350	G3AF	W.A.C. Marine Sqn - Vancouver	Curlew	M-428	Y8OF	Patricia Bay
General MacKenzie	M-639	G3AW	W.A.C. Marine Sqn - Vancouver	Fusilier	M-579	Y8OA	Patricia Bay
Gull	M-429	G3AO	W.A.C. Marine Sqn - Vancouver	Goose	M-448	Y8OK	Patricia Bay
Haida	M-206	G3AK	W.A.C. Marine Sqn - Vancouver	Kittiwake	M-290	Y8OG	Patricia Bay
Hesquiate	M-596	G3AC	W.A.C. Marine Sqn - Vancouver	Naiad	M-388	Y8OJ	Patricia Bay
Hili-Kum	M-582	G3AG	W.A.C. Marine Sqn - Vancouver	Nicola	M-11	Y8OR	Patricia Bay
Huron	M-235	G3AT	W.A.C. Marine Sqn - Vancouver	Shoveller	M-200	Y8OC	Patricia Bay
Kimquit	M-497		W.A.C. Marine Sqn - Vancouver	Coot	M-495	SL5C	Prince Rupert
Malahat	M-467		W.A.C. Marine Sqn - Vancouver	Fulmar	M-291	SL5F	Prince Rupert
Malecite	M-231	G3AQ	W.A.C. Marine Sqn - Vancouver	Atlin	M-12	3CDA	Sea Island
Montagnais	M-234	G3AB	W.A.C. Marine Sqn - Vancouver	Heron	M-157	TP3A	Ucluelet
Nimpkish	M-535	G3AI	W.A.C. Marine Sqn - Vancouver	Pelican	M-264	TP3B	Ucluelet
Naomi	M-595	G3AU	W.A.C. Marine Sqn - Vancouver	Plover	M-432	No W/T	Ucluelet
Sea Spray	M-598	G3AV	W.A.C. Marine Sqn - Vancouver	Snow Prince	M-348	G3AC	Western Air Command
Sekani	M-205	G3AA	W.A.C. Marine Sqn - Vancouver	Cape Canso	M-426	G3AL	Western Air Command
Seton	M-532	G3AN	W.A.C. Marine Sqn - Vancouver	Worshop Scow	M-159	G3AM	Western Air Command
Songhees	M-468	G3AY	W.A.C. Marine Sqn - Vancouver	Midnight Sun	M-425	G3AR	Western Air Command
Sooke	M-533	G3AD	W.A.C. Marine Sqn - Vancouver	Deerleap	M-592	G3AJ	Western Air Command
Squamish	M-469	G3AD	W.A.C. Marine Sqn - Vancouver	B.C. Star	M-427		Western Air Command
Stuart	M-531	G3AJ	W.A.C. Marine Sqn - Vancouver	Reel Fisher	M-530	G3AD	Western Air Command
Takuli	M-232	G3AX	W.A.C. Marine Sqn - Vancouver	Walter "M"	M-540	G3AY	Western Air Command
Willet	M-518	G3AP	W.A.C. Marine Sqn - Vancouver	Skeena Maid	M-536	G3AN	Western Air Command
Gadwell	M-199	PG8G	Alliford Bay	Sea-Mew	M-591	G3AP	Western Air Command
Loon	M-265	PG8L	Alliford Bay	Atlin	M-12	Y8OP	Patricia Bay
Puffin	M-430	PG8D	Alliford Bay	Teal	M-266	GH3B	Bella Bella
Brant	M-267	5NPA	Bella Bella	Jager	M-449	GH3D	Bella Bella
Scoter	M-172	5NPD	Bella Bella	Brant	M-267	SL5B	Prince Rupert
Snipe	M-433	5NPS	Bella Bella	Gull	M-429	No W/T	No. 9 C.M.U. , Vancouver
Jager	M-449	9QSA	Boundary Bay	Crash Tender (Bittern)	M-196	P19A	No. 3 R.D., Vancouver
Crebe	M-198	3CLB	Coal Harbour	Scoter	M-172	A7U	Annette Island
Whistler	M-292	3CLA	Coal Harbour				
Petrel	M-431	3CLC	Coal Harbour				

1. *M-449 "Jager" at Bella Bella before its mast was shortened by Stranraer #915.* Maude Collection
2. *M-235 "Huron" at Telegraph Cove.* CFB Comox Rowe Library
3. *M-291 "Fulmar" designed for towing. Baldwin Hydrafoil for bombing practice.* Maude Collection
4. *The Marine Section at Alliford Bay.* CFS Masset
5. *M-205 "Sekani" at Alliford Bay.* CFS Masset

7

8

10

11

6. *M-350 "Combat" in Alberni Inlet.* Stofer Collection
7. *B-160 (M-232) "Takuli" near Ucluelet.* Crombie Collection
8. *Crew of M-159 at Bella Bella, 1939.* Galbraith Collection
9. *M-232 "Takuli" heading for Marble Island.* CFS Masset
10. *Radio room on M-159.* Galbraith Collection
11. *Airmen catch a ride with Marine Section at Bella Bella.* McPhee Collection

chapter six

THE LONELY VIGILANCE

Air Craft Detection Corps

Radio Detachments

Number 1 Coast Watch Unit

WATCH AND WARN

AIRCRAFT DETECTION CORPS

RCAF

AIRCRAFT DETECTION CORPS:

Volunteers from isolated settlements, logging and fishing camps

ESTABLISHED MAY 1940

AIRCRAFT DETECTION CORPS

Although the wartime narrative of Jericho Beach concentrates on the activity at the coastal flying boat stations, there were groups of dedicated civilians who were also responsible to Air Command. The (ADC) Aircraft Detection Corps, volunteers who operated west of the 100th meridian in Manitoba were under the authority of Western Air Command. In British Columbia, the vital contribution made by the ADC members was an important element in the security of the west coast of North America. Within this context, their story deserves to be told.

The Canadian Aircraft Detection Corps was organized in May 1940. Throughout Canada, civilian volunteers took training courses in aircraft detection. They became skilled at recognizing and identifying both Allied and enemy aircraft, and they were introduced to the various communication methods that best suited the particular area they were serving in. The civilian volunteers provided a valuable, if rudimentary, early warning system at a time when radar was not fully developed. By the end of 1943 the Aircraft Detection Corps had grown to a peak enrollment of 30,000 members across the country.

On the west coast, long stretches of uninhabited coastline on the Queen Charlette Islands were particularly vulnerable. A great many sheltered, deep-water bays and inlets existed that could serve as hidden staging areas for the Japanese naval forces. Civilians living in some of these remote areas organized an Aircraft Detection Corps and appointed their own Regional Directors and Chief Observers. Enthusiastic, patriotic volunteers kept a vigilant duty watch to ensure that no aircraft passed their post unreported. From Langara Island off the northern tip of Graham Island, to Kunghit Island off the southern tip of Moresby Island, housewives, loggers, lighthouse keepers, farmers and fishermen went about their daily business with a pair of high-powered binoculars slung around their neck.

Nevertheless, the aircraft detection system was not without its problems, particularly on the west coast of British Columbia. The Deputy Chief of Air Staff, Air Vice Marshal G.O. Johnson, sent a frustrated tirade to Air Force Headquarters in Ottawa. His memorandum also offered some food for thought:

> The telephone system is inadequate and is more of an aggravation than a help. The early warning RDF chain is not yet in being and will not be ready until mid-summer. The Aircraft Detection Corps, although it is in operation, is not effective because it is dependent upon inadequate civil communication facilities, and upon the half-hearted, voluntary and unpaid efforts of civilian observers in isolated locations.
>
> The service operates - but not at the hours when it is most needed. In order that it be made effective, it will be necessary to post RCAF personnel at the most isolated points on the west side of the coastal islands to augment the civilian observers. It will be the job of those RCAF personnel to improve communications.
>
> In a specific community a solitary airman can take the early morning watch and train volunteers for the day watches. Where there is no community, for example on the west side of the Queen Charlotte Islands, it will be necessary to locate detachments of 4 airmen.

Technology progressed, and (RDF) Radar Direction Finding units were established in the most isolated and defenceless areas along the west coast, and on the coastal islands. The civilian volunteers and their ever-ready binoculars were gradually replaced by the more sophisticated radar system. On November 15, 1944, the RCAF Chief of Air Staff ordered the Aircraft Detection organization disbanded.

RADIO DETACHMENTS:

A Line of Radio Defence on the West Coast of Canada

RADIO UNITS:

No. 7 Radio Detachment: *Patricia Bay*

No. 8 Radio Detachment: *Sea Island*

No. 9 Radio Detachment: *Spider Island*

No. 10 Radio Detachment: *Cape Scott*

No. 11 Radio Detachment: *Ferrer Point*

No. 13 Radio Detachment: *Amphitrite Point*

No. 26 Radio Detachment: *Langara Island*

No. 27 Radio Detachment: *Marble Island*

No. 28 Radio Detachment: *Cape St James*

No. 33 Radio Detachment: *Tofino*

ESTABLISHED JULY 23rd, 1942

RADIO DETACHMENTS

Shortly before Japan carried out the aggressive attack on Pearl Harbor that drew the Americans into war, the United States government approached the Canadian government with a proposal to use electronic aeroplane detectors (radar) to extend the umbrella of protection north along the west coast of British Columbia. The cooperative agreement was based on Canada providing base sites along the west coast of the province, constructing the buildings, and furnishing all the necessary materials and supplies to operate each base. The Americans would then provide the detection equipment and send trained personnel to instruct the Canadian operators. An agreement of this nature would complete the chain of radio defence already in place on the west coast of the United States and on the coast of Alaska.

Prime Minister MacKenzie King acknowledged that the adoption of an "early-warning" system was necessary if Canada hoped to protect the vast length of her Pacific coastline. The Canadian Section of the Permanent Joint Board On Defence followed the Prime Minister's lead and ruled that the United States War Department's request to install the aeroplane detectors be approved. The Board issued a comprehensive outline of their conditions:

- That the United States detachments (approximately 50 of all ranks for each detector) are to be under the command of Air Officer Commanding, Western Air Command;
- That Canadian technical personnel be attached for the purpose of instruction to each United States detachment: numbers, and times to be decided jointly by the Air Officer Commanding Western Air Command and the officers commanding each United States Detachment;
- That the RCAF will take over the handling of the detectors as soon as the Canadian personnel are adequately trained, and the Air Officer Commanding Western Air Command is prepared to assume the responsibility;
- That RCAF Service Corps will provide subsistence for United States personnel on the usual accounting basis;
- That Canada shall provide the accommodation required in accordance with arrangements made between the Air Officer Commanding Western Air Command and the General Commanding Second Air Force United States Army. Such accommodation to be provided from Canadian or United States sources, in whichever may produce the quickest results, but with ownership remaining in Canada.

No 10 Radio Unit at Cape Scott, January 28, 1945. CFS Masset

Once the agreement had been ratified, two sites were initially chosen at a projected cost of $125,000.00 for each detector station: one at the northern tip of Vancouver Island at Cape Scott, and the second near Mount Arrowsmith on the Nanaimo-Alberni road. It was obvious from the start of this plan that more than two detector stations were needed. The RCAF ordered an investigation of other possible sites and prepared to expand the number of detachments.

Group Captain A.H. Hull ordered his staff at Western Air Command in Victoria to undertake an investigation of radar detection sites in the Queen Charlotte Islands. At the Department of National Defence for Air in Ottawa, Wing Commander D.G. Williams reviewed the Group Captain's recommendations submitted on June 18, 1942:

1. A party consisting of S/L G.M. Fawcett, F/L R.D. Hansen, and F/O Robinson, of the Works & Buildings Branch attached to the Works Construction Unit, have made a thorough investigation of the (Queen Charlotte Island) sites. The purpose of the investigation was to ensure that the sites were suitable for the equipment which is to be installed and also to ensure that the necessary access and camp construction was feasible from the point of view of Works and Buildings.

2. Langara Island: the site seems to be entirely satisfactory from the technical point of view. The station, when installed, will see well into Dixon Entrance and straight down the West Coast of Graham Island. The camp may be located in a natural hollow close to the operations site so that no difficulties regarding high voltage power transmission will be encountered. The only exceptions to this submission is the building site, which, it is felt, would be desirable to change in order that high voltage power transmission would not be required. In view of the urgency it is felt now that the whole job should be undertaken by the Number 1 Works Construction Unit, who are ready to commence work. Urgently required from Ottawa is the authority to proceed.

3. Buck Point: the site which was originally intended for a station, at about the entrance to the Skidegate Channel, appears to be unsatisfactory because of the difficulty in building roads. The only harbour suitable for serving such a station is Armentieres Channel, between Chaatl Island and Moresby Island. This, however, is 8 miles airline from the proposed site and, moreover, the land is so steep that it is considered that any road to the site would be at least 12 miles long, and a minimum of 3 large trestles would need to be constructed. It is the opinion of the Works and Building representative that such a road would cost a minimum of $30,000.00 per mile and take 6 to 8 months to build. No other access is available due to the steepness of the land and the heavy swell which rolls in from the Pacific continuously. It is therfore intended to put this station on Marble Island, which lies about 3 or 4 miles off the entrance to Skidegate Channel. This site will be quite good from a technical point of view and the station, which will be at a height of about 425 feet, will have a good view up and down the coast. Before any work can proceed, two small boat landings, suitable for beaching a small scow and small boat, must be contructed. These must also be provided with some sort of breakwater to keep the ordinary swell out. If these two landings are provided, it is considered that access to the island could be available at all times, except during the most severe storms in the winter - which are said to last for 2 or 3 days at a time. When landings have been provided, an aerial tramway would have to be erected in order to get to the actual site, which is on top of a knoll. The knoll descends on all sides in the landward direction, at a gradual slope to a cliff approximately 100 feet high. The aerial tramway will have to ascend this cliff and continue up the gradual slope to the site. An alternative approach would be to build a road from the landing around to the seaward side, and ascend the gradual slope which exists on that side. It is considered by the Works and Building representative that the aerial tramway would be cheaper. No water exists on the island and it would therefore have to be distilled by means of a water distilling apparatus which could be obtained local-

No. 28 Radio Unit and lighthouse, Cape St. James, 1943. CFS Masset

ly. All these serious disadvantages are considered to be easier to overcome than the larger disadvantage attached to Buck Point. Moreover the Works and Construction Unit consider this station (Buck Point) to be beyond their scope and if it is decided to go ahead, it will have to be undertaken by a contractor.

Sea conditions at Langara Island. CFS Masset

4. Cape St James: located at the southern end of the Island appears to be one of the easiest sites, in that there is no clearing to be done and certain works already exist which could be made use of. The site itself is technically the worst of the three because it is a cliff-edge site and consequently will have gaps in the vertical polar diagram. The height however is about 350 feet and so the gaps should be quite small. If the station were moved back onto Kunghit Island, though, there would be a blind spot about 30 degrees wide in the middle of the sweep. It is considered that such a blind spot would be a very serious drawback and in the present state it could not be supported. The lighthouse on the island is only manned by one keeper and is not considered by the Department of Transport to be a very important light - prior to the war consideration was being given to doing away with it. As it is, the light is useless for a large part of the time because it is in the clouds and there is no fog horn provided. After discussion with the Department of Transport Agent at Prince Rupert, it was concluded that they would accept a proposal for either allowing the Service to take over the light, or to put in an unwatched light lower down on another island. This would leave the lightkeeper's house for the Service, and the aerials could go on the present site of the lighthouse. The existing boat landing and aerial tramway would have to be improved but this would not be too expensive. Also, no water exists on this island and would have to be distilled. Moreover it is recommended that this station be heated by either coal or oil since wood will be scarce. If the Department of Transport is not open to either of these suggestions there is still room to put the aerials, operations house, and power house on the top of the island. The aerials would have to go in front of the light but they would not interfere with the light, exept at large angles of depression. The remainder of the camp would go down beside the boat landing where a certain amount of shelter is to be had.

5. It is strongly recommended that, with the exception of Marble Island, these stations be undertaken by the Works Construction Unit under S/L Aitkens. They are already doing a very good job in the fastest possible time.

In July 1942, Air Command Headquarters issued an order which established ten (RU) Radar Detection Units in strategic location on the coast of British Columbia: No. 9 RU, Spider Island; No. 10 RU, Cape Scott; No. 11 RU, Ferrer Point; No. 33 RU, Tofino; No. 13 RU, Amphitrite Point. Two radio detachments were stationed closer to the major centres of Victoria and Vancouver: No. 7 RU, Patricia Bay, and No. 8 RU, Sea Island. The sites chosen in the Queen Charlotte Islands were based on Group Captain Hull's report: No. 26 RU, Langara Island; No. 27 RU, Marble Island; and No. 28 RU, Cape St.James. The Radar Units were manned by up to 70 RCAF personnel under the command of an officer of Flight Lieutenant rank.

With the exception of Patricia Bay and Sea Island, the radar units were positioned on sites which commanded an unobstructed sweep of the open ocean. RCAF Radio Detachments found themselves perched on wind swept pinnacles of bare rock on the edge of the wild and often angry Pacific Ocean. High wind, icy rain, dense fog, and the continual bombardment of pounding waves heightened the challenge of maintaining communication with the outside world.

No one visited the coastal radar units unless they had a good reason. But if necessity brought anyone to these remote stations, it only took one trip in to appreciate the difficulty and the danger that detachment personnel dealt with every day. The arrival of the RCAF supply boat was always the highlight of the day, although unloading it was one of the greatest challenges of life on the rocky outposts. Even in calm sea conditions, transferring the supplies from the boat to the shore was a hazardous job. But the whims and moods of Mother Nature had a habit of changing the schedule, and time after time personnel existed on emergency rations because the supply boat could not reach them.

Airman Cy Luce, a clerk accountant at RCAF Coal Harbour, used to go in to Cape Scott on the supply boat to deliver the pay envelopes to No. 10 Radio Detachment:

> *"There were 50 guys there. They would come out on the beach in January and yell out 'Did you bring any beer?'. I generally brought back all the money I had taken up - they didn't want it - there was nowhere to spend it.*
>
> *One guy was so excited about getting leave that on the way out he slipped, and fell into the water. He was lucky we could fish him out of the water - then he had to strip and dry out in the hold of our converted Japanese fish boat."*

Luce philosophically regarded the trip as a "work diversion"; the boat often ended up waiting out the weather in Bull Harbour on Hope Island, and while at sea there was the added bonus of extra rations.

Many of the coastal supply boats were requisitioned vessels operated by the Marine Section of the RCAF. One of these vessels, the 70 ton seiner M 427, B.C. Star, disappeared and no official explanation was ever recorded. On July 23, 1943, the B.C. Star, manned by 10 RCAF crewmen and carrying six passengers, left RCAF Station Bella Bella enroute to No. 28 RU, Cape St James, with a second port of call at Rose Harbour on Kunghit Island. If the weather cooperated, the Star would be back in Bella Bella within the week.

By August 3rd, Number 28 RU was running short of construction material and supplies. The Radio Operator contacted RCAF Station Bella Bella and inquired about the arrival of the next scheduled supply boat. This was the first indication that the Star was in trouble. For security reasons, arrivals and departures of the Star were not broadcast, and the ship maintained strict radio silence. With no SOS to describe the search boundaries, there was a large area to be covered. In the intense and lengthy search, little trace of wreckage was found, or any conclusive evidence to explain the tragic loss of the ship.

The usual, unvaried routine at No. 11 RU, Ferrer Point, on Nootka Island, was disrupted on the evening of December 18, 1943. Security guards on duty at the docking area watched in disbelief as a barrage of gunfire strafed the surface of the water a short distance from shore. Western Air Command was immediately notified and aircraft were dispatched from both Coal Harbour and Tofino to intercept the attackers. A thorough sweep of the area produced no evidence of a Japanese submarine, and the aircraft returned to their stations. It was discovered later that the whole disturbance was caused by a passing Allied freighter. The freighter's Captain, assuming they were out in the middle of nowhere, ordered his crew to do a little gunnery practice. The incident also gave the startled Airmen at the Radar Station some practice in responding to a general alarm. Fortunately no damage was done.

In the Queen Charlotte Islands, RCAF Station Alliford Bay was the life-line for the three RU Detachments in the area. The Station's supply boat brought rations, mail, and medical assistance, and RU personnel lucky enough to get leave boarded the boat and travelled to Alliford Bay on the first leg of their journey. The tie between the Flying Boat Station and the Radar Units was mutually beneficial. Anti-submarine patrols were limited to flying in daylight hours, and bad weather often interfered with the regular patrol schedule. These factors created long periods of time when it was conceivable that the enemy task force could approach the coast undetected and establish themselves in a sheltered inlet. Alert to large, moving objects approaching the coast, the Radar Detatchments held a vital front-line position as coastal watchdogs.

Number 26 Radio Detachment at Langara Island was well situated adjacent to the extreme northwesterly tip of the Charlottes. The detachment had an excellent view to the south along the Pacific coast to Graham Island, as well as an unobstructed view of Dixon Entrance, Canada's border with Alaska. However, the small island received a constant lashing from the open sea. Swells, sometimes eight to ten feet high, exploded against the cliffs and boiled around the jagged fingers of rock that skirted the small harbour used as a landing area - a spectacular sight if you were not trying to unload a supply boat. The men got tired of watching the precious mail packet and their supplies plummet to the bottom of the sea. They shared a common determination with other Airmen living in rugged isolation - "where there's a will there's a way" - and devised an ingenious system of block and tackle connected to an overhead cable, which allowed them to lift supplies off the boat and haul them up the slope to high ground.

At 02:35 hours on August 2, 1943, two security guards on patrol at the Langara Island dock sighted a long, black oval shape about 400 yards offshore. At exactly the same time the Radio Section reported a high-pitched AC hum that jammed their service. A steady tone, estimated to be about 200 cycles on the R/T channel; and spotted directly on 3615 Kc/s, continued from 05:00 to 05:45 hours. A reasonable explanation seemed to be that a Japanese submarine was attempting to prevent the Radio Section from sending out an alarm.

The whole camp was awakened and put on full alert. The few armaments in the Station stores were handed out and patrols maintained a constant watch for several hours. Demolition charges were set in strategic locations in case the enemy felt like sending a mountain-climbing expedition ashore to invade the station.

RCAF No 27 Radio Unit Marble Island, July 31, 1944. CFS Masset

By 07:35 Canso aircraft were on hand from Alliford Bay, and eight depth charges were dropped. Two Navy patrol boats, one Canadian and one American, arrived later in the day to carry out an anti-submarine sweep of the area. No trace of the Japanese submarine was found. The excitement gradually died down and the detachment returned to its ordinary routine - but not for long.

On August 6, at 23:30 hours, another object was sighted on the surface about 300 yards offshore. It remained on the surface for a considerable time and was clearly identified as a Japanese submarine. The general alarm signal was given and patrols were quickly organized, but the Japanese appeared to be uninterested in anything happening on shore. Following these two enemy provocations, the defence capabilities on the Island were strengthened, and anti-submarine patrols, by both marine vessels and aircraft, were intensified.

The radar shack at Number 27 Radar Unit on Marble Island, anchored to a rocky knoll at an elevation of 425 feet, had an unobstructed view up and down the coast. The terrain around the site sloped down to cliffs that dropped 100 feet to the sea. During the construction of the station an aerial tramway was installed which laboured up the cliff and followed the incline to the radar shack at the top of the site. Beneath the shack, the barracks and other wood-frame buildings were constructed wherever there was a platform of level ground. In order to reach their "office", the on-duty Radio Operators, regardless of the weather, climbed rough stairs that were gouged out of the bush-covered rock.

The Detachment kept in touch with the RCAF Station at Alliford Bay and looked forward to the arrival of the Station's supply boat. It was necessary to bring the supply boat to a point some distance offshore where it was met by a rubber boat, or a dory, from the RU. Every once in a while the small boat capsized forcing the occupants to swim to shore. In one incident, Corporal Edgar A. Trethewet dove into the sea and fought the crashing waves in a courageous bid to save a fellow Airman from drowning.

It was a well-known fact that living conditions at the Marble Island Unit were much worse than they were at either Langara or Cape St. James. The Airmen at Alliford Bay easily recognized "the look" of fellows coming in from a tour of duty on Marble Island - they were really "bushed" and had a glassy stare in their eyes. Number 28 RU at Cape St. James also maintained contact with Alliford Bay.

In 1944, William Fawcett Hill, an operations officer at RCAF Station Coal Harbour, applied for a position as Personnel Counsellor at RCAF Station Alliford Bay. Upon his arrival he discovered that he was required to immediately volunteer for a week's posting to No. 28 RU on St James Island. A requisitioned whaling boat transported him to the radar site at the southern end of the island, and, since there was no dock, he stood on the deck of the whaling boat and was hoisted about 50 feet over to an elevated platform on shore. Later, someone kindly told him that the previous Personnel Counsellor lost his hold on the hoisting-rope and plunged into the surf. Unfortunately, he had drowned.

The Radar Unit diarist praised the Airmen of the Radio Detachments for their lonely vigilance in the defence of our country:

> *"The men serving on these units can be justly proud of the part they played in the defence of their country. For reasons of security their work was not mentioned, nor were they mentioned when honours and awards were being distributed. But they did not fail when faced with difficulities, dangers, isolation and monotony."*

NUMBER 1 COAST WATCH UNIT

ESTABLISHED AT:

BARRY HARBOUR

FREDERICK ISLAND

HIPPA ISLAND

MARBLE ISLAND

BIG BAY

HIBBEN ISLAND

KINDAKUN POINT

TASU HARBOUR

APRIL 23rd, 1942

NUMBER 1 COAST WATCH UNIT

On February 27, 1942, Air Vice-Marshal L.F. Stevenson, in a letter to Air Force Headquarters in Ottawa, outlined a plan to temporarily fill in the gaps in the defence organization on the west coast of the Queen Charlotte Islands. He proposed a Coast Watch Unit of ten small detachments which would act as an "early-warning system" until radar stations could be provided in sufficient numbers to give full coverage.

Coast watcher cabin, Frederick Island. CFS Masset

Air Force Headquarters received Stevenson's suggestions favourably and approval was given on April 23, 1942, which established Number 1 Coast Watch Unit with detachments at: Barry Harbour, Big Bay (now called Gougaia Bay), Frederick Island, Hibben Island, Hippa Island, Kindakun Point, Marble Island, and Tasu Harbour. The government lighthouses at Cape St. James and Langara Islands completed the coverage of the most vulnerable areas of the British Columbia coast.

RCAF Station Alliford Bay was the closest supply base, and a Flight Sergeant at the Station coordinated the re-supply and other requirements of the detachments. They were issued an outboard motor boat, camping gear, and all the necessary equipment to operate a bush-camp. A two-way radio set allowed them to communicate with the Station at Alliford Bay, and all reports went directly to the Commanding Officer, who had over-all control of No. 1 Coast Watch Unit.

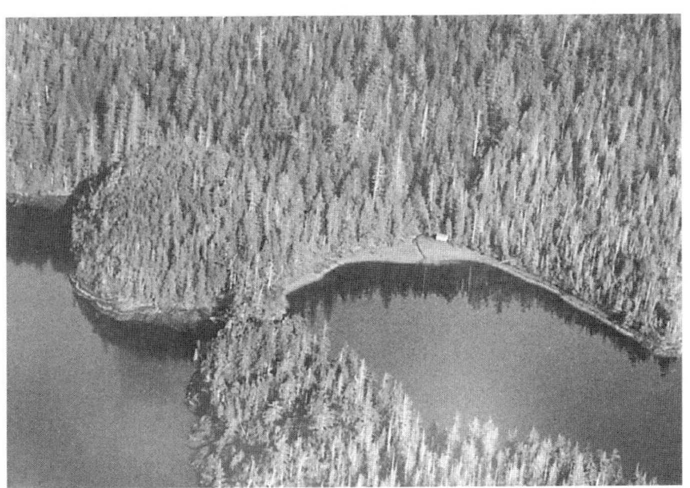

Coast watcher cabin, Tasu Sound, April 1942. CFS Masset

The detachments set up their camps on high ground at the chosen vantage points along the coast. The search for personnel to carry out the coast watch project centered on Airmen with previous bush experience, who were familiar with survival methods and first aid. The men would need to rely on each other and work as a team as they faced the extremes of climate in the Queen Charlottes. Four Airmen manned each camp: one competent woodsman, two radio operators, and one general duties Airman to maintain the quarters at the camp and do the cooking.

These detachments were an unqualified success and provided the anticipated "gap coverage" for a year and a half until the Radar Units on the Queen Charlotte Islands were fully operational. By November 22, 1943, Western Air Command began to disband No. 1 Coast Watch Unit. All detachments were disbanded by December 19, 1943.

Life at the coast watch camps was generally uneventful, except for the challenges provided by the atrocious weather and lack of any facilities. However, one returning airman, when questioned about his remote duty in the bush, replied:

"We spent the whole wartime there; never saw a thing to report; had a fine camping holiday - with pay!"

1

2

3

4

5

6

1. *Langara lighthouse, August, 1942.* CFS Masset
2. *Radar Site, Marble Island, August, 1942.* CFS Masset
3. *No 26 Radio Unit Langara Island, under construction.* CFS Masset
4. *Base camp No 27 Radio Unit (centre) Marble Island.* CFS Masset
5. *No 28 Radio Unit Cape St. James, under construction.* CFS Masset
6. *Marble Island, May, 1942.* CFS Masset

The Observer
RCAF
AIRCRAFT DETECTION CORPS
SUPERMARINE STRANRAER
1943
Vol. 1 No. 9
SEPTEMBER 1943

NO. 1 COAST WATCH UNIT
ROYAL CANADIAN AIR FORCE
1942-1943
Prince Rupert
Langara Island
DIXON ENTRANCE
Masset
Frederick Island
HECATE STRAIT
Porcher Island
Graham
Island
Hippa Island
Banks Island
QUEEN
CHARLOTTE
ISLANDS
Kindakun Pt.
Marble Island
Alliford Bay
Hibben Island
Detachment sites
Seaplane bases
Tasoo Harbour
PACIFIC OCEAN
Barry Harbour
Big Bay
N
0 10 20 30 mi
0 10 20 30 40 50 km
Cape St. James

Courtesy of DND - Directorate of History

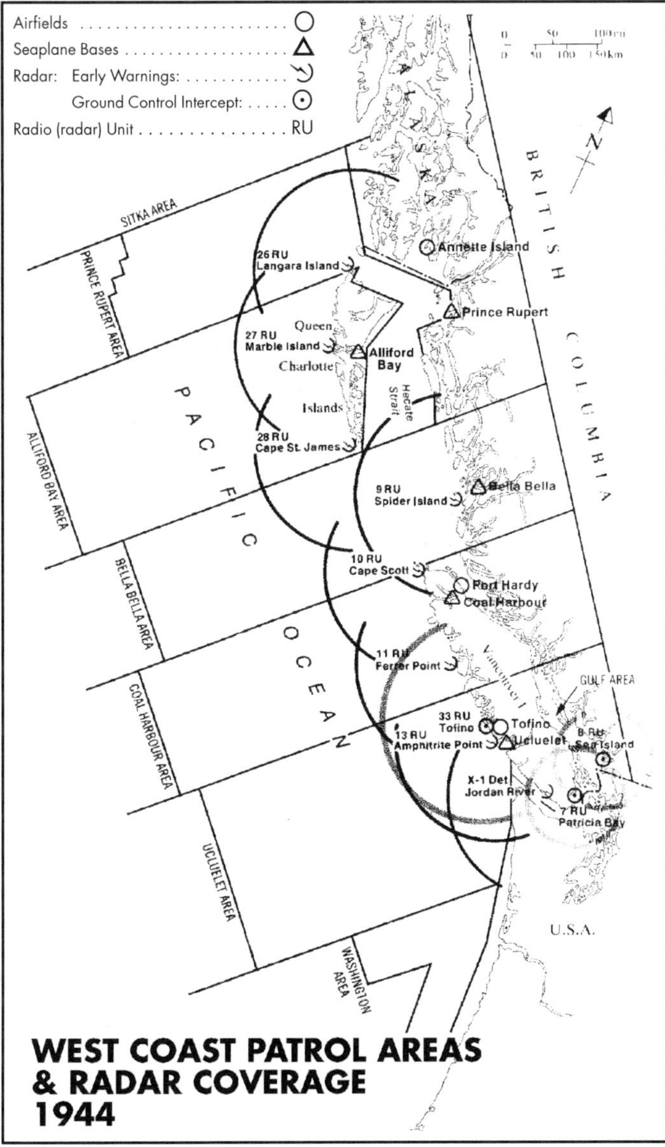
Airfields
Seaplane Bases
Radar: Early Warnings:
Ground Control Intercept:
Radio (radar) Unit . . . RU
ALASKA
BRITISH COLUMBIA
SITKA AREA
PRINCE RUPERT AREA
26 RU
Langara Island
Annette Island
Prince Rupert
27 RU
Marble Island
Alliford Bay
Queen
Charlotte
Islands
Hecate Strait
28 RU
Cape St. James
ALLIFORD BAY AREA
PACIFIC
9 RU
Spider Island
Bella Bella
10 RU
Cape Scott
Port Hardy
Coal Harbour
BELLA BELLA AREA
OCEAN
11 RU
Ferrer Point
GULF AREA
COAL HARBOUR AREA
33 RU
Tofino
13 RU
Amphitrite Point
Ucluelet
Sea Island
X-1 Det
Jordan River
7 RU
Patricia Bay
UCLUELET AREA
U.S.A.
WASHINGTON AREA
WEST COAST PATROL AREAS
& RADAR COVERAGE
1944

Courtesy of DND - Directorate of History

The Observer
RCAF
AIRCRAFT DETECTION CORPS
CONSOLIDATED CATALINA
Vol. 1 No. 10
OCTOBER
1943

THE PACIFIC ENEMY

chapter seven

THE PACIFIC ENEMY

The depression of late 1920 and early 1930 held the world in a tight-fisted grip that had governments of all nations desperately seeking ways to rebuild their countries' economies. The guidelines of democracy held fast against rising social unrest in the western world, but the economic and civil turmoil in Japan created an opportunity for the military to increase its control. As high-ranking officers in the Japanese Military became an overpowering force, the traditional positions of democratic order, Emperor, Prime Minister and Cabinet, were reduced to supporting roles.

Japan had reached a turning point. Feudalism was giving way to industrialism, and raw materials were needed to fuel the country's growing industrial strength. The military leaders viewed the subjugation of their Asian neighbours as the only solution to Japan's economic struggle. In 1931 Japan invaded and occupied Manchuria, intent on utilizing that country's resources and its people to feed Japan's rapidly expanding industrialization. The leaders of the Imperial forces agreed that Japan's strength depended on access to unlimited natural resources; and only through the domination of all other Asian countries could that power be assured.

Admiral Isoroku Yamamoto. Imperial Japanese Navy Photo

Although the leaders of the military were united in their conviction that Japan must wage war, there were a few moderates in the military hierarchy who did not approve of the plan to strike against the United States - some even harboured doubt regarding the outcome of such a move. These men held a more rational view of the Americans, and they had a higher degree of respect for the United States' military prowess. The Commander of the Combined Fleet, Admiral Isoroku Yamamoto, was one of these moderates.

One of Japan's most able military strategists, the Admiral had been in the Japanese naval service for 37 years, and his background and training gave him a unique insight into his country's capability to wage war with the western world. Ten years of his distinguished career had been spent abroad, and for much of that time he was in the United States. He enrolled in English language studies at Harvard University and travelled extensively throughout North America. He participated in the 1921-1922 Washington Naval Armament Limitations Treaty negotiations and the 1930 London Naval Conference.

Admiral Yamamoto opposed Japan's military extremists. His determination to speak his mind exposed him to threats of assassination, however, Yamamoto saw that war was becoming a distinct possibility and continued his attempts to convince his military colleagues of the folly of a clash with the United States. The Admiral met with Japan's Prime Minister Fumimaro Konoye on September 12, 1941. Konoye was also gravely concerned about initiating a war and asked Yamamoto about the probability of Japan's success. The Admiral replied that if Japan entered a conflict with the United States by attacking their

General Hideki Tojo, Japan's War Minister and later Prime Minister. Official Japanese Photo

Pacific fleet, he could promise *"to give them hell for a year or a year and a half"*, but after that time he could guarantee nothing.

Japan had been in a state of war since the invasion of China in 1937, and over the past four years the military had gained considerable power over the nation. Military leaders, aided by greedy industrialists, now dominated the country's ruling cabinet. On October 12, 1941, during a sitting of Cabinet, Prime Minister Konoye tried to reason with the War Minister, General Hideki Tojo. Tojo was bent on going to war to resolve the problems of the country and refused to negotiate further on the subject. In protest the Prime Minister resigned, after which General Tojo was recommended for the position, and Emperor Hirohito had no choice but to ratify the appointment.

Immediately the order was issued to Admiral Yamamoto to complete his plan to destroy the United States Pacific Fleet. At the same time Japanese military strategists began to plan the seizure of the Dutch East Indies, Indochina, Malaya, Thailand, and Burma, as well as the occupation of the Philippines. Success in these bold moves would constitute the basis of Japan's projected empire - the Greater East Asia Co-Prosperity Sphere.

Vice-Admiral Chuichi Nagumo. Imperial Japanese Navy Photo

The Japanese Army and Navy were in a state of readiness for war at the beginning of December 1941. In the early months of 1941, Admiral Yamamoto had already drawn up his plan to attack the unsuspecting United States Pacific Fleet at Pearl Harbor, and, while Prime Minister Tojo edged his country toward war, Yamamoto trained his selected men and established the six large carriers of his task force at Hitokappu Island in the southern Kurile Islands.

On the 27th of November Admiral Yamamoto's orders instructed him to depart with his task force for the Hawaiian Islands. At 06:00 hours on the morning of December 7, 1941, from a point 200 miles north of Oahu Island, Yamamoto launched his attack in two waves of 360 aircraft. When the last Japanese aircraft had returned to its carrier the United States had suffered the loss or destruction of 18 capital ships, 188 aircraft and 3,581 men had become the first American casualties of World War II.

Americans reacted swiftly in anger - an anger that was all the more deadly because it was laced with fear. That the Japanese had dared to conceive and then successfully carry out such ruthless destruction at Pearl Harbor shook North America deeply. Secure in their supremacy and severely overconfident, the Japanese Supreme War Council called upon Admiral Yamamoto to present a naval plan for the complete annihilation of the entire United States Pacific Fleet.

General Tojo had tasted victory. For the next six months he oversaw a phenomenal record of conquests: Japanese forces attacked Guam, Indochina, and Thailand; they sank the Royal Navy's Capital Ships, Prince of Wales and Repulse - the only major Allied warships in south east Asia; and by the end of the year Japan occupied Hong Kong and Wake Island followed by Manila, Singapore, and Malaya. In February 1942, Japan sank 10 Allied ships. In March, Burma and Java fell under Tojo's boot, and, still advancing, the Japanese took part of New Guinea and were almost within sight of Australia.

On April 16, 1942, the Imperial Headquarters issued the Midway-Aleutian Directive which included the occupation of New Guinea and Midway, as well as the destruction of the Pacific Fleet and the seizure of the western Aleutian Islands. By this time the Americans had broken the Japanese Naval Codes. Commander of the Pacific Command, Admiral Chester Nimitz, dispatched the United States Carriers, Lexington and Yorktown, to confront the Japanese invasion force. In the battle of the Coral Sea, the Japanese Navy task force sank the Lexington and severely damaged the Yorktown.

Still fully aware of the truth of his promise to former Prime Minister Konoye, Admiral Yamamoto realized the importance of completing his conquest while the Japanese fleet was still master of the Pacific. Japan must then quickly sue for peace with the Americans before America could rebuild her naval might. Yamamoto now directed the main body of the Japanese fleet - his Carrier Striking Force under the command of Admiral Nagumo - toward Midway for a projected mass attack on June 4, 1942. After the destruction of American defences at Midway, the Japanese could establish their invasion forces on the island, and Yamamoto's mission to totally annihilate the Pacific Fleet would be accomplished.

Rear Admiral Kakuji Kakuta, Commander of 2nd Fleet. Imperial Japanese Navy Photo

Meanwhile Vice-Admiral Moshiro Hosogaya, who had been given the responsibility of directing the Northern Force, dispatched a smaller task force, under the command of Rear Admiral Kakuta, into the North Pacific. The Japanese carriers Ryujo and Junyo between them carried 82 aircraft, and were accompanied by two heavy cruisers, a tanker and three destroyers. Their objective was to launch an air attack against the United States Naval Operation Base at Dutch Harbor on Unalaska Island in the Aleutian Chain. At the same time an invasion force headed further west toward the Aleutian Islands of Adak, Kiska, and Attu.

For his well-planned operation against Midway and the Aleutians, Admiral Yamamoto had amassed an armada of 190 warships and 700 aircraft. The professional Navy veteran had not altered his opinion regarding the defence capabilities of the American forces and he proposed to strike quickly to take full advantage of the element of surprise - and "give them hell".

Military intelligence had broken down the enemy's coded messages to the point where they knew the northern coastal area was in danger of an attack, but exact details of the Japanese plan still eluded them. Canadian RCAF stations reported an increase in the sightings of Japanese submarines, and both the American and Canadian defence stations on the west coast were placed on alert. But despite the vague forewarning, the operations base at Dutch Harbor was a long way from being ready for war. Even the weather - a constant and fickle foe - conspired against them. A cold front was moving in. Heavy rain and thick fog combined to build a sleety grey wall that hid the assembling Japanese strike force from the American PBY crews patrolling overhead.

At 03:25 AM on June 3, 1942, under the watchful eye of Rear Admiral Kakuta, the first Zero roared off the deck of the carrier Junyo. Fifteen minutes later the Ryujo launched its first wave of bomb-loaded Kates. Their scant and far from accurate reconnaissance information led the Japanese to expect a larger American force at the Dutch Harbor installation. However, a small but unflinching Army and Navy force of just over 6,000 men greeted the Japanese attack with fierce determination. On the 4th of June the Zeros and Kates returned and continued their raid with

EXTRA Anchorage Daily Times EXTRA

"READ BY ALASKANS EVERYWHERE"

TWENTY-SIXTH YEAR | ANCHORAGE, ALASKA, WEDNESDAY, JUNE 3, 1942 | PRICE TEN CENTS

RAID DUTCH HARBOR!

WASHINGTON, D.C., June 3. (AP)—The navy announced today that four Japanese bombers and about 15 fighters attacked Dutch Harbor at approximately 6 o'clock this morning.

The attack lasted 15 minutes, the communique said. No other details were available at this time.

The Navy announced that the Dutch Harbor attack caused no serious damage. There were only a few casualties.

The second communique based on reports received to 6 p. m., eastern time, said "further reports on the Japanese air attack at Dutch Harbor state there were but few casualties. A few warehouses were set afire but no serious damage was suffered. There is nothing to report from other areas."

BLACKOUT TONIGHT

400 Planes Hit Essen In New Raid

Call For War Against Three More Nations

City Must Be Dark As Pitch, CD Orders Say

Raid Wardens Get Patrol Instructions. Close Loop Road

Promise Nazis 30,000 Planes Every Month

"Weeping Women of Kerch" Bemoan Dead

Ask 8 Billion For 500 More

above, clipping from the Anchorage Daily News, June 3rd, 1942.
right, dive bomber pilots from carrier Junyo prior to take-off for Dutch Harbor. Imperial Japanese Navy Photo

above, the carrier Ryujo. Imperial Japanese Navy Photo

right, the flight leader of dive bomber attack on Dutch Harbor, Lieutenant Zenji Abe. Imperial Japanese Navy Photo

a higher degree of accuracy than the day before. The Americans lost 35 men, and 28 more were wounded in the attacks, but the damage at Dutch Harbor was not as devastating as the Japanese claimed it to be. The greatest losses were suffered by American bomber crews who faced perilous weather conditions to engage the enemy Zeros and attack the Japanese carriers.

According to their own reports, Japanese losses were minimal, and the Nation celebrated its victory. However, four Japanese single float Nakajima E8N2 reconnaissance aircraft did not fair as well. After catapult-launching from their carriers, the aircraft got lost in dense fog and ended up over the Aleutian Island of Umnak. Twenty-one Curtiss P-40s made short work of the trespassers. Only two of the four float planes managed to limp back to their mother ships to report the previously unknown American fighter base at Otter Point on Umnak Island.

Meanwhile, at Midway, Yamamoto suffered the first defeat of the Japanese Navy in over 100 years, a defeat that dealt a crushing blow to Japanese military pride in their superior strength and their invincibility at the hands of a preconceived weaker adversary. Japanese losses included the carrier Hiryu and severe damage to the cruisers Mikuman and Mogami, as well as 250 aircraft and 90 pilots. Yamamoto knew that his failure to secure Midway would be the turning point in the Pacific war; in that short period of time they had lost any chance they might have had to beat the Americans while they were down.

When the northern task force commander Admiral Hosogaya received the message of the disaster at Midway, the triumph at Dutch Harbor lost its significance. A disheartened Hosogaya signalled Admiral Yamamoto at 0800 on the morning of June 5, 1942, and suggested that the occupation of the Aleutian Islands be cancelled. For several hours radio transmissions travelled back and forth between the two Navy leaders. Eventually a decision was made, and Admiral Hosogaya ordered the landing to commence as planned.

At 03:00 on the morning of June 7, 1942, Japanese invasion troops landed on the shores of Kiska Island and stormed ashore, firing on the American weather station. The ten United States Navy sailors manning the station retreated into the hills, but were captured by the Japanese within a few days.

In the afternoon of the same day, Japanese troop transports steamed

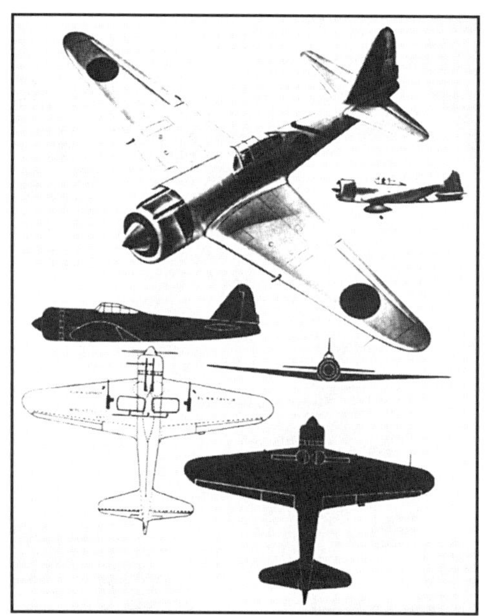

Mitsubishi Navy 0 Fighter "ZERO".

Mitsubishi Navy 2 Fighter seaplane "RUFE"

above, the Kiska Weather Detachment. U.S. Navy Photo
left, Etta and Charles Foster Jones. U.S. Navy Photo

oners of war, Etta and the Aleuts were sent to Japan on board a Japanese troop ship and spent the duration of the war interned in Japan. Etta never saw her husband again. Charles Foster died in the village and was buried there.

The communication system that connected the United States forces, the Navy weather station, and the scattered settlements located in the Aleutian Islands was often slow and unreliable, but it allowed at least a minimal contact with the outside world. Therefore, when regular radio communication from the outposts on Kiska and Attu abruptly stopped, the Navy could only assume that the western Aleutians had been overrun by Japanese troops. It was not until June 10th that a bomber from the 36th Bombardment Squadron on a patrol out of Cold Bay, discovered the Japanese entrenched on the islands.

Once the report was received, the Americans realized the serious attempt the Japanese were making to gain control of the Aleutians. By the time a search of the surrounding coastal waters began, the elusive Japanese fleet was already hundreds of miles to the south - heading home undetected, primarily because of the terrible weather that time and time again concealed their clandestine movements up and down the Pacific coast of North America.

The Aleutian Islands were not the "prize" that Japanese war leaders had thought they would be, but the success of the invasion was glorified in Japan and the Japanese

into Massacre Bay on Attu Island and discharged 1200 troops. The troops swarmed over the ridge and captured the only settlement on the Island, an Aleut village built on the wind-swept tundra at the edge of Chichagof Harbor. There were less than 50 people living in the small, isolated village, including Etta and Charles Foster Jones who were employed by the Alaska Native Services. Etta, a qualified nurse and teacher, taught school and acted as a community health worker while her husband assisted the Weather Bureau by operating a small radio station and reporting weather data.

In the disorder and confusion of the sudden attack, Charles Foster managed to send out a brief radio signal before he and Etta were separated from the rest of the villagers and questioned. Etta was left with the impression that the Japanese thought she and her husband were American agents sending information to Russia. As pris-

Rear Admiral Katsuzo Akiyama, Japanese Navy Commander of Kiska Island. Imperial Japanese Navy Photo people celebrated the victory of their illustrious military heroes.

Japan entered the 20th century with a military organization that closely followed European military standards. The well-trained army was patterned on the Prussian system, with innovative modifications based on the long-standing traditions of the samurai warriors. Military tradition was steeped in the history of the samurai warrior caste; the only class permitted to bear arms in feudal Japan, they had been treated with great respect as the military aristocracy. Without hesitation Japanese soldiers gave absolute loyalty and unfailing valour, and willingly endured the harsh discipline. They were warriors in the truest sense and Army strategists placed great importance on the infantry.

Invading Commander of Attu and his staff. Official Japanese Photo

In particular, the Officers of the Imperial Japanese Army embraced samurai legend and were strongly influenced by the Bushido code, which stressed self-discipline, bravery, and simple living. They were encouraged to regard themselves as professional warriors: invincible and superior. The Officer Cadets became dogmatic in leadership, arrogant in manner, and generally took themselves very seriously. Western nations were viewed with contempt, and they held an unshakeable belief that Americans were weak, decadent, corrupt and immoral.

The Imperial Japanese Navy had matured in less than 70 years and was modeled on Great Britain's Royal Navy. At the beginning of the Second World War Japan's Navy ranked as the third largest in the world. Japanese warships were more heavily armed and faster than their American counterparts. Japanese engineers had developed a torpedo superior to any in use by the Allies, and had built a submarine that outclassed those in use by the Americans.

The I-Class submarines were 360 feet long and had a range of 90 days, or 16,000 miles at 16 knots. On the surface they were capable of 23.6 knots, and could maintain 8.0 knots when fully submerged. They displaced 2000 to 5000 tons, and could descend to a depth of 325 feet. The I-boats carried up to 94 crewmembers across the Pacific with ease - a feat that the Americans were unable to accomplish until the end of the war.

A waterproof hangar on the forward deck was a unique feature of the I-Class submarine. Depending on the vessel's model, up to three Yokosuka E14Y1 Glen seaplanes were carried and stored in these hangars. The seaplanes were launched from the submarine deck by catapult. When the pilot returned he landed his aircraft on the ocean alongside the submarine and a crane lifted the machine back on board.

The E14Y1 Glen was a small seaplane with a metal tube structure covered with fabric. The wings had a span of 36 feet and folded rearward for storage in the deck hangar. The Glen's fully loaded weight was 3,190 pounds

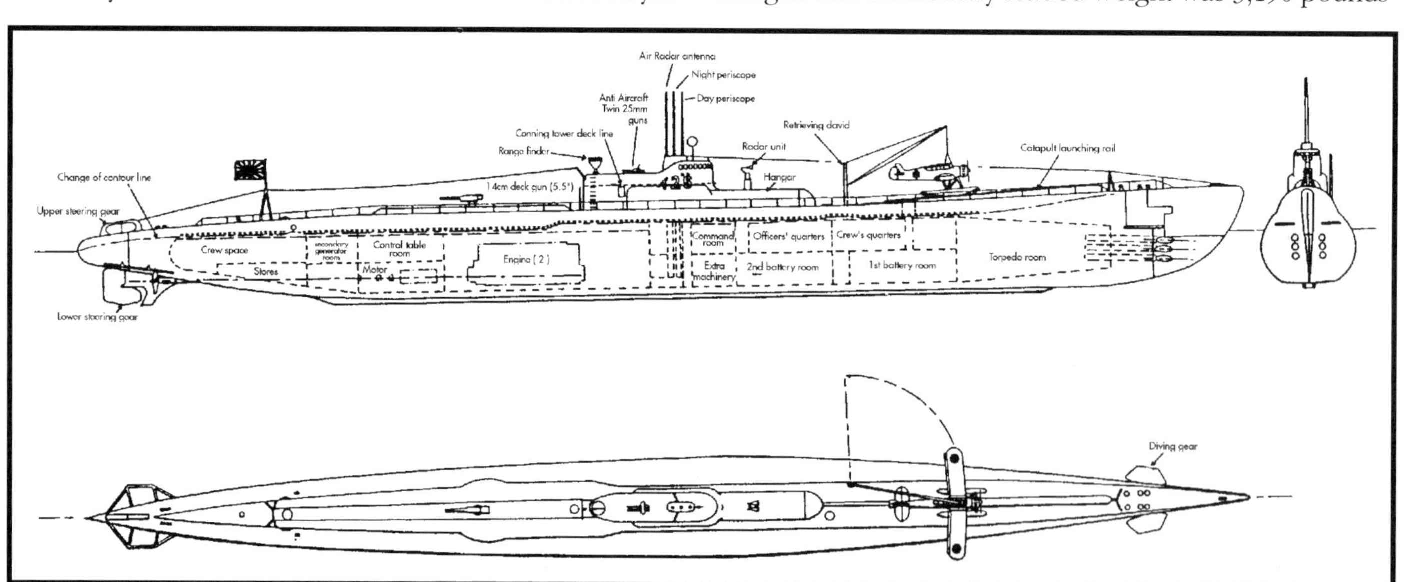

The I-25 depicted here is typical of the I-Class of submarine deployed by the Imperial Japanese Navy along the west coast of North America during WWII.

The Navy 0 Reconnaissance Seaplane "Jake"

Japanese float plane pilots on beach at Kiska with Aichi "Jake" seaplane behind.
Imperial Japanese Navy Photo

Japanese pilots (rear) and ground crew (front) at Attu. Imperial Japanese Navy Photo

The Village of Attu before the hostilities. U.S. Navy Photo

and it was powered by a single 360 hp Tokyo Gasu Amikaze nine cylinder radial engine. The aircraft was capable of a speed of 90 knots, or 105 mph, and had an endurance of 3 hours. It was crewed by one pilot and an observer/gunner, who operated a 7.7mm flexibly mounted machine gun, but there was also provision for the underwing mounting of incendiary or other bombs.

The concept of submarines carrying seaplanes was not developed by the Japanese. During the late 1920s the Royal Navy introduced the Parnell Petro, a very small byplane on floats designed to be housed in a small hangar on an M-2 Class submarine and launched by catapult. In preparation for the attack on Pearl Harbor, Japanese engineers modified the British design and adapted the I-Class submarine to carry and launch aircraft. Preliminary trials were made with the submarine I-5, and at the start of the war eleven submarines had been modified: I-7, 8, 10, 15, 17, 19, 21, 23, 25 and 26. By the end of the war twenty-four aircraft carrier submarines were in use: I-27 to I-45, and I-54, 56, 58, 11 and 12.

Launching one of the seaplanes from the deck of its mother submarine was a lengthy process. The submarine crews needed at least an hour to secure the folding wings in place and prepare the Glen for launching. The usual procedure was to surface well before dawn to begin the assembly, which allowed the pilot to arrive over his target at first light. In the meantime the submarine submerged with just its radio antenna above the surface. Once his mission was complete, the pilot reappeared at predetermined coordinates. As the submarine surfaced, the pilot landed on the water, and the recovery procedure began.

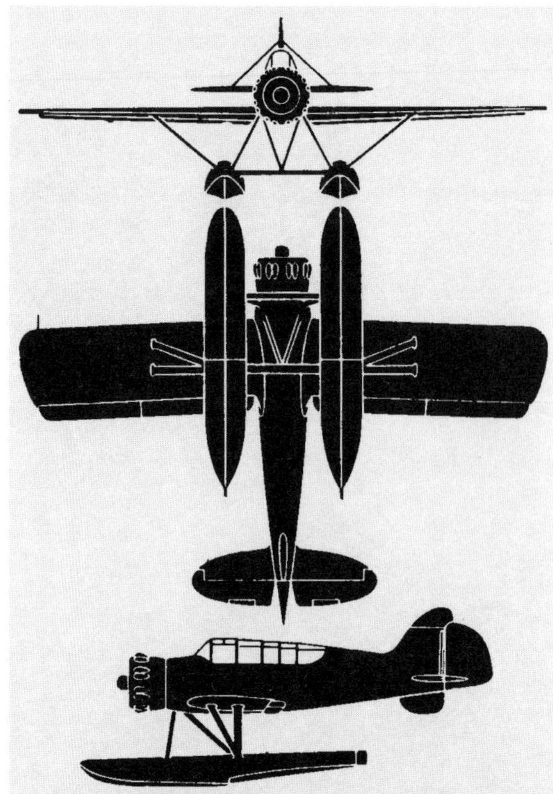

THE YOKOSUKA E14Y1 "GLEN"

Japanese Navy designation: Type 0 Small Seaplane, Model 11.

TYPE – Two-seat Light Reconnaissance Seaplane for use from submarine

WINGS – Low-wing rigidly-braced monoplane with slight sweep-back. Wings of mixed construction with light metal spars, wood ribs and fabric covering. Entire trailing-edge hinged, inner portions acting as flaps and outer portions as ailerons fold under wings and Vee struts hinged at wing attachments and fold up against lower surface of wings for stowage

FUSELAGE – Welded steel-tube structure, covered forward with light metal panels aft with fabric over light wooden formers and on the underside with metal sheet.

TAIL UNIT – Braced monoplane type. Top section of fin and vertical stabilizing surface below fuselage detachable. Tailplane braced to fin. Outer sections of tailplane fold up for stowage.

FLOATS – Twin long single-step floats attached to fuselage by transverse inverted W-struts. Floats and struts detachable from fuselage and struts from floats for stowage. Catapult points.

POWER PLANT – One 360 h.p. Tokyo Gasu Denki Amikaze 11 nine-cylinder radial air -cooled engine driving a two-blade fixed-pitch airscrew. Complete engine unit quickly detachable. Two fuel tanks in fuselage.

ACCOMMODATION – Crew of two in tandem under a continuous transparent canopy with sliding sections over cockpits.

ARMAMENT – One 7.7 mm machine-gun on flexible mounting in rear cockpit.

DIMENSIONS – Span 36 ft. (10.96 m). Length 22 ft. (8.54 m). Height 9 ft (3.68 m).

WEIGHTS – Weight empty 2,390 lbs. (1,085 kg). Weight loaded 3,190 lbs. (1,450 kg). Maximum catapult loaded weight 3,520 lbs. (1,600 kg.)

PERFORMANCE – data not available.

Hoisting the aircraft aboard and re-folding the wings for storage also required up to an hour on the surface. During both launching and recovery the I-boat was especially vulnerable to detection and attack. Crews worked quickly and efficiently but the rear-folding wing design was cumbersome. Occasionally the wings were damaged and additional time had to be spent making repairs. If an enemy aircraft or surface craft hove into view the submarine abandoned the damaged aircraft and submerged without it.

Weather also played an important part in the decision to launch the small planes. Weather changes were sudden. If a squall blew up during the three-hour flight, both landing and safe recovery of the plane turned into a dramatic challenge for pilot and submarine crew. Also, once he was aloft, the pilot needed to remain undetected as there was little hope of a successful defence in an encounter with enemy aircraft.

The many risks of using the catapulted E14Y1 on reconnaissance missions did not deter the pilots or their commanders. The Japanese relied heavily on the reports brought back by their fearless Glen pilots. On December 7, 1941, submarine I-5 launched its Glen on a dawn reconnaissance of Pearl Harbor, Hawaii. Once again, in January 1942, a Glen, launched from the submarine flagship I-9, returned to fly over Pearl Harbor and report on United States naval activity.

The I-9, Rear Admiral Shigeaki Yamasaki's flagship, was enroute north along the coast of North America. Yamasaki led his flotilla of six I-boats on a mission to gather information on American military strength in the Aleutian Islands. On reaching their destination, Yamasaki assigned each submarine to a patrol position.

On May 25, 1942, I-9 launched its E14Y1 Glen on a scout mission over Attu, Kiska and Adak. The pilot returned without observing any military activity or installations. A small party at the weather station on Kiska spotted the Glen circling overhead and contacted the Navy base at Dutch Harbor. The radio operator at the Navy base had his doubts about the identification of the aircraft, and it was obvious he didn't believe the Kiska report. Had the radio operator been less skeptical, patrols at Dutch Harbor would have been waiting for the E14Y1 reconnaissance flight that gave the Japanese what little information they did have about the base.

The E14Y1 seaplane was Admiral Yamasaki's "eye in the sky". Its scouting missions were vital to the strategic positioning of his flotilla to support the attack on the Aleutians. The Admiral's flagship was in place south of Kiska; I-15 patrolled around Adak; I-17 cruised the waters off Attu; I-19 patrolled the waters off Unalaska Island to destroy any American ships moving north in response to a call for help from Dutch Harbor; I-25 patrolled off Kodiak Island and launched an E14Y1 Glen to gather reconnaissance reports of the naval facilities there, and then, in company with I-26, headed south to the Seattle area to report on any U.S. battleships moving out of the harbour. Another Glen made an undetected flight over the Seattle harbour.

Japanese submarines made their presence known on the west coast of Canada and the United States prior to the attack on Pearl Harbor in December 1941. On the afternoon of December 11, 1941, I-9 was on patrol 800 miles east of Hawaii and crossed paths with the 5,600 ton Matson Line freighter, SS Lahaina. The submarine surfaced and fired 25 salvoes from 2,000 yards. The Lahaina went down. The submarine destroyed all but one of the freighter's lifeboats and the 34 crewmembers crammed into the remaining lifeboat. They had few provisions and were at sea for almost 10 days before they were rescued.

On December 18, 1941, the Union Oil Company tanker L.P. St. Clair, under the command of Captain John Ellison, left Seattle heading south. The I-25, under Commander Tagami, sighted the tanker and fired a volley of 10 shots at the unsuspecting ship. Captain Ellison turned the L.P St. Clair into the mouth of the Columbia River and managed to escape unharmed from the first submarine attack on the Pacific Coast.

About an hour before sunrise on the same morning, 15 miles off Cape Mendocino California, Captain Kozo

Tanker S.S. Emidio sunk by I-19 near Eureka, California, December 20, 1941.

Nishino of the I-17 ordered an attack on the freighter Samoa. Nishino decided to conserve his torpedoes and attack with the deck guns. This did not produce the desired effect, so Nishino ordered his crew to fire a torpedo. However, even though the torpedo was aimed directly amidship, it passed underneath the Samoa's hull, ran into a sandbar, and exploded. Captain Nishino took credit for sinking the Samoa but the freighter managed to make port at San Diego.

On the 19th of December the American steamship Pruss was torpedoed and sunk 100 miles southwest of Hawaii.

EXTRA

NIGHT Pictorial

RACE RESULTS

Los Angeles Times

VOL. LXI — MONDAY MORNING, DECEMBER 22, 1941 — DAILY, FIVE CENTS

22 LOST IN SUB RAID OFF CAL.

Dutch Sink Three More Transports

Hitler Ousts Nazi Army Chieftain

Ship Tried to Ram Sub.

Gunless Agwiworld Outmaneuvers Enemy, Crew Members Report

SAN FRANCISCO, Dec. 21. (AP)—The American tanker Agwiworld outmaneuvered an attacking enemy submarine after attempting to ram it, Capt. F. B. Goncalves reported when he brought his ship into port today.

Capt. Goncalves said his ship was 20 miles due west of Santa Cruz, Cal., when the submarine fired without warning or even hailing the ship.

Santa Cruz is north of Cypress Point, previously mentioned locale of the encounter.

HEADED FOR SUB

"The first thing I knew there was the explosion of a shell over our stern," he said in an interview. "I was in my room. I ran to the bridge.

"The submarine was lying about 500 yards due west of us in the path of the sun. I put

Turn to Page 2, Column 4

WAR EXTRA

L. A. TANKER SUNK; THREE OTHERS SHELLED BY JAPS

Attack 2 Tankers, 1 Flees

Sinks With Flag Flying

Japs Land on Wake

HERALD Express

SPORTS COMPLETE N.Y. STOCKS

Form Allied War Bd.

Twenty-six of her crew of 35 were able to climb into lifeboats and were eventually rescued.

At 13:30 hours in the afternoon of December 20th, Captain Nishino's I-17 engaged another tanker, the Emidio. The Sacony-Vacuum Oil Company vessel was heading south out of Seattle. Captain Farrow sent out an SOS. Minutes later the Emidio received three salvoes from I-17's deck guns and the tanker went down. I-17 submerged just as two United States Army bombers came into view. The bombers dropped depth charges without success. Thirty-one survivors from the Emidio rowed their lifeboats throughout the night in driving rain until they were taken aboard the light ship at Blunts Reef.

Meanwhile the United States Coast Guard initiated a rescue operation, but their deep-keeled cutter, Shawnee, was unable to cross the sandbar at the mouth of the Humboldt River. Undaunted, Chief Boatswain Garner Churchill launched the cutter's lifeboat across the bar, and at 01:05 AM, with four enlisted men on board, the search was underway. Two hours later, unaware that the Emidio lifeboats had reached safety, Churchill's men sighted a low vessel. Churchill signalled and received a terrifying response: the hull of a submarine reared up out of the black water - it was the I-17, and it fully intended to ram the lifeboat. Churchill and his crew escaped, but the I-17 came within 30 yards of their tiny craft.

While the I-17 blasted the Emidio, I-23, under the command of Commander Nashida, initiated an attack on the 6,771 ton Richfield Oil Company tanker Agwiworld. Tanker Captain Goncalves was jolted awake by an explosion at the stern of his ship and on immediate investigation he found that they were being shelled from about 500 yards by a Japanese submarine. In the heavy seas I-23 was unable to continue shelling and the Agwiworld escaped. Later the same day I-23 encountered a small gunboat. Nashida ordered it shelled with the 5.5 mm deck guns and the Japanese shellfire damaged the vessel's steering so that it could only go in circles. Commander Nashida left the small boat in this predicament near Monterey Bay.

Tanker Agwiworld, attacked December 20, 1941 by I-23

The I-15, under the command of Captain Nobuo Ishikawa, was in position off the coast of San Francisco near the Farallon Islands. During an eight-day patrol in the area no sightings were recorded. But William Vartnaw, Captain of the Oakland Garbage Scow, tells a more exciting story. On December 20, 1941, he was returning to Oakland in the Tahoe when he sighted a periscope about 60 yards in front of the scow. Unable to stop, the Tahoe crashed into the partially submerged submarine tearing an 80 foot gash in the scow's wooden hull. The incident wasn't recorded in the I-15 log books - apparently garbage scows did not score points in the Japanese Navy.

Although the Tahoe was leaking badly, Captain Vartnaw managed to reach the Oakland dry dock and report the incident to United States Navy authorities. His story was greeted with skepticism - perhaps it embarrassed the Navy brass that a garbage scow had struck the first blow to a Japanese submarine since the beginning of the war. However, a "eulogy" penned by a reporter on the San Fransisco Chronicle gave the Tahoe a fleeting moment of glory:

The Tahoe's back on the job today,
She's ruined a sub, her crewmen say;
The Tahoe rides the waves today,
A Queen for sure, in her own sweet way."

The I-9 had now re-positioned itself off Cape Blanco on the Oregon coast. The submarine's commander was disappointed in the lack of shipping activity but dutifully carried out his patrol for several days. His vigilance was rewarded in late December. I-9 encountered the Idaho, a small tanker owned by the Texas Oil Company, and hounded the 994-ton vessel for three days until the tanker slipped unscathed into Long Beach.

Captain Kanji Matsumura, in command of submarine I-21, lay in wait for two days for a target to present itself. On December 22, 1941, fifty-five miles north of Santa Barbara California, the unsuspecting Standard Oil Tanker, HM Story, hove into view. Matsumura let loose with his deck guns but the tanker put up a smoke screen which successfully hid her from the submarine. Matsumura ordered his crew to launch a torpedo but the tanker zigzagged to avoid being hit. Responding to the tanker's SOS, United States Army bombers arrived and dropped their bombs on the submerging submarine.

Lady Luck was with the I-21 - it escaped moving northward in search of another target. At 03:00 AM on the 23rd of December the I-21 surprised another tanker, the Richfield Oil Tanker Larry Doheney. Matsumura opened up with his 5.5 mm deck guns firing two rounds. The tanker began zigzagging frantically while Matsumura launched a torpedo, but once again his torpedo failed to hit its mark and struck the shoreline. The I-21 continued to move northward, and at 05:30 intercepted the Union Oil tanker Montebello on its way north along the coast with a cargo of fuel. This time Matsumura immediately released a torpedo, which struck the tanker amidship. After abandoning the stricken vessel the crew of the Montebello took to four lifeboats. The Japanese showed no mercy and machine-gunned the lifeboats.

By December 24th, the I-9 was back to menace the coastal shipping lanes off the shores of northern California. At 06:25 AM the I-9 discovered the lumber schooner Barbara Olson and fired a torpedo at her. Missing the vessel entirely, the torpedo struck the shore and the resulting explosion brought the nearby United States Navy subchaser USS Amethyst rapidly onto the scene, but I-9 had already quickly disappeared beneath the surface.

US Army B-25 pilot Lt. Ted Lawson attacked I-25 December 24, 1941 after he was scrambled from McChord Field, Washington. USAAC

Earlier that same morning three United States Army B-25 Mitchel bombers took off from McChord Field at Tacoma, Washington, on anti-submarine patrol. Their patrol area took them along the coast of Oregon and over the mouth of the Columbia River - one of the pilots, Lt. Ted Lawson, was involved a few months later in the Jimmy Doolittle Raid on Tokyo.

The B-25 was flying about 500 feet above the Columbia River when the crew spotted a submarine. The first 300-pound bomb deployed exploded in front of the submarine, and on the second run the crew dropped three more bombs into the swirl of the rapidly submerging submarine. Oil slicked the surface of the water, and the jubilant B-25 crew claimed their first submarine. However, the only submarine in the area was I-25, which proceeded up the Columbia River through the middle of the salmon-fishing fleet and shelled Fort Stevens, near Astoria, Oregon.

I-25 Captain Meiji Tagami later confirmed that in fact his submarine was attacked while on the surface - with nearly all his crewmembers on deck smoking, including the engine room personnel. Tagami and his crew reacted quickly and 1-25 had submerged to a depth of 20 feet when an exploding bomb destroyed the radio antenna and caused a leak in the hull. The submarine was able to continue up the river and complete its mission.

Meanwhile I-19 skulked along the California coast. A message, intercepted from I-19 to her flag ship, indignantly reported that decadent American sunbathers lined the beaches with colored umbrellas and foolishly ignored the submarine's war-like presence.

At 10:30 a.m. on December 24, 1941, the I-19 began stalking the 5,700-ton Absoroka. The McCormick Steamship Company freighter was on her way south with a load of lumber. The first torpedo I-19 fired missed its target but the second one hit the Absoroka well below the waterline and 50 feet from the stern. The freighter settled to the level of her maindeck but her cargo of lumber kept her from sinking. United States Army Bombers and a United States Navy subchaser arrived on the scene and between them they discharged 32 depth charges, with disappointing results.

The submarines of the 6th fleet received orders from Imperial Japanese Navy headquarters to indiscriminately fire on west coast cities on Christmas Eve 1941. Their action would hopefully demoralize Canadian and American citizens. I-15 was ordered to San Francisco, I-19 to Long Beach, I-10 to San Diego, I-25 to the mouth of the Columbia River, and I-26 to Victoria, British Columbia. The plan called for the submarines to surface at their assigned area and, at a coordinated time, open fire with their 4.7 and 5.5 mm deck guns. They were then to proceed immediately to their base at Kwajalein in the Marshall Islands. However, at the last minute Vice-Admiral Mitsuyoshi Shimizu cancelled the order without explanation.

After Christmas the reports of Japanese submarines sighted across the border in Canadian coastal waters slowly increased, which indicated that the Japanese were concentrating their efforts in a new direction. On December 28, 1941, the Royal Canadian Navy reported a submarine 10 miles offshore near Victoria, British Columbia. RCAF and US Army aircraft launched an attack, but the submarine slipped beneath the surface and was not seen again.

On January 1, 1942, the HMCS Outarde attacked and damaged a submarine off the northern tip of Vancouver Island. Seven days later the Outarde reported another submarine in the same location. On January 17th, two United States Army aircraft reported sighting a submarine that had cleverly camouflaged its conning tower to look like a fish boat. The information was sent out to all the RCAF coastal stations, and anti-submarine patrol crews never took another fishing boat for granted - each one was carefully inspected. At the end of January an artillery unit stationed at Ogden Point near Victoria fired at a surfaced submarine, and further proof was soon to come that the Japanese were indeed continuing to move north.

F/L George Williamson, a No. 7 (BR) Squadron Shark pilot at RCAF Station Prince Rupert recalls that in February 1942, just before dawn, a small Yokosuka E14Y1 Glen seaplane flew over the Prince Rupert harbour. It was observed to circle the various installations, including the RCAF Station at Seal Cove. The aircraft was reported by the night watchman at a city dockyard as well as a B.C. Provincial Policeman and two Canadian Army security guards. After the aircraft completed its clandestine investigation it departed northward. By the time a No. 7 (BR) Squadron Shark was airborne and in hot pursuit, the E14Y1 was long gone.

On the same day a native woman at nearby Port Simpson reported seeing what appeared to be a periscope moving through the water close to shore. Airman Cy Luce, stationed at RCAF Coal Harbour with No. 120 (BR) Squadron, confirmed that, after he arrived on January 3, 1942, Japanese seaplanes overflew the station on several occasions.

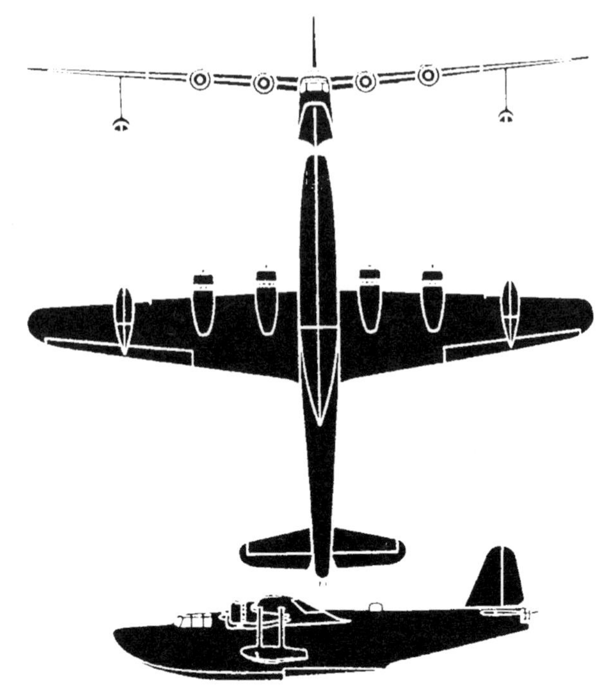

The Navy 2 Flying-boat "Emily"

On the night of February 24, 1942, Captain Kozo Narahara, in the I-17, penetrated the Santa Barbara Straits. Just before sunset, the Captain ordered a rapid fire of ten rounds from the deck guns and started what became known as the "Battle of Los Angeles". The startled shore artillery battery operators fired over 1,400 rounds in response to the attack. From his vantage point on the conning tower of I-17 Captain Narahara heard the sound of air raid warnings. Before his submarine submerged and quietly slipped away, Narahara was very pleased to witness evidence of "a great panic" on shore.

Japan's I-Class submarines assumed another duty early in March 1942. The I-22, I-9, I-15, I-19 and I-26 took up a position at French Frigatt Shoal, a small atoll, where they acted as a refuelling base for a flight of large type-2 flying boats. Commander Mochitsura Hashimoto reported that on the night of March 5, 1942, the flying boats refuelled and proceeded to Pearl Harbor where they launched an attack. On the completion of their mission, the pilots flew non-stop to Jaluit in the Marshall Islands.

The Americans hadn't recovered from the shock and disbelief over the Japanese submarine bombardment of Los Angeles in February. Now it was Canada's turn.

Late in the evening on June 8, 1942, I-26 launched a

I-26 running on surface. Imperial War Museum Photo

torpedo which sank the American freighter SS Coast Trader. The stricken vessel was between Cape Beale and Cape Flattery, at the entrance to the Strait of Juan de Fuca. A No. 4 (BR) Squadron Stranraer, #938, was dispatched from RCAF Ucluelet at 04:50 a.m. and forty minutes later pilot Sgt. E.B. Hughes sighted two life rafts carrying 22 survivors. Sgt. Hughes reported the position of the rafts and an RCN Corvette picked up the freighter's crew.

I-26 then moved up the coast of Vancouver Island, surfaced off Estevan Point, British Columbia, and on June 20, shelled the lighthouse and signal station. The submarine's commander ordered 30 rounds fired, but the first volley fell short and the rest were all long. The submarine captain remarked regretfully that, "there was not a single effective hit that night." But, the attack made a significant impact on the coastal RCAF Flying Boat Stations as word of the assault reverberated up and down the coast. June 20th was a day that all personnel would long remember.

Meanwhile Commander Togami's I-25 was not idle. At 21:55 p.m. on June 19, near Cape Flattery on the American side of the Strait of Juna de Fuca, the I-25 torpedoed the British freighter SS Fort Camousun. Earlier, on June 14th, at the mouth of the Strait, an unidentified submarine torpedoed and sank the freighter Ocean Vengance. The crew had time to deploy the life rafts, but they were machine-gunned by their determined attackers. A Royal Canadian Navy patrol boat came to their rescue from Port Renfrew and the Japanese submarine quickly submerged.

On July 30, 1942, while still laying off Vancouver Island, the I-26 intercepted two United States Navy submarines running southbound on the surface. Commander Tagami ordered the launching of the last of his torpedoes and sank one of the submarines, the USS Grunion.

Not all Japanese submarines operated on the west coast with such apparent impunity.On July 7, 1942, a Number 115 (BR) Squadron patrol flying Bolingbroke #9118, returned to RCAF Station Annette Island (Alaska). During debriefing, the pilot, F/S P.M.G. Thomas, gave a detailed report describing the one unusual, but not uncommon, incident that had occurred on their patrol. The weather was clear, visibility was good, and the sea was calm. From an altitude of 1500 feet the aircraft's second observer, P/O L.H.J. Shebeski, spotted a disturbance in the water a half mile off the starboard wing. Shebeski logged the position at 55:20 degrees north and 134:30 degrees west, on the west side of Prince of Wales Island. F/S Thomas turned the aircraft toward the object and started a descent.

As they approached the coordinates the crew could see churning water and puffs of white smoke. On the first pass, a 250 pound anti-submarine bomb was released and made a direct hit. None of the crew could make a clear identification, but they agreed there was an object just below the surface of the water - it was well over 100 feet long, cigar-shaped, and appeared to have steering vanes and an elevator at its stern.

After an excited discussion, the consensus was that they had most likely bombed a whale. As the word got around the Station, the Flight Sergeant and his crew took some good-natured rib-

RO Class submarine

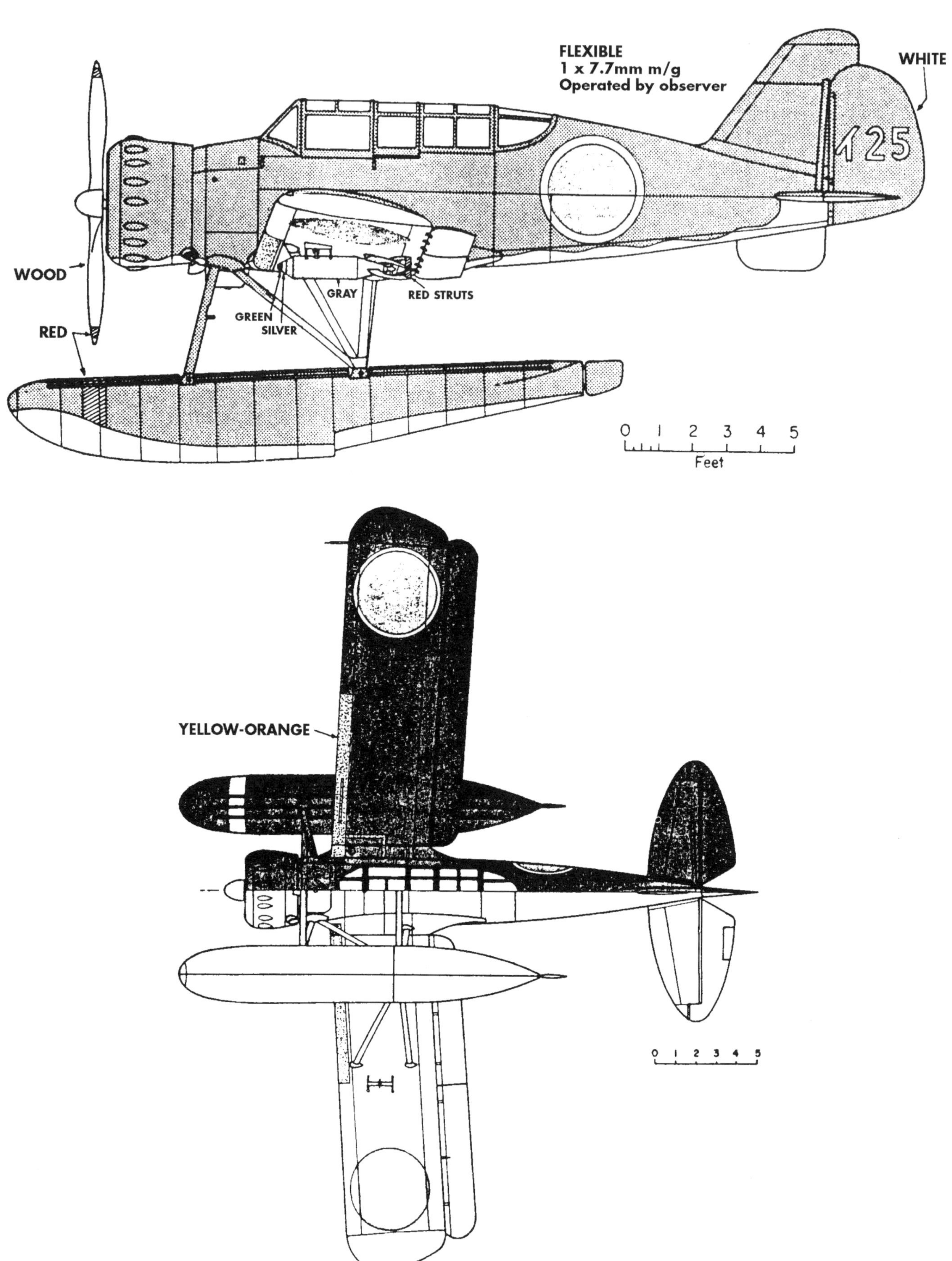
FLEXIBLE
1 x 7.7mm m/g
Operated by observer
WHITE
125
WOOD
RED
GREEN
SILVER
GRAY
RED STRUTS
0 1 2 3 4 5
Feet
YELLOW-ORANGE
0 1 2 3 4 5

bing from their fellow Airmen.

However, there was evidence to support the supposition that a Japanese submarine had run aground and the Captain was attempting to release it by blowing the tanks. A corroborative entry was discovered in the Japanese Imperial Navy's summary of official submarine losses. The summary records that on July 7, 1942, the submarine R0-32 was off of southern Alaska when it was attacked and severely damaged by an RCAF aircraft. The submarine was recorded as a loss because it was later sunk by a United States Coast Guard cutter.

On July 9, 1942, two United States Coast Guard cutters attacked and sank a Japanese submarine near the coordinates of the Bolingbroke's reported "whale" bombing. The submarine had been badly damaged and was having difficulty making headway. Bolingbroke #9118 was therefore officially credited with damaging the first submarine in any of the attacks claimed by the RCAF under Western Air Command.

Japan's RO-class submarines were smaller than the I-Class, having a displacement of 965 tons, and capable of surface speeds of up to 19 knots with a range of 11,000 miles over a period of 40 days. An RO could submerge to a depth of 260 feet, and each submarine was equipped with one 8 cm deck gun and carried 10 torpedoes.

During March 1943, the fishing vessel Oslo came upon a capsized aircraft drifting off the mouth of the Strait of Juan de Fuca. It was a small, single-engine, low wing, monoplane with twin pontoons. The Oslo took the aircraft in tow, but in the rough seas the bowline parted and they lost the aircraft 15 miles southwest of Cape Flattery, on Washington's Olympic Peninsula. The Norwegian fishermen said that the sea growth on the capsized aircraft indicated that it had been in the water for at least 45 days. A description of the aircraft was circulated but neither Canadian nor American authorities had received notification of the loss of an aircraft of this type. From the description of the aircraft it could have been a Yokosuka E14Y1 Glen seaplane abandoned at sea by a Japanese submarine.

Throughout the remainder of the war the frequency of submarine sightings and E14Y1 Glen overflights gradually decreased. Japan was concentrating her forces closer to home in defense against the gaining strength of allied forces in the Pacific. An order to carry out one of the last reconnaissance flights of an E14Y1 Glen was issued after Japanese agents in Hawaii reported a powerful build-up of United States Naval forces in Pearl Harbor.

Early in September 1943, I-36 was dispatched from Jokosuka Japan to complete a reconnaissance mission using its E14Y1 Glen. Caught unprepared two years earlier, the United States now had a sophisticated radar system in place and for over a month I-36 prowled around trying to discover a way to get within launching range and still remain undetected. Finally, in mid-October, a decision was made.

Three hundred miles at sea, at the extreme limit of the aircraft's range, I-36 launched the Glen. The pilot reached Pearl Harbor and made detailed radio reports of 4 battleships, 4 aircraft carriers, 5 cruisers, and 17 destroyers in Pearl Harbor. Knowing the risk he had been ordered to take, the pilot willingly made the supreme sacrifice for his country; somewhere over the 300 miles of ocean, between the small plane and the safety of its submarine, the Glen ran out of fuel and was never heard from again.

American and Canadian citizens knew little about the culture of the Japanese people who were living in their midst. But, thanks to Hollywood, there was at least one image shared on both sides of the border - the Japanese Kamikaze pilot in a steep dive, stoically hurtling towards his target like a human bomb. North Americans were told that in Japan this action was accorded the most profound respect. Therefore, it was concluded that this kind of unquestioning allegiance had been instilled in all Japanese people.

During the early months of 1941, RCAF intelligence officers at Western Air Command grew concerned about the loyalties of resident Japanese on the west coast of British Columbia - in spite of the fact that a large percentage were Canadian born. A year earlier, in October 1940, a secret Police-Military conference was held in Victoria to discuss questions regarding this minority group in the event of a war with Japan. Now war was a reality. RCAF defence stations were being built in isolated locations along the coast and Western Air Command was concerned about their security. Air Force Headquarters in Ottawa had information that indicated sabotage and espionage were a grave concern. As soon as any kind of accommodation was ready, or available in a nearby settlement, Airmen were posted to the station as security guards while construction continued.

On January 2, 1942, the new Air Officer Commanding Western Air Command L.F. Stevenson bypassed the Joint Service Committee and communicated directly with Air Force Headquarters to recommend that all axis aliens be removed from the west coast. A/C Stevenson received a strong reprimand for his lack of protocol. However, the following month he voiced his concerns again. This time he was supported by Air Vice-Marshal Johnson.

The Japanese attack on Pearl Harbor in December 1941

had amplified concerns about the safety of the Pacific coast, and residents of the west coast also supported A/C Stevenson's recommendations. At the end of February 1942, the Cabinet War Committee bowed to political pressure and ordered the evacuation of Japanese from the west coast of Canada. There were several actions, carried out as precautionary measures, that took place prior to the announcement of the evacuation order.

Lieutenant G.B. McKenzie of the Royal Canadian Navy Volunteer Reserve and members of the B.C. Provincial Police were ordered to Ucluelet on December 10, 1941, to seize all fishing boats belonging to Japanese fishermen. And on the 28th of December Stranraer #931 brought Wing Commander Mawdesley to RCAF Station Coal Harbour from Western Air Command Headquarters in Victoria. The Stranraer transported 22 Naval Ratings with orders to move the confiscated fishing boats to a storage area on the Fraser River near Vancouver. At the beginning of 1942, B.C. Provincial Police and the Royal Canadian Corps of Signals were sent to the west coast of Vancouver Island to take possession of all telephones owned by Japanese residents.

On Vancouver Island the evacuation of all Japanese men, women and children was completed on April 22, 1942, and 273 people were transported to the mainland aboard the SS Joan. Twelve thousand five hundred people of Japanese origin were removed. The majority of these people were born in the Victoria area and Canada was the only home they knew.

Japanese people were taken from their communities on the coast and moved to inland camps. In the British Columbia interior the war had drained the usual supply of seasonal labour, which prompted the Okanagan lumber industry to request permission to employ interned Japanese to manufacture boxes for the shipment of fruit. The provincial government argued against the use of Japanese labour. The difficulty lay in screening out those with a strong loyalty to Japan - these people were potentially dangerous and therefore Japanese employees would require close supervision. The Joint Committee promised to confer with the Federal Department of Labour to formulate long-range policies on the matter.

However, not all Japanese were interned. Cy Luce, who was stationed at RCAF Coal Harbour, recalls that two Japanese girls, one of whom was called Lotus Blossom, operated the laundry at nearby Port Alice. They took care of all the officers' cleaning needs, and the two popular girls remained in business throughout the hostilities. And in Ucluelet, two weeks before the March internment deadline, a camera captured a young Japanese woman enjoying herself on the dance floor at the Station's Valentine Day Dance.

Japanese woman dances with airman at Valentine Dance (l). RCAF Ucluelet, February, 1942. McGregor Knight Collection

Anti-Japanese feelings throughout North America were reinforced by Japan's attack on the United States. Japanese-Canadians and Americans faced a dark cloud of doubt and suspicion; rumour and misinformation about their loyalties ran rampant. It was even suggested that they might attempt to celebrate the Japanese Emperor's Birthday by staging a series of attacks against Canadian defence installations - the day passed and nothing happened.

A growing infection of distrust was directed at Japanese communities in western Canada. Property was confiscated from both the Japanese-Canadians, and from Canadians of Japanese origin (NISI); and in the United States Japanese-Americans suffered a similar fate. In Alaska there was a concern that Japanese residents might support a potential invasion, therefore all Japanese people were removed from the coast and sent to areas in the central United States. Americans on the west coast developed a strong anti-Japanese sentiment. The Kresge department store chain ordered the destruction of all products made in Japan. And in Washington D.C. an angry mob cut down and burned the Japanese cherry trees that lined the front of the capital building. Martial law was put into effect in Honolulu and the Provost Marshal dealt harshly with Yoshio Yamashita, a Japanese-born store clerk who violated the blackout regulations by using a flashlight to see inside his kitchen. He was arrested and received 100 days of hard labour.

Living in North America had become very uncomfortable for anyone whose features suggested a Japanese heritage. Members of Chinese communities were constantly being mistaken for Japanese. At first they were incensed, but as the war progressed they became increasingly alarmed, particularly in San Francisco, the home of the largest Chinese community in the United States. To identify his countrymen as Chinese, the Chinese Consul General ordered the distribution of 20,000 "I AM CHINESE" identification cards and windshield stickers.

The mounting fervour of public emotion against the Japanese swept through the Society of Composers, Authors and Publishers in New York. Members were encouraged to produce war songs with appropriate lyrics that would fuel American patriotism. In less than a week the members responded. Sam Lerner composed a catchy fox trot with lyrics that cleverly depicted Japan's "setting" sun:

So the sun will soon be setting,
For the land of the midnight sun,
While their left hand offered friendship,
Their right hand held a gun.

And a trio of music masters, Cavanaugh, Redmond and Simon, produced an amazing piece of work which predicted the sinking of Japan's rising sun:

You're a sap mister Jap,
To make a Yankee cranky.
You're a sap mister Jap,
Uncle Sam is gonna spanky.
Wait and see - before we're done,
The ABC and D will sink your rising sun.

And Perry Como crooned the tune that let us know:

"It was mighty smokey over Tokyo. A friend of mine in a B-29 dropped another load for luck. As he flew away you could hear him say, A Hubba Hubba Hubba, Yuk Yuk"

The movies featured American war heroes outsmarting Hollywood's new heartless Japanese "bad guys", and newsreels in the movie houses cranked out confirmation of Japan's cold-hearted approach to war.

Newspapers in Japan were equally eager for propaganda to bolster national pride. In the Aleutian Chain, on Kiska and Attu, the occupying forces of the Japanese Imperial Navy proudly hosted journalists and reporters intentionally brought in from Japan to report to the world that Japan's Navy was firmly entrenched on American soil, and that the Americans and Canadians seemed incapable of doing anything about the situation. Japan's presence in the Aleutians was a constant reminder of her threat to the Pacific coast.

While the industrious Japanese worked to reinforce their installations in their Aleutian stronghold, the Americans prepared a plan of attack and were now ready to act. On May 30, 1943, United States forces cleared the Japanese from Attu, and, on July 28, the Japanese quietly withdrew from Kiska prior to the final United States-Canadian assault. The tables had turned and Admiral Shigeaki Yamazaki's fleet of I-Class submarines had another job to do in the North Pacific.

Thirteen I-Class submarines from the 1st, 7th, 12th, and 19th Submarine Divisions were committed to a maximum effort to evacuate Kiska. On the night of May 26, 1943, I-7 arrived with a supply of weapons, food, and ammunition and quickly departed with 60 passengers for safe harbour at Paramushiro Island in the Kuril Islands. I-24 was not as fortunate.

Two weeks later I-24 was ordered to a rendezvous with personnel from the Attu defence forces. The United States Navy subchaser PC-487 picked up the submarine on its sonar and dropped depth charges which forced I-24 to surface. The commander of PC-487, Lt. W.G. Cornell, decided to ram the 360-foot submarine with his 170-foot patrol boat, even though the subchaser had only one-eighth the tonnage of the Japanese submarine. The PC-487 rode up on the hull of the submarine and slid back down into the water. Lt. Cornell raked the I-24 with his deck guns then rammed it again. I-24 rolled on its side and sank with a loss of all hands. [Some sources claim that it was I-9 that was rammed and sunk by PC-487. Apparently the I-9 was sunk by the United States Navy destroyer Frazier off the coast of Kiska on the 13th of June, 1943.]

The I-7, on her third trip to Kiska, was caught in the harbor by the United States destroyers Monaghan and Alwin. The destroyers fired on the submarine and severely damaged its conning tower. Unable to submerge, I-7 ran aground in dense fog, but the next day, after refloating, the submarine was escaping when three United States patrol craft attacked and forced it ashore again. I-7 and her crew were lost.

One more Japanese submarine was lost without a trace, and three more were damaged in carrying out the evacuation of 820 Japanese soldiers. However, without radar

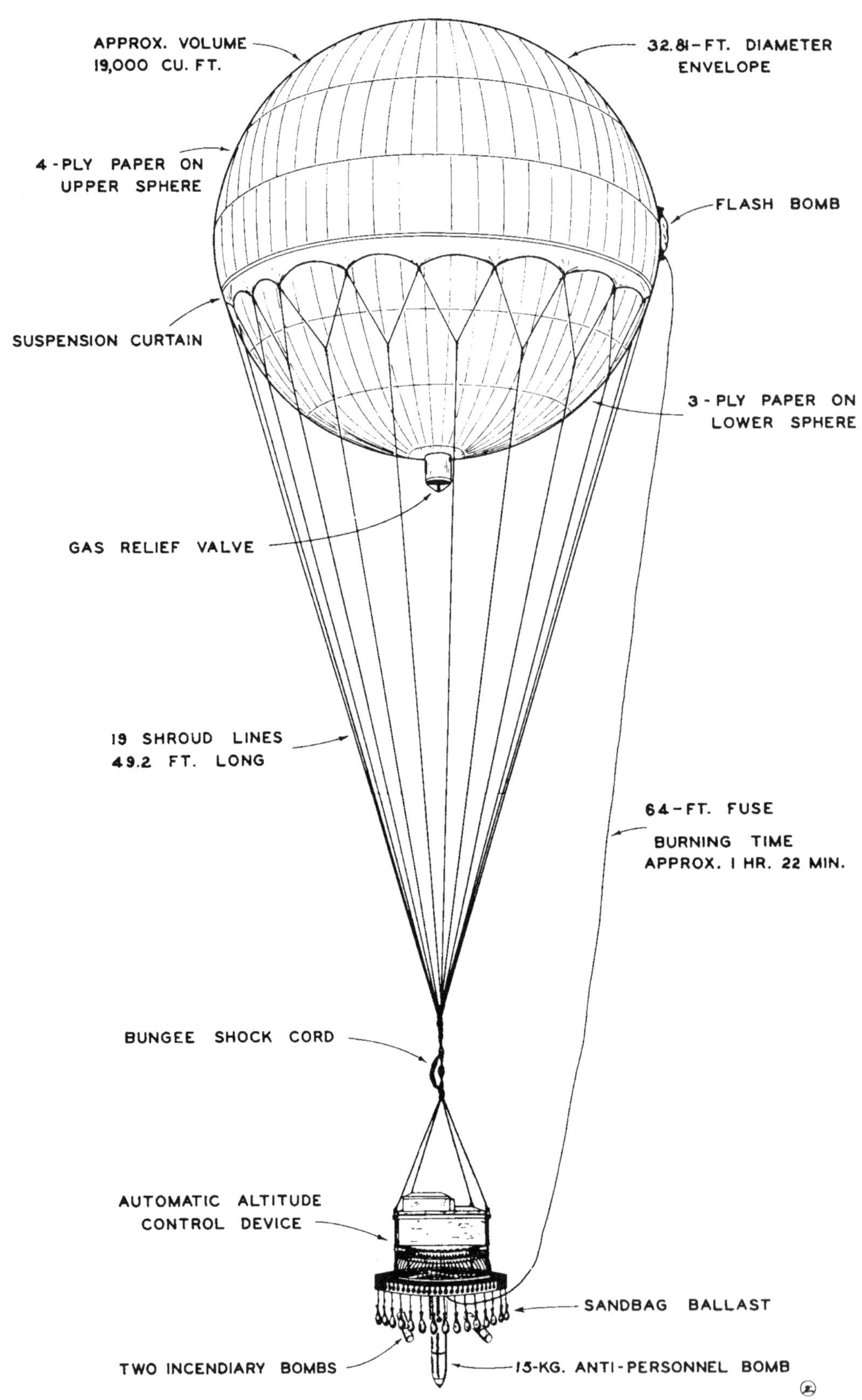
APPROX. VOLUME
19,000 CU. FT.
32.81-FT. DIAMETER
ENVELOPE
4-PLY PAPER ON
UPPER SPHERE
FLASH BOMB
SUSPENSION CURTAIN
3-PLY PAPER ON
LOWER SPHERE
GAS RELIEF VALVE
19 SHROUD LINES
49.2 FT. LONG
64-FT. FUSE
BURNING TIME
APPROX. 1 HR. 22 MIN.
BUNGEE SHOCK CORD
AUTOMATIC ALTITUDE
CONTROL DEVICE
SANDBAG BALLAST
TWO INCENDIARY BOMBS
15-KG. ANTI-PERSONNEL BOMB

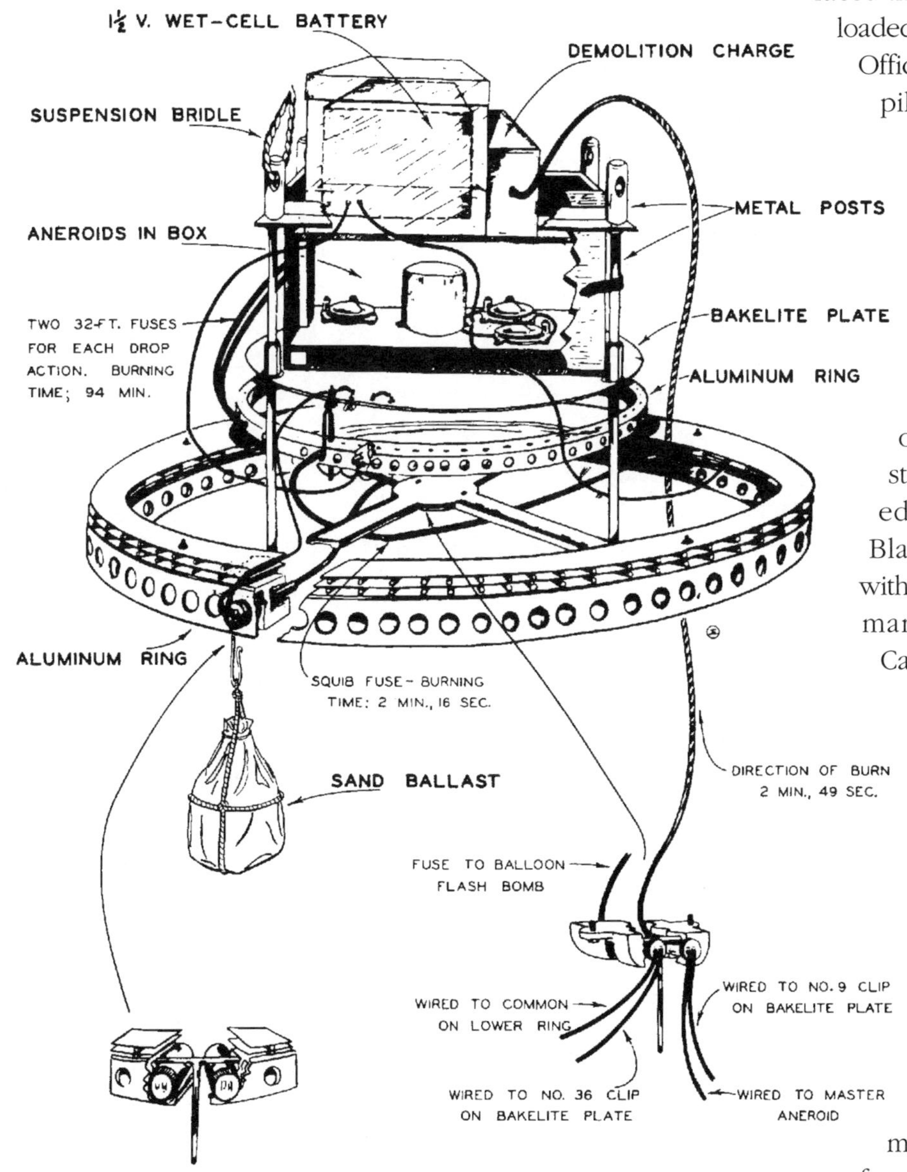

equipment, the Japanese submarine commanders were playing a dangerous game of "cat and mouse". The Americans, equipped with sonar and radar, had the advantage; this time they were the "cat". Japan's Naval leaders realized the vulnerable position of their submarines and ordered Admiral Kimura's force of surface ships to complete the evacuation of Japanese forces from Kiska.

For some time, Japanese technical researchers had been feverishly working on a unique weapon which would silently and mysteriously drop from the sky, bringing a rain of fire and destruction to the heavily forested areas on the Pacific coast. While this weapon was being perfected, the concept was put into effect using an E14Y1 Glen. On September 9th, 1942, Commander Tagami surfaced the I-25 and prepared to launch a bomb-loaded E14Y1 Glen seaplane. The pilot, Warrant Officer Nubao Fujita, was one of few Japanese pilots to survive the war.

Mounted beneath the Glen were two 147-pound incendiary bombs, and Fujita's mission was part of the Japanese strategy to achieve a new chaos on American soil. Later that same day the 13th Naval District Seattle received a report from a Forest Ranger that a single engine float plane had dropped bombs ten miles north of Brookings, Oregon - the bombs had started a fire in the vicinity. I-25 was sighted about 40 miles southwest near Cape Blanco but submerged and slipped away without incident. I-Class submarines launched many undetected Glen flights over both Canadian and American territory.

The idea of starting forest fires originated with Admiral Yamamoto, who believed that these incendiary bombs would start a holocaust of destruction that would sweep the forests of the northwest and engulf its major cities. From Yamamoto's vision, Japanese technicians devised a modification that would allow the I-Class submarines to launch the latest weapon of revenge, the fire balloon.

In March 1943, I-34 and I-35 were modified to enable them to launch a 20-foot balloon 620 miles offshore of the north American continent. Below the balloon hung incendiary bombs to start forest fires on the coast of Canada and the United States. At the last moment the plan was cancelled. The submarines were recalled for the Guadalcanal operation and the evacuation of troops from the Aleutians.

The balloon bomb concept was not abandoned. The "Fu-Go-Weapon" project, initiated in 1933 to design a constant-altitude balloon capable of carrying explosives over enemy positions, was re-established. A new prototype was developed, ingeniously designed to be launched from Japan carrying an average payload of about fifty pounds of incendiary bombs. The balloon envelope was constructed of laminated layers of paper made from the mulberry tree. Finished panels were protected with a coat of lacquer and, as production demands increased, the panels were sent out to subcontractors for final assem-

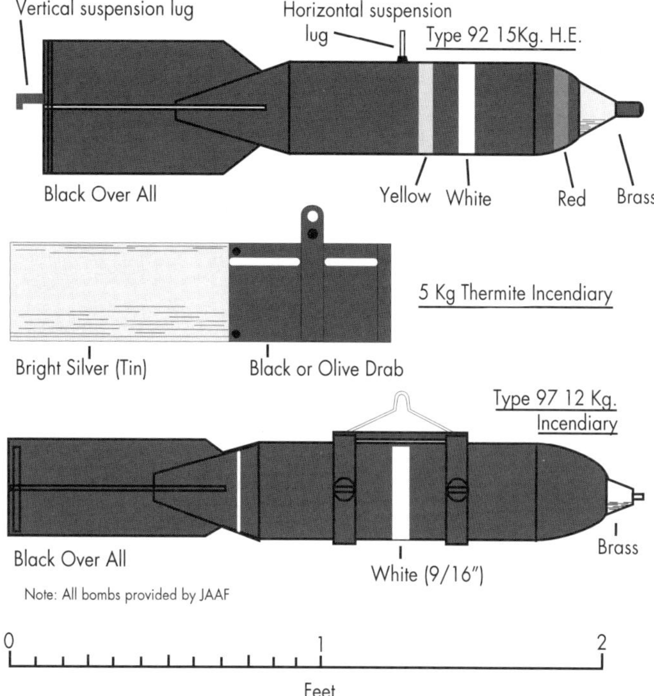

bly. The dexterity and sharp eyes of thousands of Japanese school children were involved in this part of the process.

By November 1944, the first ten thousand balloons were ready. Major General Sueyoshi Kusaba, a key figure in the various stages of the Fu-Go project, was placed in charge of the launching operation. With the release of a fire balloon on November 3rd, the Japanese air assault against continental North America began.

The first evidence that Japan had launched an offensive against the North American mainland was the discovery, on November 4, 1944, of balloon fragments floating in the ocean near San Pedro, California. Two weeks later another soggy section of a balloon was retrieved from coastal waters. In the next month balloons were found in Wyoming, Montana, and Oregon. As reports of balloon sightings increased, newspaper editors and radio broadcasters were asked to voluntarily refrain from publicizing any information that might assist the Japanese to evaluate and improve their balloon bomb technique.

Notified that Japan was launching armed balloons against the west coast, Western Air Command stationed four aircraft on Vancouver Island with orders to remain in a state of constant readiness: two aircraft at RCAF Pat Bay and two aircraft mid-island at RCAF Tofino. On February 21, 1945, 133 (F) Squadron at Pat Bay, under the command of S/L J.E. Sheppard, DFC., received a report of an object floating into the central Fraser Valley on the British Columbia mainland. P/O E.E. Maxwell was scrambled in an RCAF Kittyhawk IV and took off to investigate the report. He intercepted a Japanese fire balloon over Sumas Prairie and shot it down in a ball of flame.

The balloons that became suspended in some way without detonating posed the greatest threat to human life. On May 5, 1945, an encounter with an undetonated fire balloon claimed the lives of six Americans. The Reverend Archie Mitchell and his wife took five children on an outing to a picnic area about two hours drive northeast of Klamath Falls, Oregon. Reverend Mitchell was still in the car when his wife Elsie called out that the children had found something strange tangled in the trees. The Reverend shouted a warning but it was too late; one of the bombs exploded killing Elsie and the children. With a tragic irony the deaths occurred one month after the Japanese had discontinued the Fu-Go Weapon program.

Balloons were reported all the way from the Aleutian Island of Attu in the north, to California and Mexico in the south, and as far east as Stony Rapids, Saskatchewan. The last reported discovery was made in 1955 by a bush pilot flying along the Yukon River. A great many balloons must have landed in unsettled areas and have remained undiscovered.

According to eye witnesses, the balloon was an "amazing contraption". It was a sphere, 100 feet in circumference. When inflated it held 19,000 cubic feet of hydrogen. Its envelope, or cover, was constructed of four layers of laminated paper cemented together by a paste made from potatoes, which gave the finished product a bluish colour. After the balloon was inflated and proved air-tight, it was waterproofed with a nitro-cellulose lacquer.

Suspended below the balloon were nineteen shroud lines 49 feet in length, which supported the payload of two 11-pound incendiary bombs and a 33-pound anti-personnel fragmentation bomb, all of which were suspended from a large, circular, duraluminium ring.

The balloons were designed to be carried by the jet stream from their launch point in Japan; a river of air travelling at speeds approaching 200 miles per hour, at altitudes between 30,000 to 38,000 feet. Although radar was in use on the west coast, the low interception rate of balloons was probably due to the fact that the paper balloon presented a poor target. A properly operating balloon at 30 thousand feet would be difficult to detect except under ideal conditions. Aircraft interception usually occurred below 20,000 feet, as aircraft in use at that time had difficulty climbing to 38,000 feet.

The "Doolittle Raid" on Tokyo, April 6, 1942, was suspected as the motivation behind the Japanese balloon offensive. Lt. Col Doolittle of the United States Army Air Corps took off from the Navy Carrier Hornet, leading the North American B-25 Mitchell Bombers of the 17th Bomb

Group. Their target for the day was Tokyo, the capital city of Japan. Tokyo suffered extensive damage and Japan suffered "loss of face". For days the city was in the unrelenting grip of pandemonium as raging fires turned the night sky red. The atrocity demanded reprisals and Japan's military leaders began to plan a retaliation.

The Japanese military, their technicians, and their scientists desired to set North America ablaze. Panic and chaos would spread faster than the fires; the Japanese people would be avenged. The strength of the American and Canadian people would be undermined when they realized the extent of the sustained enemy air attack descending quietly from the sky.

The American and the Canadian government concluded that the best defence against panic was to say nothing of the new menace and play down local anxieties. In this way Japan would be deprived of any knowledge of the number of balloons that reached North America, and whether or not their new weapon had been successful - a weapon which was in effect the very first Intercontinental Ballistic Missile (ICBM).

Shortly after the war, on May 29, 1947, The New York Times published a news release that gave Americans a pat on the back for maintaining silence on the fire balloons:

> *"Japan was kept in the dark about the fate of the fantastic balloon bombs because Americans proved during the war they could keep their mouths shut. To their silence is credited the failure of the enemy's campaign."*

On March 10, 1945, RCAF Pilot P/O J.G. Patten, flying Kitty Hawk 858, intercepted a balloon at 13,500 feet near Patricia Bay on Vancouver Island. Patten shot the balloon down and no damage resulted. On the 12th of March, F/L R.L. Moodie and his crew, who had transferred to RCAF Station Coal Harbour with No. 6 (BR) Squadron, were completing the last leg of their daily patrol in Canso #9702. They sighted a partially deflated balloon slowly drifting eastward at about 500 feet over Rupert Inlet. By flying above the balloon Moodie was able to force it down on the side of Rupert Arm. Squadron personnel at Coal Harbour had also spotted the balloon from the ground and a search party was organized to attempt a recovery.

Number 120 (BR) Squadron Wireless Operator Ray E. Woolston of Calgary, Alberta, recalls his participation in the recovery of the balloon while he was stationed with the RCAF at Coal Harbour:

> *"We knew that the balloon issue was "top secret" and did not ask too many questions, knowing there would be no answers anyway. This lack of real knowledge about the Japanese Balloons, plus the rumours prevalent on all stations, made everyone more eager to catch a glimpse of one of them in the sky, through curiosity, but certainly not any real fear."*

Word was received that a balloon had been forced down three-quarters of a mile inland from the shore on Rupert Inlet. The following day Woolston was pleased to be included in an eleven-man search party assembled under the charge of an Army Captain. The Captain was a demolition expert and had participated in several previous attempts to recover Japanese Fire Balloons.

A spotter plane led the group to the site of the downed balloon which they found tangled in two small trees. On a careful, closer examination the Captain saw the intact mechanism with several sand bags still attached to it. He also identified a 32-pound anti-personnel bomb, but because of the thick brush he couldn't be sure if these were the only explosives attached to the apparatus. He then briefed the men, clearly explaining the diabolical cleverness of the balloon's construction and the mission that had motivated its creation in Japan.

Released in Japan, these balloons, with normal winter wind conditions - a continuous flow from west to east - would reach the west coast of North America in approximately 70 hours. A suspended basket held a mechanism consisting of a barometer, fuses, sand bags, incendiary bombs, anti-personnel bombs and a small self-destructing bomb of a very high-intensive explosive. The barometer controlled the sand bags and released one or more of them if the balloon lost too much altitude. The incendiary bombs were triggered to release one at a time after the required number of hours for the crossing. Next the explosive bomb was released, then the self-destructing bomb destroyed the entire mechanism.

After his briefing, the Captain decided that chopping the trees down was too unsafe so he elected to sever them with dynamite. The sticks of explosives were tied around the trunks of the trees about 4 feet above the ground. These two trees were sheared off with the explosion, falling into a small clearing. The men were relieved that the bombs had not exploded during the fall, which would have destroyed everything.

With the trees lying full-length on the ground, the Captain made a second careful inspection and determined that the incendiaries had already been released. A few tense moments later he had defused the larger bomb and had gently secured the small self-destruct unit in his shirt pocket. Woolston continued his narrative:

"The balloon itself was over 30 feet in diameter, so, by rolling it like a rug, then tying it with ropes, we made a package approximately forty-five feet long and thirty inches in diameter. The balloon had been lying out in the fog and rain for 5 or 6 days, and being made of paper was in fact very similar to a sponge; absorbing about 8 times its original weight in water. Due to the amount of glue in the paper or the type of paper it was, or possibly a combination of both, it was extremely slippery - about the same as trying to hold on to a freshly-caught fish.

To sum up the situation briefly, we had approximately eight hundred pounds of loosely-packed, slippery material, stretched into a limp snake-like package forty-five feet long and at least two feet thick with an obstacle course to traverse that only nature with Vancouver Island as a stage could produce.

We struggled through brush and under-growth normally about four feet high, but after sinking into moss-covered holes the brush became shoulder-high and more entangled. Every few feet there were old trees from decades past which had given in to the forces of nature and just lay down eventually becoming covered with a blanket of very slippery decomposed material. If they were small we could climb over but many had to be by-passed causing extra yards of struggling."

After what Woolston described as *"an endless four hours of foot by foot endeavor"* to cover the three-quarters of a mile to the inlet, the party reached the water's edge where a Marine Section motor boat was waiting for them. The balloon was shipped to Western Air Command and stored in a parachute loft at Sea Island. It was complete and undamaged, and so far it was the only one in this condition that had been recovered. At the end of March a decision was made to send this fine example of the fire balloon to the National Research Council in Ottawa. The job of flying the balloon to Ottawa was given to No. 166 (Communications) Squadron at Sea Island, Vancouver.

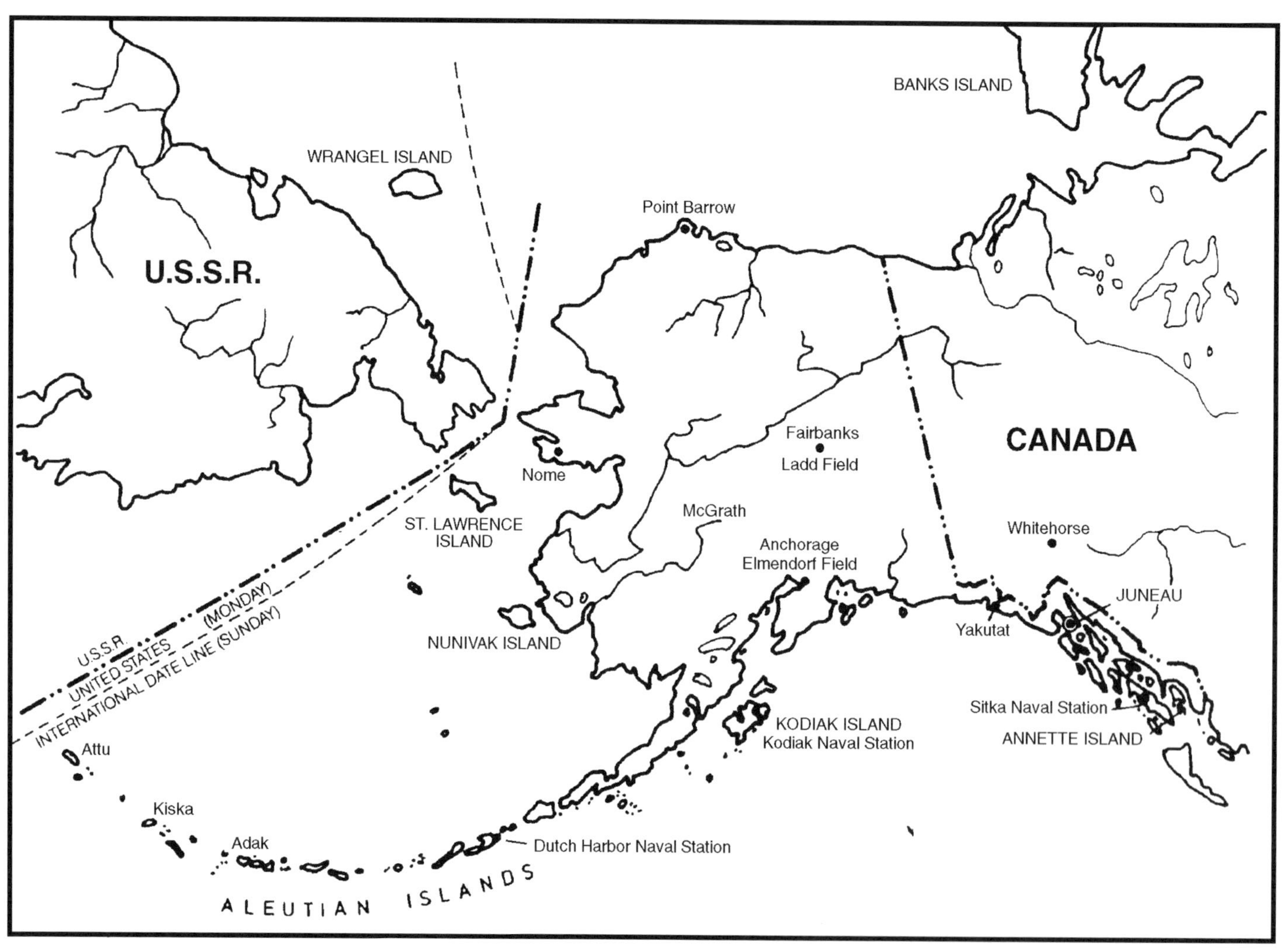

A Number 166 Squadron Beachcraft, UC45F "Expeditor", #1384, was stripped of its seats to accommodate the complete balloon assembly. Somewhere in the vicinity of Carmi, British Columbia, cruising east at 17,000 feet, the Expeditor's pilot, F/L George F. Williamson, and his co-pilot, F/O Bob Duncan, noticed an acrid smokey smell. Duncan made a quick check of their cargo and found that the heater outlets were blasting hot air onto the waxy surface of the balloon. Turning off the heat solved the problem but the first leg of the flight was, in Williamson's view, "a damn cold trip". While the aircraft was being refuelled at Winnipeg, Williamson met an old friend who was about to take off for Ottawa in an empty Douglas/Dakota C47. Completing a frigid flight across Canada was not on Williamson's list of fun things to do and he managed to convince his buddy to take the balloon the rest of the way.

From November 3, 1944 to early April 1945, the Japanese launched 9,300 balloons. Of the estimated 1,000 balloons that arrived over the continent of North America, only 285 were accounted for in reports turned in to American or Canadian authorities. Fortunately for North America the fire balloon didn't produce the violent conflagration and grand-scale devastation envisioned by its creators. Balloons were launched under the most ideal weather and wind conditions that the Japanese were able to predict; once on its way, the final destination of the balloon became a deadly game of chance.

One of the last recorded Fu-Go Weapon balloon bombs to land in North America enjoyed a somewhat ironic success. In its random descent it came to rest in brush-country between Bonneville and Grand Coulee, Washington. In a capricious twist of fate, the incendiary bombs detonated inside the security fences surrounding the Hanford, Washington Atomic Energy Plant. The brush fire caused by the exploding balloon triggered the elaborate safety mechanisms surrounding the Plant. The power supply automatically shut down, and it took several days to reactivate the system.

Unknown to the citizens of Hiroshima and Nagasaki, the floating Japanese time bomb caused a delay in the production of the Atomic Bomb that was destined to end the Second World War in August 1945.

chapter eight

THE BATTLE FOR JERICHO
"And The Walls Come Tumbling Down"

Up until the late 1930s Jericho Beach Air Station was the only permanent military establishment at Vancouver. With the beginning of hostilities in 1939 activity at Jericho Beach increased, creating a shortage of space and forcing the Department of National Defence to increase its property holdings. The Federal Government began to expropriate and purchase some of the smaller, privately owned properties in the area. One of these properties, the estate of Colonel Victor Spencer, was purchased for the sum of $94,446.00, and the family home was used as the Officers' Mess until 1972.

In 1941 Vancouver City Council passed a resolution which allowed DND to acquire land at Jericho Beach, and also at Kitsilano Beach - a site which DND agreed to vacate at the end of the war. In 1942 the Federal Government purchased 7.8 acres of freehold property from the Jericho Country Club, complete with furnishings and equipment, for the sum of $45,000.00 and, to keep pace with the demands for more space, a further 140 acres was leased from the Province of British Columbia.

In 1942 the Army Headquarters moved to Vancouver from the Workpoint Barracks at Esquimalt. The Navy, Air Force, and the General Staff portion of the Army were located in adjoining buildings at Jericho Beach, but Pacific Command Administration Headquarters was located in the old Vancouver Hotel, at Granville and Georgia Streets in downtown Vancouver - the site of the present-day Eatons Department store.

During the war there was also a Joint Naval/Air Force "Ops Room" at Jericho Beach, with an Army liaison officer in attendance. The functions of the Navy and the Air Force were closely related, being primarily concerned with the approach of the enemy from a seaward direction. However, the Army role was somewhat different in that they were responsible for maintaining shore defences to repel enemy landing parties.

In 1945 the Army was faced with a decision: remain at its Vancouver Headquarters at Jericho Beach (Pacific Command Administration Headquarters had now vacated the old Vancouver Hotel), or move back to Esquimalt, as recommended by Major General Pearkes, the former General Officer Commanding Pacific Command. Pearkes, now an elected Member of Parliament, felt that a move back to Esquimalt would save additional construction expenditures at Jericho Beach. However, the decision was made to consolidate Army Headquarters in Vancouver at Jericho Beach.

On January 23, 1946 the existing Army Commands in British Columbia, Alberta, the North West Territories and the Yukon were incorporated into British Columbia Area Command Headquarters. Also included were the former Military Districts No. 11 and No 13 Headquarters, which were relocated to Jericho Beach.

In May 1946 the Department of National Defence decided to create a permanent military establishment in Vancouver and purchased, at a cost of $351,000.00, the 140 acres of land they had leased from the province. In March 1947 Jericho and Kitsilano were established as permanent military bases. The Federal Government now owned 154 acres of waterfront real estate at Jericho Beach, with an additional 40 acres at Kitsilano Beach.

In the 1950s the Jericho Beach location on Fourth Avenue became the Army Headquarters for the British Columbia area, responsible for the administration of all permanent and Militia units in British Columbia, including the garrison at Victoria and the Engineering School at Chilliwack.

An Air Force presence, under the command of A/C J.L. Plant, remained at the 4th Avenue Headquarters, Jericho Beach, in the form of No. 12 Group of North West Air Command. A/C J.A. Easton, Commanding Officer at the time No. 12 Group was disbanded in June 1951, remained as CO of the redesignated No. 12 Air Defence Group which was reassigned to Air Defence Command on

July 1, 1951. On September 1, 1955, No. 12 Group was redesignated No. 5 Air Division with A/C W.A. Orr in command.

The 5th Air Division administered the affairs of RCAF Station Sea Island and Comox, as well as Holberg, No. 121 Search and Rescue Unit at Sea Island, and was also home to the RCAF Search and Rescue Coordination Center. The RCAF Station at Kitsilano housed No. 2 Supply Depot, the Accounting units, the RCAF Investigative Department, No. 19 (Auxiliary) Wing, and three Air Cadet Squadrons.

But, despite the meaningful activities at Jericho Beach the area was fast becoming a political "hot potatoe" destined to provide the impetus for lengthy political manoeuvring for years to come. Vancouver politicians and journalists have had a field day with the "Battle Of Jericho Beach" for almost 40 years. Now, in 1996, the walls are "tumbling down", but the battle rages on.

In early 1960 the City of Vancouver, in concert with its resident newspapers, began an intense and escalating campaign to persuade the Federal Government to release its military land holdings to the city. The news headlines conjured up images of a general siege: *"Give Jericho Back", "Keep Fighting for Jericho", "Return Our Waterfront".*

The June 19, 1961 edition of the Vancouver Sun newspaper ran an article quoting Member of Parliament John Taylor, Conservative, Vancouver Burrard, who demanded that the defence installations at Jericho Beach and Kitsilano be removed to make way for recreational facilities. The persistent Taylor was carrying on a campaign he initiated in 1959. From his seat at the Council table, Vancouver City Alderman Bill Rathie exuberantly pounded the same drum.

Taylor and Rathie's vision of a housing and park development on the Jericho lands seemed almost reasonable in comparison to the grandaddy of all plans submitted in 1957 by the visionary Neville Beaton. Beaton, a professional engineer, proposed a Marine Drive Parkway connected to a four-lane waterfront road along Point Grey Road, pedestrian overpasses, and parking for 450 cars. His plan was quietly filed at City Hall under "Waikiki Beach Plan".

In August 1961 Brigadier General J.W. Bishop, area commander, made an effort to defuse the situation by assuring Vancouver's Mayor Alsbury that the Army was intent on co-operating with the city. Bishop made it clear that Ottawa had received an Army recommendation to allow the Vancouver Parks Board to lease a section of Jericho land.

The Department of National Defence was ready to relinquish some of its land holdings and leased two small parcels of land to the city. The first site was three-quarters of an acre adjacent to Locarno Beach, on Trimble Street, and the second property was a sixteen and one-quarter acre parcel just east of the Jericho Beach hangars, along the beach to Point Grey Road. This property release was the tip of the iceberg, and set the stage for a long and drawn-out process of DND property erosion.

On February 22, 1964, Bill Rathie, now Vancouver's Mayor, dusted off Beaton's "Glamour parkway scheme" and suggested it could become the city's 1967 Canadian Centennial contribution. But first the battle of Jericho had to be fought and won. Early in May Rathie met with Defence Minister Paul Hellyer in Ottawa. The Province newspaper carried Mayor Rathie's confident interpretation of the outcome of this meeting of two politicians: *"part of the former Jericho Beach Air Station will be turned over to the city in the near future"* and *"eventually the city will obtain the area"*. And, slowly, nothing changed.

In mid-1964 Liberal MLA for Point Grey, Doctor Pat McGeer, also climbed on the Jericho bandwagon with an address to the Point Grey Liberal Association. On Wednesday, May 13th the Province dramatically implied that Dr. McGeer was launching a simultaneous campaign that would "wrest" the Kitsilano area from the defence department, and "blow down the walls of Jericho". But, the day before, buried at the bottom of an article that wondered in typical pigeon-journalese, "Jericho next target?", a responsible journalist devoted two inches of column-space to an interesting quote from McGeer. However, what McGeer said was so sensible and non-aggressive, so rational and unlike a battle cry, that it was quickly forgotten:

> *"Leasing surplus defence property for park purposes is in the best tradition of serving the public interest. It adjusts the use of public lands to meet the needs of the times. Leased land can be quickly recaptured for national defence in times of emergency."*

In August 1965 Prime Minister Lester Pearson visited Vancouver. He publicly acknowledged that the Federal government was prepared to give the city of Vancouver waterfront property at no cost. Minister of Defence, Paul Hellyer, who accompanied the Prime Minister on his western tour, visited Jericho Beach and was given a full orientation tour in company with British Columbia Area Engineer Lieutenant-Colonel L.G. MacDonald. MacDonald arranged for Lieutenant-Colonel R.R. Buckley, Command Engineer, to prepare a confidential memorandum on the subject for Western Command Headquarters, Edmonton, Alberta.

CONFIDENTIAL WCC 5150-J45

MEMORANDUM

HEADQUARTERS WESTERN COMMAND

AQMC EDMONTON ALTA 13 SEP 65

Background on Hand-Over of Jericho Beach Property

1. During my recent familiarization visit to 8 C Area, Lt Col L.G. MacDonald, Area Engineer, outlined the situation concerning the possible hand-over of a portion or all of the DND property at Jericho Beach to the City of Vancouver.
2. On 25 August 65 the MND viewed the entire property, and the $12,000,000 value placed on the facilities was derived from the enclosed estimate provided by the Area Engineer. This estimate gives a rough approximation for the replacement of existing buildings and services with standard accommodation at another location. It does not include a Militia Armoury, which will be needed to replace shared accommodation at Jericho. In addition, there are other hidden benefits that DND now receives at the Jericho location (ie. bunker oil for the Central Heating Plant is delivered by barge at a substantial saving over truck delivery.)
3. Although this has been given considerable newspaper publicity, no firm proposal has been received by Headquarters BC area from the city of Vancouver. If and when such an offer is made, DND is considering three alternatives:
   a. Retain the existing property
   b. Grant an easement from Point Grey Road to Marine Drive dividing the current holdings in accordance with the enclosed plan. Such a move would relieve City traffic congestion in the area and would not interfere with DND use of the property if access between the two portions is provided.
   c. Release all property north of Fourth Avenue. There is not sufficient space in the remaining property to permit construction to provide for buildings given up under such a scheme. Consequently, it would be necessary to relocate the supporting services and the price of $12,000,000 is considered realistic, varied by the scale of service accommodation needed.
4. Until such time as a firm proposal is received from the City of Vancouver and the ultimate establishment for this location is known, a comprehensive estimate of costs cannot be prepared.
5. On return trip from BC Area, the outline costs given in the annex were shown to the GOC.

R.R. Buckley Lt Col
Command Engineer

The Vancouver Sun reported on August 27, 1965 that Mayor Rathie was going to Ottawa the following week and was once again fully confident that he would receive, on behalf of the city, 60 acres of the 176.2 acres that remained of the Army base at Jericho Beach. Rathie said a public beach and walkway would be constructed and land would be designated for road allowance. Hellyer indicated at that meeting that the Federal Government was concerned with the whole property and that he would like to see a realistic long-term redevelopment plan for the area that included some re-zoning. Creating pockets of residential zoning would allow DND to recover funds through sale of the properties to private sector developers. Did people think that the military could simply fold their tents in the night and disappear? Hellyer laid it on the line, stressing that relocating the present military installations would require financing.

So far, the politicians and the public they represented had shown little concern for the casualties in the continuing battle over Jericho lands. The military personnel working and living on the base were caught in the middle of the cross-fire; their lives and careers were affected by the years of uncertainty created by political manoeuvring and manipulation.

On September 9, 1965 Vancouver Quadra MP Grant Deachman charged that Rathie "blew it" in his dealings with Ottawa. Deachman accused Rathie of being more concerned with getting Defence Minister Paul Hellyer to agree to giving public access to the beach by way of a 150-foot road allowance, than he was with long range development of the entire Jericho Beach military holdings. The MP later softened his rebuke by giving Rathie credit for his sincere desire to give the waterfront back to the people of Vancouver.

A week later the Vancouver Sun announced in bold print that "Battle of Jericho 'Not Necessary'"; "Hellyer, Rathie 'Not Far Apart' On Beach Deal Says Deachman".

Deachman pointed out that the Federal Government had offered to send a top government planner to consult with city planners on the best use of the land involved at Jericho Beach, and Deachman continued with a very reasonable summary of the situation: *"if he [Hellyer] has offered to sell off a portion of the defence lands at Jericho in order to remove the structures from the beach, surely the planners of his department and the city can work out a satisfactory zoning arrangement."* In retrospect, Deachman was possibly referring to controlled development, a difficult concept for any democratic/political body to commit to.

In February 1966, Ottawa assigned a planner to begin the final stages of settlement and "advise" on the disposition of the remaining 150 acres of land held by the Department of National Defence. Gilbert Hardman of Grosvenor-Laing bravely stepped into the arena in the role of private consultant/investigator for the DND, but he found it was impossible to shed the sinister shadow of Grosvenor-Laing's "Big Developer" image. Wearing a different "hat" didn't wash with Vancouver City Council. They reasoned that a developer always had the glint of large-scale commercial development in his eye, a disease for which there was no known cure.

In May 1966 four city Aldermen took Defence Minister Hellyer and Mayor Rathie to task over a statement that a development proposal for the Jericho land "could include high-rise apartments". The Sun newspaper assisted the cause in an article titled *"Aldermen Assail Jericho Land Plan; Fear High-Rise Development Under Study by Federal Gov't"*. Alderman Hugh Bird described such a proposal as *"outrageous and disgraceful"*, Alderman Ernie Broome labeled Hellyer *"a huckster, a second-hand buy-sell-and-trade man"* for his part in the scheme. Alderman Bob Williams accused Mayor Rathie of *"treating the council like children"*. Alderman Halford Wilson stated that if Grosvenor-Laing was involved, *"the firm will be doing it for its own benefit"*.

The article revealed that the Northwest Point Grey Homeowners Association was spreading high-riseophobia despite the fact that Council had not yet received Hardman's preliminary report on his investigation of the various uses of the land in question. Mayor Rathie, still focused on the 150 feet of Jericho beachfront he wanted turned over to the city, defended the Federal Government's plan to raise money to remove the buildings from this section of their property. And Liberal MP Grant Deachman calmly reiterated that no final decision had been made on the use of the property. Nevertheless, in an exercise of caution, Council passed a resolution that discontinued Hardman's studies.

At the same time, Vancouverites were encouraged to vent their growing resentment against the wartime actions of the Federal Government - resentment based on the assumption that during the Second World War DND had acquired land from the city and from the Jericho Golf and Country Club for a nominal payment, therefore, the Vancouver taxpayers deserved to have their land returned for an equally nominal sum. Past history was not consulted and as a result the whole argument received a surprise twist at the October 1966 Council meeting.

At that meeting Council was informed by its planning director, Bill Graham, that the 150-foot strip of land, the main focal point of contention between the city and the Federal Government, did not belong to the Federal Government in the first place; it wasn't theirs to give away. In fact, a strip 200 feet wide would revert to the Province of British Columbia when the defence department discontinued military use of the shoreline property. The Aldermen listened in shocked silence as Graham explained that provincial ownership was only discovered after his department had completed a detailed investigation of the complex property exchanges that were part of the history of Jericho Beach.

Two waterfront lots under provincial jurisdiction stretched from Discovery Street to the edge of the Jericho Beach base. The remaining 100 acres of the Jericho Beach Army base, north of Fourth Avenue, was owned by the Federal government. Acting on this "new" information, Council submitted a brief to both the Federal and the Provincial governments giving notice of the city's intention to acquire both properties for park and recreational facilities.

Until the Armed Services Unification Bill had successfully passed through the House of Commons, the Minister of National Defence was unable to respond to any gauntlets thrown down by Vancouver City Council. Liberal MP Grant Deachman cautioned that even after Defence Minister Hellyer resolved the problems of the unification process he still had no intention of surrendering all of the Jericho Beach land.

On June 24, 1967 Vancouver Sun reporter Allan Fotheringham added a dash of satirical spice to the stewing "Jericho" pot. In a half-page spread, embellished by Peterson's clever cartoons, Fotheringham presented a tongue-in-cheek review of the military establishment at the Jericho Beach base. Keen to apply his masterful quick-wit-and-retort to re-kindling political pressure on the Federal government, Mr. Fotheringham moved into over-gilt on the proverbial lilly.

Jericho personnel were referred to as *"squatters"*, *"paper-*

shufflers", and "pencil-pushers", on some of the *"most valuable real estate in Canada".* No one on civvy street understood the damage to morale caused by the lampoonist's gibes: *"Join the army and get your own exclusive foreshore."...."grass grows and corporals putter with engines"...."There is not a fighting man on the place."...."What's wrong with booting them out to Surrey?".* Regardless of individual opinions on either side of the tug-of-war over Jericho Beach, a proud force of Canadian men and women were made to look like members of "Sgt Bilko's Motor Pool".

Tom Campbell, now Vancouver's Mayor, joined the furor in support of Allan Fotheringham's "call to arms" by announcing in June 1967 that he, together with a delegation of council members, would proceed to Ottawa to establish a Jericho "beachhead". The chairman of the Vancouver Park Board, George Puil, volunteered to be a member of Campbell's "commandos". The advance force planned to land on hostile Ottawa shores in mid-July prepared to man the trenches in a renewed battle for the surrender of Jericho - unfortunately the trip was delayed because Parliament was not in session.

At the end of June 1967 Defence Minister Hellyer invited a Sun reporter-photographer team to visit Jericho Beach in an attempt to give the Army and the Department of National Defence an opportunity to respond to Fotheringham's criticisms. The article appeared in the Vancouver Sun on Friday, June 30. The headline read, *"At Jericho Quartermaster's Store You Can Find Antiques, and More"*; the opening line read, *"Maybe the Canadian Armed Forces should go into the antique business."*; a three-column wide photograph, a close-up of a stack of old chairs, was captioned *"Jericho chairs...in nuclear-defence base's warehouse".* A misleading lead-in to an article that went on, almost reluctantly, to allow the military to fill in the background in some of the half-pictures captured by Fotheringham's jaundiced eye.

Flight Lieutenant Vic Keating, the establishment's integrated Public Relations Officer, gave the group a tour of the base and introduced the reporter to F/L Ralph Madden of the Search and Rescue Centre operations room. F/L Madden explained the function of his department and pointed out that SAR helicopters now landed on the concrete apron once used by the RCAF seaplanes and flying boats - an interesting titbit of history left hanging without any further explanation.

Past history held another interesting piece of information that Mayor Campbell could have used a few days earlier, before he made his "off-the-cuff" offer to compensate DND for their surrender of Jericho land: *"When there's a war on they can have Stanley Park if they want, but when the fighting stops we want it back."* Now, as the Vancouver Sun team prepared to leave the military base, F/L Keating produced a document relating to the history of Stanley Park.

Keating wished to inform the Mayor that records of the Royal Canadian Engineers showed that the land which comprised the present-day Stanley Park had been a military reserve since 1859. The land was leased to the city of Vancouver in 1908, but the Minister of Defence had the power to take possession of any part, or all, of Stanley Park at any time for military purposes. Campbell's response was not documented.

Mayor Tom Campbell wasn't the only one to come out with less than brilliant tactical plans to win the Battle of Jericho. Garde Gardom, the Liberal MLA for Point Grey, suggested that the city should lay siege to the military's occupation at Jericho Beach and perhaps cut off the base's water and light.

In 1968 the process of Unification of the Armed Forces downscaled the role of Jericho Beach from that of Army Headquarters to a Detachment of CFB Chilliwack. Jericho Beach was now known as Vancouver Detachment, CFB Chilliwack; a name change that was related to the integration of Canada's armed forces in that command of all support services on the mainland went to the Commander of CFB Chilliwack; the Army Headquarters became Pacific Militia Area Headquarters - Reserve only; regional operations were run by MARPAC in Esquimalt.

With this change of responsibility it was even harder for the Federal government to justify the need for keeping their large holdings in Point Grey. On June 17, 1969 Prime Minister Trudeau signed the document that transferred ownership to the city of Vancouver of all properties north of Fourth Avenue: approximately 77 acres. The token cost of this real estate transaction was $1.00, with the condition that the property be exclusively used for a public park. However, in a further concession to the Federal government, the city agreed to a re-zoning of the remaining federally owned 38 acre parcel. Sale of this property would allow the Department of National Defence to recover some of the taxpayers' money that had been invested in Jericho Beach over the last fifty years.

The land was transferred to the City in three parcels, a transaction which took the best part of three years to complete. When the last parcel of land was turned over in the spring of 1972, the City held title to a total of 72 acres of the land they had been fighting for since the late 1950s, land that a succession of Mayors and Aldermen said belonged to the people of Vancouver, prime waterfront in one of Canada's most beautiful cities. The current City council could now get on with the construction of the long-promised public park.

The negotiated "land deal" ended the Battle of Jericho, 'Vancouver City Hall vs the Federal government', but all was not quiet on the western front. Storm clouds massed over the drawing board as it became apparent that a "park" meant many different things to many different people. The Battle of Jericho: "Two" was underway: 'Everyone-and-his-dog vs Vancouver City Hall'.

The flood-gates of contention reopened, rushing in another series of "developers' designs for paradise". Planners proposed a six-lane freeway along the beach; the Vancouver Parks Board toyed with the idea of constructing a playland, complete with games, rides and exhibits; two aquatic playlands; an 18-hole pitch-and-putt golf course; marina facilities including large boatsheds, offshore moorage and a breakwater island; an ice palace; tennis courts; picnic and free activity areas and parking for about 1,200 cars - a simple public park, a quiet place, a refuge from the frantic pace of the city.

Small skirmishes broke out like hives: representatives from the Jericho Tennis Club and the Royal Vancouver Yacht Club brought forward plans for expansion of their facilities on the waterfront and also called for more parking space; and a controversial plan was under consideration to turn No. 4 Barrack into a youth hostel.

This time around the taxpayers city-wide vehemently condemned proposals that would pave the beach to provide parking or allow development that would clog the area with high-density residential and commercial uses. And residents living north of Fourth Avenue were very unhappy: they didn't want a six-lane expressway along the beach to the University, and they took the greatest exception to the amusement park concept, which they envisioned as a Coney Island affair. *"We are trying to attack the philosophy that got Los Angeles into a mess"* reasoned a spokesman.

Slowly over a period of several years the remaining Army and Air Force Units of the Unified Armed Forces removed their equipment and material from all of the buildings and property lying to the north of Fourth Avenue. The majority of the buildings were razed and all sign of them removed.

Some of the personnel who had served at Jericho Beach many year ago came forward to express their bewilderment at the wholesale destruction of the former Air Station. On April 17, 1977 the Vancouver Province published an interview with two highly respected Jericho veterans: 82 year-old Air Commodore Earl Macleod, a commanding officer at Jericho Beach on several occasions during his career; and 81 year-old Howard Hines, an employee at Jericho Beach from 1920 to 1922, who later served with the Vancouver School Board from 1930 until 1958. Neither men could understand why at least one of the original hangars could not be preserved in the new park.

Hangar number 7 dated from 1938 and number 3, 5, and 6, dated back to 1924. And, to attach a deeper sense of past history to the newly created park, both Hines and MacLeod felt that the site should be named in honour of Major Claire MacLaurin, DFC, the first Superintendent of Jericho Beach and the determined force behind the construction of the Jericho Beach Air Station in 1920.

After all the years of the off-again-on-again Battle of Jericho, the Department of National Defence still occupies 53 acres of land south of Fourth Avenue, which, up until the summer of 1996, was home to the Vancouver Detachment of CFB Chilliwack. VAN DET provided support to over 700 regular force, and 100 class B reservists, as well as DND civilian employees from five different commands. It also supplied technical services to the British Columbia District Headquarters, 74 Comm GP HQ, 403 CFTSD, PDSIU, CFRC, 744 Comm Regt, 12 MED COY Unit, and seven lower mainland armouries, as well as HMCS Discovery located on Deadman's Island at Stanley Park.

Today building number 13, the RCAF Stores and Marine building, is a sailing instruction centre and storage complex for a local boating operation. Building number 4, the NCO quarters, is a youth hostel. Building number 22, previously a recreation hall, is an amateur theatre. Building number 1, originally the Spencer estate residence and later the Officers' Mess, is now a community centre.

The concrete apron at the waterfront, north of the former locations of hangar number 2, 3, 5, and 6, still remains intact. This apron now provides a viewpoint to English Bay. Cyclists and pedestrians pass along the series of pathways and stop to enjoy the view of the north shore mountains and the city itself. No markers exist to tell the visitor of the origins of the viewpoint or the deeds and accomplishments of the thousands of airmen and soldiers who have served at Jericho Beach. Perhaps this is the legacy of the bitter battle between the Federal Government and the City of Vancouver.

Once the Battle of Jericho is over the politicians and the bureaucrats, professing to carry out the will of the electorate, will have removed all vestiges of a military presence. A rich and meaningful segment of Vancouver history, and of our collective Canadian history, will be erased from the public conscience.

In 1996 the discussions continue. The Vancouver Detachment is gone but the British Columbia District Headquarters Land Force is still in operation, for the time being, at the Fourth Avenue location. Everyone knows that the writing is on the wall and it is just a matter of time before the property will be vacated in favour of future development, as yet undecided. The Battle for Jericho Beach is far from over.

It is fitting that L/Col Crober, one of the last military commanders of the military installation at Jericho Beach, and presently Chief of Staff of British Columbia District Headquarters has the last word on what will transpire as his command prepairs for its final days at Jericho Beach.

Vol. 87 No. 90 • November 10, 1996 • Established 1908

Remembrance Day

Search for HQ, native land claims forestall military detachment's move

Jericho waits for other shoe to drop

By Ann Sullivan
Contributing writer

NINE BUILDINGS ARE FALLING to the wrecking ball at B.C. District army headquarters at Jericho. You can see the demolition from West Fourth Avenue, wooden buildings sitting half toppled on a wide expanse of grass.

Getting rid of the ramshackle buildings is logical. They were constructed for temporary use during World War II and were crumbling anyway. Knocking them down will save the federal government taxes and maintenance costs.

However, the razing of the rickety structures mirrors the dismantling of the army in B.C. and the military in general.

For the first time since 1887 B.C. will have no regular army units. The Princess Patricia Canadian Light Infantry moved to Edmonton; the officer candidate school (CFOCS) moved to St. Jean, Quebec; and the Canadian Forces School of Military Engineering is set to leave for Gagetown, N.B. by Dec. 10.

"The media have dumped on these people who have gone overseas and put themselves in harm's way."
—Lt.-Col Paul Crober

A few regular army personnel and 14 reserve units are all that's left to run the show in B.C. District, the largest of four districts in the army's Land Force Western Area.

The Jericho detachment was supposed to close by the summer of 1995, the result of budget cuts announced by the federal government earlier that year. Almost two years later, personnel are still living on borrowed time while the army searches for a new location for headquarters. Jericho is the logistics nerve-centre for all military bases in the Greater Vancouver Regional District

The restructuring is part of a plan to consolidate military operations in Canada's western region. While it may save the federal government money, it does nothing for morale at bases like Jericho.

Budget cuts are not the only problem facing the army. The death of Somalian Shidane Arone, reports of brutal hazing rituals and the highly publicized Somalia inquiry have affected public perception of the military and lowered morale.

Lt.-Col. Paul Crober, chief of staff for B.C. District, blames the media. "The media have dumped on these people who have put themselves in harm's way and gone overseas," said Crober.

"(Soldiers) have been killed, wounded and psychologically wounded. It appears as if the public doesn't give a damn."

It also appears the public doesn't understand or want to accept the primary role of the Canadian military: "To close with and destroy the enemy."

"'Peacekeeping' has a benign ring,

Canada in danger of lapsing into isolationism and meaninglessness

conjuring up an image of peace and harmony that is simply not accurate.

"People say, 'You're going peacekeeping,'" Crober said. "You're not. You're going into a war zone."

As chief operations officer in Bosnia, Crober was almost killed on four separate occasions. Soldiers in the thick of the conflict faced death every day.

Douglas Ross, a professor of political science at SFU, agreed the general attitude toward the Canadian military is in drastic need of change.

"I see (our attitude) as very sad, very distressing and potentially very unstable," Ross said. "I think it's reinforcing a general idea that the military is not needed...There's the attitude of 'Let the Americans do it for us.' That is a big mistake."

Ross said more cuts will leave the military ineffective and unable to fulfill its peacekeeping obligations to the UN.

"We're on the leading edge of isolationism," Ross said. "It's tragic, it's foolish and it's dangerous."

Crober admits civilians and the military have a long way to go in understanding one another.

"We are a society amongst ourselves and there's no doubt about that," he said. "If you have an army that's the same as the people it serves, then you don't have an army."

EPILOGUE

To the Readers:

As I sit here in my family's married quarter at Jericho, composing the epilogue for what I believe is a very necessary chapter in the history of the Armed Forces in this province, I can see one of the designated buildings on the south side of 4th Avenue being demolished. As you read in the last chapter, all of the Jericho lands north of that street were given back to Vancouver by 1970 and now form the second largest park (next to Stanley Park) in the city. Very few people under the age of 40 who run, walk, cycle or simply enjoy the fresh air off English Bay have any idea that on and near the beach there was once a large and meaningful Air Force and Army presence.

The Federal Government budget of 1995 severely cut defence spending. The Canadian Forces' only solution for finding the necessary funds to train and equip the decreasing number of operational units, particularly for the never-ending overseas multi-national missions, was to cut infrastructure. Many critically important bases, service schools, colleges and administrative units have been closed or will be by time of publication of this book. Amongst them is every Regular Force facility on the Mainland including CFB Chilliwack (which had just completed construction of several new complexes) and the remaining site at Jericho. At time of writing, all Regular Force Army units have departed the province (for the first time since 1887) and are now in newly-built accommodation in Edmonton or St-Jean, Que.

The CF School of Military Engineering will move to CFB Gagetown, NB in 1997, CFB Chilliwack will close and there will be no Regular Force operational or training units of any kind on the Mainland.

At the time of the decision, Jericho housed British Columbia District Headquarters (successor to Pacific Command, BC Area, Pacific Militia Area and which commands all regional operations in the province as well as 2500-3000 Militia or Reserve Army soldiers spread throughout BC), 74 Communications Group (which commanded all Regular and Reserve signals units in BC), 12 Medical Company (a Militia field medical unit), the Militia Training Detachment for Vancouver (which runs several types of courses that cannot be conducted in armouries), the 8th Canadian Forces Quality Assurance Region (a large name for a small but important unit that performs quality control with provincial defence contractors), BC headquarters for the leagues that support Army Cadets, Air Cadets and Sea Cadets and finally, Vancouver

EPILOGUE

Detachment itself which was an administrative/logistic unit under CFB Chilliwack control that supported all military activities in the Greater Vancouver Regional District (GVRD).

Vancouver Detachment and 74 Communications Group disbanded in the spring/summer of 1996 which was also the original period when all other tenants were to have departed for other sites. Because the site is the subject of native land claims involving the Musqueam, Squamish, Capilano and Burrard bands, and because the process to resolve said claims will take some consideration and time, it was clear that the Federal Government would continue to pay to the city "Grants in Lieu of Taxes" or GILT.

To pay this as well as enormous leasing costs ($1.5M +) to temporarily house the displaced units from Jericho was considered excessive and unnecessary. Thus, all the foregoing units that were not disbanded are still resident in the large headquarters building. The completely renovated single quarters building and the married quarters are also still in use as well as one very modern vehicle maintenance hangar. Eight other buildings, all of World War II vintage, continue to come down, generating much comment amongst the married quarters residents, local neighbours and of course, the media.

The present plan is that all units will be out of the site by summer 1997, that is if appropriate permanent accommodation is found (moves to temporary sites are deemed to be ultimately wasteful of taxpayers' money). Certainly, the one remaining headquarters of the Canadian Forces on the Mainland and the only Army Headquarters in BC will likely remain somewhere within GVRD, although some valid arguments exist to co-locate with Maritime Forces Pacific Headquarters in Esquimalt. The married quarters will be vacated once a workable housing solution for Regular Force members and their families can be found - one that takes into account the fact that no one on Forces' wages can afford to rent or buy in Vancouver.

Hopefully, once the military has vacated completely, the Canadian Forces and the City of Vancouver can agree on an appropriate monument that would commemorate the thousands of service men and women who called Jericho home during war and peace - perhaps to be erected on the original seaplane site in Jericho Park and therefore able to serve in both a commemorative and educational manner for all who use the park but are unaware of its history.

November, 1996

F.P. Crober
Lieutenant-Colonel
Chief of Staff
British Columbia District
Land Forces Western Area

APPENDIX

Jericho In The News

Prominent Airmen of the Dominion Air Station Jericho Beach

Aircraft of Jericho Beach Air Station

JERICHO IN THE NEWS

1930 to 1947

The Chilliwack Progress

The Vancouver News Herald

The Vancouver Sun

June 3, 1931

[illegible]-FIRST YEAR, VOL. No. 7

Chilliwack's New Airport To Be Formally Opened By Squadron Leader MacLeod on Wednesday

Many Planes Will Take Part in Thrills, Stunts and Surprises Planned For Afternoon

Wednesday, June 3, promises to be a day of outstanding interest to Chilliwack, when the airport on Sumas Prairie will be formally opened by Squadron Leader Earl MacLeod, of the Jericho Air Station. The formal opening of the airport will be made the occasion of an airplane demonstration in which it is expected that fifteen planes will take part. The planes will be on the grounds about 10 a.m., when they may be inspected. Shortly before 1 o'clock a formation flight over the city and valley is planned, to be followed by the formal opening. The heavier planes will land and the light machines will participate in a dog fight, each machine being in command of a former war pilot. Bombing, shooting balloons, and stunting will contribute to the program, while some genuine surprises are in store for visitors. At 4:15 a parachute jump will be made. Airplane gliding and model airplanes may also be demonstrated.

With the assistance of H. J. Barber, M.P., the Chilliwack airport has been declared a customs port of entry, thus permitting planes from across the line to take part in the opening formalities.

All details for the opening are being prepared by the executive committee, several of whom are experienced in these matters. Four members of the provincial police will assist the committee on the grounds in parking cars, keeping the runways clear, and in generally safeguarding the interests of all concerned. For those without cars a bus service from town has been arranged.

A flight of planes from the Dominion air station at Jericho Beach, under Squadron Leader MacLeod, will take part in the flight over the valley, using Cultus Lake as a base, while three club planes and three commercial machines from Vancouver have also promised to attend. Victoria will send at least one plane, probably more, and Seattle one to three, while it is expected that planes will be present from other points across the line. Pilot R. L. Coote's plane and the Brett's Ltd. plane will also take part in the "show."

Pilot Coote took part in a demonstration at Victoria on Monday in connection with that city's forthcoming airport bylaw, being accompanied across the gulf by Ronald Wells, son of Reeve Wells, and Monty Hall. The trip to Victoria was made in an hour and five minutes and the return trip in fifty-eight minutes. While on the Island, Pilot Coote urged and received assurance of Victoria's participation in the Chilliwack ceremonies.

Catering at the airport has been taken over by the Canadian Legion. There will be strict control over airways and the public will not be allowed near machines during the afternoon in the interests of safety to pilots and visitors.

Gas for the visiting planes is being donated by Home and Shell distributors, while other firms are making contributions toward the success of the occasion.

The airport committee will entertain the pilots at luncheon and dinner, together with Mayor Manual and Reeve Wells, and other active supporters of the movement to provide an airport for Chilliwack.

The committee has also arranged for a dance to be held in the Legion hall in the evening, to which an invitation has been extended to all pilots to attend.

Mr. C. L. Worthington is chairman of the committee and is being assisted by an executive comprising Frank Edwards, Russell Coote, Earl Brett and Harry Spull.

ROUTINE AT JERICHO BEACH THRILLS

PLANE, CRASH BOAT IN RESCUE

Army Flyers Demonstrate Correlation of Air, Sea and Land Forces

Jericho Beach air station is no training ground for rookies, but a defense base guarding the whole of Canada's Pacific Coast. Peter Stursberg, staff reporter, accompanied by Lloyd Turner, staff photographer of The Vancouver Daily Province, flew with the airmen from Jericho in order to record their splendid work. In two previous articles Mr. [St]ursberg related his experiences [in a] dive-bomber and on a formation flight. Today he tells of the [...] of hundreds of airmen at [the] Jericho base. He will describe the net- [...] [wi]lderness of the West [...] the thrills of patrol- [...] in the worst flying [...] world.

[...]TURSBERG.

[...]inary day—a [...] Jericho Air [...] spluttering [...] [sw]erved over [...] [Burr]ard Inlet [...] [da]y work. [...] [co]mbined [...] in the [...] Air [...] and [...] [e]asy test- [...] [d]ocks on the [...] [inspec]tions. [...] [...]y hours' flying an [...] given a much more [thorou]gh going over, and some [...] the men were stripping the engines and tearing off the major components on the periodical inspections.

Only a few of them, just four master mechanics and four helpers, were working on one plane which had flown 300 hours. They were taking it to pieces; for this "line" inspection calls for every smallest nut and bolt to be checked.

All of them dropped their work, though first making quickly but thoroughly sure that not a tool or a part was misplaced, when the siren screamed.

A big flying boat had just taxied out to the centre of the Bay. Its engines had shattered the dull calm of the wintry afternoon, then stopped, and, like a dying bird, had thrown up its Verey light ghost.

One of the two powerful crash boats attached to the Jericho Air Station was idling a little distance from the dock. It had picked up the signal and was knifing its way to the rescue, an Aldis lamp flashing from its bow.

Out in the Bay a brilliant answering wink came from the flying boat.

The Aldis lamp is among the finest signalling lights, as it has a range of several miles and, at that distance, can be focussed to within twenty-five yards, so that the message can only be seen by the person to whom it is sent.

It has a handle like a revolver butt, and is sighted in much the same way as a miniature camera. The Morse is ticked out by a trigger switch.

Just as the crash boat opened up its powerful Diesel engines, which can drive it at 35 knots, the unearthly hoot of the siren sounded across Jericho Air Station.

Overalled mechanics and ground crews fell in in front of their hangars and officers lined up beside them.

Across the dock raced army ambulance men attached to the R.C.A.F., shouldering first aid equipment. Out from behind the hangars a grey ambulance sneaked up on to the wharf.

The second crash boat was now racing toward the scene of the accident, but the first had already reached the plane.

In a trice it had turned around and was speeding back, its throttles opened wide. As soon as it reached the dock, two men on stretchers were hoisted ashore and slipped into the ambulance, which moved quickly away. The siren hooted again—in short blasts giving the "all clear" signal.

"It was just a practice," Wing Commander Earl MacLeod, officer commanding Jericho Air Station, told me. "The two men volunteered to fall in the water."

But I doubt if anyone else realized it was a practice, not even the men on the crash boat. It was so well carried out. And the whole rescue from a flying boat three-quarters of a mile out in Burrard Inlet took about the same time as it has taken you to read about it.

Canadian Press

The Vancouver Daily Province

JAN 19 1939

New Bombing Planes And Flying Boats For Jericho

(See map on Page 6.)

By TORCHY ANDERSON.

OTTAWA, Jan. 19.—Important steps will be taken this year in the defense programme of the Pacific coast and Western Canada. Both advanced, and secondary defenses of British Columbia and supporting defenses on the prairie will be strengthened by steps which include:

1. The torpedo bomber squadron based at Jericho Beach air station will be brought up to full strength with the most modern craft.
2. Jericho flying boat squadron will be re-equipped with Stranraer aircraft, now being built in Montreal.
3. Development of floating mobile flying-boat bases on the B. C. coast will continue.
4. Work on Ailford Bay (Queen Charlotte Islands), and Patricia Bay (Vancouver Island), air bases will be pressed.
5. Additional "close-in" defense armament around Vancouver will be provided.
6. Development will be continued at Esquimalt and at other points on the coast.

Additional undertakings and details of these projects will be known when defense estimates are tabled.

The most important step in the programme on the west coast is the modernization of the flying units based at Jericho Beach. The Stranraer aircraft are the latest type in their class and are identical with those in use in the British air service.

DEFENSE WEAPON.

The bombers are capable of attacking both with bomb and torpedo, and are a formidable defense against raiding naval craft with either weapon.

These bombers are essentially a defense arm and are regarded as highly important in the defense of the maze of sequestered waters which lie in the great coastal indentations north of Vancouver to the Alaskan boundary.

(Continued on Page 6.)

Bomber Lands For Re-fuelling

Royal Air Force Plane Makes Easy Landing Here On Sunday

Judging by the crowd at the wharf, Sunday's dinner must have been a somewhat sketchy affair for many, but the sight of the latest model "Stranraer" reconnaissance bomber is not a thing to be lightly missed.

Piloted by Squadron Leaders J. F. Mawdesley and A. J. Ashton, R.C.A.F., the big flying boat, weighing some nine and a half tons when fully loaded, made a beautiful landing soon after one o'clock on its way from Ottawa to Vancouver. It will be used on coastal reconnaissance work.

The plane stopped here to refuel with some 400 gallons of gas to replenish tanks which normally contain 500 gallons and 26 gallons of oil.

An unequal span biplane with monoplane type tail and twin rudders, it is powered with a pair of Bristol "Pegasus X" radial air-cooled motors, developing some 1800 h.p. It is rather interesting to note that each cylinder provides something like four times as much power as the entire motor used by some of our early pioneers of aviation, who flew with a 25 h.p. Anzani engine, staggering through the air at some 45 miles per hour instead of the 150 miles of our Sunday visitor.

Many of the younger members of the community as well as some of the older ones were privileged to inspect the aircraft and see what makes it "tick," returning ashore fully determined in some cases, to fly a Stranraer themselves some day.

One of the aircraftsmen standing on a wing-tip fending off from a light pole in the channel failed to stop when the craft did and gave the spectators a thrill when he took an involuntary header, and it was noted that his "opposite number" stationed on the port wing, lost no time in donning a life preserver lest a similar fate befell him.

It took considerable skill in piloting the plane up the narrow channel since it measures some 85 feet from tip to tip, but boats were available and the manoeuvre was executed with little mischance.

Some criticism was heard amongst the crowd as to the lack of facilities for refuelling visiting aircraft at the wharf but it should be realized that no request was made by the authorities for anything but gas and oil, and these were promptly supplied.

NEW BOMBER AT JERICHO BEACH

The large Stranraer bomber which left Ottawa on Friday for Vancouver arrived at the Royal Canadian Air Force station at Jericho Beach at 5 p.m. Sunday. Flown in easy stages to the coast, the flying boat, piloted by Squadron Leader F. J. Mawdesley with Squadron Leader A. J. Ashton as co-pilot, will augment the present force at the local station. JUL 17 1939

Aliford Bay

JAN 17 1939

By RONALD KENVYN.

WORK is to commence this month on a Royal Canadian Air Force station to cost $119,000 at Aliford Bay in the Queen Charlotte Islands. So this snug harbor will again boom with activity reminiscent of the days when British capital attempted to establish a fishing industry there.

A year or two before the Great War, Sir George Doughty, a big figure in British and South African fisheries, had his attention drawn to British Columbia as a field for investment. He came here, he was convinced and he launched a big project.

Everything worked quite according to plan with one fatal exception. The fish were not available, and after a year or so the operation closed down.

Sir George paid $90,000 for a site at Aliford Bay and also bought an existing oilery at Skidegate. He paid $150,000 for a German fertilizer plant and erected this at Aliford with wharves, houses, stores and other necessary buildings. From England came two fine trawlers, the Canada and the Triumph.

The plan was to get Indians to catch dogfish to be rendered into fertilizer and to take sockeye for canning. The pack was to be shipped via nearby Prince Rupert.

But the Indians refused to fish, the sockeye did not run and without fish the ambitious scheme came to an end and Aliford relapsed into a quiet harbor.

Now hammers will ring again and the roar of seaplanes wake the echoes along the rocky shores

Jericho In The News: 1930-1947

Jericho Airmen service Stranraer #912 after its flight from Ottawa, July 16th, 1939

TENDER FOR CONSTRUCTION OF STORES AND MARINE BUILDING. R.C.A.F. STATION, JERICHO BEACH VANCOUVER, B. C.

SEALED TENDERS, enclosed in envelope marked, "Tender No. 2847—Construction of Stores and Marine Building, R.C.A.F. Station, Jericho Beach, Vancouver, B. C.", and addressed to the Chairman, War Supply Board, Ottawa, Ontario, will be received until 12 o'clock noon, Wednesday, January 24th, 1940, for the construction of Stores and Marine Building, at the Royal Canadian Air Force Station, Jericho Beach, Vancouver, B. C.

Tenders will not be considered unless made on the forms supplied by the Board, and in accordance with the conditions set forth therein. These forms, together with plans and specifications and form of contract are on exhibition at the offices of the War Supply Board, Ottawa, Ontario, and at the offices of the Officer Commanding, Western Air Command, Belmont Building, Victoria, B. C., at which offices plans and specifications may be obtained upon the deposit of $50.00 in the form of a certified cheque, made payable to the Receiver General of Canada. This deposit will be returned when the plans and specifications are returned in good condition.

Each tender must be accompanied by a certified cheque on a chartered bank in Canada, payable to the Receiver General of Canada, or Bearer Bonds, as specified in the form of tender, for ten per cent. (10%) of the amount of the tender.

The cheque or bonds of the successful tenderer will be forfeited should he decline to enter into a contract for the work or should he fail after accepting the contract to complete same in accordance with the plans and specifications.

The Board does not bind itself to accept the lowest or any tender.

W. R. CAMPBELL.
Chairman.

War Supply Board
Ottawa, January 4, 1940.
Tender No. 2847.

 5 - 1939

TENDER FOR THE CONSTRUCTION OF A 25 YARD MACHINE GUN RANGE AT THE R. C. A. F STATION, VANCOUVER, B. C.

SEALED Tenders, enclosed in envelope marked "Tender for Machine Gun Range, Vancouver," and addressed to the Director of Contracts, Department of National Defence, Ottawa, Ontario, will be received until 12 o'clock noon (D.S.T.) Thursday, July 27, 1939.

Tenders will not be considered unless made on the forms supplied by the Department and in accordance with the conditions set forth therein. These forms, together with the plans and specifications, may be obtained on application to the Officer Commanding, Western Air Command, 715 Hastings St. W., Vancouver, B. C., or to the Director of Contracts, Department of National Defence, Ottawa.

Each tender must be accompanied by a certified cheque on a chartered bank in Canada, payable to the order of the Honourable the Minister of National Defence for ten per cent (10%) of the amount of the tender.

The cheque of the successful tenderer will be forfeited should he decline to enter into a contract for the work, or should he fail, after accepting the contract to complete same in accordance with the plans and specifications.

The Department does not bind itself to accept the lowest or any tender.

L. R. LaFLECHE.
Deputy Minister.

Department of National Defence,
Ottawa, June 24, 1939.
(H.Q. 921-5-7 Vol. 4).

JUL 19 1939

NEW DEFENSE UNIT—First of several long-distance reconnaissance and bombing planes which will be stationed at Jericho Beach, the Stranaer flying boat pictured above was flown from Ottawa to Vancouver last week. It is shown receiving attention from R. C. A. F. engineers after its long flight.

The machine, a twin-engined flying boat, has three gunnery stations—in the bow, amidships and in the tail—carries a crew consisting of two pilots, navigating officer, wireless operator and air engineer.—It has facilities for living on board, including sleeping and cooking equipment.

Below are the two officers who piloted the machine across Canada—Squadron Leader A. J. Ashton (left), who will take command of the flight of Stranaer flying boats at Jericho Beach, and Squadron Leader F. J. Mawdsley of Ottawa.

New R.C.A.F. Bomber Coming

JUL 14 1939

OTTAWA, July 14. — (CP)—Destined for the Royal Canadian Air Force station at Vancouver, a large Stranraer bomber left Ottawa today to be flown in easy stages to the Pacific Coast. It is piloted by Squadron Leader F. J. Mawdesley, with Squadron Leader A. J. Ashton as co-pilot.

The flying boat will make stops at Sudbury, Ont.; Sioux Lookout, The Pas, Man.; Edmonton and Salmon Arm.

LETHBRIDGE, July 14.—(CP)—Work has begun on construction of a large airways building at Cowley airport, seventy five miles west of here.

Tenders are also being called by the department of transport for construction of an emergency landing field at Wasa about thirty-five miles north of Cranbrook. Both points being improved are on the Lethbridge-Vancouver airline.

R.C.A.F. Bombing "Sinks" Boat In Bay

JUN 27 1939

Police were puzzled on Monday afternoon when they received a report from a citizen that a boat was seen going up in smoke in English Bay and then sinking without a trace.

When the information was checked it was found that the R.C.A.F. planes were holding bombing practice over the Bay and the person who had phoned in had seen one of the smoke bombs exploding on the water.

Tenders Are Called For R.C.A.F. Hangar

Construction of a landplane hangar at the R.C.A.F. station at Patricia Bay, Saanich, is planned by the Federal Government, and bids for the work will be received by the director of contracts, department of national defense, Ottawa, until 1 noon (daylight saving), August 14. JUL 20 1939

Flying Officer To Receive Full Military Honors At Funeral

JUN 9 1939

Board of Inquiry Set Up By Western Air Command

An air force funeral with full military honors will draw the curtain across the tragic death of Flying Officer Thomas G. Fraser, who was killed instantly Thursday morning when his parachute began to blossom too late when he leaped from Hawker Hurricane "317" as it plummetted earthward near Mission.

A coroner's jury in Mission City yesterday concluded that the young pilot was killed "in an attempt to save his life by means of his parachute which seems to have had insufficient time to open."

Wing Commander E. L. McLeod and four other officers attended the inquest in Mission at 3:30 p.m. yesterday, nine hours after the powerful fighter plane shattered itself on the Sylvester Road, 12 miles north of Mission.

Indications were that the pilot fell out of the formation of four planes heading toward Calgary and crashed when he came out of the clouds about 800 feet above the ground.

Meanwhile a board of enquiry was set up by the R. C. A. F. Western Air Command to investigate the crash. A report will be made to the Department of Defence in Ottawa.

Last night the body lay in Gillie's Undertaking Parlors, Mission. The date or place of the funeral had not been set.

Witnesses who were beginning their farm chores in the Fraser Valley Thursday morning said that when they first saw the plane it seemed to be skimming the bottom edges of a cloud, with the motor throttled back, and then disappeared into a thicker layer.

Suddenly the olive colored ship emerged from the far side of the cloud bank with motor full on, made a steep, sharp turn and swung away from the mountains and toward the valley as if looking for a field.

As it glided earthward at high speed they heard the pilot cut the motor and saw him bail out at an altitude which witnesses said was about 500 feet. Then they saw the white plume of the pilot chute and he "seemed to fall in an arc behind the plane." Then both disappeared behind trees and spectators heard a dull thud, as the plane ploughed an eight-foot furrow in a gravel road.

Squadron Leader Fullerton arrived in Calgary at noon yesterday, and said he had learned of the accident at Lethbridge. He said he had noticed that Fraser's ship was missing from the formation, but thought that he had had engine trouble, and made a landing somewhere.

Fraser's plane had left Sea Island 15 minutes after the Squadron Leader took off, Fullerton said. "We were flying in open formation in the shape of a "V," with Fraser on my right and Davis on my left. The last time I saw Fraser he was about 150 yards in the rear."

"I turned and looked around and he seemed to be flying in perfect order with everything under control. The next time I turned a minute or so later, he was not in sight.

Flying Officer Fraser was a graduate of the University of Saskatchewan.

He was born in Suriamamale, India, and came to Canada to study agriculture. His parents, Mr. and Mrs. C. Fraser, live in Ootacamund, India. He was unmarried. He joined the R. C. A. F. January 3, 1938, as a pilot officer, and was promoted 12 months later to flying officer.

A $30,000 INVESTMENT JUL 19 1939

First Of Canada's Speedy Training Planes Lands Here

All-Metal 200-Mile-an-Hour Craft Flown From Los Angeles—More Coming.

FIRST of fifteen North American "Trainers" ordered by the department of national defense for the use of R.C.A.F. pilots landed at Vancouver airport today from Los Angeles.

It was piloted by P. B. Balfour, former New Westminster resident, who is the factory pilot for the manufacturers. He was accompanied by a mechanic, George D. McCauley.

The remaining fourteen Trainers will be delivered by air from Los Angeles.

Pilot Balfour will remain here for several days and give Flight Lieut. Ernest MacNab instruction in handling the planes. MacNab, in turn will instruct R.C. A.F. pilots from the East in handling the planes which will be flown east to Trenton, Ont., for instruction purposes.

Flight Lieut. F. L. Johnson of Ottawa is here to take delivery of the training ships.

A fast low-wing all-metal monoplane, the Trainer is capable of 200 miles per hour and is fully equipped with radio. There are mountings for two machine guns and bomb racks. Each machine is said to have cost nearly $30,000.

R.C.A.F. Cadets Receiving Preliminary Training Here

JUN 17 1939

Four Probationary Officers Start On Course With Aero Club at City Airport

PRELIMINARY training of probationary officers for the R.C.A.F. is now in full swing by several of the flying clubs in Western Canada, including Vancouver. Four officers have been assigned to the Aero Club of B.C., and Instructor "Hal" Wilson has taken them under his experienced wing.

The young men, who will receive fifty hours' flying instruction during the next twelve weeks, are F. B. Curry of Toronto, P. W. S. Lochnan, Ottawa, D. F. Manders and W. J. G. Clarke, both of Vancouver.

Besides instruction in flying, the young officers receive daily lectures on such subjects as airmanship, engines, navigation, signalling and raidio rigging. Instructor Frank Hawkridge has been appointed assistant to Mr. Wilson.

GUARDIAN OF THE PACIFIC—Silhouetted against the sky, the air gunner, his muffler streaming and his great flying suit bulging in the howling gale of the big bomber's front cockpit, takes aim with his Lewis gun. This dramatic picture was taken by Lloyd Turner, Vancouver Daily Province staff photographer, during a five-day patrol flight with the R. C. A. F. on the B. C. coast.

NEWSMEN TASTE AIR WAR

JUST PASSENGERS ON "BOMBER"

JAN 4 1940

Battling Storms Along B.C. Coast Anything But a Tea Party

In order to record the splendid work of the airmen guarding Canada's Pacific frontiers, Peter Stursberg, staff reporter, and Lloyd Turner, staff photographer, became the first Canadian newspapermen to go on wartime patrol duty, when they flew for five days in a ten-ton bomber up the storm-tossed B. C. coast.

Today, Mr. Stursberg describes how they left Jericho Air Station, main Pacific base, and battled the worst type of B. C. weather to reach an R.C.A.F. outpost.

By PETER STURSBERG.

The cup stayed in my hand, but the tea stayed where it was. For a moment it was a cylinder of brown liquid frozen in the air. Then it fell back into the cup, almost all of it, only a little splashing out.

Another bump, this time sideways, and the stove and pots and pans came clattering down in the narrow galley. The storm was tossing the great ten-ton bomber around like a feather in a gust of wind.

The "graveyard of planes," they call the British Columbia coast. Yet for five days, Lloyd Turner, The Vancouver Daily Province staff photographer, and I flew over 2000 miles in the worst kind of flying weather along this coast with the airmen from Jericho Air Station, who patrol it daily.

We "went to war" with the R.C.A.F. For five days we ate and slept and worked with them, searching for submarines and enemy vessels. And at first hand we saw the aerial defense net which has been stretched along Canada's Pacific Coast.

• • •

On a sunny morning we took off from Jericho Air Station in a Stranraer flying boat, manned by a crew of seven under Squadron Leader F. J. Mawdesley.

There was the thunder of the waves hitting the hull, the hiss of spray pouring over the many bombs which hung from our wings, and the twin-engined ship, which takes off and climbs as fast as any flying boat in the world, was sailing over Vancouver.

Circling over Jericho, Flight Sergeant Bob Wilcock, the head fitter or engineer, flashed "goodbye" with an Aldis lamp. "Leaving for Victoria," Corporal E. W. Pierce, sitting in front of the radio, signalled the base.

Out in the Straits it was bright and clear. The plane wheeled and dropped a small marker bomb which made a white puddle of aluminum powder on the sea. Then diving, it loosed three practice bombs—one, two, three, they hit the target.

That would have made short work of a submarine," said the navigator, Flight Lieutenant Con Farrell with a grin.

A sharp rat-a-tat sounded above the drone of the engines. Standing in the front cockpit, the wind howling around him, a helmeted air gunner sprayed the white puddle with machine gun bullets.

• • •

Without anyone so much as touching the pilot's controls, the automatic pilot brought us straight to Victoria. A blanket of fog covered the Capital City.

The pilot pulled the Supermarine Stranraer over the fog, and we were in another world, a Christmassy world of snow, whipped into ice-cream cone peaks, and lit by the soft rays of a wintry sun.

Finding a hole in the fog, we returned to earth. Beneath us stretched the great runways of the new R.C.A.F. base at Patricia Bay. Landing on the bay we picked up Major G. R. Chetwynd, an army engineer officer attached to the Western Air Command.

"Will try to reach No. 3 base," Squadron Leader Mawdesley instructed the radio operator, after studying weather reports which were not altogether favorable. I sat beside the pilot as we cruised across Vancouver Island at a steady 95 knots.

Though the sun was out, a wind was beginning to catch us, and as we bumped along a mysterious valley, I saw storm clouds gathering.

• • •

"It looks pretty black ahead," I yelled to make my voice heard above the engines' roar.

"If anyone can get through, we can get through," Squadron Leader Mawdesley shouted in my ears, and though we turned back once, I knew then we would reach our destination.

Now the plane was pitching and tossing so that the notes I jotted down became squiggly hieroglyphics. Mist swept past us and began to fuzz up the scenery.

In the swaying tail, the crew were cooking a hot meal, and we had fun trying to put the stew into our mouths. Suddenly the plane dropped hundreds of feet in a particularly violent air bump, like a stone in a vacuum, and it was then that my tea stayed up in the air.

• • •

Now we were in the centre of the storm and the rain sounded like steel rods hitting the plane. In the gloom the pilot leaned out of his cockpit and yelled to the navigator: "Turning back."

For a few minutes we headed for the safe haven of a sheltered inland lake. Then the pilot shouted "Trying again."

Opening a window in the cockpit, he peered out at the murky landscape. He was steering the

ALL SHIPS MET BY AIR PATROLS

JAN 3 1940

In order to record the splendid work of the airmen guarding the Pacific Coast, Peter Stursberg, staff reporter of The Vancouver Daily Province, and Lloyd Turner, staff photographer, became the first Canadian newspapermen to go on war-time patrol duty when they flew for five days in a ten-ton bomber up the storm-swept B. C. coast.

Today Mr. Stursberg describes a routine inspection of a ship which they made, and their flight to Prince Rupert.

By PETER STURSBERG.

In the early light of the dawn, the sea was grey and the ship a pencil mark in the distance. Bundled up in a thick "teddy-bear" flying suit, I sat beside the pilot of the Supermarine Stranraer bomber as we went out to inspect it.

For five days I flew with the R.C.A.F. on war-time patrol duty, and inspection of all shipping was one of our most important jobs in guarding the British Columbia coast.

A crew man crawled beneath us into the front cockpit. In a few minutes we were on top of the ship. Evidently the captain had seen us coming, for, as we wheeled over it, we saw a sailor walking away from the British flag he had just raised.

"We are now reporting all particulars of that ship by wireless," the pilot, Squadron Leader F. J. Mawdesley, said to me, "and if it was in any way a suspicious ship it would be further investigated by surface craft and aircraft."

We were completing a patrol off the west coast of Vancouver Island and had just received orders to proceed to Esquimalt and go from there to Prince Rupert.

Sitting beside the pilot, I watched the rows of dials on the dashboard—air speed meter, altimeter, thermometer, oil gauges. One quivering panel of six instruments was worth $5000, the pilot told me.

Just one of the instruments on this panel, the direction finder, cost $1000. By means of this the plane could be kept on its right course, the squadron leader explained.

"The navigator gives me a compass reading to travel on," he said. "I put the aircraft on that reading, then I adjust the direction finder to zero, and all I have to do is to keep it at zero."

At the entrance to the Alberni Canal, tiny fishing boats bobbed around in the heavy swell. In Esquimalt a naval tug pulled us out so we could take off.

• • •

Between Nanaimo and Qualicum I drank a cup of tea. This flying fortress had all the comforts of home. Beside a galley there were half a dozen bunks and hammocks, though more than six men had slept on board during an emergency.

There was a desk where the navigator worked. At regular intervals he reported the position of the plane, its direction and ground speed. So that, if it was forced down, the base would know its exact whereabouts.

The sun was not shining over Seymour Narrows and storm clouds hung menacingly over Vancouver Island. Logging camps made a bright splash of red and yellow against the dull green of the forests that came down to the sea.

From an island below, a signal light flashed at us. We replied with our Aldis lamp, then wheeled around and landed. After a few minutes we took off again, the choppy water on the hull making a noise like a barrage of heavy guns.

• • •

Over the open sea again, the pilot dropped a heavy bomb. It made a great churning in the water below, but, strangely enough, was not as spectacular as a 20-pound practice bomb with its smoke.

Looking out over the snow-clad mountains around Namu, I ate the stew which the crew had made on the kerosene stove in the tail of the plane. This flying home had all the comforts except that it was a bid cold.

We were now at 4000 feet and the temperature inside was two degrees Centigrade. However, we didn't feel it in our warm "teddy bear" suits.

On we sped over the half-land, half-sea of Smith Sound, the muskeg and forest of the northland toward Prince Rupert. Wind blowing through mountain gaps jolted us.

• • •

The weather was dirty and we flew low through Grenville Channel. Again I sat beside the pilot and I held a map for him to follow.

In a blinding rainstorm we wheeled over Prince Rupert and landed. After eight hours' flying my ears were still humming as I went ashore, and I could still feel the plane swaying under my feet.

But I didn't dream about flying. I slept like a log in this northern city where the street lights stay on till 9 o'clock in the morning.

Jericho In The News: 1930-1947

DAWN PATROL WITH R.C.A.F.

JAN 10 1940

In order to record the work of the airmen guarding the Pacific Coast, Peter Stursberg, staff reporter of The Vancouver Daily Province, accompanied by Lloyd Turner, staff photographer, became the first Canadian newspapermen to go on war-time patrol duty when they flew for five days in a ten-ton bomber up the storm-swept B. C. coast. Today Mr. Stursberg describes a reconnaissance flight around the Queen Charlotte Islands and life at an R.C.A.F. outpost.

By PETER STURSBERG

They work over uncharted waters and unsurveyed coasts whose forbidding shores and angry seas equal in cold ferocity Tierra del Fuego and all the horrors of the Horn.

They live in a rain-soaked wilderness where a haircut is a luxury and the dawn comes up at 10 o'clock in the morning.

After five days' flying with the R. C. A. F. on wartime patrol duty along the British Columbia coast, I got to know how these airmen who guard Canada's Pacific shores work and live.

• • •

One day in Prince Rupert our orders were to fly around Queen Charlotte Islands on a reconnaissance patrol. At 9 o'clock in the morning, while the street lights were still on, we drove the couple of miles to Seal Cove, where contracts have just been let for an R. C. A. F. base.

There our Supermarine Stranraer bomber was riding at anchor in the lake-like calm of this sheltered bay.

The fitters (engineers on a plane), Sergeant Bob Wilcock and Aircraftsman J. Cooper, had made their daily check of the great Bristol Pegasus engine, and in a few minutes we were off.

Exactly on the calculated minute our nose was over the long needle of sand which is Rose Point. Mile after mile we flew along the east side of the island a flat, desolate wasteland of muskeg and forest.

• • •

At Tlell a road cut a straight line across the muskeg and forest. Somehow it seemed like a canal on Mars and we talked about the road till long after we had passed it.

Skidegate Inlet and the flat muskeg and forest began to roll into hills and then mountains. Again exactly on the minute, according to the navigator's calculation, we reached Cape St. James, the end of the Queen Charlottes.

Around one of the loneliest lighthouses in the world, perched on a bare rock in the Pacific, we came upon the most awe-inspiring sight. The sea boiled white and angrily on jagged rocks and the land steamed with mist and fog.

It was a mariners nightmare, a Dantes Inferno, and out of its maw two golden eagles winged their way toward us as if to warm us away from their abode.

"A sight for the gods, was how the commander of the bomber, Squadron Leader F. J. Mawdesley, described it. According to the Canadian Pilot, bible of all airmen of the Pacific, the forbidding shores of the west coast of Queen Charlotte Islands have never been completely surveyed.

• • •

Those who have seen this coast, and they are few, consider it worse than Tierra del Fuego and Cape Horn. The westernmost barrier of Canada, the Queen Charlottes ramparts jut out in serried lines like rocky teeth gnashing in fury at invaders.

Over Langara Lighthouse we saw the faint lines of Alaska, and, more distinctly, Rose Point, where we started our reconnaissance flight. At Naden Harbor, a famous old-time whaling station, we swooped down to come to rest on the calm waters.

There I met S. L. Simpson, manager of the Queen Charlotte Cannery, which is reputed to put up the best canned crab in the world. He gave me a couple of tins of his toothsome delicacies.

While Haida Indians from the Masset Reserve, who work at the cannery, waved good-bye, we took off and sailed back to Prince Rupert.

• • •

That's how they work. Now, how do these airmen who guard British Columbia live? Up and down the coast in odd havens and at strategic spots are a network of R. C. A. F. outposts.

At one outpost somewhere on the coast we followed the commanding officer, Flight Lieutenant Mike Doyle, up a steep path. It was a dark night, without a star showing, and our only light was the narrow beam of a torch.

The men lived in a house which the R. C. A. F. had rented for $10 a month, but which, with new oil stove, plumbing and other improvements, was warm, comfortable and clean.

Some of the men were playing darts, while others were sitting around in chairs reading, writing, or just listening to the radio. The only inconvenience the airmen suffered was that in this little fishing village they couldn't get a haircut.

BOMBER BUCKS A HURRICANE

JAN 13 1940

• • • • • •

Newsmen Thrilled As Seaplane Tackles 100-Mile-An-Hour Gale

In order to record the work of the airmen guarding the Pacific Coast, Peter Stursberg, staff reporter of The Vancouver Daily Province, accompanied by Lloyd Turner, staff photographer, became the first Canadian newspapermen to go on wartime patrol duty when they flew for five days in a ten-ton bomber up the storm-swept B. C. coast.

Today, Mr. Stursberg concludes the series by describing the hurricane which forced them to take shelter at an R.C.A.F. emergency station in a lonely northern cove.

By PETER STURSBERG.

Angel cake weather isn't the sort of stuff for storms. And I didn't think there was much wrong — except that our big bomber seemed to take such a long time to pass those islands beneath us.

Not until we turned tail and ran for shelter to a lonely cove further north did I realize we had been battling a hurricane

The sky was all blue and gold the brightest we'd had in five days of flying on war-time patrol duty with the Air Force, though the wind was screaming around the pilot's high cockpit where I was sitting.

It was kicking up the waters of the Sound beneath us but the weather was so clear and we were so high it didn't seem much. Later, when Squadron Leader F. J. Mawdesley asked me how big I thought the waves were, I guessed five feet.

"They were at least twelve feet high," he said, "And the wind must have been tossing the spray a good hundred feet."

The first inkling I got of the hurricane was when the navigator, Flight Lieutenant Con Farrell, remarked: "We're getting nowhere."

Our 2000 horsepower Bristol Pegasus engines were making only fifteen knots against the gale.

When we turned around and ran with it, our speed was 185 knots.

So the wind was blowing at 100 miles an hour.

The sky was overcast as we dropped down on the murky water beside an R.C.A.F. floating dock in a lonely cove. We had beaten the storm—but only by a few minutes.

As we clambered aboard the scow, the crew rolled drums of gasoline to the plane. After refuelling, the big flying boat taxied to a mooring.

• • •

Just in time. The hurricane hit us, whipping the waters of the sheltered cove into a froth. Spray whistled over white caps racing past the dock.

Everything seemed to lean before the storm. Two ducks flying forward were going backward. The Air-Force ensign which had been new two weeks before was torn in shreds.

In oil skins and sou'westers, Corporal C. M. Martin, who was in charge of the crew of five manning the floating station and Aircraftsman J. Munn were crouching at the end of the dock.

"My God, they're going out in an outboard," someone said.

It was the most daring thing I had ever seen. Suppose the puttering engine failed . . . With bated breath we watched them clinging to their boat which was sometimes thrown into the air by the waves, and sometimes lost to sight in the spray.

But the engine didn't fail, and they reached the plane with a rope to attach it to another mooring, in case one slipped.

• • •

On board the bomber, Squadron Leader Mawdesley was actually flying at anchor. The air speedometer which works on air pressure was showing sixty-five knots. The wind was blowing at seventy-five miles per hour in a sheltered cove.

On board the scow we stood in the door of the men's cozy quarters, watching an island only 100 yards away, swing back and forth.

"This is worse than the storm which blew the scow across the bay, despite the fact we had out six anchors," said Corporal A. E. Thomas.

At that moment we felt the bumping drag of the anchors. Again and again—we stood by the door and watched the island get closer.

• • •

Beside a battery radio was a tinselly invitation. On it was written in childish script: "To the boys at the scow. We at the Rural School invite you to our Christmas concert."

There was another grinding crunch. "It's jumped a rock," someone said.

After three hours the wind died down. At 5 o'clock we had our first meal since breakfast of bully beef, carrots, potatoes canned peas, and bread and butter.

That night I slept on the floor of the scow with my "teddy bear" flying suit as a comforter and a gunny sack as a pillow.

Death Ends Norse Flyer's Plan for Week-end Ski Jaunt

FEB 22 1941

"If nothing unsuspected happens I will compete in the Red Cross tournament next Sunday, and I hope to see you there."

These seemingly prophetic words were penned to Don Tyrell, ski editor of The Vancouver Daily Province, by Student Pilot Erling Jorgensen of the Royal Norwegian Naval Air Force a few hours before he flew to his death.

Jorgensen, 25-year-old student flyer, and Sub-Lieut. Harald Kruse, instructor, met sudden death late Friday afternoon when a new Northrop N-3PB bomber, which they were piloting, crashed into the water off Point Atkinson.

The plane struck with terrific force and sank almost immediately in more than 400 feet of water, leaving only a few scraps of wreckage on the surface.

There was no chance for the two flyers to escape from the plane, even if they had survived the crash.

Jorgensen and Kruse, who had escaped from the Nazis in their native Norway, came to Vancouver with the Royal Norwegian Naval Air Force. They had been here only a short time, but had made many friends in ski and social circles.

Erling Jorgensen's death brought tragedy to a young bride of less than two months. Mary Loosemore of Toronto, had met the young flyer in the eastern city and married him on December 29.

She was excited and happy when she saw the Pacific Coast for the first time with her handsome husband.

"We expect to have the happiest lives in the world," she said.

Today, widowed by the tragic crash, she says she will probably return to her parents in the East.

The death of the two Norwegian flyers cast a pall of gloom over the 31st anniversary banquet and dance of the Sons of Norway. They were to have been guests of honor on Friday evening.

"I watched the plane for more than a minute before it fell" stated J. H. MacDonald, 2415 Yew, this morning: "It was certainly in distress and the engine was missing badly.

"The motor seemed to be hitting on about two cylinders. The plane seemed to be having a lot of trouble, for it kept wobbling and circling down towards the water. Another plane was following it not far behind."

Mr. MacDonald was unable to see the plane hit the water as his view was temporarily obscured.

Four Are Missing As RCAF Plane Crashes On Coast

DEC 30 1941

Flying Boat Ir Crack-up At Ucluelet

STRIKES TREES

(By Canadian Press.)

VICTORIA, Dec. 30. — Western Air Command of the Royal Canadian Air Force announced today four men are missing and four are injured slightly, following the crash of a large flying boat at Ucluelet, on the west coast of Vancouver Island, this morning.

In a brief statement, Western Air Command said the flying boat crashed into trees soon after taking off half a mile south of Ucluelet station, and added that next-of-kin are being notified.

Ucluelet is about 100 miles up the west coast of Vancouver Island, at the mouth of Barkley Sound.

S-HERALD, WEDNESDAY. DECEMBER 31, 1941

DEC 31 1941

Believe Four Fliers Perished In Fire As RCAF Plane Crashed On Island

VICTORIA—(BUP)—The charred, twisted wreckage of a giant Royal Canadian Air Force flying boat which crashed and burned near Ucluelet, on the west coast of Vancouver Island, was searched last night for the remains of four airmen who were trapped and perished in the flames.

The Western Air Command announced Tuesday morning that four airmen were slightly injured and four others were "missing" in the crash, but Tuesday night they said that the four reported missing were believed to have been burned to death in the plane.

The giant plane crashed into a clump of trees a half-mile south of the air base at Ucluelet shortly after taking off, and burst into flames. It blazed and smouldered for hours.

The air command said that next of kin of the victims were being notified and an inquiry was being held into the disaster—the third major one involving R.C.A.F. planes in British Columbia in two months.

The names of the victims are expected to be released at noon today, and the extent of the injuries suffered by the four airmen who escaped death and how they escaped will be revealed at the inquiry.

Officials said the plane was leaving the air station at Ucluelet on a routine flight when it crashed. It was believed the four survivors were thrown clear of the wreckage as the plane struck the tree tops, but the four others were trapped.

Name Crewmen

SEEK BOMBER NEAR ALBERNI

NOV 12 1941

Identity of the crew of an R.C.A.F. flying boat which disappeared a week ago on a flight from Penticton to Patricia Bay was revealed today by Ottawa, as planes from the island station continued the search, concentrating in the Alberni district.

R. C. A. F. headquarters announced that the names of the five flyers were in Tuesday's casualty list.

They are: LAC. Charles Murray Ross, whose wife lives at Vernon, Sgt. Jack Fenton Bliss, father living in San Diego; Sgt. Gerald Searing Palmer, whose mother is in Raymond, Alta.; Cpl. John Robert Bruce Fernie, whose wife lives at Rimbey, Alta.; and LAC. Gilbert Fowler Willett, whose wife lives at Hampton Station, N.B.

FEAR BOAT SANK.

Numerous flights over the Alberni Valley were made today on the strength of a report the missing Stranraer flying boat was seen flying low on November 4, the day the pilot radioed he was lost in a snowstorm.

Fears that the plane continued westward out to sea and sank were expressed by R.C.A.F. officers but the search continued throughout the eighth day.

Rev. F. E. Pitts, former principal of the Indian residential school in Alberni, said he saw a large plane fly over his farm, about two miles from Port Alberni, on November 4.

He said he had a good view of the machine from a distance of about 300 yards and that it appeared to be flying in the direction of Mount Arrowsmith.

POOR VISIBILITY.

Mr. Pitts said fog and darkness made visibility poor. The plane was flying so low that he at first feared it would not clear the trees surrounding the pasture.

After viewing pictures of various types of planes, Mr. Pitts said the machine he saw was a Stranraer flying boat.

Reports have reached Port Alberni from McCoy Lake, 12 miles northeast, and from Franklin River, south of Alberni, stating that a plane was heard circling in low-hanging clouds last Tuesday

Fail In Search For Missing Plane

VICTORIA, B.C.— (BUP).— Royal Canadian Air Force officials announced Sunday night after a day of searching for the lost air force flying boat that planes had returned to their bases without sighting signs of the giant craft. NOV 10 1941

BELIEVE SIGNALS FROM LOST PLANE

NOV 14 1941

Hopes that an R.C.A.F. flying boat missing since November 4 may be down in the wilds of the Alberni district were strengthened late Thursday by a report of what may be smoke signals.

Two men working in the Great Central Lake area reported to B. C. Provincial Police in Victoria they had seen smoke puffs rising from the bush, on a bearing of 10 degrees north of west from Great Central Lake mill.

The report was handed to the R.C.A.F. command at Victoria, who have been searching continuously since November 4 for a Stranraer flying boat with a crew of five, missing on a flight from Penticton to Patricia Bay.

The smoke report was the most direct of several from individuals in the Alberni district. All clues, it was said, are being tracked down as the search proceeds.

REPORT LOST PLANE AT GARIBALDI LAKE

NOV 22 1941

Rumors that an R.C.A.F. flying boat with a crew of five, missing since November 4 on a flight from Penticton, has been located at Garibaldi Lake, were heard in the city today.

The rumors stated that a member of the crew had made his way out to civilization and revealed the fate of the big Stranraer plane.

No confirmation of this was given by Western Air Command headquarters of the R. C. A. F.

Persons reached by telephone at settlements on the P.G.E. Railway near Garibaldi Lake denied the report that an airman had appeared there.

It had been reported, early in the search for the lost aircraft, that it was seen over Garibaldi Park, 60 miles north of Squamish, about the time the pilot radioed he was in a snowstorm, running out of fuel and look for a place to land.

Plane Wreck, Body Found Near Squamish

Oct. 11 1947.

RAYMOND, Alta. (CP)—Mrs. F. Marion Palmer of Raymond said she has been advised that the body of her son, Gerald Palmer, 22, pilot of an RCAF amphibian plane missing since the spring of 1941 has been found near Squamish.

The plane carried five men on a flight between Lethbridge and Vancouver and it was indicated that by the appearance of the wreckage, spotted 10 miles east of Squamish, all aboard died instantly.

A party has been sent to hold memorial services and erect a cairn to the dead airmen.

RCAF officials earlier this week announced the finding of the plane, but said they could not release details until all next-of-kin of lost personnel had been notified. They refused to say how many persons had been aboard

R.C.A.F. PLANE LOST

Seven Flyers Die In Crash Near Nanaimo

DEC 16 1941

Stanraer Patrol Boat Drops Into Water At Nanoose

STORMY SEA

Seven young flyers are dead—their bodies trapped in the cabin of a flying boat that hit the water and sank, yesterday off Nanoose Bay—the Western Air Command of the R.C.A.F. announced today.

Dead are: SERGT. G. H. ANDREWS of Abbotsford.

FLT.-LT. D. C. MACDOUGALL, Winnipeg.

SGT. R. T. MITCHELL, Strasbourg, Sask.

SGT. R. WOOD, Norwood, Man.

LAC. W. D. RILEY, REGINA.

AC1. R. W. ADAMS, Edmonton.

AC1. R. A. BLAKELY, Kamsack, Sask.

TEN-FOOT WAVES.

Today, as high winds whipped up 10-foot waves across the reef-strewn bay, 10 miles north of Nanaimo, work parties of the Air Force and police grappled for the stricken Stranraer and the seven lads in the cabin.

Recover Bodies Of 7 RCAF Men

NANAIMO, B.C. — (BUP) — A navy crash boat left Nanoose Bay at 11 p.m. Friday, carrying the bodies of seven of the R. C. A. F. airmen who lost their lives when a bomber plane crashed into Nanoose Bay last Monday afternoon, provincial police reported.

DEC 20 1941

(The Western Air Command Friday announced there were eight men and not seven as previously announced aboard the plane.)

The salvage boat Skookum No. 2 of Vancouver hooked the sunken plane and towed her three-quarters of a mile under water to a shallower place in the bay where she was raised.

PARACHUTED TO RIVER

Flyer Missing As Planes Crash at Mouth of Fraser

DEC 24 1941

A student pilot who parachuted from his plane when it was in collision with another at the mouth of the Fraser River is missing and may have been drowned.

Details of the accident, which occurred at 12:30 p.m. Tuesday, were released today by Leslie J. Martin, manager of No. 18 Elementary Flying Training School at Boundary Bay.

LEADING AIRCRAFTMAN DENNIS PERCIVAL FROUDE, 22, of Regina, a R.C.A.F. student pilot, bailed out of his Tiger moth training plane when it was hit by another and spun out of control.

He was seen as he floated down to the surface of the river, Mr. Martin said, and the parachute was recovered a few minutes later by a crash boat.

Froude had discarded the chute and could not be found.

It is thought probable that he has drowned. He wore a heavy flying suit, boots and gear. The next of kin in Regina have been notified.

Fraude's machine fell out of control when the wing of another plane, piloted by LAC. W. Holland, hit the tail end of the fuselage, smashing the tail assembly.

Froude bailed out immediately and reached the surface of the river near Westham Island at the mouth of the Fraser.

Holland's machine was undamaged and he landed immediately, unhurt.

Both aircraft were in routine flight, Mr. Martin said, at about 2000 feet. Weather was good with ceiling unlimited.

He said three boats are searching the area today and dragging operations for the body are under way.

NEED MORE AIRMEN JAN 3 1942

RCAF Unit to Seek Recruits On Tour of Coastal Centres

A mobile recruiting unit of the R.C.A.F. with facilities for medical examination and attestation of new men will visit Prince Rupert, Ocean Falls and Powell River January 5 to 14 inclusive.

Specified quotas of classes of recruits are set for each locality and applications will be accepted only on the first two days of the visit in order to allow time for enlistment procedure and attestation on the last day.

The unit will be in Ocean Falls January 7, 8 and 9, in Powell River January 10 and 11, and in Prince Rupert January 14, 15 and 16.

SET QUOTA.

The quota set for immediate enlistment in Prince Rupert includes nine aircrew (pilots and observers), five standard tradesmen, 20 general duties and 1 radio mechanic (for university training).

For Powell River it is six aircrew, five standard tradesmen, 15 general duties and one radio mechanic (U.T.)

Ocean Falls has been allotted five aircrew, five standard tradesmen, 10 general duties and one radio mechanic (U.T.)

There is also a call for young men with a minimum of one year high school, but with not sufficient educational qualifications for aircrew, who may be enrolled in the youth training school for airframe mechanics, aero engine mechanics and wireless operators (ground).

Those with two years high school completed, who are physically fit for aircrew may be enrolled in the pre-enlistment school for pilots and observers in order to bring their educational qualifications up to standard.

VISIT ISLAND.

Another R. C. A. F. recruiting party will visit a number of Vancouver Island points early in January.

The itinerary is: Port Alberni, City Hall Council Chambers, January 5 and 6; Courtenay, Legion Hall, January 7; Nanaimo, Eagles Hall, January 8 and 9; Duncan, City Council Chambers, January 9 and 10.

Besides air crew candidates, applicants are also desired for training as aero engine mechanics, air frame mechanics and wireless operators (ground). Educational requirements are one year of high school.

There are also openings for steam engineers and firemen (works and buildings). These men should have experience and valid certificates.

GENERAL DUTIES.

There is also a need for men between the ages of 18 and 50, with grade eight standing, to be enlisted for general duties. Men with two years' high school, who are physically fit, can be enrolled in the pre-enlistment school for pilots and observers in order to bring their educational qualifications up to standard.

A medical officer will accompany the mobile recruiting officer so that applicants will be medically examined as they submit their applications.

13,000 B.C. Men Join Army, RCAF

VICTORIA, Dec. 31.—(CP)—Figures released today showed that during 1941 in British Columbia 6711 men enlisted in the army and 6300 in the Royal Canadian Air Force. Naval figures were not available, but enlistments in the senior branch were greatly stimulated during December by Japan's declaration of war. DEC 31 1941

Sky Scrapings

From No. 1 Recruiting Centre, R.C.A.F.
Royal-Bank Building, Vancouver

MAY 30 1942

By FLYING OFFICER "BOB" WILLIAMS

Among recruits recently enlisted by the No. 1 recruiting centre of the Royal Canadian Air Force in the Royal Bank Building were:

Vancouver—Arthur S. Burket jr., Neville C. Holman, Charles Pawlett, Jean Phillipe Rene Bourget, Stuart W. Boucher, Bruce E. Tees, Joseph B. Loftus, Thomas K. Cunningham, Joseph W. Nevison, Gerald Michael Doyle, Robert F Jones, Hans B. Pedersen, Harry F. Miles.

Victoria—Vincent C. Knox, George H. Birnie, Douglas W. Smith, Lory A. Gaetz, Aikman E. Todd.

Others—Herschell E. Simmons and Edgar T. Wilton, North Vancouver; Percy Gladstone, Skidegate Mission; Donald E. McLean, Cloverdale; Walter M. Jefferd, Port Moody; Thomas Hughes, Courtenay; Douglas H. Aitchison, Daly J. Dorgan Allan L. Burris, New Westminster; Gilbert S. Swain, Saskatoon; Francis A. Clarke, Los Angeles; Wilfred F. Fletcher, Duncan; Robert W. Fulton, Dauphin, Man.

Badge of Two Wars

Pilot Officer Vernon H. Johnson, son of Mr. and Mrs. C. G. Johnson of Golden, who is now serving overseas as an observer in a Royal Canadian Air Force Lockheed Hudson squadron of the coastal command, wears an old and battered observer's wing on his chest.

The wing is exactly 24 years old, and was worn during the Great War by Pilot Officer Johnson's father, who served as an observer in the Royal Flying Corps and the R.A.F. from late 1917 to the Armistice.

The elder Johnson, now employed by the Canadian Pacific Railway Company at Golden, enlisted in the Canadian Railway Corps and later transferred to the R.F.C. His son, an employee of the Royal Bank of Canada in New Westminster, is 22 and enlisted in January, 1941.

"Bruin" Squadron

A Royal Canadian Air Force Spitfire Squadron of fighter command, commanded by Squadron Leader R. E. Morrow, formerly of Vancouver, is adopting the snarling head of a Canadian black bear as the squadron crest.

"We've been thinking about getting ourselves a crest for some time," says the squadron leader, "but we couldn't make up our minds what the crest would be.

"For a while, we thought about using a Canadian grey goose, but the colors don't stand out well enough. So we decided on the bear's head."

Women's Division

The first two meteorologists to be enlisted in the women's division at the Vancouver recruiting centre are Miss L. M. Cooper, 1066 West Twelfth, and Miss Nora Nedden, 6507 Cypress street, who leaves for a specail course of training at Rockcliffe.

Current requirements include applicants for enlistment as general duties, clerks (general), cooks and laundrywomen.

It is claimed by those who know—the men on stations—that the standard of cooking has greatly improved since the ladies moved in.

Need Skilled Tradesmen

A limited number of vacancies for enlistment in the R. C. A. F. have been announced for the following trades.

Pumpman and fireman, first class (works and buildings).

Fitters (diesel) and fitters (general).

The necessary qualifications and application forms can be obtained from the Vancouver recruiting office

Air Gunner's Song

Lads who are selected as wireless air gunners instead of pilots are sometimes disappointed until they discover how important their duties are. Their theme song, written by Sergeant Gunner "G. H. H.", shows pretty well how they feel:

I wished to be a pilot,
And you, along with me,
But if we all were pilots
Where would the Air Force be?

It takes GUTS to be a gunner,
To sit out in the tail,
When the Messerschmitts are coming
And the slugs begin to wail.

The pilot's just a chauffeur,
It's his job to fly the plane;
But it's WE who do the fighting
Though we may not get the fame.

If we must all be gunners,
Then let us make this bet:
We'll be the best darn gunners
That have left this station yet!

"Mobile" Moves Again

The Mobile Recruiting Unit is looking forward to its approaching visit to the sunny Okanagan, preceded by two days at the City Hall, New Westminster, on June 2 and 3.

After servicing the Royal City they move on to the armories in Kamloops, June 8 and 9, and then proceed according to the following itinerary:

Kamloops—June 8, 9 a.m. to 9 p.m.; June 9, 9 a.m. to 5 p.m.

Salmon Arm—June 10, 9 a.m. to 8 p.m.

Armstrong—June 11, 9 a.m. to 8 p.m.

Vernon—June 12, 9 a.m. to 9 p.m.; June 13, 9 a.m. to 5 p.m.

Kelowna—June 15, 9 a.m. to 9 p.m.; June 16, 9 a.m. to 5 p.m.

Penticton—June 17, 9 a.m. to 9 p.m.; June 18, 9 a.m. to 5 p.m.

Princeton—June 19, 9 a.m. to 8 p.m.

Merritt—June 20, 9 a.m. to 8 p.m.

AUG 7 1942 THE VANCOUVER DAILY PROVINCE, FRIDAY, AUGUST 7,

Royal Canadian Air Force Bombers Patrol Coast Waters

FLYING BOATS SPEED TO SEA

AUG • 7 1942

By LLOYD TURNER.

Just let's suppose that you were a Japanese submarine all prepared to go to work in the waters off British Columbia's coast.

In the first place you would cruise cautiously up to some vital spot in the shipping lanes, aided of course, with maps provided by a former fishing relative. Then you would sit back quietly and wait for your first victim.

This sounds simple, and in fact it would be simple but for one or two things.

After a tour of a secret west coast air base last week, I found out just how much trouble you are going to have.

SLEEP LIGHTLY.

Now as you are still a sub, and are rolling safely in the pretty green Pacific swells somewhere off the coast of Vancouver Island, you feel smug. You're the early-bird that gets the pay-off, and you'll never be troubled by lazy Canadians, you think.

But haven't you forgotten something? Yes. It's the Royal Canadian Air Force, and as dawn comes clamily out of the liquid mists at our air station, the motors of its huge reconnaissance bombing planes awake. They're doing it all up and down the coast. They sleep lightly and little these men and machines.

Piloted by a fair-haired youth from Washington, D.C., **who has** been in the R.C.A.F. for two **years, and who doesn't like Japanese submarines one little** bit, we take off for routine patrol duty.

Seven of a crew and myself are on board. We have a huge chunk of the ocean and shoreline to search and we don't want to miss you if you are there.

CAN SEE SHADOW.

Still secure in your early-risen tin fish, you loll through the waves waiting for victims. But wait. There's something in the sky.

"It's too big for a seagull. No Zeros around here. It must be a Canadian airplane."

You hiss orders, and your sub dives. But the roaring, zooming bomber has seen you and can still see your shadow below the nice green Canadian sea. There are explosions and eruptions and for a little while the sea loses its color and is full of holes and boiling spray.

Well that's the end of your success as a Japanese raider, and the sea returns to its pleasant rolling greenness once more.

You didn't want to be a successful Jap sub anyway, did you?

This is just about the way I had it explained to me with gestures by the R.C.A.F. And to prove their points they took me flying on one of their actual war patrols looking for submarines.

Early one morning, in a rugged type of reconnaissance ship we took off from a camouflaged seaplane base, somewhere on the coast. We rose fearlessly into the perpetual mist of the coastline and started off on a search for the enemy.

Pilot Officer E. L. "Buck" Buchanan, a 22-year-old veteran of the R.C.A.F. and a one-time resident of Washington, was at the controls. We circled carefully along the coastline, checking each bay and inlet. Nothing was there. At a pre-designated spot we shot out to sea, here was the part of the ocean we had to cover.

All was peaceful at sea and the powerful engines lulled us sleepily along. Suddenly with a roar we were off in a sweeping dive. The airgunners of the plane started swinging their weapons and P.O. Alex MacDonald, a Sydney boy, and the navigator-observer, grabbed his camera gun.

RETURNS SIGNAL.

It was a ship and before we were within a thousand feet of her, lights flashed from the bridge and signals raced back and forth to the plane.

"She's okay. Just a coastwise craft," said Alex, in a faked New Zealand accent, as he took identifying pictures of her.

If the ship hadn't returned the right signal or had turned out to be an enemy, the plane would have blazed into action with bombs, depth charges and machine guns.

Everything returned to normal again, and every head in the plane scanned every foot of the water below. But before long there was another dive, and this time the ship turned out to be a freighter—also friendly.

The process was repeated for large and small fishboats, navy vessels and cargo ships, until our patrol seemed to take on the excitement of a roller coaster ride.

Lunch was served between dives from a compact galley stove on the plane. After one especially steep dive and close examination of a big fish packer, we heard a plaintive voice on the plane's intercommunication system:

"Please, I'd like to drink my coffee, not wear it." We levelled off for lunch.

PO. Harry Hudson from London, co-pilot, was in charge of the Aldis signaling lamp.

"We identify ships with this lamp rather than radio," he said, "because in a war zone we try to maintain silence at all times."

LIKES REAR SEAT.

A lot has been said about the danger of being a rear gunner, but aboard our ship the two boys in the tail would rather be there than anywhere. They were PO. Gordon Lee of Whonnock and PO. Russell Monck of Ottawa, both wireless air gunners.

"I like the back of the ship. It makes you feel better to have a gun in your hand. You can fight back with that," said 20-year-old Russell. He and Gordon, who is 19, both graduated from air school at the same time and were slated to go to England until the Japanese war resulted in them coming to the Coast.

Fog, which hangs constantly over the waters of the coast closed in 50 miles or so from the shore and we sank down to nearly 50 feet above the level of the waves.

"WE'LL BE BACK."

It's an interesting experien but a chilling one to thun along in a never-ending cav between a roof of mist an floor of whitecaps.

"As we flew over the hang PO. MacDonald took a roll film from his camera gun, sea

it in a rubber container dropped it over the side attac to a brilliant streamer. It immediately picked up by crash boat.

"Those films will be develo and printed as soon as we re the base, and if any of the bo show the slightest signs of picion, we'll be right back visit them," he said.

This is just a safety check shipping. There is always the mote possibility that an en ship will disguise herself a coastal boat, learn the pro signals and then approach coast. The pictures would be final proof if anything w wrong.

Under Buck's careful hand plane sat down easily in water and we skidded to a s "Well, that's all for to chums," he said, and we left plane relectantly.

"No Jap subs?"

"Not today, but soon we ho they said. And you could that each of these happy efficient young men were itching to criss cross a patt of death on the stomach of first enemy sub or plane t could find.

PATROLS OF THE PACIFIC—Thundering out of hidden air bases along the coastline of British Columbia, pl of the Royal Canadian Air Force carry on wartime patrol duty. These photos, taken by Lloyd Turner of The V couver Daily Province staff on a recent tour of coastal air defenses, show some scenes on patrol.

Night time means nothing to the hard-working crews who look after the reconnaissance bombers. In the photo the midnight shift, in the light of powerful searchlights, get to work on a big flying boat which has come in from patrol work far out over the ocean and will soon be ready to take to the air again.

Officer commanding this secret air base is shown in the centre panel. He is Flt.-Lt. Eric Beardmore, who f Hurricanes through the Battle of Britain, and was once shot down in flames over the Thames.

PROMINENT AIRMEN OF THE DOMINION AIR STATION AT JERICHO BEACH

The Airmen who served at Jericho Beach Air Station contributed significantly to the future development of both the RCAF and civil aviation in Canada. Overseas, the men had served in the Great War of 1914-18 with the RAF and its predecessor services, the RFC and the RNAS, and many of them served in military service during World War II. Their military aviation careers survived the peacetime afflictions of economic depression, political procrastination, and public apathy, and a number of these early aviators rose in rank to the top of the RCAF.

Time and space allows only a few to be listed as examples of the excellence in calibre and esprit-de-corps that was especially evident at the Jericho Beach Air Station.

CLARENCE "CLAIRE" C. MACLAURIN:

Major Claire MacLaurin at Jericho Beach, 1920.
DND/PL-143828

Claire MacLaurin grew up in East Templeton, Quebec. In 1915 he graduated in engineering from McGill University in Montreal. That year the Curtiss Flying School opened its doors in Toronto and MacLaurin signed up for flight training. He quickly earned his wings accreditation and applied to join the Royal Naval Air Service. In July 1915 he was accepted by the RNAS and events in his life began to move swiftly.

The following month he arrived in England and received a posting, on September 13, 1915, to the Naval Flying School at Chingford. On November 20 he reported for duty at Calshot Naval Air Station where he remained until posted, on January 10, 1916, to Bembridge Air Station. On August 7, 1916 he was promoted to Flight Lieutenant and served in Flying Boats on anti-submarine patrols and bombing sorties against enemy shipping and shore installations.

MacLaurin was given the position of Flight Commander on June 30, 1917, and on October 1st he was awarded the Distinguished Service Cross "for acts of gallantry in the face of the enemy". Only 48 DSCs were issued to Canadian flyers in World War I.

Early in 1918 F/L MacLaurin was posted to Felixtowe, but three months later, in May 1918, he was selected for special service in Ottawa with the Canadian Department of Naval Service. On his arrival in Ottawa, he was given the acting rank of Wing Commander.

In August W/C MacLaurin received orders to proceed to Washington, D.C. on special service duty. At the end of this tour of duty he returned to the RCNAS in Nova Scotia and was given the position of Acting Director of the Royal Canadian Naval Air Service.

After the Armistice in 1918 MacLaurin eventually remained as the sole member of the RCNAS, and spent his time inspecting the only two Canadian stations and nostalgically test-flying their aircraft, at Baker Point and at Kelly Beach in Nova Scotia.

On December 10, 1919 the Air Ministry cancelled MacLaurin's tour of duty as Canada's one-man Naval Air Force and selected him as a founding member of the newly constituted Air Board. At this point in his military career, MacLaurin had the opportunity of returning to civilian life and taking over his family's successful timber business at Lachine, Quebec. But flying was in his blood and he decided to make aviation his career.

MacLaurin accepted the appointment to the Air Board, and, as a key member of the Board, and in concert with another former Director of the RCNAS, J.A. Wilson, made many submissions to the Federal government respecting the future of aviation in Canada.

Early in 1919, MacLaurin proposed an aerial forest survey experiment in Quebec to prove that the use of aircraft increased productivity. Wilson arranged for the loan of two Curtiss HS-2Ls to carry out the project which was an unqualified success and acclaimed in a report published in the British aviation journal, THE AEROPLANE. That fall the Air Board commissioned Major J. W. Hobbs, MacLaurin, and one other officer, to conduct a national survey to determine what other services aircraft could supply, and how these services could economically be provided.

The results of this survey shaped the origins of the government Air Stations, and MacLaurin was given an appointment as a Station Superintendent. Because of his significant contribution to the Air Board, he was allowed the privilege of selecting the base of his choice, and MacLaurin requested a posting to Jericho Beach, at Vancouver. In May 1920 he and his staff began the construction of their Air Station on a site previously selected by Major J.W. Hobbs.

On September 11, 1922, Major MacLaurin was killed in the crash of HS-2L C-GYEA off Point Grey while attempting to return to Jericho Beach after experiencing multiple mechanical difficulties.

Major MacLaurin was survived by his infant son. MacLaurin's English war bride had previously died in 1918 soon after the birth of their only son.

C.A.F. Officers E. MacLeod, E. Godfrey and T. Cowley at Jericho, 1922.
DND/PMR79-288

EARL L. MACLEOD:

Earl MacLeod was born in 1894 at South Sumas in the Fraser Valley of British Columbia. He entered Chilliwack High School in 1908 and after graduation attended the Vancouver Normal School in preparation for a career in teaching. In 1913 MacLeod won his first teaching post at the one-room school at Glen Valley. From there he moved on to General Wolf, and John Norquay schools in Vancouver, and then returned to Chilliwack in 1916 as a teacher at the Atchelitz Road school.

Teaching was MacLeod's "bread and butter", but aviation was his "passion". MacLeod avidly read the Popular Mechanics magazines and anything else he could lay his hands on that nurtured his fascination with flight. In 1914, an item on the Annual Dominion Day program brought the young teacher a step closer to turning his fantasies into reality.

On Dominion Day, July 1, 1914, William "Billy" Stark, flying his Curtiss Flyer biplane, gave the folks in Chilliwack their first look at an airplane in flight. An applauding crowd at the Chilliwack fairgrounds gazed skyward as the small biplane carried out its demonstration. Stark, the Vancouver shoe merchant who had learned to fly from American Glen Curtiss only two years previously, was unaware of the impression he was leaving with one of the spectators below - a lasting impression that would eventually change the direction of young Earl MacLeod's life.

Two years later, in 1916, MacLeod responded to an advertisement inviting applications to the Royal Naval Air Service. He was summoned to Esquimalt, near Victoria, and interviewed by Admiral Kingsmill of the Royal Navy. MacLeod was accepted, but before the appointment could take effect he faced a major prerequisite, a certificate of flight training, at his own expense.

The cost, four hundred and fifty dollars for ten hours of flying time, did little to discourage MacLeod, who immediately set about the business of registering himself in a flight training school. Training schools were few and far between; the Curtiss Flying School in Toronto and several schools in the United States all heard from Earl MacLeod. He was willing to try almost anything in order to get the necessary qualification for his wings, but vacancies for new students were scarce.

Several months of continued inquiry led the undaunted MacLeod to the Vancouver waterfront and the boatbuilding yard of Jim and Henry Hoffar. That fall the brothers were involved in constructing a seaplane of their own design, the H-1, patterned on an Avro 500 tractor biplane.

Earl Godfrey is flanked by Jericho Staff Officers Tom Cowley (l) and Earl MacLeod, 1923 at Jericho. DND Photo

As soon as their aircraft was finished, the Hoffars would be happy to qualify Macleod to wings standard at the reduced price of $400.00. Negotiations were underway with an instructor who would instruct all three men. On January 4, 1917 a telegram arrived that ended MacLeod's potential adventures in flight with the Hoffar brothers.

The telegram instructed MacLeod to report immediately to Ottawa. He wasted no time in settling his affairs, and booked a seat on an east-bound train. In Ottawa MacLeod and a group of fifty-one fellow pilots were ordered to embark from Halifax, Nova Scotia, on the S.S. Scandinavian, enroute to England. All were hopeful of a position as a Royal Naval Air Service officer. Unlike MacLeod, most of the other men had their wings, and a number of them had already built up considerable flying experience. Their sea voyage behind them, the Canadians were temporarily posted to Crystal Palace, near London, for indoctrination, and were then assigned to various RNAS flying training stations.

Meanwhile, Jim and Henry Hoffar carried on with their experiment. The pilot instructor arrived in Vancouver to begin flight instruction, but found that the aircraft wasn't complete, and he left. The Hoffers were not easily discouraged. The lack of an instructor was a minor detail. The brothers agreed that a "step by step" approach was the best and safest way to learn to fly the aircraft, and flipped a coin to settle which one of them would taxi the H-1 on its first run up and down the harbour: Jim won. Securing a rope from their speed boat to the H-1, Henry towed his brother out to the centre of Burrard Inlet. A few minutes later Jim unintentionally turned the day's "first practice run" into the "first flight", and from there Jim and Henry taught themselves to fly.

In Europe, far from the self-taught aviators and their successful H-1, MacLeod approached a similar hurdle in his own determined efforts to fly. He was posted to Vendome Air Station in France and assigned to a British flight instructor, W.G. McMinnies. McMinnies had trained a succession of Canadians who all had previously flown and he assumed that young MacLeod was in this category.

The first day of MacLeod's flight instruction ended abruptly after a short period of difficult flying. During the flight McMinnies delivered a constant stream of what MacLeod interpreted as "fantastically colourful and extremely uncomplimentary remarks". Suddenly, the instructor landed the aircraft and walked away, shouting out that he had no intention of risking his life further. If MacLeod wished to risk his own life, he would have to carry on, solo. Placed in the same predicament as the Hoffar brothers, MacLeod taught himself how to fly.

Earl MacLeod spent the rest of the war flying various seaplanes and flying boats on coastal patrol and reconnaissance flights over the North Sea and the Irish Sea. In 1918, when the Royal Naval Air Service and the Royal Flying Corps amalgamated, he was attached to the Royal Air Force.

Returning to Canada after the war, MacLeod obtained a pilot license from the Aero Club of Canada and received aviator certificate #486, dated September 17, 1919. MacLeod joined the growing number of returning aviators who were doing their best to convince various government agencies that the aircraft had a multitude of civilian uses. Their reasoning was simple: if the government got involved in aviation they would need pilots. The Airmen would then have an opportunity to build a new career in peacetime aviation.

The organization of the Canadian Air Board in 1919 was followed by a decision to establish Air Stations in chosen locations across Canada. Lieutenant MacLeod was appointed to Jericho Beach Air Station as an Air Pilot Navigator. He arrived on July 1, 1920 as one of the first three officer pilots at the Vancouver Station. However, his first assignment was at ground level. Station Superintendent Major Claire MacLaurin assigned MacLeod to the Station's small Cletrac Caterpillar tractor to clear logs and other debris from the beach in preparation for the construction of a ramp, hangar and slipway at the site of the new Jericho Beach Air Station. In November 1920 MacLeod was appointed as a Flying Officer in the Canadian

Earl MacLeod and Howard Hines prepare to send a message by carrier pigeon, 1922. CFB Comox Rowe Library

Air Force (non-permanent).

While at the Air Station MacLeod flew Curtiss HS-2L and Felixstowe F-3 Flying Boats on forestry patrols, customs surveillance, fisheries inspections, aircraft licensing inspections, and a host of other projects for both federal and provincial government departments.

On April 1, 1924 the Air Board ceased to exist and Jericho Beach Air Station became an RCAF Air Station. MacLeod was awarded his pilot's badge and proudly wore the new uniform of the Royal Canadian Air Force. Serving as a Flight Lieutenant, he carried on with the season's current flying schedule with no disruption to his duties.

On May 14, 1925 F/L MacLeod was assigned temporary command of Jericho Beach and he held this position for six months until S/L J.H. Tudhope took command on December 8th.

On June 5, 1926 MacLeod was transferred to RCAF Station Camp Borden, and the following month he was posted to Ottawa Air Station where he was engaged in air photographic flying in Ontario and Quebec. For the first three months of 1927 he served as an exchange officer with the RAF in England where he was selected for a Flight Command position and given Flying Boat duty. In 1928-29 he was Flight Commander of an RAF Coastal Reconnaissance Training Flight, operating four Southampton Flying Boats on a tour from the south of England to the Isle of Skye in Scotland.

Vancouver City Archives

On his return to Canada, MacLeod was promoted to Squadron Leader, and in March 1929 he was given command of RCAF Station Vancouver at Jericho Beach, replacing F/L A.Hull. One of MacLeod's first official functions was to open the new Chilliwack Airport on Sumas Prairie in the eastern Fraser Valley. He led a flight of Flying Boats from Jericho Beach which circled over the new airfield and later landed in nearby Cultus Lake. This was an especially enjoyable event for MacLeod who still considered this part of the Fraser Valley as his home.

For three years, 1932 to 1935, he commanded RCAF Station Winnipeg. While he was at the Winnipeg Station, he carried out an extensive inspection flight of the North West Territories and the Yukon, in company with the head of the RCMP and a representative of the Royal Canadian Corps of Signals. During this trip he landed at Old Crow, Yukon Territory. The arrival of an airplane caused great excitement in the area and marked the first time an aircraft had ever landed there.

From 1935 to 1938 MacLeod was posted to Military District Number 11 at Esquimalt, serving as Air Staff Officer. He was selected to lead a flight of four aircraft which flew the Governor General of Canada and his party on a tour of British Columbia.

In 1938, following a promotion to Wing Commander, MacLeod returned to command RCAF Station Vancouver. In 1940 he served as Deputy Air Member at the RCAF Headquarters in Ottawa and then received an appointment as Senior Air Staff Officer and Director of Personnel at RCAF Overseas Headquarters in London, England. In 1942 he served as Air Officer Commanding No.2 Group Western Air Command, Victoria, British Columbia, a position he held until his retirement on September 1, 1944.

Air Commodore Earl L. MacLeod returned to his home in Chilliwack and maintained an active association with the Chilliwack Flying Club and the Chilliwack branch of the Royal Canadian Air Force Association; named the "Earl MacLeod" Wing, in his honour.

Earl MacLeod recognized that flying was "in his blood". His early fascination with the mystery of flight proved to be a solid foundation on which he built a life-long career in aviation. His standards were high, but he surpassed them. Determination, hard work, and loyalty, earned him a respected place in Canadian aviation history.

WILLIAM (BILL) TEMPLETON:

William Templeton was born in Vancouver, British Columbia in 1890. At age 21, Bill's interest in aviation sparked a unique project. Bill, his brother Winston, and their cousin, William McMullen, designed and built their own Curtiss light tractor biplane powered by a 35 hp British Humber engine. The three young men, from the Fairview district of Vancouver, set up their workshop in the basement of the McMullen home. As assembly progressed, the aircraft out-grew the McMullen's basement. On April 23, 1911 the boys moved the partially assembled biplane to Minoru Park on Lulu Island. There they completed the final assembly, and at the beginning of May Bill successfully flew their Curtiss biplane for the first time.

In 1914 young men across Canada responded to the call to serve their country. Bill Templeton joined the Royal Naval Air Service and saw active service flying seaplanes and flying boats on submarine patrols over the North Sea. His next posting took him to the Mediterranean, and during this tour of duty he contracted malaria. He was invalided home to Vancouver to convalesce at the Shaughnessy Veteran's hospital.

In spite of periodic attacks of his illness, Templeton attempted to get back into aviation. In 1920 he was accepted by the Civil Service Commission as an Air Pilot Navigator at Jericho Beach Air Station and was one of the first three Officer Pilots at the Station: in company with Second Lieutenant Earl MacLeod, and under the Command of Major Claire MacLaurin. However, Lt. Templeton continued to suffer from the recurrence of malaria, and in the mid-summer of 1921 a particularly serious bout forced young Templeton to give up his flying career.

At the close of the 1920s, Templeton's knowledge of aviation, and his avid enthusiasm for airplanes, opened the door to a whole new career. In 1929, Bill Templeton was hired as the Manager of the City of Vancouver's Airport on Lulu Island. The airport was, at that time, only a rough pasture and its poor condition caused the city considerable embarrassment when Charles Lindbergh refused to land there.

Under Templeton's guidance the Vancouver Airport slowly began to develop, but the city was growing rapidly and the small airport struggled with increasing demands for more space. Finally Templeton was successful in convincing the city to purchase the site of the present airport on Sea Island. On July 22, 1931 he was officially in charge of the opening of the new airport. He remained as Manager of the Vancouver Airport until he retired in 1949. William Templeton, one of Vancouver's most dedicated aviation pioneers, died in 1966 at age 76.

The tractor biplane built by William Templeton, his brother Winston and cousin William McMullen and flown in 1911 at Minoru Park. Vancouver City Archives

A. EARL GODFREY:

Earl Godfrey was born at Killarney, Manitoba, on July 27, 1890 and, soon after, moved with his parents to Vancouver, British Columbia. At age 12 he was selected by the 6th Duke of Connaughts Own Rifles as a bugler. In 1911 he assisted Vancouver pilots Bill Stark and Bill Templeton in the construction and maintenance of their two aircraft.

S/L Earl Godfrey in CAF uniform, November 1922. DND photo

In January 1915, the twenty-five year old Godfrey joined the 11th Canadian Mounted Rifles and was sent to France in November of that year. A year later he transferred to the Royal Flying Corps and became an air gunner with No. 10 and No. 25 Squadrons. Now a Second Lieutenant, Godfrey decided that he would rather be in the pilot's seat, and applied for, and received, pilot training. He served overseas with No. 10, 25, 40 and 44 Squadrons where he destroyed 17 enemy aircraft and 2 observation balloons.

Godfrey was promoted to Captain and posted to No. 78 Squadron as a Flight Commander. He arrived in December 1917 and within that year he faced the enemy in 53 air engagements. His courage was rewarded with the Military Cross. After returning to

Sgt. Earl Godfrey with the 1st Canadian Pioneer Batallion, 1915. DND RE21011-1

Canada in July 1918, Captain Godfrey received an appointment as Chief Instructor of the Aerial School of Gunnery at Beamsville, Ontario. He was given the position of Commanding Officer in October 1918, and in the fall of that year he was awarded the Air Force Cross. When the war ended on November 11, 1918, training ceased at Beamsville and the camp was closed.

Returning to England, Godfrey served in the RAF until his release in December 1919. He went home to Vancouver, British Columbia and spent the next several years involved in the aircraft business. He accepted an invitation to return to the Canadian Air Force as a Flight Lieutenant, and in the spring of 1922 F/L Godfrey was given the position of Commanding Officer at Camp Borden, Ontario.

Arriving at the Jericho Beach Air Station on October 18, 1922, Godfrey was appointed as the new station Superintendent. He replaced Major Claire MacLaurin after his fatal crash in September 1922. One month later Godfrey became the Station's first Commanding Officer and received a promotion to Squadron Leader. History had a hand in Godfrey's promotion. With the demise of the Air Board on November 22, 1922, the Canadian air stations became units of the Canadian Air Force operating under the authority of the Department of National Defence.

Shortly after taking over as Commanding Officer, S/L Godfrey heard about the formation of the International Air Force Club. The Club gathered together a veteran group of British, French, Italian, American, and German aviators under a broad mandate to promote the development of aviation in Canada.

S/L Godfrey, a keen supporter of the multiple uses of aircraft in peacetime, organized a "Flying Services" Reunion Dinner and Sunday Air Meet to be held at Jericho Beach Air Station in April 1923. Veteran aviators of the First War, and local flyers and aviation enthusiasts, received an invitation. The success of the reunion resulted in the creation of the Air Force Club of British Columbia, with Major A.D. Bell-Irving, MC as President. The Club later evolved into the Aero Club of Vancouver.

In May 1925 Godfrey was posted to Andover England where he took a staff course at the Royal Air Force Staff College. After graduation he returned to Ottawa in mid-1926 to take a position as Superintendent of Civil Government Operations. On September 19, 1926 Godfrey and James McKee completed the first trans-Canada seaplane crossing in McKee's Douglas M0-2BS seaplane. The 3,000 mile journey from Montreal to Vancouver was accomplished in 35.08 hours and allowed Godfrey to assess the practicality of using seaplanes in cross-country flights. Godfrey was involved in a second historic flight in 1928, when he carried the first trans-Canada airmail in a flight from Ottawa to Vancouver.

In April 1930 Godfrey was promoted to Wing Commander, and a year later he took command of the Ottawa Air Station at Rockcliffe, Ontario. He was commander of the Trenton Air Station from 1936 to 1938, where he received a promotion to Group Captain.

In the fall of 1938 G/C Godfrey organized #1 Training Command in Toronto, Ontario. At the end of that year he once again paid a visit to Great Britain. He attended the Imperial Defence College in London, and at the end of his studies the Group Captain took a tour of RAF bases in France before returning to Canada at the end of 1939.

A posting to Western Air Command Headquarters at Jericho Beach as the Air Officer Commanding brought Godfrey back to his home town of Vancouver. However, two years later he was on his way back east to RCAF Headquarters Ottawa as Deputy Inspector General for Western Canada.

In June 1942 he was promoted Air Vice-Marshal and in this capacity visited every RCAF establishment in Canada. Air Vice-Marshal A.E.Godfrey retired from the RCAF on June 8, 1944 after a long and exceptional career in aviation.

In May of 1977 he was awarded the McKee trophy in honour of his trans-Canada flight in 1926. In 1978 he was admitted to the Canadian Aviation Hall of Fame.

HARRY BROWN:

Harry Brown spent much of his early life in Victoria,

British Columbia. Before the First World War, he had launched himself into a career as a bank clerk. The young Mr. Brown spent countless days and months laboriously checking balance sheets and making other mundane calculations. This was about to change and the unpretentious bank clerk would become a hero.

Brown enlisted in the Canadian Expeditionary Force

Lt. Harry Brown (r) and Lt. Robert Rideout are given a letter by Victoria Mayor Porter for delivery to Seattle, Washington May 18, 1919. Victoria Colonist

early in 1914 and received six long months of infantry training at Valcartier, Quebec. In September 1914 he sailed to France on a troop ship, the converted Liner "Athena". Brown fought in some of the bloodiest battles of the war, and was a survivor of the Battle of Vimy Ridge.

Sickened by the stench of death and the filth in the trenches, Brown remustered to the Royal Flying Corps in 1917. He was sent to England for flight training and after graduating as a Pilot Officer, Brown returned to France to fly Royal Aircraft Factory B.E.s and de Havillands on fighter reconnaissance patrols.

Lt. Brown quickly learned the flying skills required to survive a challenge by an enemy fighter. His experience grew and by mid-March 1918 he had earned the status of "Air Ace", and the admiration of his fellow Airmen in Number 84 Squadron. On March 25, during the Ludendorff offensives, Brown scored two kills. He was awarded the Military Cross, the first to be awarded to a Canadian Airman. His seventh victory was the last to be recorded by the Royal Flying Corps before it became the Royal Air Force through an amalgamation with the Royal Naval Air Service on April 1, 1918.

After the Armistice of 1918, Brown returned to Canada. Considering his adventures in the last 4 years, there was little chance he could again assume the existence of a bank clerk. Those days were gone forever and aviation was now the only career that interested the twenty-eight year old pilot. Brown gravitated to Victoria's fledgling Aerial League of Canada, a group that sprang up in the latter stage of World War I, with the purpose of advancing the cause of aviation in Canada. Their activities included exhibition and formation flying at various air meets throughout the country. The Aerial League welcomed the participation of a pilot with Brown's experience, and Brown was more than pleased to offer his services.

An exciting opportunity presented itself on the morning of May 18, 1919. Flying the Aerial League's "Pathfinder", a Curtiss JN-4 two-seater biplane, Lt. Robert Rideout and Lt. Harry Brown set out on the first flight from Victoria to Seattle, Washington. Victoria's Mayor Porter entrusted the Airmen to deliver a letter to the Mayor of Seattle. Mayor Porter wished to invite his American peer to attend the Victoria Day celebrations held annually in the British Columbia capital.

Poor weather conditions halted the flight at Coupville, Washington, on Whitby Island, but later in the afternoon the cloud cover lifted, and at 5:50 p.m. the JN-4 arrived in Seattle. The next day Brown and Rideout brought back a number of unofficial letters, including a letter of acceptance from the Seattle Mayor. This flight was made non-stop.

An aviation entrepreneur at heart, Brown went into business with Norman A. Goddard. Together they founded the Vancouver Island Aerial Service: British Columbia's first practical, commercial air service. Incorporated at 3 Arcade Building in downtown Victoria, the air service offered flights from Victoria, and later from Courtenay. The company also offered fire protection patrols to the British Columbia Forest Service, as well as a complete course of flight instruction under the auspices of the Aerial League of Canada.

The Vancouver Island Aerial Service's first aircraft was the same Curtiss JN-4 previously operated by the Aerial League of Victoria: G-CABU, the "Pathfinder". Its wheel landing gear was replaced by twin pontoons, converting the machine to a seaplane. In August 1920, Yarrows shipyard at Esquimalt sheathed the "Pathfinder's" pontoons in copper and tested them to ensure that they were watertight. The plant superintendent was very proud that a local company had played a part in this unusual experiment. He accompanied Brown on the test flight and had the honour of being the first passenger to ride in the converted Curtiss seaplane.

Brown and Goddard's aerial enterprise was the first

company to operate seaplanes on the West Coast. Along with the Curtiss JN-4, their air service and flight training school also operated a former United States Navy Curtiss HS-2L Flying Boat, as well as two early Boeing Model C float aircraft (C-300 and C-700). The two men felt satisfied that they were well set up and ready for anything. But they didn't count on having to translate flight instruction into Chinese. A group of twelve Chinese students signed up for flight training and one of them managed to totally destroy his machine in a landing accident. It is possible that these students served with Generalissimo Chang Kai Shek's Nationalist Air Force during its battles with the Japanese in the 1930s and 40s.

The Vancouver Island Air Service flourished for a short while, but eventually Brown and Goddard were forced to abandon their dream and look elsewhere for employment. Goddard headed to the United States and established himself as chief designer, builder, and pilot of his own small aviation company in San Diego, California. Harry Brown was reluctant to leave his home province and made a decision to offer his services to the new CAF Air Station at Jericho Beach.

In mid-1921 Superintendent Major Claire MacLaurin hired Brown to replace William Templeton in the position of Air Pilot Navigator at Jericho Beach. Major MacLaurin apparently appointed Lt. Brown as Chief Pilot at a substation at Kamloops, British Columbia during the summer of 1921 but no official record was made of his duties there.

The peacetime Air Force was not for Brown. At the end of the season at Jericho Beach he returned to Victoria and spent several months as an instructor working for the Commercial Aviation School at Esquimalt. Jobs in aviation were hard to come by in Canada and the level of pay did nothing to encourage pilots to remain in the country. California had been good to Goddard, who still kept in touch with his old partner, and Brown made up his mind to emigrate to the United States. Like so many other disillusioned aviators, Harry Brown was lost to Canadian Aviation. However his move to California opened another chapter in Brown's career. At the end of 1923 he established a flying school at Oakland, California which operated successfully for many years. Harry Brown retired in 1946 at Claremont, California.

Lt. W.H. Brown contributed significantly to aviation heritage. His visionary approach to developing commercial aviation motivated him to experiment with new ideas and test what had never been done before. Trying and flying were two things Harry Brown understood. He left behind a long list of solid accomplishments as one of British Columbia's pioneer aviators.

THEODORE (TED) HENRY CRESSY:

Ted Cressy in 1932 at Vernon, B.C. CFB Cmox Rowe Library

Ted Cressy was born in London, England in the late summer of 1900. He was fourteen when Great Britain entered the First World War, but at the age of seventeen Cressy volunteered for service with the British Red Cross. While serving as an orderly in France he was gassed and had to return to England for medical care. On his release from the hospital in December 1917, he immediately joined the Royal Naval Air Service as a Boy Mechanic, and received an automatic transfer to the newly-formed Royal Air Force on April 1, 1918. Cressy remained in the RAF until August 1922, serving in Egypt, Palestine and Africa.

Following his release from the RAF, Ted Cressy emigrated to Canada and chose British Columbia's capital city, Victoria, as his home. His first job entailed precision tuning of high speed launches for maximum performance. After several high speed crossings of the Straits of Juan de Fuca in the middle of the night, he realized that his employers were in the rum-running business.

In December 1922 he enlisted with the Canadian Air Force at the Jericho Beach Air Station as a fitter. On April 1, 1924, Corporal Cressy received his second automatic transfer with the formation of the Royal Canadian Air Force. He was then transferred to Victoria Beach, The Pas, Cumberland House, and Norway House.

Cressy obtained his release from the RCAF in May 1926 and joined Central Canada Airways in Kenora, Ontario, as an Air Engineer. In January 1928 he joined B.C. Airways at Victoria as an engineer until that company ceased operations. In 1930 he joined Alaska Washington Airways of B.C. for a short time before joining the newly-formed Air Land Manufacturing Company, where he became an active participant in the October 1930 search for Lieutenant Paddy Burke - previously with the Jericho Beach Air Station. Cressy and two other pilots, Bill Joerss and R.VanDerbyl, in Junkers F-13 CF-ALX, were stranded on Thutade Lake and had to snowshoe 185 miles, taking 35 days to reach civilization at Fort St. James on December 17, 1930.

In the late 1930s Cressy joined the Shell Oil Company, and in 1940 he volunteered for duty with the RCAF at the outbreak of the Second World War. Once again his age was a stumbling block and he was turned down. However, he was referred to Bristol Aero Engine Limited where he was employed as a factory representative. He later worked for the Canadian Wright Company in the same capacity at Vancouver, British Columbia.

In 1950 he was retained by the RCAF Western Air Command as a service representative. After he retired Ted Cressy maintained an active interest in aviation. He was a member of the B.C. Aviation Museum, as well as a proud member of 800 (Victoria) Wing of the Royal Canadian Air Force Association, where he received the distinction of being made Honourary President and Life Member. At the 1993 RCAFA convention in Winnipeg, Manitoba, Cressy, at age 93, was sworn in as an Airman in today's Air Force by AIRCOM heritage officer, Major Bill March. Airman Ted Cressy passed away on April 28, 1994 at age 94 years young.

HAROLD DAVENPORT:

Harold Davenport left England in 1915 and emigrated to Canada. In 1923 he was hired by the Air Board as an air mechanic at Jericho Beach Air Station, where he rose to the position of Sergeant Mechanic. He resigned from the RCAF in 1925 and became a flight engineer for Don MacLaren at Pacific Airways. The company had a contract for fisheries patrols and operated from Jericho Beach with a HS-2L Flying Boat. In 1928 Pacific Airways was taken over by Western Canada Airways, and Davenport continued with the new company as an engineer.

A layoff in 1929 gave him some time to consider his future and he decided to try a business of his own. In 1931 he formed a partnership with Gordon Ballentine and the two men opened Aircraft Service of B.C., a flying school and aircraft repair shop. In 1932 they leased, and in turn rented, an Aerenca C-3, CF-AQK, as well as C-3, CF-ATL. By the end of 1934 Davenport and Ballentine closed their business. Davenport later worked for White Pass, and Yukon Route Airways in the Yukon and Alaska. During World War II he worked for Pan American Airways and Canadian Pacific Airways, and later became an Aviation Airworthiness Inspector with the Department of Transport.

Harold Davenport in 1928 at Swanson Bay, B.C.
CFB Comox Rowe Library

DONALD RODERICK MACLAREN:

Born in Ottawa in 1893, MacLaren and his family moved to the Peace River area of British Columbia and operated a fur trading post. Young MacLaren became an excellent marksman. In 1911 he returned to eastern Canada to attend McGill University. In the spring of 1917 MacLaren took flying instruction with the Royal Flying Corps Canada, at Longbranch, Ontario. After training, Second Lieutenant MacLaren was posted to No. 46 Squadron in France in November 1917.

On March 6, 1918 he shot down his first enemy aircraft, a Pfalz Scout. Four days later he recorded his second victory, and he continued this distinction, recording 54 victories in only eight months. During the course of the War he was promoted to Major and his effort and skill earned him several honours: the Distinguished Service Order, Military Cross, Distinguished Flying Cross, the Croix De Guerre, and Ribbon of the French Legion De Honneur.

Donald MacLaren in 1925. CFB Comox Rowe Library

Major Donald MacLaren ranked fifth as an RAF "ace", and third in Canada, after Bishop and Collishaw. Because of his commendable actions, he was rewarded with the command of No. 46 Squadron in France.

Major MacLaren was selected for service in the fighter wing of the Canadian Air Force, however, the demise of that organization in 1919 ended his involvement. Before his release from the RAF he was given a permanent commission, but MacLaren chose to leave military service. He returned to civilian life and moved to Vancouver, British Columbia.

Early in 1924, he entered a partnership with the Vice-President of the B.C. Sugar Refinery, Ernest Rogers. The two men purchased an HS-2L Flying Boat from the United States Navy and shipped it by boat to Vancouver. With a sharp eye for business, MacLaren and Rogers recognized that the government would be looking for private companies to continue contracts no longer being handled by the RCAF at Jericho Beach. They called their new company Pacific Airways Limited.

MacLaren paid a visit to the Commanding Officer of Jericho Beach Air Station, Squadron Leader A.E. Godfrey. S/L Godfrey supported the fledgling company by allowing Pacific Airways to base its HS-2L at the Station, and recommended to the Federal government that MacLaren's company be given some of the government's aviation contracts. The government agreed by awarding Pacific Airways a fisheries patrol contract in 1926.

In May 1928 Western Canada Airways took over the operation of Pacific Airways and retained MacLaren as Superintendent of West Coast Operations. Later, Western Canada Airways merged with the James Richardson controlled Canadian Airways, and as Superintendent of the Pacific Division, MacLaren remained with the company for nearly ten years. In 1937 he left Canadian Airways and was the first employee hired by Trans Canada Air Lines, where he stayed until retirement in 1957.

FREDERICK JOSEPH MAWDESLEY:

Group Captain F.J. Mawdesley was born in Tyrone, Ireland, in 1891. He was educated at Beaconsfield College at Plymouth, and later at Rossall, Lancashire, England. As a youngster he accompanied his father, a civil engineer, to South America, the British West Indies, as well as the Orient.

In 1914 he emigrated to Canada and obtained work as an accountant with the Grand Trunk Railway. After the declaration of war Mawdesley enlisted in the Royal Canadian Artillery at Niagara Falls, Ontario, as a gunner. He was promoted to sergeant and posted overseas, but after two years he transferred to the Royal Canadian Engineers, and in 1918 he transferred to the Royal Flying Corps as an Observer with the 49th Day Bombing Squadron.

At the end of hostilities, Mawdesley, now in the RAF, returned to England and took a course in wireless communications, and later enrolled in a pilot's course. On his return to Canada in 1920 he resumed his position with the Grand Trunk Railway, but in 1921 with the formation of the Canadian Air Force, Mawdesley was invited to join the CAF and was appointed adjutant at Camp Borden. There he requalified for his pilots wings, after which he was posted to Vancouver, British Columbia, where he completed the seaplane training course at Jericho Beach. Mawdesley remained at Jericho Beach until 1926, when he was sent to the Royal Air Force Air Pilotage School, Calshot, Hampshire, England.

On returning to Canada, Mawdesley was appointed to command RCAF Station Cormorant Lake, Manitoba. He flew in support of forestry operations at Lac du Bonnet and Norway House. In the course of his forestry flights, Flight Lieutenant Mawdesley noticed widespread sickness at many of the Native settlements.

He took it upon himself to fly in a doctor, the Indian Agent and the RCMP to attend to the needs of the isolated Native people.

On May 3, 1929 he flew a doctor and two Nursing Sisters to York Factory to assist in the evacuation of a missionary sick with typhoid fever. A blizzard forced the party to remain at York Factory for three days before they were able to return to Cormorant Lake. In December 1929 F/L Mawdesley was appointed Superintendent of Operations for RCAF Headquarters in Ottawa.

During the late summer of 1930 Mawdesley and F/S Harry Winney, flying a Fairchild 71B, G-CYVX, and a Vedette, departed on a survey flight of the North West Territories. They flew west to Fort McMurray, then north down the MacKenzie River to Aklavik, and west to Herschel Island on the Beaufort Sea. The pair then flew eastward via Great Bear Lake, Coppermine on Coronation Gulf, then to Thelon River and Churchill on Hudson Bay, and continued north to Repulse Bay on Melville Peninsula before heading south, via Winnipeg, to land at Rockcliffe, Ottawa, on October 1, 1930.

The two pilots had completed a survey of over 15,000 miles and took more than 3,000 photographs. At the time, this was longest exploratory flight ever accomplished in Canada.

During winter 1930, and early spring 1931, Mawdesley was again at Jericho Beach as an instructor on the seaplane course, and later in 1931, he was posted to Camp Borden to command the Air Navigation School.

In the spring of 1932 Mawdesley was posted to Havre St Pierre, Quebec, where he participated in an experimental air mail service. During the Ottawa Economic Conference the mail was picked up from a ship inbound from England and relayed by a series of aircraft to the capital.

In March 1933 Mawdesley was selected as an exchange officer with the RAF and sent to England to join No. 210 Flying Boat Squadron which was equipped with Supermarine Southampton Flying Boats. Mawdesley had the opportunity of flying on a trip that left England and flew south to the equator, then north to Singapore and Hong Kong, and crossed the North Pacific back to Canada.

In May 1935 Mawdesley was posted to Jericho Beach to assist in a survey of harbours, lakes and inlets on the British Columbia coast; a precursor to the British Columbia Reconnaissance Detachment formed the following year under W/C Shearer. In December 1936 Mawdesley led the Detachment in a survey of Patricia Bay.

Under the command of W/C E. MacLeod, S/L Mawdesley was selected to fly one of four Fairchild 71s from Jericho Beach to the Chilcotin area of British Columbia. On August 12, 1937 the aircraft provided transportation for Lord Tweedsmuir, the Governor General of Canada, and his party, on a two week visit to the recently established Tweedsmuir Park. During their stay at a lodge at Susan Point, S/L Mawdesley earned quite a reputation as a skilled card player and was recognized officially as the top player in the group. However, the official record did not disclose the amount of his winnings.

At the end of August MacLeod and Mawdesley flew the Fairchilds to Prince Rupert to begin a selection of possible Air Force stations on the west coast. They returned to Jericho Beach on August 31, 1937 after making a stop at Alert Bay on August 30th. In the fall of that year S/L Mawdesley was assigned as Officer Commanding a temporary detachment at Seal Cove, Prince Rupert, flying one of Jericho's Fairchild 71s.

During 1938 Mawdesley took command of the Air Navigation and Seaplane School at Trenton. On November 9, at No. 7 (BR) Squadron, Ottawa, he officially received the first RCAF Stranraer, #907, delivered from Canadian Vickers in Montreal, and in December he went to Halifax as an instructor on the new Stranraer Flying Boats. Mawdesley returned to Trenton in April 1939 to command the Air Navigation School.

On July 14, 1939 Mawdesley, in company with S/L A.J. Aston, flew Stranraer #912 from Ottawa to Jericho Beach with stops at Sudbury, Sioux Lookout, The Pas, Edmonton and Salmon Arm, arriving at RCAF Vancouver on July 17. Number 912 was the first Stranraer on the west coast.

In preparation for the establishment of an RCAF Station on the Queen Charlotte Islands, Mawdesley was appointed Officer Commanding a detachment of No. 4 (BR) Squadron at Alliford Bay in September 1939. In October he was appointed Commanding Officer of No. 4(BR) Squadron at Jericho Beach, a position he held until March 11, 1940.

Later in 1940 Mawdesley was attached to Western Air Command at Victoria, and, as Posting Officer, he was responsible for seeking out prospective aircrew for the RCAF. Early in 1943 W/C Mawdesley was given command of RCAF Station Patricia Bay. He later undertook the responsibility of training officers to assume administrative positions in the various schools operated by the British Commonwealth Air Training Plan. His last posting was as Station Commander at No. 5 (B&GS) Bombing and Gunnery School at Dafoe, Saskatchewan. In 1945 he was awarded the Air Force Cross. His citation read:

> "This officer, as commanding officer of a Bombing and Gunnery School, by his energy and good leadership, has brought the functioning of this station to a high level of efficiency. Throughout a long flying career he has made an excellent record as a pilot and instructor and has at all times taken a keen and active interest in the progress and welfare of those undergoing flying training. By his personal example of leadership, ability and devotion to duty he has set a high standard for all officers to follow."

Group Captain Mawdesley retired from the RCAF in 1945 after 27 years of flying service in the RFC, RAF, CAF and RCAF. He relocated to the United States and served with ICAO at the United Nations.

During 1958, Mawdesley visited Winnipeg, Manitoba at the invitation of the RCAF. Mawdesley proudly opened the new home of the RCAF Observers' School, officially named Mawdesley Hall.

A biography of F.J. Mawdesley would be incomplete without a sample from the legion of "Mawdie" stories fondly told and retold by those who knew him. Mawdie's sense of humour and generous nature added colour and character to the history of the RCAF in the pre-war years. Jack Hunter provided the following anecdote in a tribute to Mawdesley published in the CAHS Journal in 1995:

> *". . . at Jericho, when things were quiet, Mawdie approached Earl MacLeod, the Commanding Officer: 'I'm coming up for my promotional exams very shortly, Earl, and I can't study down here at the station. Do you mind if I stay at home? I'll call you every morning and if there's anything doing, I can be down here in just a half an hour.' 'No, go ahead,' MacLeod replied, 'things are quiet. I'll let you know if I need you.' So, Mawdie phoned in every morning. But when he called the station switchboard, he had to tell the Corporal not to let the 'old man' know that he was calling long distance. And, by a strange coincidence, the Hialeah Race Track in Los Angeles had just opened. 'How are things Earl?' Mawdie would ask, 'Remember, if you need me, I can be there in a half-hour.'*
>
> *But, unfortunately for Mawdie, Earl MacLeod and his wife went to see a movie a little later in the week. In those days they showed Pathe News-of-the-World between films. The MacLeods were at the theatre when footage of the opening ceremonies for the new race track was flashed on the screen. Lo and behold, sitting right in the front row at Hialeah Park, larger than life, was Mawdesley! And he was still calling in every day, offering to be right down if he were needed. MacLeod just about fell out of his seat!"*

Sgt. Harry Bryant and F/L Mawdesley aboard RCAF Vancouver.
DND RE-19227 Jack Hunter Collection

HARRY BRYANT:

Harry Bryant was born at Innisfail Alberta in 1910. He received his early education in central Alberta before moving with his family to Vancouver, British Columbia where he attended high school.

In 1927, at the age of 17, he responded to an advertisement in the Vancouver Daily Province encouraging young men to join the Royal Canadian Air Force. Bryant's application was accepted, and he was ordered to report to Camp Borden, Ontario, but at his own expense. At Camp Borden he trained as a fitter and rigger (engine and airplane mechanic) and then received a posting to Winnipeg in the rank of Airman Second Class. During the summer season Bryant flew as crewman on Vikings, Varunas, and Vedettes.

In 1928 Bryant was transferred to Fort Churchill as a crewman on Fairchild FC-2s, but a year later he was posted back to Vancouver to serve as a crewman on Vedette and Vancouver Flying Boats carrying out fisheries and anti-smuggling patrols on the west coast. At the end of the 1929 summer flying season, Bryant was recommended for pilot training. Early in 1930, and this time at RCAF expense, he returned to Camp Borden where he received his pilot wings and a promotion to Sergeant.

In early 1931 Sergeant Bryant attended a seaplane and flying boat course at Jericho Beach, on the completion of which he returned to Camp Borden to receive one of the first Blind flying courses given in Canada. A variety of interesting work followed Bryant's move into the left seat. During 1932 he was given command of a Vickers Vancouver Flying Boat and the job of flying the mail from Red Bay Labrador to Rimouski, Quebec. In 1933 he was attached to the RCMP and flew patrols in search of rum-runners in Nova Scotia, New Brunswick and Quebec. In 1936 he completed the Flying Instructors course at Trenton, Ontario, and on completion he was commissioned as a Flying Officer.

F/O Bryant was appointed the Squadron Commander at No. 8 Service Flying Training School (SFTS) at Moncton, New Brunswick, and received a promotion to Flight Lieutenant. Early in 1941 he became Chief Instructor at No.6 SFTS at Dunville, Ontario, and was promoted Squadron Leader. Late in 1941 he was posted to the British Empire Flying Training School in England and on completion returned to Canada to attend Staff College in 1942.

During 1943 Bryant received a promotion to Wing Commander, and in 1944 he was posted to the RAF Heavy Transport Pilot Course in England. On completion, he was posted to No. 216 RAF Transport Squadron at Cairo Egypt, and later, W/C Bryant served as the Commanding

Officer of RAF Base Rabat Sale in Morocco.

On December 3, 1945 Bryant returned to Vancouver and was appointed as Commanding Officer at Jericho Beach Air Station. The Station closed on March 1, 1947, giving W/C Bryant the honour of being the last Commanding Officer of the Air Station.

A number of appointments as Commanding Officer moved W/C Bryant throughout the western Provinces before he retired in 1959: Camp Commandant, North West Air Command in Edmonton, Alberta; RCAF Station Dawson Creek, British Columbia; RCAF Station North Battleford, Saskatchewan; RCAF Station Edmonton as Chief Technical Officer; and RCAF Station Edgar, his last Command posting.

Wing Commander Harry Bryant and his wife retired in 1959 to live in the Comox Valley on Vancouver Island. Although he was "officially" retired, the former Wing Commander was a familiar face at the Air Force Indoctrination School at Comox. His rich background in the evolution of the RCAF was a valuable resource, and, until the unit was transferred to eastern Canada, he willingly passed on this wealth of knowledge to the next generation of Airmen.

JOHN HENRY TUDHOPE:

CFB Comox Rowe Library

John Henry (Tuddy) Tudhope, MC, COF, was born at Johannesburg, South Africa on April 17, 1891. His early education was at the St. Johns College in Johannesburg, but his schooling was completed in England at the Tonbridge school in Kent. He returned to South Africa to oversee the family farm and also took an engineering position in the family-run diamond mine.

At the outbreak of World War I Tudhope enlisted in the British Army as a Trooper and served in German South West Africa. In 1917 he transferred to the Royal Flying Corps, earned his pilot's wings, and flew as a fighter pilot with No. 40 Squadron, RFC. He was awarded the Military Cross and Bar for destroying 15 enemy aircraft in combat. At war's end he retired from the Royal Air Force with the rank of Major. Tuddy emigrated to Canada at the urging of several of his Canadian Airmen friends, who had a dream of starting a farm at Lumby, British Columbia.

In 1920 Tudhope joined the Canadian Air Force as a Flight Lieutenant. He then served as a flying instructor at Camp Borden, Ontario until 1923 when he was promoted to Squadron Leader and given command of the CAF's Dartmouth, Nova Scotia Air Station. The following year the Royal Canadian Air Force was established, and S/L Tudhope was appointed to Command the Jericho Beach Air Station, where he oversaw the administrative details involved in the transfer over to an RCAF unit. He also held command of No. 1 Operations Squadron RCAF at Jericho Beach until transferred to Air Force Headquarters at Ottawa in 1927.

As a serving officer, he was detailed for duty to the Directorate of Civil and Governmental Air Operations to work with the controller of civil aviation, and with this background, Tudhope was selected as Inspector of Airways in 1931. He was then seconded from the RCAF to continue serving civil aviation authorities through the Department of Transport until his retirement from the RCAF in 1938.

During his extended career with the civil aviation authorities, he became primarily responsible for surveying and planning trans-continental air routes. Tudhope pioneered numerous airmail flights and flew many of the initial mail delivery flights to and from trans-Atlantic Ocean liners docking at ports in the Gulf of St. Lawrence. The successful experimental airmail flights from Rimouski, Quebec, and his supervision of the Prairie airmail service in 1930, earned Tudhope the McKee Trophy for that year.

In 1937 he commanded the Lockeed 12A aircraft which flew government officials on the first pre-inaugural inspection flight of Trans-Canada Airlines' air routes. This was known as the "Dawn to Dusk" flight and was purposely flown through the most severe weather conditions that future pilots of the airline might encounter.

In 1943 Tudhope became General Manager of Operations for Trans-Canada Airlines, the company which he helped to establish. Five years later he was appointed the first Civil Air and Communications Attache to the government's High Commissioner at London, England.

"Tuddy" Tudhope died in England on October 12, 1956. His ashes were brought back to the Canadian Rockies and released from the Lockeed 12A that he had commanded on the "Dawn to Dusk" flight in 1937. The official ceremony was conducted jointly by the RCAF and the Department of Transport. In 1973, a final and fitting honour was bestowed on John Henry Tudhope: he was inducted into the Canadian Aviation Hall of Fame.

THE AIRCRAFT OF JERICHO BEACH AIR STATION

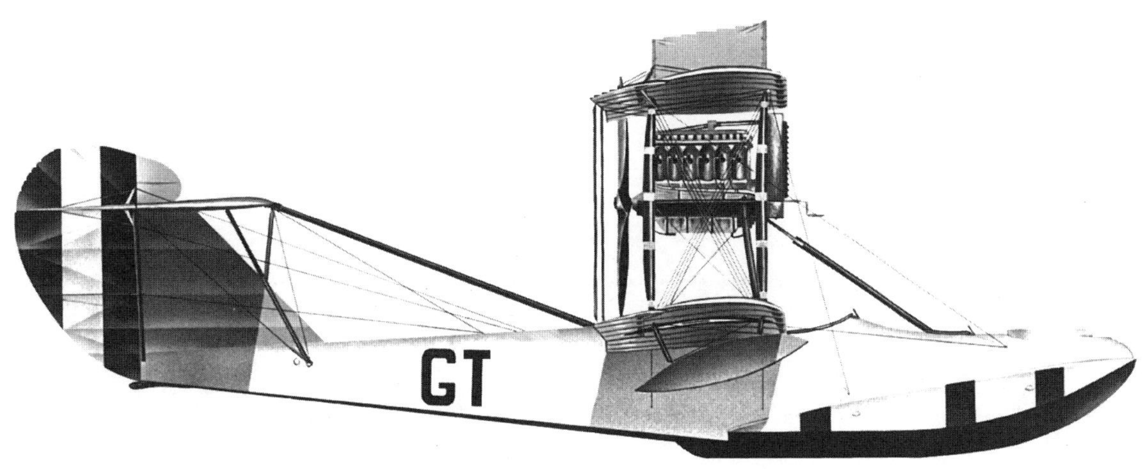

CURTISS HS-2L:

The HS-2L was an improved version of the earlier HS-1L developed by Curtiss as a patrol bomber after the United States entered into the First World War in April 1917.

The main difference between the two types was an additional 12 feet of wing span on the HS-2L to allow for the transport of two 230 pound depth charges. Curtiss couldn't keep up with the demand for the HS-2L and subcontracted their construction to six other American aircraft factories. At the end of the war in 1918, 1,121 examples of both variants had been produced.

The HS-2L first appeared in Canada when the United States Navy established two Air Stations in Nova Scotia: one at Dartmouth, with six HS-2Ls; and one at Sydney, also with six HS-2Ls on strength. The newly formed Royal Canadian Naval Air Service anticipated that they would assume the duty from the United States Navy but the war ended before this took place.

When the United States Naval contingent went home, they left the twelve HS-2Ls behind, and in late 1919 the aircraft were donated to the Canadian government.

The slow, often unwieldy, and, by later standards, uneconomical Flying Boat was the pioneer bush aircraft in Canada. The HS-2L became the principal Flying Boat in use during the first half of the 1920s.

PERFORMANCE DATA:

Maximum speed	91 mph at sea level	Ceiling	5,200 feet
Cruise speed	65 mph	Range	517 miles
Landing speed	51 mph	Weight empty	4,359 pounds
Rate of climb to 1,800 feet	180 ft/min	Weight loaded	6,223 pounds

After the Air Board was formed during 1919, many of the HS-2Ls donated by the United States Navy were assigned to Air Board Stations across the country. Other HS-2Ls were also acquired from the United States, and in all 30 of these aircraft were in use by the Air Board, and later by the Canadian Air Force and the Royal Canadian Air Force, for Civil Government Air Operations.

Eighteen HS-2Ls served at the Jericho Beach Air Station at Vancouver, British Columbia, and the last two were struck off strength on September 25, 1928. The last HS-2L in Canada was retired during 1933.

The Curtiss HS-2L was powered by a single 360 hp Liberty V-12 engine; it had a wingspan of 74 feet, 1 inch; a length of 38 feet, 6 inches; and a height of 14 feet, 7 1/4 inches.

CURTISS HS-2L AT JERICHO BEACH

Canadian Registration & Serial #	MFG#	U.S. Navy #	T.O.S.	S.O.S.	Remarks
G-CYBA			24-09-20	29-07-22	First aircraft assembled at Jericho Beach
G-CYBB			30-05-21	27-03-23	Listed as spare hull
G-CYDS	9327	A-1986	08-07-21	08-08-21	Destroyed by fire on first test flight
G-CYDT	9331	A-1990	23-07-21	26-02-24	Air Board and CAF use Coast to Coast
G-CYDU			07-07-21	10-09-25	Cat."A" crash B.C. Coast 23-7-25
G-CYDX	439	A-1993	27-06-21	26-01-24	First a/c flown Jericho to Prince Rupert
G-CYEA	9360	A-2019	12-02-21	09-04-23	Cat."A" crash at Jericho Beach 11-9-22 killing Major C.C. MacLaurin & passenger
G-CYEB	950	A-1994	06-08-21	10-09-25	On strength at Jericho Beach
G-CYED		A-1985	27-09-21	01-07-28	On strength at Jericho Beach
G-CYGA		A-1307	13-10-24	01-07-28	On strength at Jericho Beach
G-CYGM		A-1290	19-06-25	01-07-28	Cat."A" crash at Klemtu, B.C.
G-CYGN		A-1312	31-05-25	25-10-26	On strength at Jericho Beach
G-CYGO		A-1152	25-05-25	01-07-28	On strength at Jericho Beach
G-CYGP	107	A-1159	08-06-25	01-04-26	On strength at Jericho Beach
G-CYGQ	119	A-1303	12-08-25	25-09-28	On strength at Jericho Beach

Canadian Registration & Serial #	MFG#	U.S. Navy #	T.O.S.	S.O.S.	Remarks
G-CYGR	142	A-1315	12-08-25	25-09-28	On strength at Jericho Beach
G-CYGS	210	A-1392	12-08-25	08-05-28	On strength at Jericho Beach
G-CYGT	97	A-1279	12-08-25	01-07-28	On strength at Jericho Beach

HS-2L YGA on slipway at Jericho Beach, January 6, 1925. NAC PA140637

The author Captain Chris Weicht stands with sole surviving HS-2L G-CAAC at the Canadian Aviation Museum in Ottawa, February 1995 DND REC 95-02-21-1

HS-2L G-CYBA during assembly, 1920. DND PL143822

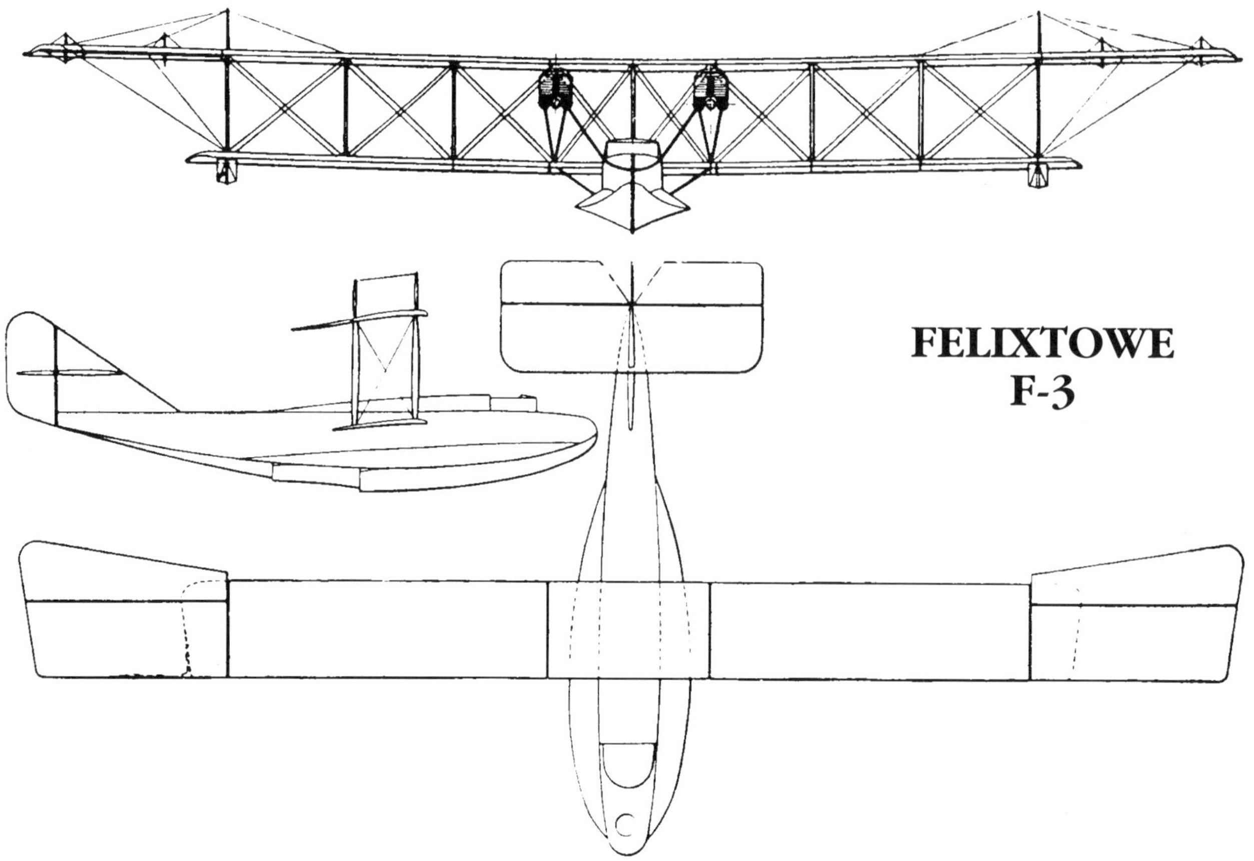

FELIXTOWE F-3

The Felixtowe had its beginnings in the Curtiss H "America" series of aircraft. In 1914 Rodman Wanamaker agreed to finance the construction of an aircraft to mark the 100th anniversary of the Peace of Ghent, the 1815 accord between Great Britain and the United States. It was intended that a trans-Atlantic flight would celebrate the completion of the aircraft and commemorate the centennial.

The aircraft was a flying boat, reminiscent of the Curtiss type, designed by a thirty year old Royal Navy Lieutenant, John Cyril Porte. Tuberculosis forced Porte to leave the Royal Navy in 1911, but instead of accepting a slow death, he learned to fly and became a prominent figure in the development of the flying boat.

On June 28, 1914 the Archduke Francis Ferdinand was assassinated in Sarajevo and in the following 39 days most of Europe was emeshed in the bloody conflict of World War I. When war was declared, Porte returned to England and was accepted back into the Royal Navy. He convinced Captain Murray Sueter, the director of the Admiralty's Air Department, that the Curtiss American design would provide the Royal Navy with an excellent patrol flying boat.

The Admiralty quickly reached an agreement with Curtiss and the design went into production as the Porte-Felixtowe Flying Boat. Porte, now a Squadron Leader, supervised the construction of the Felixtowe and incorporated improvements to the F-1 and F-2A, and, later, the F-3, of which 71 were produced up to the end of the war in 1918. The Felixtowe F-3 served as an anti-submarine patrol flying boat at British Stations as well as serving in the Mediterranean. The F-3 was powered by two Rolls-Royce Eagle engines initially of 275 hp, although larger horsepower models, up to 360 hp, were later used.

A later model of the Felixtowe, the F-5, became the RAF standard Flying Boat in post World War I. In 1921 Short Brothers of Belfast built 15 F-5s for the Imperial Japanese Navy. In early 1918, Canadian Aeroplanes Limited received an order from the United States Navy to produce 50 Felixtowe F-5-Ls. The order was later reduced to 30 and the last aircraft was shipped January 21, 1919.

After the war S/L Porte joined the Gosport Aircraft Company of Hantshire, England. The company soon offered a variant of the F-5 and attempted to market the aircraft in the United States.

The F-3 had a take-off weight of 10,650 pounds and a maximum level flight speed of 93 mph with a range for endurance of 6 hours. The Gosport G-5 (F-5) claimed a fully loaded ceiling of 14,000 feet and a landing speed of 42 mph. Its gross weight was increased to 12,500 pounds.

Eleven Felixstowe F-3s were included in a British Imperial gift to the Dominion of Canada on June 4, 1919. The eleven aircraft were withdrawn from service in 1923. Only one F-3 was in use at the Jericho Beach Air Station: G-CYDI.

FELIXTOWE F-3

Reg #	Manufactured	Previous Reg. #	T.O.S.	S.O.S.	Remarks
G-CYDI	Short Bros., Belfast	N.4010	30-05-21	12-09-23	At Jericho Beach

F-3 YDI being launched after assembly, 1922. DND PL143826

F-3 G-CYDI by the slipway at Jericho, 1922.
Elwood White Collection VPL

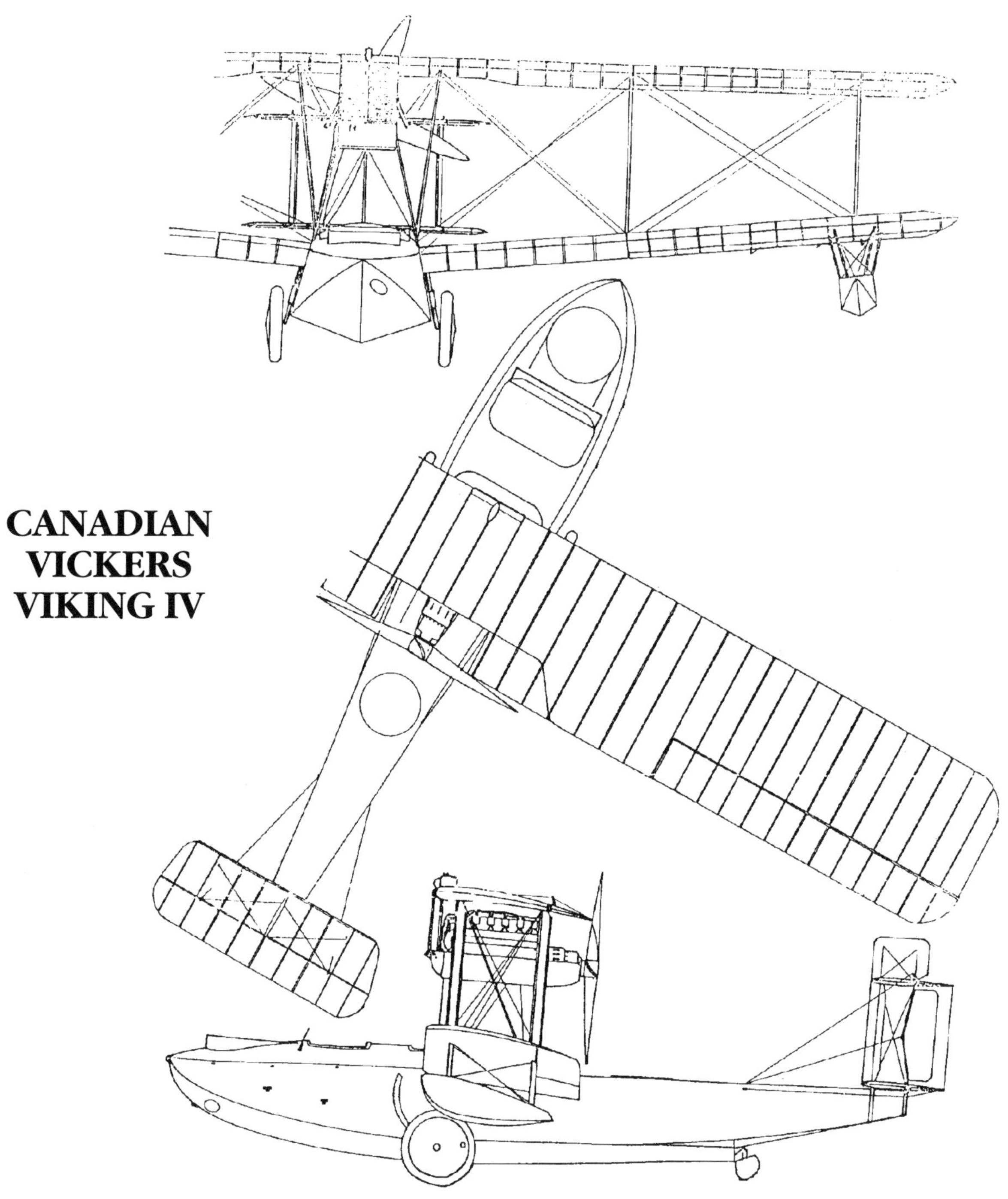

CANADIAN VICKERS VIKING IV

In late 1922 the Canadian Air Force was looking for a replacement for the Curtiss HS-2L Flying Boats. Canadian Vickers offered their Viking IV design and on February 23, 1923 they were awarded a contract for the construction of eight aircraft. Two aircraft fuselages were shipped from the parent company in England, and the remaining six were made by the Montreal company. These Canadian-built single-engine amphibians were powered by a 360 hp Rolls-Royce Eagle engine.

The Viking IV was used as a general transport aircraft and in survey work, but after the introduction of the Canadian Vickers Vedette and the Fairchild FC-2 in the mid-1920s, the Viking was assigned to transport use only. Pilots reported that the aircraft had poor water-handling characteristics and took an excessively long time to become airborne. They also found the Viking very difficult to control in any kind of rough water. In August 1924, Group Captain Scott notified Canadian Vickers that it was impossible to stop the aircraft from porpoising on landing, and when taxiing for take-off - in even a moderate sea the cockpit filled up with water.

In the hopes of improving performance and increasing the Viking's power, the RCAF installed a 400 hp Liberty engine in October 1924. The modified aircraft was test flown by Wing Commander A.B. Shearer early in 1925. However, the introduction of the Vedette led to the retirement of the Viking IV and the last one was struck off strength in May 1931.

Official records indicate that only one Vickers Viking, G-CYEW, came to Jericho Beach Air Station It crashed on July 31, 1926 in a category "A" crash.

A civilian-owned Viking IV, G-CAEB, operated in the Vancouver area. The aircraft was previously operated by Laurentide Air Service. AEB was a British-built Viking powered by a 450 hp Napier Lion engine. The aircraft, registered in Canada on June 5, 1922, was sold to a Calgary, Alberta mining syndicate in June, 1926 and was then purchased three years later by B.F. Lundy of Vancouver. The new owner made the mistake of using the wrong grade of castor oil, and piloted by R.I. Van der Byl, AEB's engine seized over Howe Sound and Van der Byl barely made it back to Jericho Beach. The aircraft was abandoned behind the hangar at the Vancouver Air Station where it was sadly neglected until Aero Mineral Locators Limited of Vancouver bought the Viking from Lundy in February, 1932. They operated the Viking until August 8, 1932. At that time it was taken to Boeing of Canada at their Vancouver location for a complete overhaul.

Two Vancouver boys, Captain Fred Clark and his brother Herman, were the last owners of the machine. On September 16, 1932, on a flight over the Fraser River estuary, with pilot Gilbert E. M. Jenkins at the controls and three passengers on board, a fuel line broke and the engine burst into flames. Jenkins immediately put G-CAEB into a sideslip, which kept the flames away from the fuselage until he flared the blazing aircraft close to the water, landed and everyone safely escaped. Fortunately for Jenkins and his passengers there were several small boats in the vicinity which immediately came to their rescue.

C.V. VICKERS VIKING IV

PERFORMANCE DATA:

Maximum speed	102 mph	Ceiling	9,000 feet
Cruising speed	80 mph	Empty weight	3,750 pounds
Initial rate of climb	1,000 ft/min	Loaded weight	5,600 pounds

RCAF#	MFG#	T.O.S.	S.O.S.	Remarks
G-CYEW	CV 3	31-08-23	15-10-26	Transferred from Jericho Beach to Victoria Beach, Manitoba, Spring 1925 Cat "A" 11-07-26

Vickers Viking IV G-CAEB at Jericho Beach, 1930. Madill Collection

CANADIAN VICKERS VEDETTE

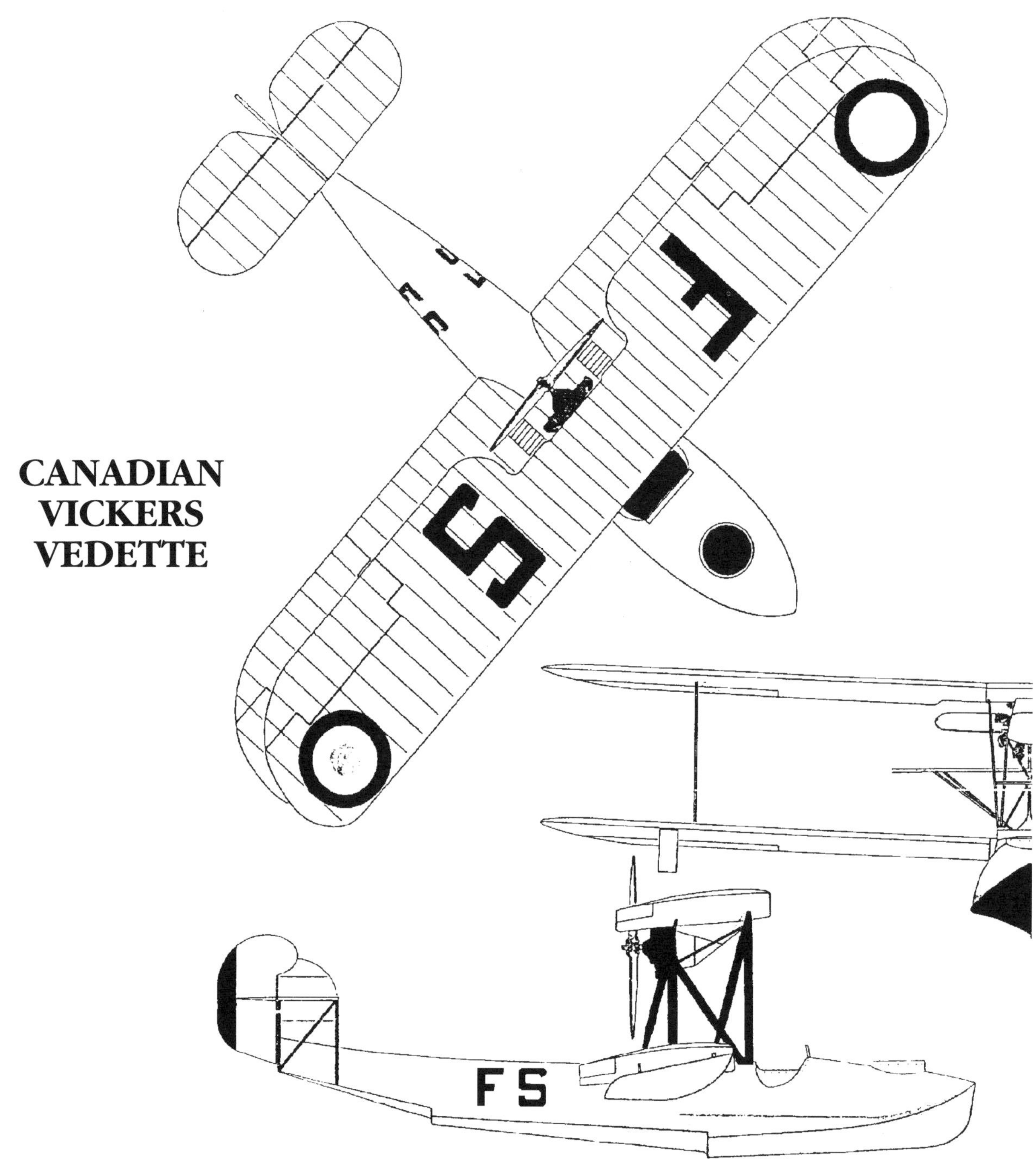

The origins of the Vedette can be traced back to 1922 and the Canadian Vickers Viking IV, the larger Flying Boat used as a forestry patrol aircraft by Laurentide Air Services of Montreal. At the time, Laurentide employees recommended reducing the size of the Viking in order to make it more serviceable in their forestry patrol work. Vickers British parent company acted quickly. R.K.Pierson designed a small flying-boat and in the summer of 1924 W.T. Reid arrived in Montreal with the design layout. He took the position of Chief Engineer with the Canadian Vickers company and had the project well in hand by mid-July.

Laurentide then suffered a financial setback and the RCAF entered into the design picture intending to use the seaplane for forestry survey and fire protection patrols. The original concept of the Vedette was kept but, after a battery of tests had been completed, the RCAF stipulated the use of the air-cooled, 215 hp, Armstrong Siddeley Lynx engine. The Wright Aeronautical Corporation came forward with a money-back guarantee on their J-4 Whirlwind engine, and the cost-conscious RCAF took their offer.

On the morning of May 9, 1925 the Wright-powered Vedette was taken on a successful test flight by Squadron Leader B.D. Hobbs. The RCAF put the aircraft into active service on forestry patrols and received very favourable reports on its performance during the 1925 forestry season. Canadian Vickers put the Vedette into production in 1926.

The Vedette Flying Boat was well-liked by the RCAF for both forestry patrols and photographic work. The small, single-engine pusher biplane was in use from coast to coast and remained in service with the RCAF until the early days of World War II. At Jericho Beach the Vedettes were represented in several different models.

In 1929 the Vancouver Seaplane School received RCAF #108, 109, and 110 - the last MK II produced. In 1930 Jericho Beach Air Station acquired three MK VAs, which were amphibian aircraft: #115, 123, and 124. Ten years later, and with the approach of war, the demand for training personnel in flying boat operations had created a shortage of aircraft. At a request from RCAF Station Jericho Beach, the surplus Vedettes at RCAF Trenton were transferred to the west coast. Between January and March of 1940 two metal hull models, #816 and 817, and two wooden hull models, #809 and 812, arrived at the Seaplane School. These Vedettes remained in use instructing neophyte flying boat pilots of No. 4 (BR) Squadron, as well as No. 119 and No. 120 Squadrons, until 1941 when they were retired from service.

In 1928 two civilian Vedettes started to operate out of Jericho Beach. Canadian Vickers leased the aircraft to Don MacLaren's Pacific Airways, which became Western Canada Airways: G-CASW, serial #CV-91; and G-CAUT, serial #CV-93, both Mark V models powered by a Wright J-5 Whirlwind engine. However, a crash on August 28, 1928 ended the short working history of the brand-new G-CASW.

The last Vedette in Canadian service was retired in 1946 by the Ontario Provincial Air Service. Unfortunately Canada has no surviving Vedettes but there is an example of the type taking shape at the Western Canadian Aviation Museum in Winnipeg. The replica incorporates some original parts and thousands of hours of volunteer time and skill.

CANADIAN VICKERS VEDETTES USED AT JERICHO BEACH

PERFORMANCE DATA: Vedette MK II

Maximum speed	92 mph	Rate of Climb	650 ft/min
Cruising speed	87 mph	Ceiling	13,000 feet
Landing speed	48 mph	Range	6 hours

Vedette on slipway.
CFB Comox Rowe Library

C.V. Model #	R.C.A.F. Serial #	MFG#	Previous R.C.A.F.#	T.O.S.	S.O.S.	REMARKS
II		CV32	G-CYGW	20-08-26		
II	108	CV100	G-CAUW	31-12-28		
V	109	CV101	G-CAUX	05-01-29	14-06-33	
V	110	CV118	G-CAVZ	10-01-29	17-09-34	Cat."B" crash 05-03-31 Vancouver
V		CV123	G-CYZD	12-06-29		Cat."B" crash 23-08-29 Vancouver
V	806	CV124	G-CYZB	05-07-29		
V	116	CV130	803	29-07-29	27-12-35	Cat."A" crash 04-11-35 Point Grey, Vancouver Rebuild of RCAF 116
VA	115	CV152		20-01-30	26-08-30	Cat."B" crash 17-06-30 B.C. Coast
VA	123	CV153		30-01-30	23-07-35	Cat."B" crash 09-02-31 Vancouver
VA	124	CV154		04-02-30	16-06-31	Cat."A" crash 02-03-31 Vancouver
VA	813	CV156	G-CYWP	07-05-30		Vancouver Seaplane School
VA	812	CV157	G-CYWO	04-05-30		Vancouver Seaplane School
VA	809	CV160	G-CYWL	04-05-30		Vancouver Seaplane School
V1	817	CV163	G-CYWI	10-05-30		Vancouver Seaplane School
* VAM	816	CV170	G-CYZD			Vancouver Seaplane School

*Canadian Vickers metal hull to rebuild CV123 (G-CYZD)

ACCIDENTS RECORDED CANADIAN VICKERS VEDETTE

Canadian Vickers Vedette 2 109 — **05-03-31** — **Vancouver**

No details. Cat. "B" crash.

Canadian Vickers Vedette 2 110 — **23-08-29** — **Vancouver**

No details. Cat. "B" crash.

Canadian Vickers Vedette 2 115	**17-06-30**	
No details. Cat. "B" crash.		
Canadian Vickers Vedette 2 116	**04-11-35**	**Vancouver**
No details. Cat. "A" crash.		
Canadian Vickers Vedette 2 123	**09-02-31**	**Vancouver**
No details. Cat. "B" crash.		
Canadian Vickers Vedette 2 124	**02-03-31**	**Vancouver**
No details. Cat. "A" crash.		

Vedette #803 beaching at Jericho Beach, 1935. Madill Collection

Vedette FY-F #816 at dock at Jericho Beach.
DND PMR77-156

Vedette #816 in hangar at Jericho.
Madill Collection

CANADIAN VICKERS VARUNA

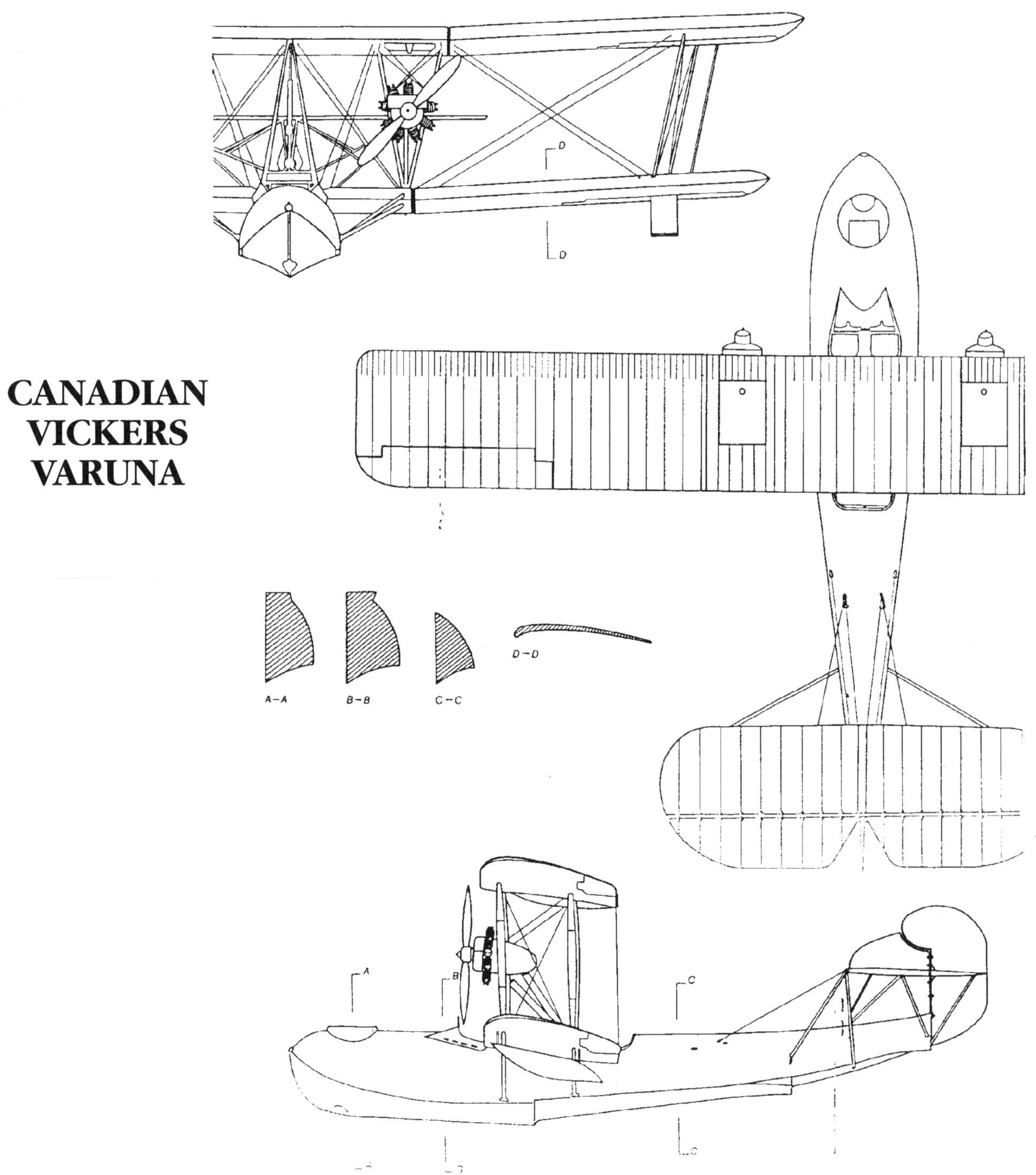

In 1925 the Department of National Defence issued a requirement for a twin engine flying boat to transport men and equipment to fight forest fires. Canadian Vickers developed a prototype, the Varuna I, and after test flights were completed it was taken on strength by the RCAF on June 2, 1926. The Varuna I was powered by two Wright J-4 Whirlwind engines and seated seven people. The aircraft was flown to Rockcliffe for further testing and never left. After a very short career of four years, the Varuna was put into storage and eventually taken off strength in 1932.

New specifications were drawn up and a second prototype, the Varuna II, was accepted by the RCAF. Seven of these aircraft were delivered in the spring and summer of 1927. The 200 hp Wright engines were replaced in the Varuna II with two 180 hp Armstrong Siddeley Lynx IVs; and the RCAF requested a number of other design changes which, in the end, greatly affected the performance of the aircraft.

The Varuna IIs spent most of their service time in Manitoba, with the exception of G-CYZV. It was shipped to eastern Canada and taken on strength at Dartmouth Air Station in Nova Scotia. By 1930 the RCAF acknowledged that what they needed was a more powerful machine, and redesigning the Varuna was not the answer. The Varuna IIs were gone by the end of 1930. Although there is no official record of a Varuna at Jericho Beach, Wing Commander Harry Bryant states that there was one present for a short period of time.

A photograph in the Public Archives of Canada collection (HC 843 see chapter one) depicts a Varuna at Shirley's Bay, B.C. The registration markings are not visible save for a "V" on the underside of the left wing. The propellers are left turning (American), and the engines are probably Wrights. The lower wing is set low on the hull, unlike the Varuna IIs with their nine inch, higher wing. The above implies that the aircraft is the prototype Varuna I, G-CYGV.

However, J.A. Griffen's book CANADIAN MILITARY AIRCRAFT - Serials and Photographs 1920-1968, lists Varuna II, G-CYZP in a catagory "A" accident at Shirley's Bay on August 19, 1927. Another source shows that YZP, after being modified in an attempt to improve its performance, crashed at Ottawa, and the date given is also August 19, 1927.

PERFORMANCE DATA: Varuna 1

Maximum speed	90 mph	Empty weight	3,860 pounds
Ceiling	14,000 feet	Loaded weight	5,850 pounds

PERFORMANCE DATA: Varuna 11

Maximum speed	81 mph	Empty weight	4,325 pounds
Ceiling	7,800 feet	Loaded weight	6,315 pounds

Varuna II in Manitoba. Madill Collection

Varuna I G-CYGV.
CFB Comox Rowe Library

AVRO 504NS

Avro 504NS Number 32 moored at Jericho Beach. Madill Collection

The basic trainer used by the RAF in Canada during World War I was the Curtiss JN-4 (Canadian). The RAF recognized that the Canuck, as the JN-4 was known, was not capable of giving the student pilots the experience they needed to competently operate the rotary-engined service types in use overseas.

To overcome this problem, Major Robert R. Smith-Berry demonstrated that students could, with little difficulty, graduate directly from the AVRO 504NS to service-type machines. Based on this information, the RAF in Canada ordered 500 AVRO 504s from Canadian Aeroplanes Limited. The order was placed in the late summer of 1918 to be completed by April 1919.

The Canadian prototype was delivered to the School of Aerial Fighting at Beamsville, Ontario on October 1, 1918 and tested by Captain A.E. (Earl) Godfrey. Godfrey later became the Commanding Officer at Jericho Beach Air Station in Vancouver, British Columbia, and eventually rose to Air Vice-Marshal in the RCAF.

The test flights were satisfactory and the aircraft went into production. However, only two AVROs reached the end of the production line before the war in Europe came to an end with the signing of the Armistice and the rest of the order was cancelled. Very soon after the war, Canada received a gift of aircraft and equipment from Great Britain which included sixty-two AVRO 504s. The aircraft became the standard Canadian Air Force trainer, and carried on in this role with the RCAF.

In 1925 Canadian Vickers started to manufacture the AVRO 504. The first three aircraft were "N" models equipped with a Wright J-4 engine, and with a single float. Two years later the RCAF ordered a further 12 180 hp Armstrong Siddeley Lynx powered "N" models. Three of this group had the single float installations: RCAF serial # 32, 33, and 34. They were given the RCAF designation of AVRO 504NS, and were completed by mid-January 1928. The three AVROs were shipped by rail to the seaplane training school at Jericho Beach in Vancouver, British Columbia.

Lock Madill, a former fitter at Jericho Beach recalls the day that Sergeant Pilot Harry Bryant took one of the station's AVROs on a flight up Howe Sound. On the return trip, Sgt. Bryant decided to do a low pass at Fishermans Cove near Horseshoe Bay. Unknown to Bryant someone had strung a telephone wire out to a small island. As the AVRO streaked low over the channel, the propeller struck the telephone wire and wrapped it around the hub. There was also some damage done to one of the wing-tip floats.

Sgt. Bryant managed to reach the Air Station where he took the fitters into his confidence. His fellow Airmen sympathized with his predicament should the Commanding Officer find out about his deviation from the normal route. Airman Madil assisted in the operation to remove the wire and repair the damage. The wire was tossed into English Bay and the incident was forgotten - but only for sixty years. Another former Airman at Jericho Beach, Sergeant Pilot Jack Hunter, also remembered the day.

AVRO 504NS

PERFORMANCE DATA:

Maximum speed	85 mph	Empty weight	1,848 pounds
Ceiling	12,000 feet	Loaded weight	2,676 pounds

RCAF#	MFG#	T.O.S.	S.O.S.	Remarks
32	CV59	12-07-28	21-09-29	Jericho Beach Seaplane School
33	CV60	22-02-28	07-05-29	Jericho Beach Seaplane School
34	CV61	05-03-28	28-08-29	Jericho Beach Seaplane School

Avro 504NS seaplanes #32 and #33 moored at Jericho Beach. CFB Comox Rowe Library

DE HAVILLAND DH-60 MOTH

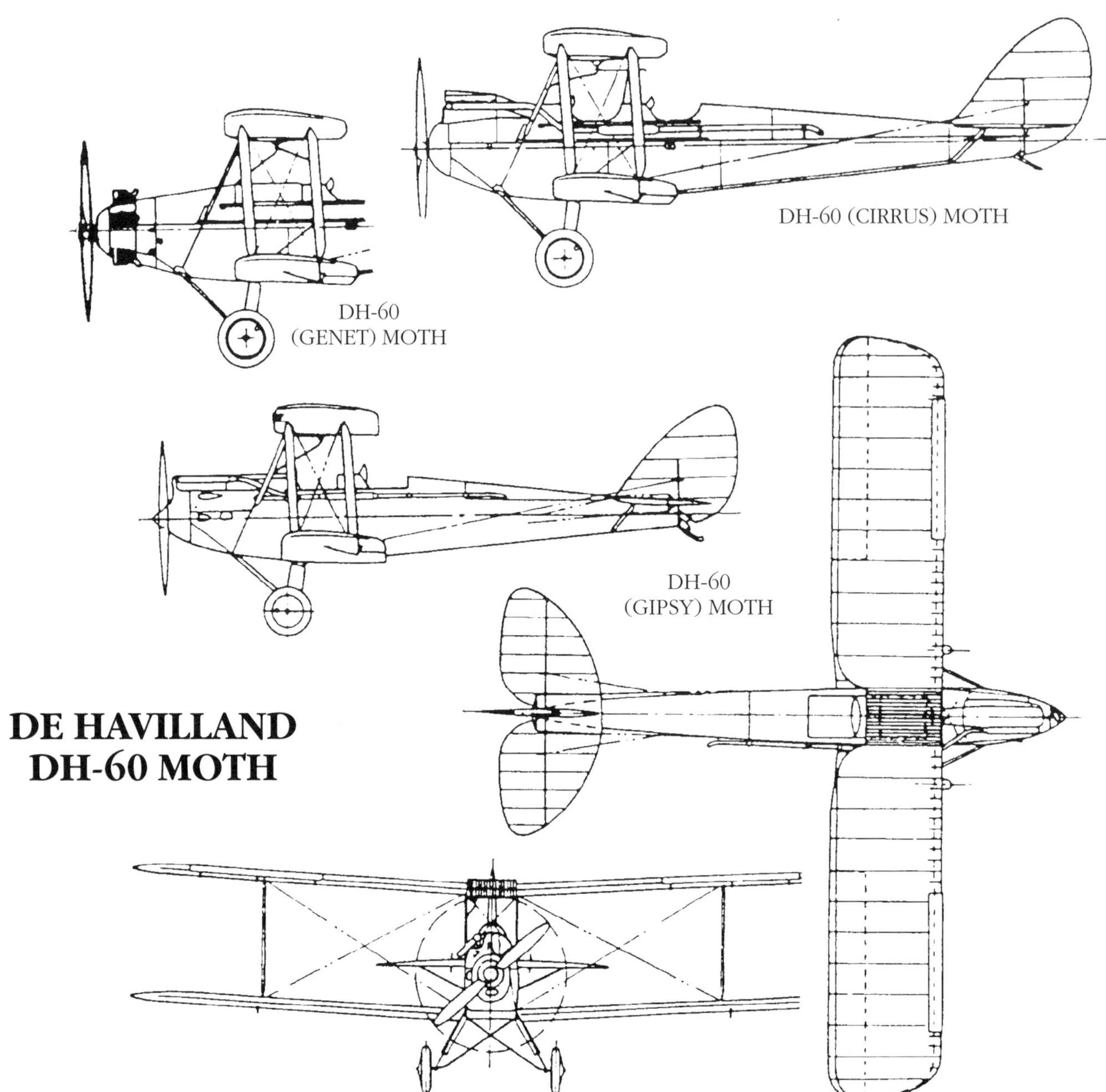

Throughout the British Commonwealth, beginning in the mid-1920s, "Moth" aeroplanes became associated with training.

During World War II, 1,546 "Tiger Moths", a descendant of the earlier Moths, were used in association with the British Commonwealth Air Training Plan.

The first prototype of the DH-60 was flown by Captain (later, Sir) Geoffrey de Havilland, at Stag Lane Aerodrome, England, on Sunday, February 22, 1925.

The Moth's first Canadian use was by the Ontario Provincial Air Service in 1927. Subsequent to this the RCAF took delivery of at least 3 DH-60X Moths, powered by a Genet engine, and one Moth on floats, #3177, powered by a Cirrus II engine. This aircraft was registered to the Department of Marine and Fisheries, Ottawa and was destined for use by the Hudson Strait Expedition.

The RCAF assigned serial numbers 55, 56, 57, and 58, to its first four Moths. In 1928 the DH-60M, or Metal Moth, was evaluated and an initial order for 50 aircraft was placed. In all the RCAF received 17 DH-60X model Cirrus Moths, and 72 DH-60M Moths with a Gipsy engine.

Twelve DH-60 Moths were on strength at Jericho Beach where they were used extensively for seaplane training. Later, several of these Moths were transferred to Number 11 (AC) Army Cooperation Squadron at Sea Island for use by the (NPAAF) Non Permanent Active Air Force Unit.

At Jericho Beach, Moths number 102, 104, 105, 106, and 107 were converted from Cirrus III power to Gipsy I. The conversion took place between October 10, 1930 and October 16, 1931. At the same time de Havilland converted these Moths to a metal fuselage before returning them to RCAF Vancouver.

The Metal Moths at Jericho Beach suffered from salt water corrosion. By October 1931 numbers 151, 152, 153, 155, and 156, were also modified as well as corrosion-proofed by Boeing of Canada at their Vancouver location.

Number 154 received the same treatment after it was returned to service-use on March 16, 1936. It was previously used by the DND Controller of Civil Aviation, District Inspector Carter Guest.

DH-60 MOTHS AT JERICHO BEACH

PERFORMANCE DATA: Powered by a single ADC Cirrus II 85 hp engine

Maximum speed	95 mmph	Ceiling	17,000 feet
Cruise speed	85 mph	Empty weight	890 pounds
Rate of climb	650 ft/min	Loaded weight	1,550 pounds

RCAF#	MFG#	Civil Reg.#	Other#	T.O.S.	S.O.S.	Remarks
102	740			23-05-29	16-03-31	RCAF Vancouver
103	741			15-03-29	08-10-29	Cat, "A", 29-08-29 at Vancouver
104	742			23-05-29	30-09-31	Cat. "A", 23-07-31 at Vancouver
105	743			22-05-29	16-03-31	RCAF Vancouver
106	744			23-05-29	16-03-31	RCAF Vancouver
107	745			27-05-29	16-03-31	RCAF Vancouver
151	DHC107			26-04-30		RCAF Vancouver
152	DHC108			22-04-30		RCAF Vancouver
153	DHC109			25-03-30		RCAF Vancouver
154	DHC110	CF-CCD		25-03-30		RCAF Vancouver, transferred to District Inspector Carter Guest at Vancouver, B.C. 08-02-33
				05-10-34		RCAF No. 11(AC) Sqd. NPAAF Vancouver (Sea Island)

RCAF#	MFG#	Reg.#	Civil Other#	T.O.S.	S.O.S.	Remarks
		CF-CFT	A 105		21-12-44	To Aero Club of B.C. as CF-CFT
155	DHC111			21-03-30		No. 4(FB) Sqd. - Jericho Beach 30-10-34, 11(AC) Sqd. Sea Island 23-11-34 N.P.A.A.F. Sea Island
		CF-CFV	A 106		25-05-44	To Aero Club of B.C. as CF-CFV
156	DHC112			25-03-30		No. 4(FB) Sqd. - Jericho Beach 30-10-34, No. 11(AC) Sqd.
					18-11-36	23-11-34, Cat. "A" 25-05-36

ACCIDENTS RECORDED DE HAVILLAND DH60 MOTH

De Havilland DH-60G 103 **28-08-29** **Vancouver**

No details. Cat. "A" crash.

De Havilland DH-60G 104 **23-07-31** **Vancouver**

No details. Cat. "A" crash.

DH-60 Gipsy powered Moth #151, Jericho Beach. Hunter Collection

CANADIAN VICKERS VISTA

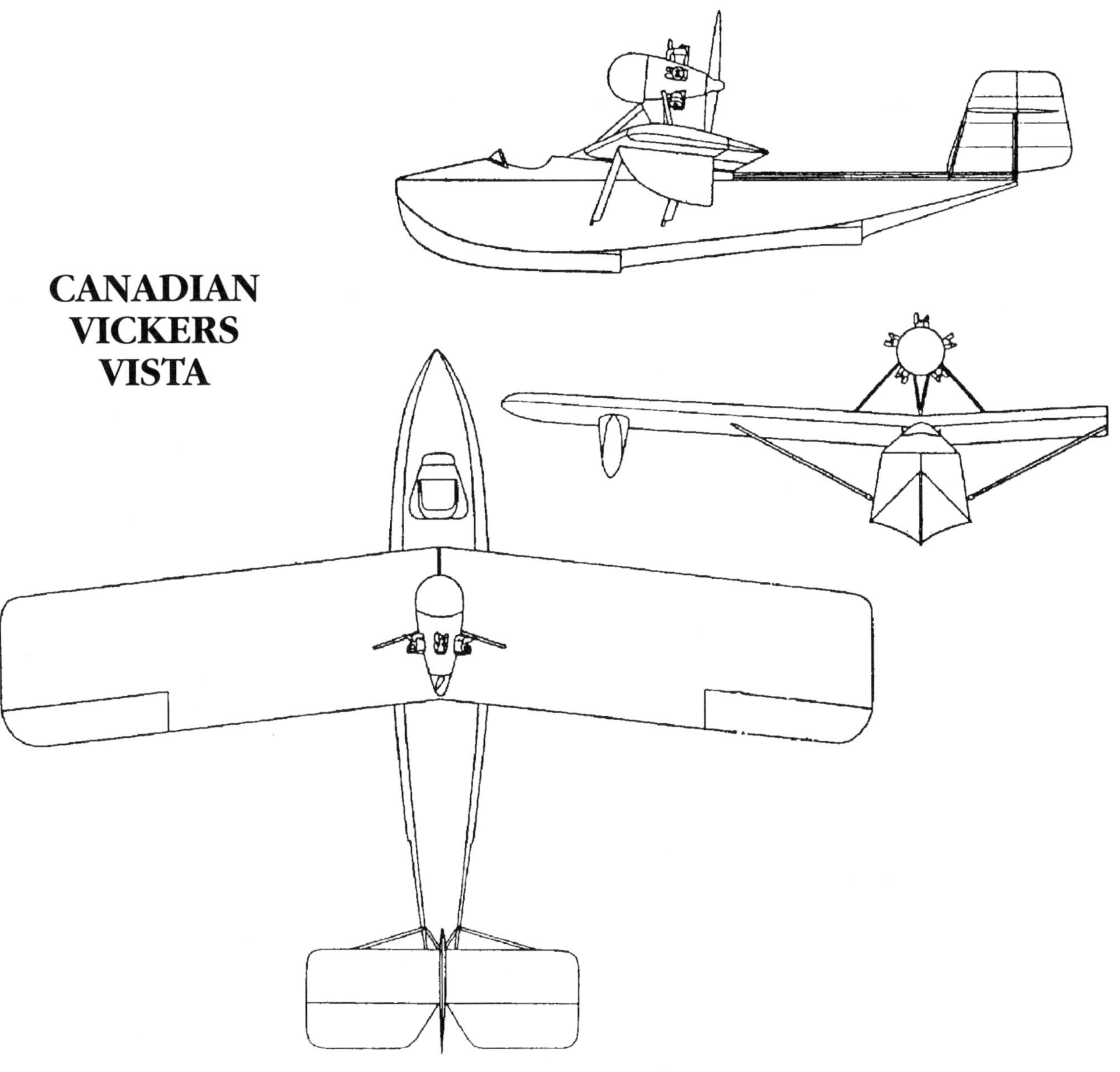

On September 17, 1926 the RCAF ordered two Vistas from Canadian Vickers. The Vista was powered by one 60 hp Armstrong Siddeley Genet engine and had a wing span of 29 feet, 6 inches. However, its poor performance in test flights reduced the order, and only one Vista was completed. G-CYZZ was shipped to Jericho Beach and put to use at the seaplane school, but, due to the aircraft's extremely sensitive controls, its use was restricted to taxiing practice.

Wing Commander Harry Bryant remembered that wing fabric was removed from the outer wing panels to prevent the aircraft from becoming airborne. As Murphy's Law suggests, there is an exception to every rule. During a high-speed taxi practice Pilot Officer A. O. Keith managed to encourage the Vista to fly.

In under nine months of constant exposure to salt water the Vista's duralumin hull developed a dangerous degree of corrosion. The aircraft was scrapped in May 1931, and apparently it was not missed.

C.V. VICKERS VISTA

PERFORMANCE DATA:			
Maximum speed	88 mph	Range	550 miles
Cruise speed	66 mph	Empty weight	655 pounds
Rate of climb	590 feet/min	Loaded weight	1,005 pounds
Ceiling	12,000 feet		

RCAF#	MFG#	T.O.S.	S.O.S.	Remarks
G-CYZZ	CV 42	09-11-27	04-05-31	To Jericho Beach Seaplane School, September 1930

Vista G-CYZZ being lowered into water. CFB Comox Rowe Library

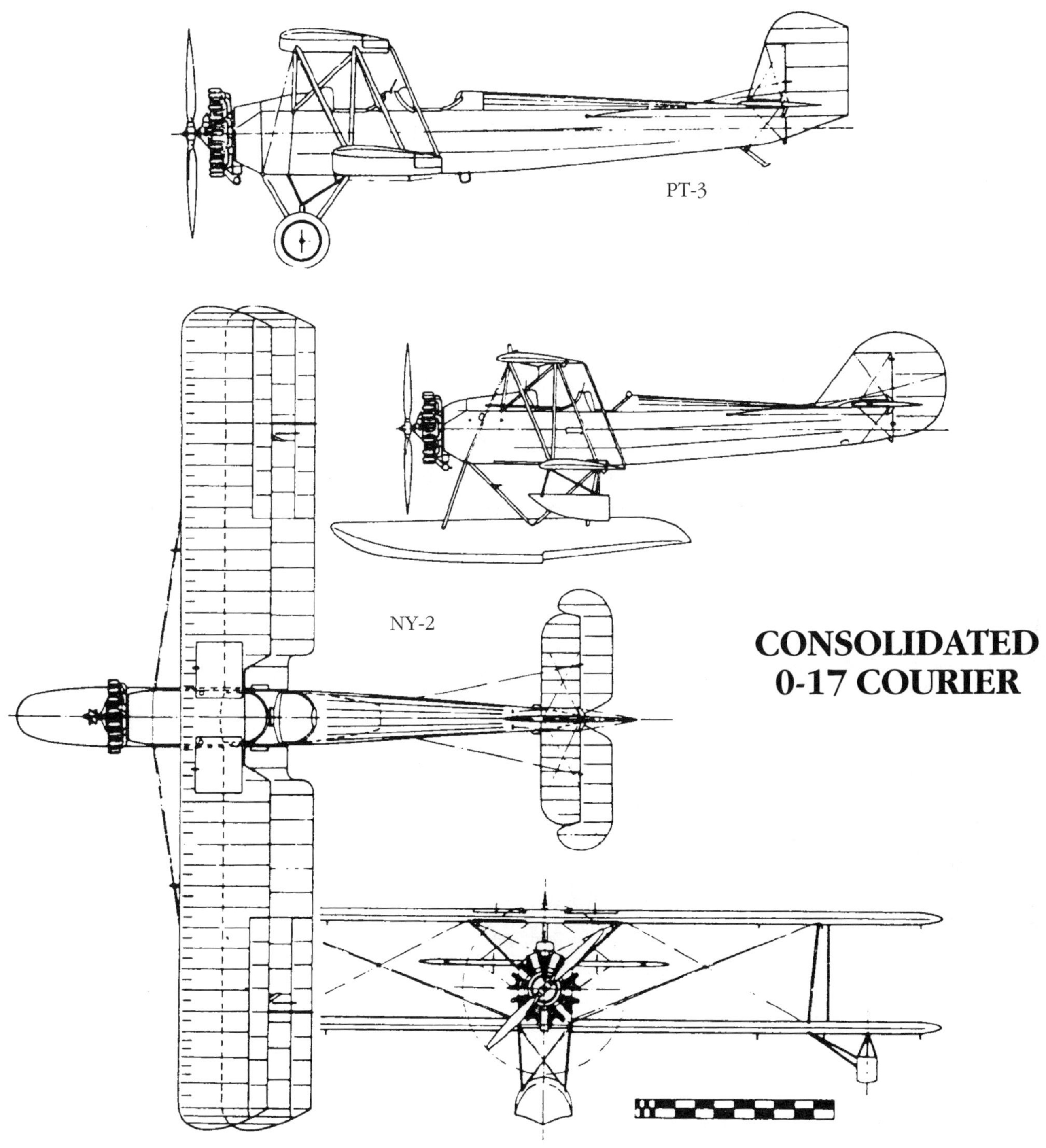

CONSOLIDATED 0-17 COURIER

Following a flight demonstration by Fleet Aircraft of the Consolidated 0-17 Courier in July 1928, three Couriers were purchased by the RCAF. One of these aircraft was a single float model 8 (0-17), which was assigned RCAF serial #24. This aircraft was powered by a single Wright R-790-1 nine-cylinder 225 hp Whirlwind engine.

The 0-17 Courier was a development of an earlier model PT-3 (in turn, an improved NY-2) but with fuselage streamlining, oleo shock absorbers, wheel breaks, balanced elevators, and increased fuel capacity. The other 0-17 Couriers, RCAF #25 and 26 were model 7 wheel-equipped aircraft.

Wing Commander Harry Bryant; fitter, Lock Madil; and Sergeant Jack Hunter, all relate that #24, the single float Ruben Fleet designed Courier, was used at the Jericho Beach Seaplane Training School during 1929, 1930.

CONSOLIDATED 0-17 COURIER (Model 8)

PERFORMANCE DATA:

Maximum speed	118 mph	Range	550 miles
Cruise speed	100 mph	Weight empty	1,881 pounds
Rate of climb	865 feet/minute	Weight loaded	2,723 pounds
Ceiling	12,000 feet		

RCAF#	MFG#	T.O.S.	S.O.S.	Remarks
24		27-02-28	18-06-30	Jericho Beach Seaplane School

Courier #26 model 7 (note square tail) at Camp Borden, 1928. Hunter Collection

The only model 8 Courier #24 at Rockcliffe (Ottawa) in 1930, after its service at Jericho Beach.
DND HC 1546 (via BCMFT)

FAIRCHILD FC-2, 51, 71

During World War I, Sherman Mills Fairchild invented an advanced aerial camera. At the end of the war Fairchild set up his own aerial survey company, but soon found that existing aircraft did not suit his photgraphic needs. He designed a high-wing aircraft, the Fairchild FC-1 (Fairchild Cabin #1) to satisfy his purpose.

The FC-1 was powered by a Curtiss OX-5 engine which was later replaced with a 200 hp Wright J-4 Whirlwind engine. This aircraft went into production as the FC-2 and was an instant success. It had many features that were popular with both the purchaser and the pilots who flew the machine: an enclosed, heated cabin, shock-mounted undercarriage, quick conversion to floats and skis, and an arrangement that allowed the wings to fold back alongside the fuselage for easy storage. The aircraft had excellent forward and side visibility as well as the provision for the convenient mounting of aerial cameras.

Early FC-2s had a razorback or triangular shaped fuselage with only three longerons. However this did not prove satisfactory and later aircraft were produced with four longerons.

The RCAF became interested in the FC-2 in 1927, and, after Canadian Vickers obtained the Canadian manufacturing rights, the company built 12 FC-2s for RCAF service use. The RCAF eventually purchased 27 of these small, yet flexible and hardy aircraft.

Because of its size and comparably low-powered engine many of the FC-2s were converted to Model 5ls by the addition of a 300 hp engine: either a Wright R-975 engine, or a Pratt and Whitney Wasp JR engine. The modification made it necessary to add a fourth longeron to earlier FC-2s.

The FC-2 was again enlarged to have a greater wing span and a larger carrying capacity - first to six seats and later to seven. This Model became the Model 71. The success of his design in Canada prompted Fairchild to establish Fairchild Aircraft Limited at Longueuil, Quebec in 1929.

The Canadian-built FC-71B was test-flown in mid-June 1930 and delivered to the RCAF on June 26th. The gross weight in the 71B was increased to 6,000 pounds, and an innovative design feature allowed the occupants of the aircraft to exit through the roof skylight in the event of an emergency.

The RCAF used the FC-2 and the FC-71B for photographic and transport work and several were in service at Jericho Beach during the 1930s and the 1940s. Thirty-four model 7ls were used by the RCAF from 1929 to 1946.

In August 1937 Wing Commander Earl MacLeod led a tour of four Fairchild 71s from Jericho Beach to Tweedsmuir Park. The Fairchilds and their pilots, W/C Macleod, F/L F.J. Mawdesley, Captain Ted Dobbin, and Captain Charley Elliot, provided air transportation for the Governor General Lord Tweedsmuir and his entourage.

Several 71s were still in use in the Vancouver area after World War II. Early in 1956 Chris Weicht, employed by Central B.C. Air Services, flew out of Vancouver in CF-BVK. The aircraft, manufactured in the United States in 1929, was a Fairchild 71C powered by a 420 hp Pratt and Whitney Wasp B engine. It had served with the RCAF as serial #625 with the previous registration of G-CYXB. In the late 1950s, BVK was damaged beyond repair during take-off out of Ocean Falls, British Columbia.

The last operational Fairchild 71 in Canada was CF-BXF manufactured in 1928 as a FC-2W2. It was converted to a FC-71 in October 1949 by installing a Pratt and Whitney R-985 engine. The aircraft, operated by Sechelt Air Service at Sechelt, British Columbia, was damaged beyond repair on take-off from Deserted Bay, Jervis Inlet on June 27, 1963.

Canadian-built model 71B #647 taxiing off English Bay, Vancouver. Driscoll Collection

FAIRCHILD FC-2 AND 71

PERFORMANCE DATA: Fairchild FC-71C

Maximum speed	132 mphs	Service ceiling	11,000 feet
Cruising speed	106 mph	Empty weight	3,168 pounds
Rate of climb	600 ft/min	Loaded weight	6,000 pound

Aircraft I.D. #	Model	MFG#	RCAF#	Other#	T.O.S.	S.O.S.	REMARKS
XN	FC2W	90	615	G-CYXN	04-06-28	23-07-35	
XP	FC2W	94	617	G-CYXP	13-06-28	05-04-35	
XQ	FC2W	84	618	G-CYXQ	04-06-28	21-07-36	

Aircraft I.D. #	Model	MFG#	RCAF#	Other#	T.O.S.	S.O.S.	REMARKS
YU	FC2W	92	619	G-CYYU	21-05-28	11-06-37	
VX	71B	1/764	633	G-CYVX	09-07-30	13-03-41	
WC	71B	688	638	G-CYWC	03-03-30	16-10-41	
WF	71	687	641	G-CYWF	25-03-30	17-04-45	6 (BR)
	71B/C	FAC8	647	183/CF-BXG	25-06-31	16-10-41	Converted to 71C (02-44)

CF-BXF was the last operational model 71 in Canada, seen here in the livery of BC Airlines at Sea Island, Vancouver, 1946. Elwood White via Rowe Library

XQ a model FC-2W (later RCAF #618) flies over Port Alberni, B.C. CFB Comox Rowe Library

An example of a 71, (#644) on skis. CFB Comox Rowe Library

RCAF #625 (previously G-CYXB) on wheels. This aircraft later became CF-BVK. The author flew in this aircraft in early 1956. Driscoll Collection

IIIF RCAF #J9172 tied to Jericho Beach Cletrac tractor.
Madill Collection

FAIREY IIIF MKIV GP

#J9172 parked on ramp at Jericho Beach in front of fuel tank.
Madill Collection

An interesting aircraft, at Jericho Beach from late fall 1929 until the fall of 1930, was on loan from the Royal Air Force for evaluation.

A development of the World War I Fairey IIIA reconnaissance biplane which was built for the Royal Naval Air Service, the IIIF MKIV was highly modified and streamlined from the original model and was powered by a 570 hp Napier Lion XIA engine. Two hundred and fifteen of this model served with the RAF between 1927 and 1933, as a general purpose aircraft. The reliability of this aircraft led to its use for a series of long distance flights.

The Fairey III IV had a wing span of 45 feet 9 1/2 inches. Its T.O. Weight was 6,040 pounds.

RCAF #J9172 was equipped with a Rolls-Royce Kestrel engine and performance figures are unavailable. Airman fitter Lock Madil states that this aircraft was rarely, if ever, used.

FAIREY IIIF MK1VGP

PERFORMANCE DATA:

Maximum speed . . . . .120 mph
Landing speed . . . . .50 mph
Maximum range . . . . .1,520 miles

RCAF#	T.O.S.	S.O.S.	Remarks
J9172	07-10-29	16-09-30	On loan from Royal Air Force for evaluation

CANADIAN VICKERS VANCOUVER

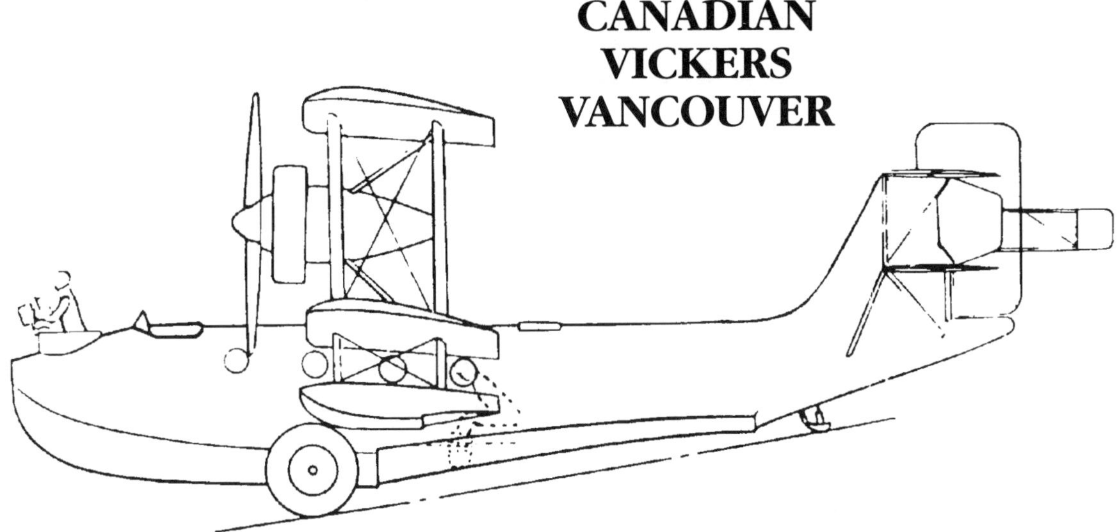

The RCAF was not happy with the outcome of the design modifications it had imposed on the Varunas. However, specific requirements were necessary to develop an effective and efficient transportation aircraft for use in fire-suppression. In May 1928, after consultation with the RCAF, Canadian Vickers provided a new design. The Vancouver I was an equal-span biplane powered by two Armstrong Siddeley Lynx IVB engines. The prototype was flown in April 1929, and accepted by the RCAF in September of that year.

With the Vancouver I, the RCAF felt they were finally on the right track and that many of the design flaws evident in the Varunas had been solved. After sorting out some design changes, the RCAF requested Canadian Vickers to produce five Vancouver IIs. Three Vancouver IIs were powered by a 240 hp Lynx IVC, a geared version of the Armstong Siddeley, and two with the 300 hp Wright J-6 Whirlwind. Delivered in the summer of 1930, the aircraft were sent to Manitoba for operational trials. For several years the machines satisfactorily performed a valuable service for the forest industry.

By 1932 fire protection was no longer a federal responsibility and the RCAF decided to convert the Vancouvers to a Service type. Lewis guns, external bomb racks and other military equipment were installed, which brought about the replacement of the Lynx engine with the more powerful Armstrong Siddeley Servals. All of the converted aircraft eventually served on coastal patrol duty with No. 4 Squadron at Jericho Beach Air Station.

Vancouver #903 on ramp at Jericho Beach.
CFB Comox Rowe Library

CANADIAN VICKERS VANCOUVER IN SERVICE AT JERICHO BEACH

PERFORMANCE DATA: Vancouver I

Maximum speed	96 mph	Empty weight	4,632 pounds
Rate of climb	565 ft/min	Loaded weight	6,700 pounds
Ceiling	12,500 feet		

PERFORMANCE DATA: Vancouver II (W)

Maximum speed	114 mph	Empty weight	4,632 pounds
Cruising speed	92 mph	Loaded weight	7,600 pounds
Rate of climb	565 ft/min		

PERFORMANCE DATA: Vancouver II (AS)

Maximum speed .... 120 mph
Cruising speed .... 85 mph
Rate of climb .... 570 ft/min
Ceiling .... 8,800 ft
Empty weight .... 5,385 pounds
Loaded weight .... 7,600 pounds

PERFORMANCE DATA: Vancouver IIS/W

Maximum speed .... 110 mph
Cruising speed .... 75 mph
Empty weight .... 5,678 pounds
Loaded weight .... 10,000 pounds

PERFORMANCE DATA: Vancouver IIS/S

Maximum speed .... 94 mph
Cruising speed .... 86 mph
Rate of climb .... 200 feet/minute
Ceiling .... 4,800 feet
Empty weight .... 5,960 pounds
Loaded weight .... 10,000 pounds

CV Model #	RCAF Serial #	MFG#	Previous RCAF #	T.O.S.	S.O.S.	REMARKS
Vancouver I	901	CV107	G-CYXS			4(BR) Jericho 1936
Vancouver II	902	CV164	G-CYVQ	16-07-30	25-11-40	Jericho
Vancouver II	903	CV165	G-CYVR	24-07-30	23-11-40	Jericho, 6BR (at Ucluelet)
Vancouver II	904	CV166	G-CYVS	28-08-30		Jericho
Vancouver II	905	CV167	G-CYVT	15-08-30	05-05-36	Jericho
Vancouver II	906	CV168	G-CYVU	02-09-30		Jericho 1941

Vancouver with rear Lewis Gun installation. CFB Comox Rowe Library

#906 parked next to Jericho's fuel tower. CFB Comox Rowe Library

NORTHROP (C.V.) DELTA

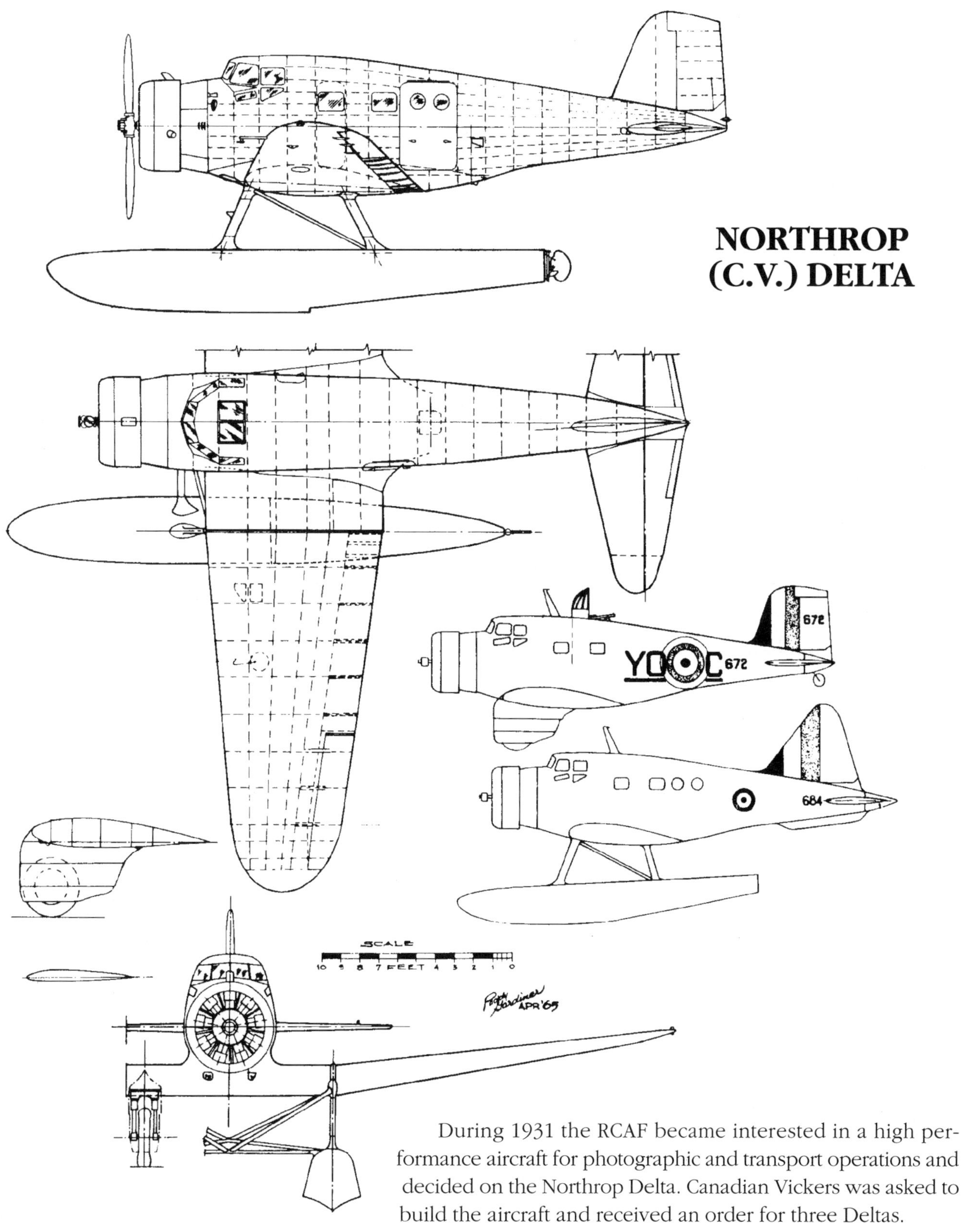

During 1931 the RCAF became interested in a high performance aircraft for photographic and transport operations and decided on the Northrop Delta. Canadian Vickers was asked to build the aircraft and received an order for three Deltas.

RCAF Deltas were modified to accept three camera installations in the aft cabin. The cabin floor was also strengthened to accommodate heavy freight loads and an upward-rising freight door was installed on the left side of the aircraft. Canadian Vickers also designed a special set of floats to fit the three Deltas.

The RCAF prototype, #667 on floats, was first flown on August 21, 1936 and taken on strength on September 1st. Eventually 20 MK1 and MKII Deltas were produced in Canada for the RCAF.

By 1940 most of the Deltas were transferred to British Columbia for use as operational trainers by No. 13 Bomber Reconnaissance Training School at Sea Island. RCAF 675 was used by No. 1 (F) Squadron to give duel instruction to pilots converting to Hawker Hurricane fighter aircraft.

Delta on floats over west coast. Maude Collection

Wing Commander Harry Bryant reported that the Deltas were frequent visitors at Jericho Beach during the early days of World War II. The Northrop Delta series of aircraft, as manufactured by Canadian Vickers for the RCAF, were powered by a single 725 hp Wright SR 1820-52 Cyclone engine.

NORTHROP DELTA

PERFORMANCE DATA:

Maximum speed . . . . .205 mph
Cruising speed . . . . .170 mph
Ceiling . . . . .22,000 feet
Empty weight . . . . .4,566 pounds
Loaded weight . . . . .7,350 pounds

Model	MFG#	RCAF#	Other#	T.O.S.	S.O.S.	Unit	Remarks
I	CV177	667	A-143	01-09-36	26-04-44	120(BR)	13 O.T.U.
I	CV179	669	A-145	31-10-36	26-04-44	6(GP)	Detachment at Jericho
II	CV180	670		04-11-37	16-12-40	120(BR)	Cat."A" 8-8-40 Discovery Passage near Campbell River
II	CV181	671	A-146	05-11-37	26-04-44	W.A.C.	
II	CV192	675	A-158	18-10-38	14-02-45	No.1(F)	Sea Island
II	CV193	676	A-157	04-11-38	14-02-45	120(BR)	MX-C
II	CV196	683	A-156	01-06-40	14-02-45	120(BR)	MX-D
II	CV198	685	A-149	24-06-40	14-02-45	120(BR)	
II	CV199	686	A-150	24-07-40	24-10-44	120(BR)	
II	CV200	687	A-151	24-07-40	14-02-45	120(BR)	
II	CV201	688		14-08-40	16-12-40	120(BR)	Cat."A" 10-10-40 Bella Bella
II	CV202	689		23-09-40	11-08-43	120(BR)	Cat."A" 16-01-42 Lethbridge (MX-H)
II	CV203	690		28-10-40	30-05-42	13 OTU	

ACCIDENTS RECORDED CANADIAN VICKERS DELTA

Delta II RCAF#670 120(BR) Sqd. **08-08-40** **Near Bloedel, Discovery Passage (N.W. Campbell River)**

On August 7, 1940, #670 was at the Queen Charlotte Islands and departed from Alliford Bay the following morning in search of the suspicious vessel "Southern Cross", which it eventually sighted in Discovery Passage, 8 miles northeast of Bloedel. While pilot S/L R.S. Proctour was circling low above the vessel, the aircraft stalled and crashed into the sea killing its crew and passengers.

2nd Pilot: F/O J. George Desbiens; Crew & Passengers: F/O A.L. Gordon, Cpl. R.G. Brown, Cpt. Bourne R.C.O.C.

Delta II RCAF #688 120(BR) Sqd. **10-10-40** **Bella Bella**

En route from RCAF Patricia Bay to Alliford Bay, the crew of #688 spent the night on the seaplane tender, RCAF Scow M-159, at Bella Bella. On the morning of October 10, S/L Fred Ewart, in company with Sgt. Jack McMahone and F/O J.A. Gagnon, took off to the southeast into low cloud and drizzle. At an altitude of 500 ft., as Pilot Ewart turned right over the shoreline of Denny Island, the Delta's engine started to backfire and then stalled. S/L Ewart managed to reach the water near Shearwater Island, striking the trees during his attempt to land on the water. The plane crashed and overturned in 7ft. of water. Ewart and his 2nd Pilot were uninjured, but Sgt. McMahone has a bad cut to his forehead. The crew of the seaplane tender had witnessed the whole event and were soon on the scene. They took the Delta crew to the R.W. Large Memorial Hospital in the Native village of Bella Bella.

Delta #689 (MX-H) at Patricia Bay 120 (BR) Sqdrn. Maude Collection

Refuelling Delta at Pat Bay, 1940. Maude Collection

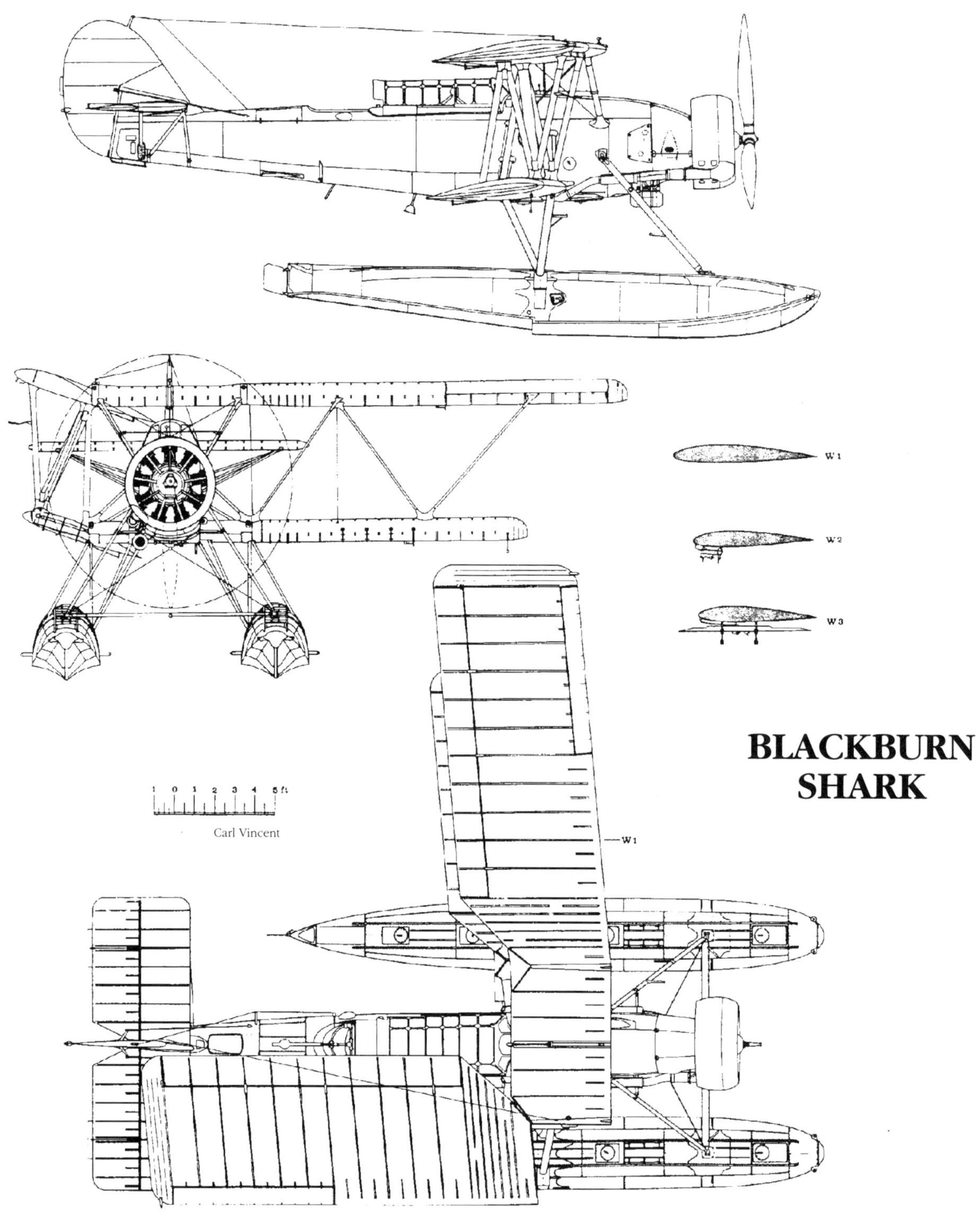

During 1935 the RCAF, on the recommendation of the British Air Ministry, ordered seven British-built Blackburn Shark IIs for use as dive bombers. The Sharks arrived in eastern Canada during 1936-37, and the seven aircraft formed a nucleus for No 6 (Torpedo Bomber) Squadron at Trenton, Ontario.

The Shark II was originally powered by a 760 hp Armstrong Siddeley Tiger VI engine, but was later changed to a Bristol Pegasus 1X engine of 840 hp. An arrangement was made with the British manufacturer, Blackburn Aircraft Limited of Brough, East Yorkshire, which allowed Boeing Aircraft of Canada at Vancouver, to manufacture the Shark III under license from the British company.

The Boeing contract with the Canadian Government was on a "cost, plus 10%" basis and held Boeing harmless from any increase in the price of materials. Boeing-built Shark IIIs were given RCAF serial numbers 514 to 524, and 545 to 550.

The first Boeing-built Shark, RCAF number 514, was delivered to Jericho Beach following its test flight in July 1939. At the end of July, William J. Holland, from Ginger Coote Airways, performed a second successful test flight, and the Shark was then delivered to Sea Island where it was converted to wheels. Edward C. Dobbin completed the RCAF acceptance flight on August 2, 1939. Boeing delivered the last of the Shark III aircraft, RCAF #550, on April 4, 1940.

The Sharks, primarily mounted on floats, served almost entirely on the west coast. They were operated by the RCAF Flying Boat Squadrons: No. 4 (BR), No. 6 (BR), No. 7 (BR), and by No. 122 (K) Squadron at Patricia Bay.

In RCAF use, the Shark III was powered by a Bristol Pegasus 1X engine of 840 hp. But it was not lack of power that squashed the idea conceived by the fertile minds of the Airmen of No. 4 (BR) Squadron. At the outbreak of war with Japan, No. 4 (BR) proposed making a night fighter out of their Shark IIIs. However, sanity prevailed and the idea died a natural death.

On July 27, 1940, F/O Halpenny, flying Shark #517, shed his upper wing on a divebombing practice at RCAF Station Alliford Bay. The three occupants of the Shark were killed but the accident tragically pointed out a weakness in the aircraft. All the Sharks were ferried to No. 3 RD at Jerico Beach where a two foot strengthening section was added to the upper wing spar.

The characteristics of the Blackburn floats caused a great deal of grief. Squadron Leader Allan H. Hull, Commanding Officer of No. 6 (TB) Squadron at Jericho Beach, found his temper taxed to the limit when one RAF exchange officer, F/L Herington, crashed Shark 514 shortly after encountering a severe porpoising condition on take-off. Five days later the same pilot landed Shark 507 too fast and down wind. The aircraft was written off, and the pilot had earned himself a nickname - "Crasher Herington".

Twenty-three percent of all RCAF Sharks were written off through accidents in some way connected to the unstable landing and take-off characteristics of the aircraft. F/O G.A. Doolittle, attached to No. 7 (BR) Squadron at RCAF Station Prince Rupert, inadvertently produced a desperate solution to the problem. On September 3, 1942 Doolittle wrote off Shark #526 in a glassy water landing: his float tips dug in and the aircraft executed a somersault.

The Commanding Officer, Squadron Leader L.H. (Doc) Brooks suggested that if F/O Doolittle wrote off all the Sharks, without injury to anyone, Brooks would recommend him for the Air Force Cross. Doolittle declined the offer.

During 1944 five Sharks were transferred to the Royal Navy. By July that year, all Sharks were retired from RCAF use and struck off strength.

BLACKBURN SHARK

PERFORMANCE DATA:

Maximum speed	152 mph	Empty weight	4,948 pounds
Cruising speed	135 mph	Loaded weight	8,300 pounds
Ceiling	16,100 feet		

RCAF#	MFG #	T.O.S.	S.O.S.	Units	Remarks
BLACKBURN BUILT SHARK II					
501	B3/M723	17-11-36	23-09-43	6(TB) 4(BR) 7(BR) 3RD	Reduced to spares 8-11-43
502	B3/M726	26-10-36	05-06-44	6(TB) 122(K) 3RD	To Royal Navy 5-6-44
503	B3/M729	15-10-36	13-08-44	6(TB) 4(BR) 7(BR) 3RD	Reduced to spares 13-4-44
504	B3/M732	17-11-36	03-08-44	7(GP) 6(TB)122(K) 3RD	Reduced to spares 13-4-44
505		03-05-37	08-03-39	6(TB)	Crashed Trenton 7-10-38
506		27-04-37	03-11-42	6(TB) 4(BR) 122(K)	Crashed Sea Island 18-7-42
507		03-05-37	16-02-40	6(TB)	Crashed Jericho 10-9-39
BOEING BUILT SHARK III (CANADA)					
514	501	02-08-39	16-02-40	6(TB)	Crashed Jericho 5-9-39
515	502	22-08-39	16-02-40	6(TB)	Crashed Jericho 5-9-39
516	503	16-09-39	16-02-40	6(TB)	Crashed Jericho 17-10-39
517		17-10-39	14-11-40	6(BR)	Crashed Alliford Bay 27-7-40
518	506	24-10-39	04-02-42	6(BR) 7(BR)	Crashed Prince Rupert 4-1-42
519	507	22-11-39	13-07-44	6(BR) 7(BR) 122(K)	Reduced to spares 13-7-44
520	505	14-12-39	25-05-43	6(BR) 7(BR)	Crashed Prince Rupert 2-3-43
521	504	05-12-39	13-07-44	6(BR) 7(BR)3RD	Reduced to spares 13-7-44
522		22-12-39	05-06-44	6(BR) 7(BR) 122(K)	To Royal Navy 5-6-44
523		08-01-40	13-07-44	6(BR) 7(BR) 122(K)	Reduced to spares 13-7-44
524		24-01-40	13-07-42	6(BR) 7(BR)	Crashed at Kitkatla, 20-6-40
545		14-02-40	03-07-44	6(BR) 4(BR) 7(BR) 122K	Reduced to spares 13-7-44
546		20-02-40	05-06-44	6(BR) 4(BR) 7(BR) 3RD	To Royal Navy 5-6-44
547		05-03-40	02-02-43	4(BR) 7(BR)	Crashed Prince Rupert 27-1-43
548		19-03-40	09-10-43	4(BR) 7(BR)	Destroyed Prince Rupert 21-9-43
549		19-03-40	05-06-44	4(BR) 7(BR) 122(K)	To Royal Navy 31-5-44

RCAF#	MFG #	T.O.S.	S.O.S.	Units	Remarks
550		04-04-40	05-06-44	6(BR) 7(BR) 122(K)	To Royal Navy 5-6-44
BLACKBURN BUILT SHARK III (CANADA)					
525		22-03-39	04-10-40	6(TB)	Crashed Alliford Bay 19-7-40
526		14-03-39	04-12-42	3RD, 7(BR)	Crashed Prince Rupert 3-9-42

Boeing-built Shark III #522 at Alliford Bay, 1940. Baribeault Collection

ACCIDENTS RECORDED BLACKBURN SHARK

Blackburn Shark 2 506 122(K) Sqd. 18-06-42 Sea Island

Aircraft left Pat Bay for Sea Island and, as the aircraft touched down on water, one float touched a submerged mudbank, the aircraft cartwheeled, shedding the floats and sections of the wings. The fuselage came to rest with the pilot, still strapped in, uninjured save for a "splitting headache".

Pilot: F/O R.T. Heaslip

Blackburn Shark 2 507 6(TB) Sqd. 10-09-39 Off Jericho Beach

Aircraft, with pilot alone aboard, was landed too fast, out of the wind, and crashed. Pilot not seriously hurt.

Pilot: F/Lt. "Crasher" Herington, RAF

Blackburn Shark 3 514 6(TB) Sqd. 05-09-39 Off Jericho Beach

Aircraft porpoised on take-off and crashed after becoming airborne. Crew not seriously hurt. Aircraft sank.

Pilot: F/Lt. "Crasher" Herington, RAF

Blackburn Shark 3 515 9(BR) Sqd. 05-09-39 Off Jericho Beach

Aircraft crashed on take-off from porpoising, and sank. Crew not seriously hurt.

Blackburn Shark 3 516 6(BR) Sqd. 17-10-39 Jericho Beach

Aircraft crashed on take-off for bombing practice.

Blackburn Shark 3 517 6(BR) Sqd. 27-07-40 In Alliford Bay

Aircraft was on local flight and was being dived on test when the top wing twisted and broke off. The aircraft plunged into the water and was totally destroyed, killing the 3 aboard. Cause due to rib buckling and spar twisting.

Pilot: F/O K.H. Halpenny; Crew: F/L A. Simpson; Passenger: LAC R.L. Richardson

Blackburn Shark 3 518 7(BR) Sqd. 54.30N 130.25W 04-01-42 Finlayson Island

Aircraft, with 3 aboard, was formatting with Shark 550 when it collided with it, the fin and rudder striking 550's floats and tearing off. The aircraft went out of control, the gunner baled out safely at low altitude, but the aircraft crashed and burned on Finlayson Island, at Big Bay, killing the two crew remaining aboard.

Pilot: F/O R.E. "Barny" McLeod; Gunner: Sgt. T.H. Collins; Passenger: Sgt. E.E. Cormier

Blackburn Shark 3 520 7(BR) Sqd. 02-03-43 Prince Rupert

Aircraft swerved on take-off, dug in float and flipped over, destroying the aircraft. The crew escaped unhurt.

Blackburn Shark 3 524 7(BR) Sqd. 54.23N 130.35W 20-06-42 Off Kitkatla

Aircraft ran into slipstream of another Shark, lost control and crashed into the sea, killing both aboard. Aircraft sank, one float later retrieved by HMCS Courtenay.

Pilot: F/Sgt. H.E. Phillips; Crew: F/Sgt. H.W. Baum

Blackburn Shark 3 525 6(TB) Sqd. 19-07-40 Alliford Bay

Aircraft crashed on landing in glassy water in Alliford Bay. The crew were not seriously hurt.

Blackburn Shark 3 526 7(BR) Sqd. 03-09-42 Prince Rupert

Aircraft overturned on landing and was destroyed. The crew escaped without injury.

Blackburn Shark 3 547 7(BR) Sqd. 27-01-43 Prince Rupert

Aircraft, with 3 aboard, crashed on landing, depth charges broke loose and detonated, igniting fuel. All crew seriously injured; one died the next day.

Blackburn Shark 3 548 7(BR) Sqd. 21-09-43 Prince Rupert

Aircraft had returned from last anti-sub patrol for Sharks and was tied up. A routine maintenance was carried out by two mechanics in a dinghy, and two more inside the aircraft.

The arming and release circuits for the depth charges were accidentally switched on and one depth charge dropped from the aircraft; upon reaching the appropriate depth it blew up. The aircraft capsized from the explosion and the wing containing the other charge sank to the same depth, whereupon the second charge detonated. The aircraft was totally destroyed and two mechanics were killed.

Mechanics: LAC L.O. Dorge, AC1 J.A. Fraser

Shark II #507 on wheels. Driscoll Collection

Shark III #520 at Jericho Beach. Madill Collection

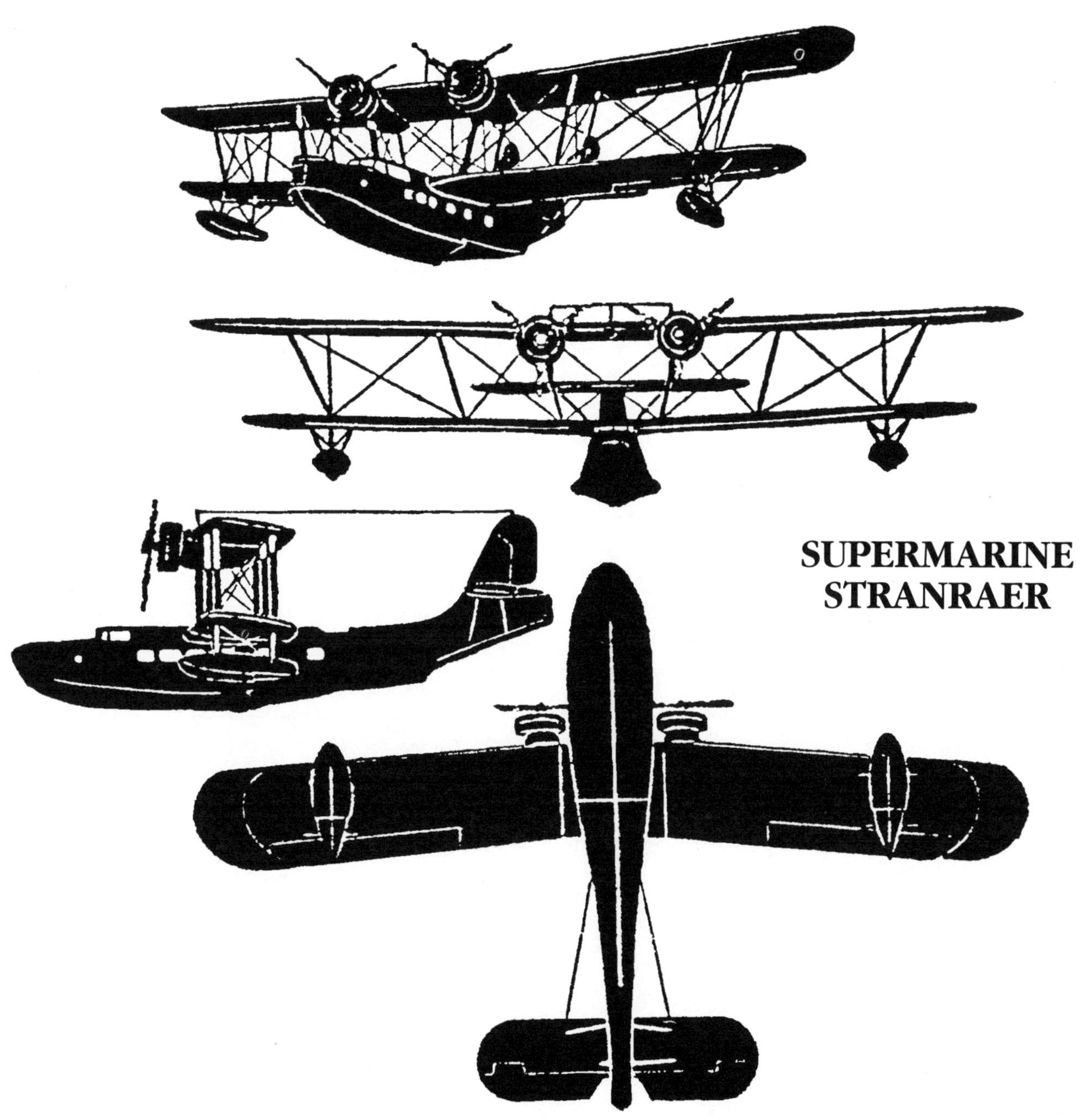

SUPERMARINE STRANRAER

In December 1931, RCAF Headquarters completed a review of its needs to meet the requirements of National defence. The primary mandate was coastal defence, which included reconnaissance, anti-submarine patrols, cooperation with coastal artillery, and the defence of ships moving up and down the Pacific west coast.

The RCAF believed that it was prudent to utilize aircraft of British origin. Therefore, in 1936 Canadian Vickers of Montreal received an order to build five Stranraers. The aircraft had been designed in England by R.J. Mitchell - of the Spitfire fame - and was a development of the 1925 Supermarine Southampton Flying Boat. Eighteen twin-engine, biplane Stranraers were produced by the Supermarine Aviation Works Limited in Southampton. In 1935 these Flying Boats went into service with the RAF.

Following the test flight of the Canadian prototype, RCAF #907, on October 21, 1938, a total of forty aircraft were ordered from Canadian Vickers. At Jericho Beach, No. 4 (BR) Squadron received its first Stranraer, RCAF #912, on July 16, 1939. Stranraers were used by eight Squadrons on the west coast: Numbers 4, 6, 7, 9, 13, 117, 120, and 166.

The “Stranies” gave good service to the RCAF for six years, particularly in carrying out anti-submarine patrol schedules for the newly established west coast Flying Boat Stations. In 1944 most of the Stranraers were withdrawn from service and replaced with the Canso and Catalina aircraft. The sole surviving example of the Stranraer is RCAF #920, later CF-BXO, which now reposes in the RAF Museum at Hendon in southwest London.

In RCAF use the Stranraer had a range of up to 1,750 miles and was powered by two 810 hp Bristol Pegasus X or XXII engines. In post-war years five Stranraers were purchased by Queen Charlotte Airlines. Two Stranraers, ex-RCAF #915 and #920, were modified by fitting two 1,000 hp Wright GR-1820-G202GA Cyclone engines and became Super Stranraers. These aircraft had an empty weight of 14,560 pounds and a loaded weight of 22,000 pounds.

SUPERMARINE STRANRAER

PERFORMANCE DATA:

Maximum speed . . . . 152 mph
Cruising speed . . . . 135 mph
Ceiling . . . . 16,100 feet
Empty Weight . . . . 14,948 pounds
Loaded Weight . . . . 18,300 pounds

CV#	RCAF#	T.O.S.	S.O.S.	Unit	Civic Reg.#	Remarks
184	907	09-11-38	07-02-45	6BR, 13 OTU	CF-BYI	Alliford Bay, 1941
185	908	03-12-38	26-01-44	9BR		Bella Bella, Cat."B", 5-2-42
186	909	11-05-39	07-02-45	120 BR	CF-BYL	Coal Harbour, 1942
187	910	30-05-39	07-02-45	4BR	CF-BYE	Ucluelet
189	912	06-07-39	07-02-45	4BR		Also 120BR (MX-E) & Jericho Beach
190	913	05-08-39	07-02-45	120BR 7(BR)	CF-BYF	Coal Harbour
204	914	31-08-39	07-02-45	4BR 120(BR)	CF-BYH	Ucluelet, 1942
205	915	27-09-39	07-02-45	4BR, 9BR	CF-BYJ	Jericho Beach, 1939, Bella Bella
206	916	12-11-39	18-07-43	3 OTU, 6(BR)		Cat."A", 18-7-43 Crofton, B.C.
207	918	23-10-40	02-09-44	9BR 4BR		Cat."B", 2-10-42 Bella Bella
208	919	18-11-40	29-11-44	166BR 6BR	CF-BYA	Sea Island, 1944
209	920	28-11-40	10-05-44	7BR, 9BR	CF-BXO	Cat."B", 16-9-43 Prince Rupert
210	921	06-02-41	29-11-44	13BR OTU	CF-BYD	Patricia Bay
211	922	15-02-41	18-02-42	6BR		Cat."A", 31-12-41 fire at Alliford Bay

CV#	RCAF#	T.O.S.	S.O.S.	Unit	Civic Reg.#	Remarks
212	923	19-03-41	07-02-45	6BR	CF-BYG	Alliford Bay
213	927	27-05-41	18-02-42	13 OTU		Cat."A" Nanoose Bay, 15-12-41
214	928	25-06-41	18-02-42	4BR		Cat."A" crash 30-12-41, Ucluelet
215	929	26-06-41	06-11-43	120BR		Cat."A", 13-9-43 Coal Harbour
216	930	04-07-41	07-02-45	6BR		Alliford Bay 1942
217	931	10-07-41	04-12-43	13 OTU 6BR		
218	932	10-07-41	02-11-41	4BR		Destroyed in fire on take off 2-11-41
219	933	10-07-41	03-11-43	13 OTU		
220	934	10-07-41	07-02-45	4BR 7BR 9BR		Ucluelet 1941
221	935	09-08-41	08-03-43	6BR, 13 OTU		Cat."A", 14-2-43 Skidigate Channel
222	936	12-08-41	07-02-45	13 OTU 6BR 9BR	CF-BYK	Bella Bella damaged Rose Harbour QCI
223	937	14-08-41	08-03-44	9BR		Bella Bella
224	938	10-08-41	30-11-43	166COM 4BR 6BR		Sea Island 1941
225	946	07-10-41	01-06-42	5BR		Lost on flight from Penticton, BC, to Jericho Beach 4-11-41
226	947	17-10-41	02-09-44	4BR		Cat."A", 22-4-42 at Vancouver
227	948	21-10-41	29-11-44	6BR 4BR 13(OT)	CF-BYB	Cat."C" 28-4-42 Pat Bay
228	949	22-10-41	20-01-46	9BR	CF-BYM	Cat."B", 29-7-42 Bella Bella
229	950	22-10-41	07-02-45	120 BR		Coal Harbour 1941
230	951	01-11-41	26-09-42	120 BR		Cat."A", lost at sea 23-8-42
231	952	01-11-41	16-10-46	120 BR		Coal Harbour (MX-C)
232	953	17-11-41	07-25-45	166 COM 9BR	CF-BYC	Sea Island
233	954	17-11-41	25-11-43	7BR 4BR 166		Cat."A" 26-9-43 Annette Island, Alaska
234	955	17-11-41	07-02-45	4BR, 13 OTU		Cat."C" 20-7-42 Patricia Bay
235	956	17-11-41	07-02-45	9BR, 7BR, 13(OT) 6BR		Cat."C" 29-4-42 Patricia Bay

CV#	RCAF#	T.O.S.	S.O.S.	Unit	Reg.#	Civic Remarks
236	957	17-11-41	07-02-45	13(OT)		
	* 924			120 BR		Coal Harbour

* R.C.A.F. #923 was assigned CV #212. CV #213 was R.C.A.F. #927. Thus #924, 925, 926 were not built. However, # 120(BR) Squadron records show #924 on strength at Coal Harbour. This is probably an error.

No 4(BR) Stranraer #915 at dock at RCAF Ucluelet.
Baribeault Collection

ACCIDENTS RECORDED CANADIAN VICKERS STRANRAER

Canadian Vickers Stranraer 916 30TU 48.53N 123.37W 18-07-43 In Stuart Channel

Aircraft left Pat Bay on blind flying exercise, with 6 aboard, and landed and sank in Stuart Channel, one mile offshore from Crofton, two crew were missing, the others rescued. The body of LAC Bell was later found.

Pilot: F/Lt. L.G. Larsen; Crew: P/O J. Chesney, F/O P. Hertsley, Sgt. J.E.C. Rogers, LAC J.M. Bell, F/Sgt. W.K. McCarty - missing.

Canadian Vickers Stranraer 922 6(BR) 31-12-41 Alliford Bay, QCI

Aircraft destroyed by fire while receiving maintenance.

Canadian Vickers Stranraer 927 130TS 49.15N 124.08W 15-12-41 Nanoose Bay

Aircraft left Pay Bay, with 8 aboard, and crashed at entrance to Nanoose Bay, killing 7, one missing. Wreck recovered and transported aboard scow to Jericho Beach to be broken up. Bodies removed from hull.

Pilot: F/Lt. D.C. MacDougall- missing; Crew: Sgt. R.T. Mitchell (Pilot), Sgt. G.H. Andrews (Pilot), Sgt. R. Wood (WAG), Sgt. J.C. Gunn (WAG), LAC W.D. Riley (Air Mechanic), AC1 R.A. Blakely, AC1 R.W. Adams (Air Mechanic)

Canadian Vickers Stranraer 928 4(BR) Sqd. 48.55N 125.33W 30-12-41 Half mile south of Ucluelet

Aircraft crashed in woods half mile south of Ucluelet Base and sank, killing four of the 8 aboard.

Pilot: F/O R.J. Gray killed; Crew: Sgt. M.N. McKay (2nd Pilot) - killed, P/O A.C. Scruton (Navigator) - killed, Cpl. W.J. Zenkie (Aircraft Mechanic) - killed, Sgt. F.A. Rogas, Cpl. G. Atkinson, Sgt. L.A. Davies, Sgt. A.V. Gordon.

Canadian Vickers Stranraer 929 120BR Sqd. 13-09-43 Coal Harbour

No details. Cat,"A" crash. Landing accident

Canadian Vickers Stranraer 932 4(BR) Sqd. **02-11-41** **Patricia Bay**

Destroyed by engine fire on take-off.

Canadian Vickers Stranraer 935 6BR Sqd. **53.12N 132.02W** **14-02-43** **Alliford Bay**

Aircraft left Alliford Bay on training flight, with 6 aboard, and crashed on landing in Skidegate Channel between Maude and Lina Islands, killing all aboard.

Pilot: P/O D.S. MacLennan; Crew: P/O L.G. Thompson (Pilot), P/O E.W. McConkey (WAG), Sgt. J.O. Gilmour (Aircraft Mechanic) (N.K.G.), Cpl. J.P. Sperling (Aircraft Mechanic) (N.K.G.), F/Lt. C.W.T. Field (ROC)

Canadian Vickers Stranraer 946 5(BR) **49.36N 123.00W** **04-11-41** **Squamish**

Aircraft left Penticton for Vancouver, with 5 aboard, and disappeared without trace. The aircraft had crashed 10 miles southeast of Squamish, breaking up on impact, covering a 100 yard circle. It is not known if any of the crew survived the crash as no trace of them was ever found. Wreck located in 1947 at the headwaters of Indian River at the 4,400 ft. level. A cairn was erected at the site. Part of wing and float remain at site, visible from the air.

Pilot: Sgt. J.F. Bliss; Crew: Cpl. G.S. Palmer (WAG), Cpl. J.R.B. Fernie, LAC C.M. Ross (Aircraft Mechanic), LAC G.F. Willet (Aircraft Mechanic)

Canadian Vickers Stranraer 947 4(BR) **22-04-42** **Jericho Beach**

No details. Cat. "A" crash

Canadian Vickers Stranraer 951 120(BR) **49.30N 130.30W** **23-08-42** **Off Coal Harbour**

Aircraft left Coal Harbour on patrol, with 8 aboard, and had an inflight problem causing forced landing out at sea. Crew survived ditching but were never found.

Pilot: F/Sgt. E.T. Cox; Crew: F/Sgt L.A.B. Horn (Pilot), LAC M.R. Cram (WAG), Sgt. R.B. Stuart (Navigator), Sgt. K.E. Hope (Aircraft Mechanic), Sgt. A.W. Anderson (WAG), Sgt. L. Oldford (Aircraft Mechanic), Sgt. C.F. Beeching (Aircraft Mechanic)

Canadian Vickers Stranraer 954 166 Sqd. **25-09-43** **Tongas Harbor Annette Island, Alaska**

3 fatalities, 1 missing, 10 injured. Aircraft on mail and passenger flight to No 135(F) Squadron, many on board were P-40 pilots.

Pilot: F/O R.T. Johnstone, injured; Crew: W/Operator F/S F.N. Connelly, injured; LAC F.E.S. Hammerton, injured; LAC R. Haslett, missing.

The last Stranraer built, #957, on the slide. Schofield Collection

#937 of No. 9(BR) Squadron Bella Bella on patrol. LaRamée Collection

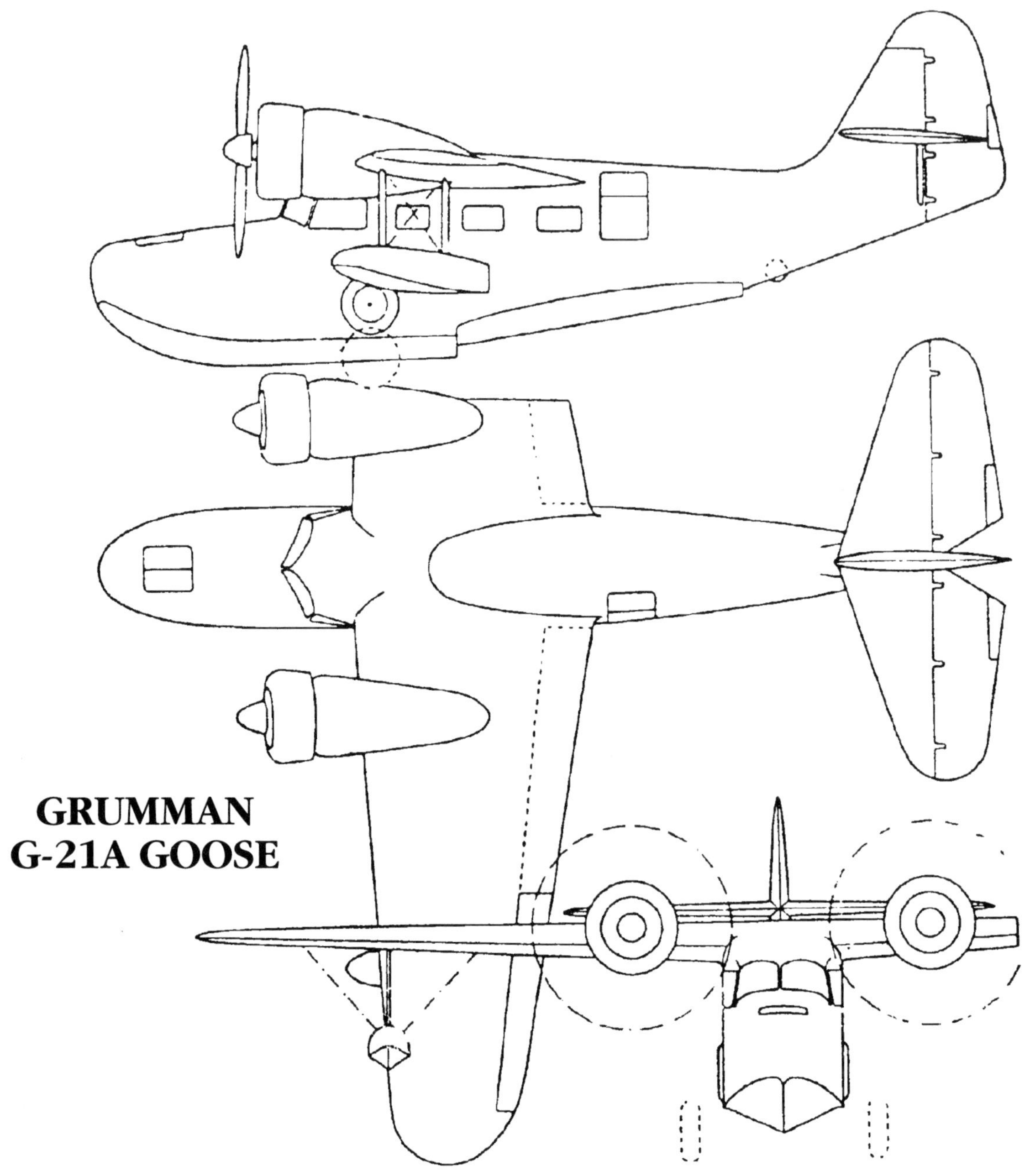

GRUMMAN G-21A GOOSE

First produced in the spring of 1937, the Grumman Goose was the company's first venture in constructing an aircraft for the private and the commercial market. The aircraft was an immediate success and 11 were completed during the first year of production, with another 31 under construction.

The model under various designations was later ordered in quantity by the United States Navy and Coast Guard. Production ended in September 1945.

The RCAF operated 31 G-21As for general utility purposes, many of which served on the British Columbia coast. Some of these aircraft were requisitioned from private users.

At least two former RCAF Goose aircraft are still in service on the British Columbia coast with Pacific Coastal Airlines at Port Hardy; CF-IOL and CF-HUZ were for many years well known in the livery of MacMillan & Bloedel Forest Product Limited until the aircraft were sold in 1995.

The Goose served as a utility aircraft with the RCAF, and was a frequent visitor to all of the west coast Flying Boat Stations, as well as Jericho Beach.

GRUMMAN GOOSE II

PERFORMANCE DATA:

Maximum speed . . . . .201 mph (at 5,000 feet)
Cruise speed . . . . .190 mph (at 5,000 feet)
Rate of Climb . . . . .1,100 ft/min (at sea level)
Ceiling . . . . .21,000 feet
Range . . . . .640 miles

Grumman Goose RCAF #924 at Alliford Bay, 1940. Baribeault Collection

MFG#	RCAF#	T.O.S.	S.O.S.	Previous Reg.#	Civil Reg. #	Unit	Remarks
B 60	388	30-05-44	19-07-45	USN 37807		WAC	Cat. "A"
B 76	392	24-08-44	16-01-47	USN 37823	CF-BAE	WAC	
B 83	393	02-10-44	14-02-36	USN 37830	CF-HUZ		
B 90	394	03-11-44	30-01-52	USN 84795			
B 98	395	05-12-44	25-09-47	USN 84803	CF-GEC	WAC	
B 99	396	16-12-44	13-01-46	USN 84804		WAC	
B 107	397	20-01-45	08-01-48	USN 84812	CF-IOL		
1003	942	29-03-41	09-05-45	NC 16912		13(OTU)	122 (K) Cat. "B" 03-10-41 Pat Bay
1013	924	12-09-39	01-01-45		CF-BKE	13(OTU)	122 (K)
1016	917	26-07-38	23-10-42			122(K) 6(BR)	Cat."A", 27-07-42 Pat Bay

MFG#	RCAF#	T.O.S.	S.O.S.	Previous Reg.#	Civil Reg. #	Unit	Remarks
1018	798	17-04-42	05-01-45	NC 20648		122(K)	No. 166 Sqdrn
1020	796	21-04-42	29-08-44	NC 20650		122(K)	
1061	941	01-11-40	05-01-45		CF-BQE	13(OTU)	
1083	940	16-10-40	05-01-45	CF-BTF		7(BR)	Cat."C" 14-03-41 Pat Bay
984						4(BR)	

Grumman Goose lands at Masset Strip. Furlong Collection

Goose CF-IOL (ex RCAF #397) climbs slipway at Sea Island, 1994. Weicht Collection

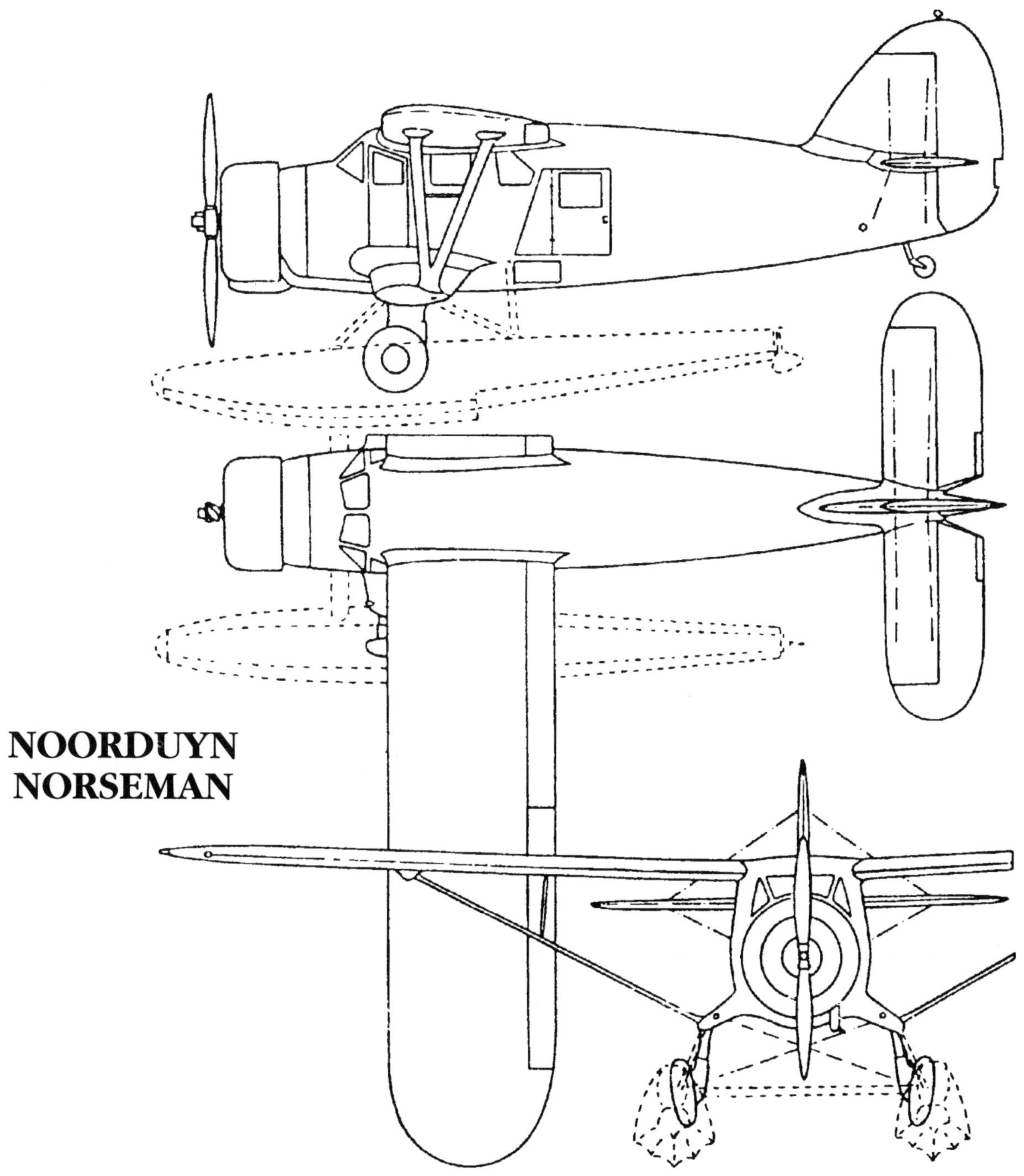

The Norseman design had its beginnings in 1934. Bob Noorduyn consulted Canadian bush pilots and aircraft operators in an attempt to produce the right aircraft for the job.

Noorduyn was born of British/Dutch parents and apprenticed at the Sopwith Aviation Company in England. He emigrated to the United States in the 1920s and took employment with both Fokker and Bellanca Aircraft companies. It was during this period that he became interested in the specialized aircraft requirements that would assist bush pilots flying in the north.

The Norseman I, first flew on November 14, 1935. It was powered by a 420 hp Wright Whirlwind engine and accommodated a pilot and up to nine passengers. The production Norseman II followed on May 2, 1936, but, like the prototype, it was under-powered.

September 4, 1936 saw the first flight of the Pratt and Whitney-powered model III, with a WASP SL engine. Only one model was built. The model III was followed by the Norseman IV with a Pratt and Whitney 550 hp R-1340 engine. This model first flew on November 5, 1936.

Several IVs were sold to Canadian bush operators, and in 1938 the RCAF ordered four of these models. By the end of 1941 the RCAF had 18 Norseman IVs on order.

In July 1941, Burnt Belchen, the Norwegian-born pilot who had accomplished extensive arctic flying, was enlisted by the United States Army Air Force. Belchen had the job of establishing a ferry route across Labrador and Greenland to transport aircraft for use in the war in Europe. Belchen specified the Norseman aircraft for his use. Six Norseman were diverted to him from the RCAF's order.

Following Belchen's use of the Norseman, the United States Army Air Force ordered a considerable number of the aircraft and some were also ordered by the United States Navy.

The manufacturing rights were sold in 1946 to Canadian Car and Foundry in Montreal, who continued the manufacture of model V. The CCF developed a model VII in 1951 with all-metal wings and tail section. However, the prototype Norseman VII was destroyed in a hangar fire in 1958.

In 1979, 46 Norseman aircraft were still in active use in Canada. Many more of the stalwart aircraft performed useful service in other parts of the world. The last Norseman in use on the British Columbia coast was CF-KAS, a model VI/C-64A, operated by Hannah Air of Ganges on Salt Spring Island. However, in 1995 CF-KAS suffered its final blow. A float strut separated in flight and the aircraft sank on landing.

Many Norseman IVs and VIs served with the RCAF at Jericho Beach and also at the various Flying Boat Squadrons on the British Columbia coast.

NOORDUYN NORSEMAN

PERFORMANCE DATA:

Maximum speed . . . . .170 mph
Cruising speed . . . . .150 mph (on wheels)
Ceiling . . . . .22,000 feet
Empty weight . . . . .3,675 pounds
Loaded weight . . . . .6,450 pounds

Model#	RCAF#	MFG#	T.O.S.	S.O.S.	Civil#	Remarks
II	695	02	24-02-40	20-07-44	CF-AZA	No.6(BR) 166 Sqd, Cat."A" Port Alice 4-2-44
III	694	05	10-02-40	07-03-46	CF-BAM	122K Sqdrn, 13 OTU 6(BR)
IV	697	08	24-02-40	08-05-46	CF-BAN	No. 6(BR), 166 Sqdrn
IV	696	15	24-02-40	08-05-46	CF-BFR	No. 6(BR), 166 Sqdrn
IV	2470	43	12-02-41	14-03-45		122K, 166 Sqd, Cat."B" Chilcotin & Fraser Rivers
IV	2480	53	02-05-41	08-05-46	CF-CRS	6(BR), 122K, 13 OTU, 166 Sqdrn
IV	2481	54	02-05-41	10-06-43		6(BR), 13 OTU, Cat."A" Annette, Alaska
IV	2488	61	07-05-41	17-10-47	CF-GHH	No. 166 Sqdrn
IV	3536	87	26-01-42	17-11-53		No. 166 Sqdrn

Model#	RCAF#	MFG#	T.O.S.	S.O.S.	Civil#	Remarks
IV	3539	90	04-04-42	06-01-46		No. 166, Cat."A" 15-10-45 Porcher Island
VI	361	234	14-11-43	25-11-55	CF-INK	No. 166 Sqdrn
VI	362	235	14-11-43	23-06-52		No. 166 Sqdrn
VI	363	236	14-11-43	28-06-45		No. 166 Sqdrn
VI	364	237	14-11-43	23-06-52		No. 166 Sqdrn
VI	37	432	03-04-44	20-01-56		W.A.C. (1944)
	3531	75	08-01-42	29-11-44		7(BR) Cat."A" 23-10-44, 166 Sqdrn

#680 tied down on ramp for servicing.
Driscoll Collection

ACCIDENTS RECORDED NOORDUYN NORSEMAN

Noorduyn Norseman 4 3539 166 Sqd. **53.58N 130.20W 103 G16W** **14-10-45** **Kitkatla Inlet Porcher Island**

Aircraft left Alliford Bay for Prince Rupert, with 6 aboard. Aircraft force-landed in trees near Kitkatla Inlet on Porcher Island, tearing off both wings and causing other damage. All occupants escaped. Wreck still at site, visible.

Pilot; F/O R.A. Kirkwood; Passengers: W02 G. Lepp, Sgt. C.H. Aitken, Cpl. D.C. McEachern, LAC A.B. Carlson, LAC Lind.

Noorduyn Norseman 4 2470 166 Sqd. **51.43N 122.23W** **02-02-45** **Junction Chilcotin and Fraser Rivers**

Aircraft left Anaheim for Prince George, with 6 aboard, but force-landed on river ice on west bank of Fraser River, one mile south of the junction of the Chilcotin and Fraser Rivers. Occupants survived; aircraft later salvaged.

Pilot: F/O J.Bell; Passengers: Sgt. F.J.M. Foley, F/Sgt. A.D. Henderson, Cpl. A.R. McLennan, Cpl. A.H. Borne, Sgt. N.J. Wilkie

Noorduyn Norseman 4 695 166 Sqd. **50.23N 127.28W** **04-02-44** **2 miles west of Port Alice**

Aircraft left Port Alice, with 5 aboard, on local flight and crashed shortly after takeoff and burned, killing 4 occupants. SAR list wreck as badly damaged, yet it may have been removed circa 1946, as this was the second Norseman built, Reg. CF-AZA, and was re-registered in 1946 as AZA.

Pilot: F/O J.J. Eccles; Passengers: Sgt. L.A. Powell (WAC) - killed, Major J.G. Moore - killed, L/Bdr E.C. Scrivenor - killed, Sgt R.R. Barker

Noorduyn Norseman 4 2481 122 Sqd. **26-03-43** **Annette Island, Alaska**

Aircraft left Ketchikan on return to Annette and was forced down in heavy snow near Metlakatla, Alaska, killing crew and passengers.

Pilot: S/L F.B. Currie; Crew & Passengers: F/L I.M. Dowling, F/L E.B. Stapleford, LAC E.K. McMichael, plus three women members of concert group visiting RCAF Annette Island.

Norseman is brought up ramp at Jericho Beach.
Madill Collection

A No. 6(BR) Norseman #696 on beaching gear.
Driscoll Collection

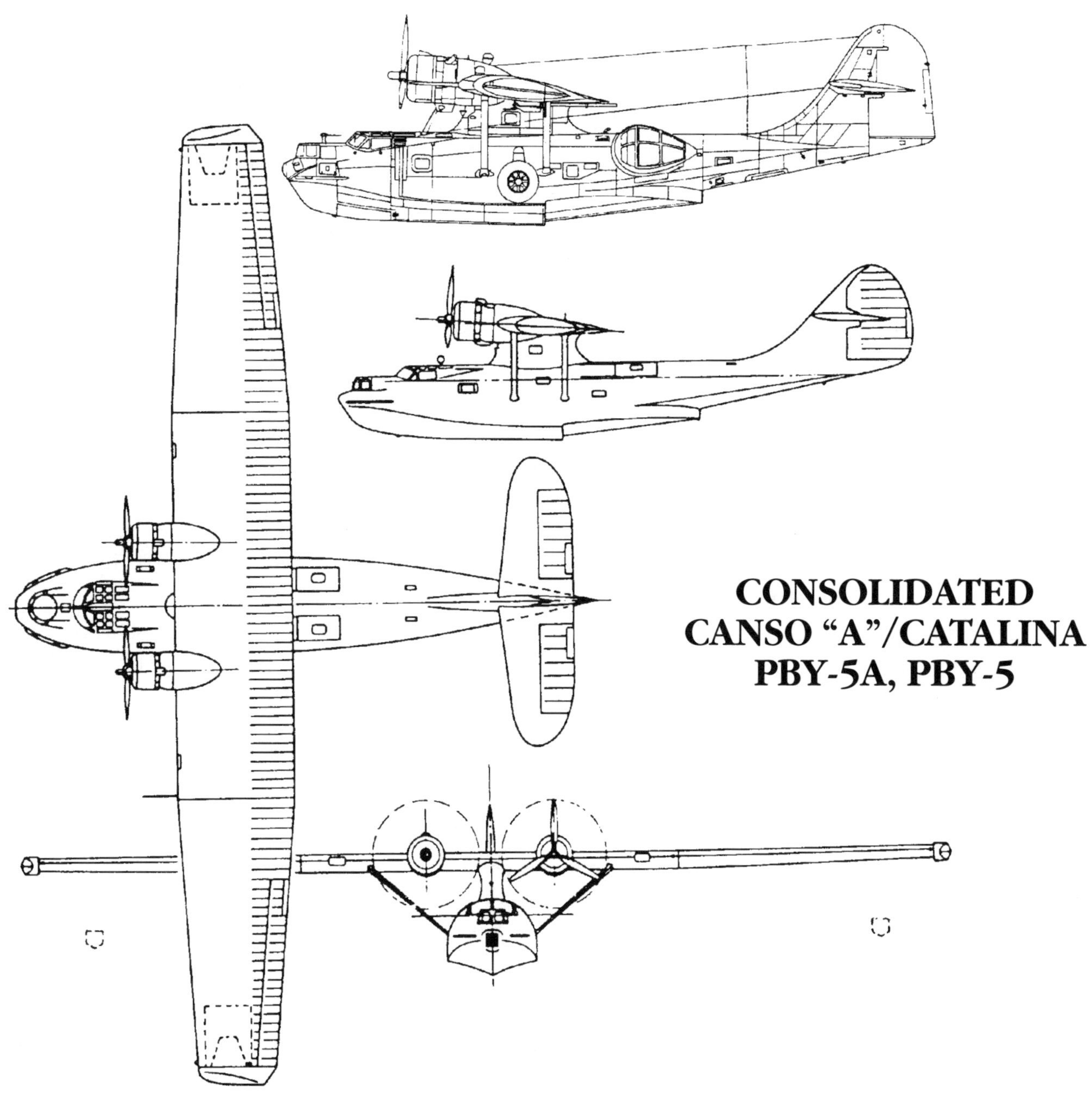

CONSOLIDATED CANSO "A"/CATALINA PBY-5A, PBY-5

In 1939, when the RCAF started to receive the first of 40 Stranraers that had been on order since 1936, a decision was made to start investigating a suitable successor. In December 1939 the Consolidated PBY was selected as the next generation of flying boat for RCAF service use. The prototype of the PBY was ready for its first flight on March 28, 1935 and was in service with the United States Navy in October of the following year.

Late in 1940 the Vancouver location of Boeing Aircraft of Canada entered into an agreement to assemble 55 PBY-5As from parts supplied by Consolidated. Canadian Vickers in Montreal also had a contract to construct PBYs as soon as the Stranraer orders were completed.

The name "Catalina", denoting the flying boat version of the PBY, was used by the United States Navy and the Royal Air Force, but the RCAF rejected the name in favour of "Canso". The amphibious PBY-5A was dubbed by the RCAF as the Canso A. In spite of this official nomenclature, confusion often arises over which aircraft is being referred to in Station diaries and other recorded information. Generally speaking, a Catalina was a Flying Boat, and Canso was the amphibian.

Except for a few early models of the PBY-5, the RCAF only used the PBY-5A Canso. The first Boeing built Canso A was RCAF 9751, flown at Vancouver on July 26, 1942. Boeing Aircraft at Vancouver also built a substantial number of other Consolidated-designed Flying Boats and amphibian aircraft for the Royal New Zealand Air Force, the Royal Australian Air Force, the United States Navy and the United States Army Air Force.

In 1942 Canadian Vickers started to produce Canso "A"s and the prototype, RCAF 9806, was given a test flight on December 2nd of that year. The PBY-5A Canso "A" was powered by two 1,200 hp Pratt and Whitney Twin Wasp R-1830-92 engines.

Canso As were used on the west and the east coasts of Canada for anti-submarine patrol and convoy protection. Eventually the Canso A replaced the Stranraer at the Flying Boat Squadrons on the coast of British Columbia: No. 4 (BR), No. 6 (BR), No. 7 (BR), No. 9 (BR) and No. 120 (BR). The aircraft also served with No. 3 (BR) Operational Training Unit at Patricia Bay, and with No. 160 (BR) formed at Sea Island.

The RCAF believed that the advantages of the amphibious PBY-5A Canso over the PBY-5 Catalina Flying Boat were considerable - even though the amphibian had a 2,800 weight penalty. Therefore, the only Flying Boats used were early-model Catalinas loaned by the RAF.

In post-war years the Canso continued to be popular with west coast airlines. Many of these airlines used the Canso successfully on scheduled operations on the British Columbia coast: Queen Charlotte Airlines, Pacific Western Airlines, and Canadian Pacific Airlines. The Flying Firemen Limited, based at Patricia Bay, also made good use of the Canso in their water bombing operation.

During the early 1980s the last Canso on the coast of British Columbia flew sport fishermen from Vancouver to Hakai Passage, in the vicinity of the former RCAF Station Bella Bella.

PERFORMANCE DATA:

Maximum speed . . . . .179 mph
Cruising speed . . . . .117 mph
Ceiling . . . . .20,000 feet
Empty weight . . . . .20,910 pounds
Loaded weight . . . . .33,975 pounds

CONSOLIDATED CATALINA

Model	RCAF#	T.O.S.	S.O.S.	Unit	Remarks
	202	24-11-41	17-05-46	6(BR)	(This A/C either FP or DP 202)
1B	FP 290	04-12-42	24-09-46	6(BR)	
	FP 291	04-12-42	08-08-46	4(BR) 3 OTU	
	FP 292	04-12-42	03-09-46	6(BR)	
	FP 293	10-12-42	21-08-46	9(BR)	
	FP 294	04-12-42	08-08-46	4(BR) 120(BR)	
1B	FP 296	04-12-42	24-09-46	6(BR)	

Model	RCAF#	T.O.S.	S.O.S.	Unit	Remarks
	FP 297	10-12-42	18-12-46	9(BR) 6(BR)	Cat."C" 10-1-45 Coal Harbour
MK4	JX 206	29-05-43	17-05-46	7(BR)	
MK4A	JX 207	29-05-43	16-05-45	9(BR) 7(BR)	Cat."B" 17-4-45 Dead True Point, Queen Charlotte Islands
MK4	JX 209	08-05-43	17-05-46	7(BR)	Cat."B" 23-3-44
	JX 211	08-05-43	04-09-46	4(BR)	
MK4A	JX 212	08-05-43	27-08-46	7(BR) 3 OTU	
MK4	JX 213	08-05-43	08-08-46	7(BR)	Cat."D" 29-7-44 Alliford Bay
	JX 217	08-05-43	17-08-46	9(BR) 6BR	
	JX 293	10-12-42	21-08-46	9(BR)	
	JX 294	04-12-42	08-08-46	4(BR) 120 BR	
MK4A	JX 571	08-05-43	18-12-44	120(BR)	
	JX 572	08-05-43	17-05-46	6(BR)	
MK4A	JX 579	08-05-43	04-09-46	120(BR)	
MK4	JX 584	08-05-43	04-09-46	W.A.C.	Cat."C" 4-5-45 Pat Bay
	W8431	13-06-41	03-09-46	3 OTU	
	W8432	13-06-41	26-07-44	9(BR)	Cat."A" 16-6-44 Bella Bella
	Z2139			120(BR)	

ACCIDENTS RECORDED CONSOLIDATED CATALINA

Consolidated Catalina 4A JX207 7BR Sqd. 53.21N 131.56W **17-04-45** **Dead Tree Point, Queen Charlotte Islands**

Aircraft left Prince Rupert for Alliford Bay, with 21 aboard, and force-landed on sea off Dead Tree Point, Queen Charlottes, and drifted ashore during which aircraft was damaged. All occupants escaped unhurt and removable equipment was salvaged. Parts of wreck wedged in rocks still visible at low tide.

Pilot: F/O W.R. Whitby; Crew & Passengers: F/O W.E. Love, F/O H.F. Rogers, O'Connor, F/Sgt. R.M. Dionne, F/Sgt. D.H. Wilson, F/Sgt. G. Gorrie, F/Sgt. J. Camp, Sgt. W.S. Cooper, Sgt. R.E. Alcombrack, Cpl. P.F. McDougall, Cpl. G.G.H. Scott, LAC V.C. Tremola, LAC D.R. Richter, LAC A.D. McLean, LAC G.H. Weller, AC1 J.W. Currie

Consolidated Catalina 1 W8432 **16-06-44** **Near Bella Bella**

Few details. Cat. "A" crash.

CONSOLIDATED CANSO A

MFG#	RCAF#	T.O.S.	S.O.S.	Unit	Civil#	Remarks
282	9701	25-08-41	30-04-45	3 OTU 4(BR)		Cat."A" 12-2-45 Patricia Bay
283	9702	28-08-41	20-08-46	6(BR) 116 Sqdrn		
290	9709	17-09-41	11-08-45			W.A.C. Crash
	9742	02-11-42	05-09-46	7(BR)		Cat."B" crash
	9752	03-12-42	04-10-46	120(BR) 4(BR)		Also with No. 3 O.T.U. and 160 Sqdrn
	9753	08-02-43	22-08-46	120(BR)		Cat."B" crash
	9761	18-02-43	27-04-54	9(BR) 7(BR)		
	9762	18-02-43	03-10-46	3 OTU 6(BR)		Cat."B" crash
	9771	20-04-43	21-12-44	4(BR) 120(BR)		Also with No. 160 Sqdrn
	9784	20-04-43	16-02-46	7(BR)		Also 3 O.T.U. and 160 Sqdrn
	9785	28-04-43	04-10-46	160 Sqdrn 7(BR)		
	9786	28-04-43	24-09-44	7(BR) 160 6(BR)		Cat."A" crash 19-12-43 Prince Rupert Harbour
	9787	14-07-43	19-03-45	6(BR)		Cat."B" fire
	9788	28-04-43	20-08-46	6(BR) 7(BR) 4(BR)		
	9789	28-04-43	02-10-43	9(BR) 160 120(BR)		Cat."A" crash 30-7-43 Alarm Cove, Bella Bella
	9790	02-05-43	20-08-46	9(BR) 6(BR) 3 OTU		

At least 13 Canso As on ramp and moored at Pat Bay.
NAC PA136642

MFG#	RCAF#	T.O.S.	S.O.S.	Unit	Civil#	Remarks
	9792	02-05-43	01-10-46	120(BR) 3 OTU		
	9800	21-07-43	20-08-46	9(BR)		
	9801	26-07-43	08-09-45	4(BR)		
	9802	21-06-43	20-8-46	4(BR)		Cat."B" crash 12-7-43
	9803	01-07-43	04-09-46	7(BR)		Also 3 O.T.U.
	9804	15-07-43	21-12-44	4(BR)		
	9805	15-07-43	04-10-46	120(BR)		
CV260	9826	10-07-43	04-09-46	9(BR)		Cat"B" 18-12-44
CV261	9827	10-07-43	28-01-44	4(BR)		Crashed at Sitka, Alaska 5-12-43
CV262	9828	26-07-43	20-02-47	3 O.T.U.		Cat."B" crash 14-12-44
CV272	9838	20-09-43	31-10-46	3 O.T.U.		Cat."C" crash 25-03-45
CV281	11003	16-11-43	06-01-61	9 (BR)		
CV282	11004	25-10-43	18-11-46	7(BR)		
CV283	11005	27-10-43	25-05-61	9 (BR)		
CV284	11006	28-10-43	01-05-50	4(BR) 9(BR)		
CV285	11007	30-10-43	30-04-45	6(BR)7(BR)		Cat."A" crash 3 miles west of Tofino Airport
CV286	11008	04-11-43	01-05-50	3 OTU		Cat."A" crash
CV287	11009	05-11-43	04-10-46	3 OTU		At Patricia Bay
CV288	11010	06-11-43	07-05-47	7(BR)		Also 3 O.T.U. & 60 Sqdrn
CV289	11011	10-11-43	26-10-44	3 OTU		Cat."A", 4-8-44 Satellite Channel
CV290	11012	12-11-43	01-05-50	6(BR)		Cat."C", 26-9-44
CV291	11013	19-11-43	04-10-46	4(BR)		Cat."C", 11-6-42
CV292	11014	19-11-43	04-09-46	W.A.C.		Cat."C", 26-4-44 Pat Bay
CV293	11015	27-11-43	22-06-62	3 OTU	CF-FFX	Cat."C", 8-11-44
CV294	11016	27-11-43	20-08-46	4(BR)	CF-1HB	

MFG#	RCAF#	T.O.S.	S.O.S.	Unit	Civil#	Remarks
CV295	11017	27-11-43	11-01-45	4(BR)		Missing 14-11-44 (06-04-46 wreckage drifted ashore at Forrestor Island, Alaska)
CV296	11018	27-11-43	31-10-50	4(BR) 9(BR)		Cat."C", 21-9-44
CV297	11019	27-11-43	14-07-44	4(BR)		Cat."A", 9-6-44 Ucluelet Inlet
CV298	11020	03-12-43	04-10-46	7(BR)		Cat."B", 26-3-45
CV299	11021	03-12-43	19-08-46	3 OTU		
CV300	11022	04-12-43	10-01-45	3 OTU		Cat."A", 13-11-44
CV302	11024	07-12-43	20-10-61	3 OTU	CF-VAW	
CV303	11025	08-12-43	01-05-50	3 OTU		
CV312	11030	06-01-44	12-08-49	3 OTU		
CV313	11031	06-01-44	04-10-46	3 OTU		
CV314	11032	06-01-44	21-08-45	3 OTU		Cat."B" 02-29-44 Pat Bay converted to synthetic trainer
CV317	11035	16-01-44	06-07-49	3 OTU		
CV319	11037	16-01-44	19-08-46	3 OTU		Cat."C", 12-12-44

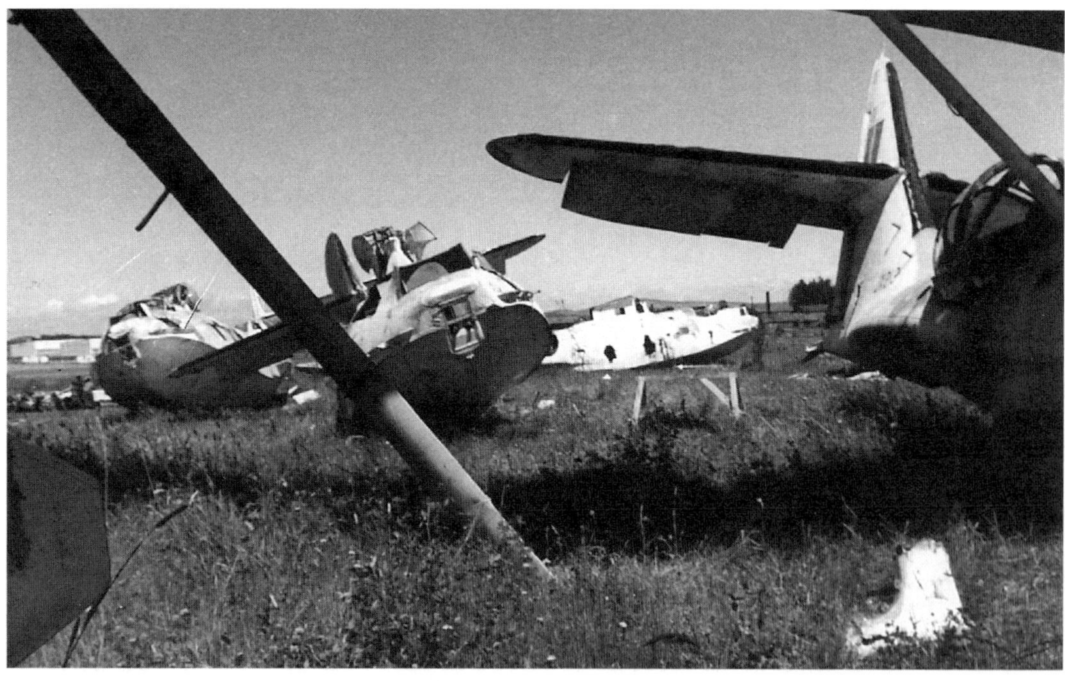

Catalinas being broken up at Pat Bay, 1952. JX 209 at front right formerly with 7(BR) Sqdrn. Schofield Collection

MFG#	RCAF#	T.O.S.	S.O.S.	Unit	Civil#	Remarks
CV320	11038	19-01-44	04-05-45	W.A.C.		Cat."B", 20-7-44
CV331	11041	12-02-44	12-07-59	3 OTU 6(BR)		Converted to freighter 29-08-48
CV335	11043	17-02-44	31-08-45	4(BR) 6(BR)		Cat."A", 31-07-45 Holberg Inlet
CV337	11044	18-02-44	22-12-44	4(BR)		
CV341	11046	24-02-44	24-10-52	W.A.C.		
CV351	11051	07-03-48	13-11-48			Cat."B", 14-4-48 Pat Bay
CV385	11068	20-04-44	04-10-46	3 OTU		
CV387	11069	22-04-44	24-08-50	3 OTU		Cat."B", 05-11-44 Destruction Island, Washington, USA
CV389	11070	23-04-44	24-10-52	6(BR), 3 OTU		
CV391	11071	14-04-44	01-05-50	3 OTU		
CV393	11072	29-04-44	04-10-46	3 OTU		
CV395	11073	30-04-44	22-12-55	3 OTU		Cat."A", 11-55 Johnstone Strait
CV415	11083	22-05-44	01-10-46	3 OTU	CF-FAR	Cat."C", 13-9-44
CV417	11084	24-05-44	26-09-61	3 OTU		
CV419	11085	27-05-44	07-10-46	3 OTU		Cat."C" 02-08-44
CV421	11086	29-05-44	05-06-45	3 OTU		Cat."A", 02-12-44 Night crash 5 miles north of Kennedy Lake
CV439	11095	02-01-45	23-08-55	Sea Island		Cat."A" crash 19-7-55 Sea Island
CV447	11099	03-07-44	14-05-51	W.A.C.		
CV449	11100	03-07-44	10-04-61	3 OTU	CF-NJP	

ACCIDENTS RECORDED BOEING I CANADIAN VICKERS CANSO

Canso A 9701 3 OTU **12-2-45** **Patricia Bay**
Few details. Cat."A" crash
Pilot: P/O R.B, Fraser (RCAF)- killed

Canso A 9786 7BR Sqd. **19-12-43** **Prince Rupert**
Few details. Aircraft crashed in water, broke up and partly burned.
Pilot: P/O E.S. Fereday - killed

Canso A 9789 9(BR) Sqd. **52.07N 128.07W** **30-7-43** **Llama Passage**

Aircraft left Bella Bella on patrol, with 9 aboard, and crashed into mountainside and burned at Alarm Cove, Llama Passage, Bella Bella. 8 crew survived, one missing. Status of wreck not given.

Pilot: P/O A.J, Joseph; Crew: F/Sgt. K.L. Brown, F/O R.B. Shirra, P/O L. Jones, W01 L.R. Travis, Sgt. H.A.S. Robinson, Sgt. E.A. Kewshaw, LAC W.J. Johnston, Sgt. J. Cowman- missing presumed dead.

Canso A 11007 6BR Sqd. **49.04.15N 125.4n'V** **08-02-45** **3 miles west of Tofino Airfield**

Aircraft left Tofino for Coal Harbour, with 12 aboard, but shortly after becoming airborne the engines stopped and the aircraft crash-landed 3 miles off the end of Runway 28. The occupants escaped. SAR notified wreck was to be salvaged by private party 21 February 1966, but recent reports indicate wreck still at site.

Pilot: F/O R.J. Scholes; Co-Pilot: F/O L.C. Laker; Crew & Passengers: F/O E.E, Knechtel, P/O C.C. Sartouris, W02 L.H. Malcomston, W02 J.B. Campbell, W02 C.H. Henningsen, F/Sgt. R.W. Hacker, Sgt. R.F. Bell, Sgt. W.A. Hooge, AW1 R.J. Pike, Mr. D.F. Marlett

Canso A 11011 3 OTU **48.43N 123.26W 92 B11** **04-08-44** **in Satellite Channel**

Aircraft, with 4 aboard, landed in Satellite Channel, the wingtip floats were damaged and the aircraft turned over. The crew escaped, but the aircraft was written off.

Pilot: F/O G.E. Cohoe; Crew: F/O N.T. Taylor, W02 C.F. Howe, Sgt. E.E. Ulvann

Canso A 11017 4BR Sqd. **app. 54.50N 133.32** **14-11-44** **Off Dixon Entrance**

Aircraft left Tofino on sea patrol, with 10 aboard, and disappeared without trace. On June 4, 1946, wreckage from the aircraft drifted ashore on the east side of Forrester Island, Southern Alaska. No trace of the crew was ever found.

Pilot: F/O G.E. Butler; Crew: F/O A.B. Georghe, F/O J.L. Westphal (WAG), F/O F.W.J. Lynam (Navigator), P/O M.H. Blesky (WAG), P/O J. Welsh, P/O G.F. Patterson (F.T.), F/Sgt. E.P. Gartley (Armourer), Sgt. R.C. Thomson (WAG), LAC E.G. Feil (Armourer)

Canso A 11019 4(BR) Sqd. **09-06-44** **Ucluelet Inlet**

Aircraft was returning from patrol when it crashed, killing the crew.

Pilot: F/LJ.G. Kee; Crew: P/O G.R. Morrison (Pilot), P/O E.O. Herlen (Flight Engineer), F/S J.C. Barfoot (Navigator), WO C.F. Coleman (WAG), Sgt. F.J. Wyatt (Flight Engineer), Sgt. A.E. Rydholm (WAG), Sgt. T.M. Edwards (WAG)

Canso A 11022 3 OTU **13-11-44**

Few details. Cat."A" crash

Canso A 11043 6(BR) Sqd. **31-07-45** **Holberg Inlet**

Few details. Cat."A" crash. Moving detachment from Prince Rupert to Coal Harbour, crashed one mile from entrance to Holberg Inlet.

Navigator: F/O B.G. Hamilton - killed

Catalina Z2139 on mooring buoy.
Schofield Collection

Canso A 11051 **14-04-48** **Patricia Bay**

Written off. Cat."B" crash.

Canso A 11070 3 OTU **47.40N 124.28** **05-11-44** **near Destruction Island Washington, USA**

Aircraft left Pat Bay, with 8 aboard, on navigational training flight and force-landed in vicinity of Destruction Island, USA. Crew escaped injury.,

Pilot: P/O A.A. Mackenzie; Crew: P/O W. Whelan, P/O J.H. Harris, Sgt. R.J. Milroy, Sgt. W.E. Whitelton, Sgt. J.C. Young, LAC J.V.M. Karouac, LAC C.I.M. Hilleby

Canso A 11073 **-11-55** **In Johnstone Strait**

Aircraft, with 19 aboard. crash-landed in Johnstone Strait. 16 survived and were picked up by vessel "Western Challenger".

Canso A 11086 3 OTU **49.09N 125.30W** **02-12-44** **5 miles off Kennedy Lake**

Aircraft left Pat Bay, with 9 aboard, on night navigation exercise and disappeared. Aircraft had crashed 5 miles north of Kennedy Lake, near top of 4,000 ft. mountain. Fire broke out and aircraft burned as far back as the mainwheels. All aboard were killed. Wreck was located on July 1, 1945, and the bodies were buried at the site marked by a white cross with names and date.

Pilot: F/O R.L. Nash; Crew: F/Lt. G.B.L. Ramsay, P/O L,O. Day, P/O A.I. Staples, P/O J.A. Mahoney, P/O F.F. Porter, Sgt. J.R.A. Trudel, Sgt. J.R.M. Patenaude, Sgt. R.W. Davidson

Canso A 11095 **19-7-55** **Sea Island**

Few details. Cat."A" crash

Seven Canso As lined up at Pat Bay awaiting ferry flight to Moose Jaw, Saskatchewan for storage, August 1, 1945. Canso #'s 9792, 11010, 11021, 11083, 11085, 11100, 11037. Schofield Collection

Three Canso As take off in formation, Pat Bay. D/HIST DND

Canso flies southbound along coast range on British Columbia coast. D/HIST DND

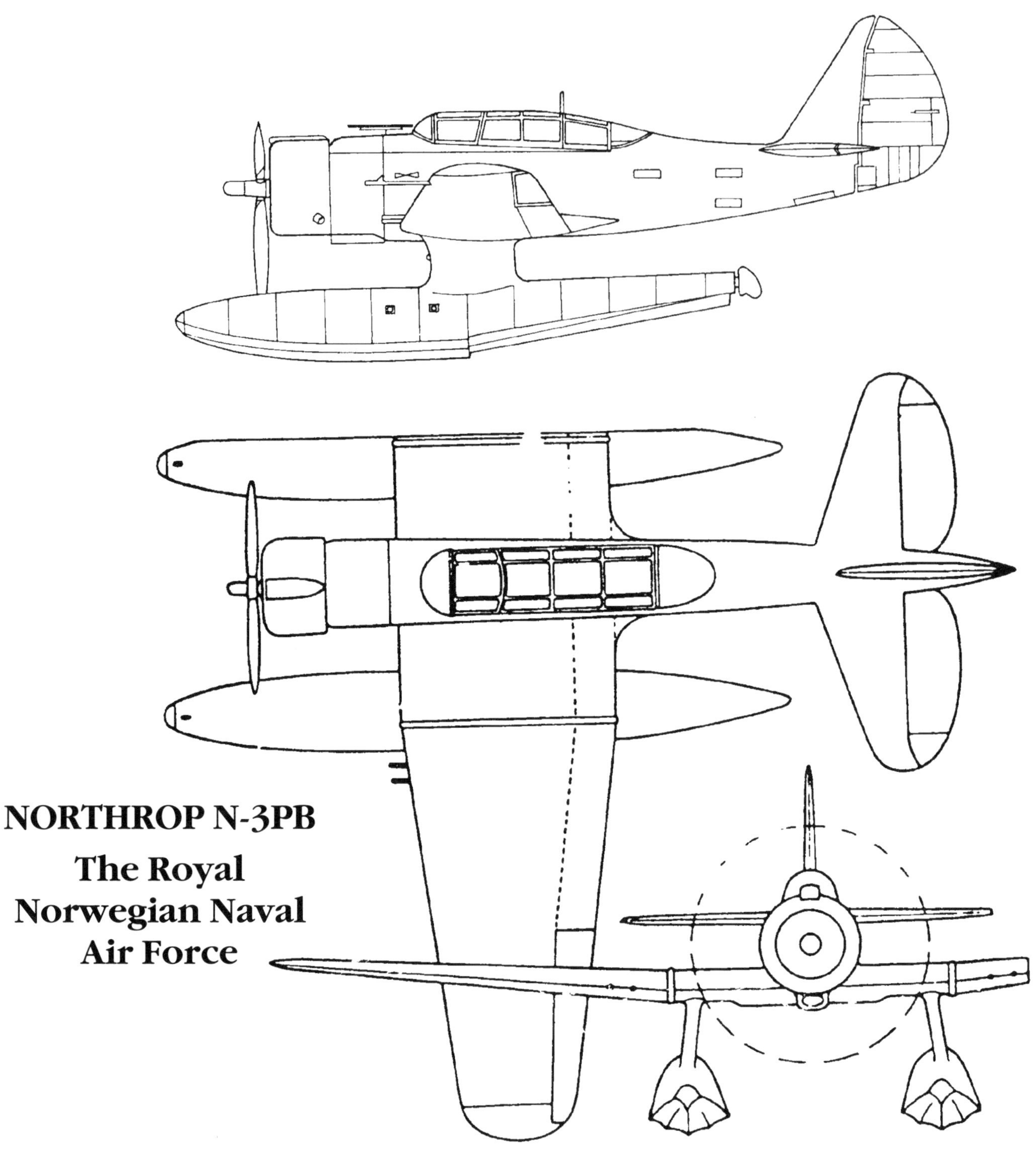

NORTHROP N-3PB

The Royal Norwegian Naval Air Force

In 1941 RCAF Vancouver (Jericho Beach) hosted the (RNNAF) Royal Norwegian Naval Air Force. The Norwegian pilots arrived at the Toronto Island Training Establishment in the late fall of 1941 to begin training on seaplanes. As the harsh Ontario winter approached they soon found that training was impossible. The RNNAF appealed to the RCAF for an ice-free location and were offered the facilities at Jericho Beach.

At the beginning of World War II, Norway chose to remain neutral. Nevertheless, the Norwegian government recognized that it was in the country's best interest to modernize Norway's airpower. Several orders for aircraft were placed with United States manufacturers, and discussions took place regarding a particular type of seaplane which could be used for both reconnaissance and attack.

The Norwegian Purchasing Commission decided on a model offered by the newly incorporated Northrop Aircraft Inc. at Hawthorne California. The company was formed by John K. Northrop after his departure from Douglas Aircraft Corporation in 1939. The Norwegian government's first contract with Northrop was signed on March 12, 1940 and production began on 24 single-engine, patrol-bomber seaplanes. The Norwegians requested that the N-3PB be constructed with a single pedestal float mount, which was an advanced feature at the time.

Germany marched into Norway on April 19, 1940, and forced the Norwegian government into exile. Determined to fight back in any way possible, the Norwegian government-in-exile sent pilots to Canada for flight training, which included seaplane conversion.

The first N-3PB rolled off the assembly line on December 30, 1940, and was assigned serial number 301. The initial N-3PBs were flown to Jericho Beach, via Portland, Oregon. On February 19, 1941, an entry in the station diary at Jericho Beach records that two N-3PBs were expected to arrive on that date. Between February 19 and March 5, 1941 six aircraft arrived in pairs: serial numbers 302 to 307.

Northrop #303 commenced a training flight on the afternoon of February 21, 1941 with student pilot Erling Jorgensen and his instructor, Sub-Lieutenant Harold Kruse. On take-off from Jericho Beach, the aircraft climbed to approximately 1000 feet and entered a dive, ending in a crash at Point Atkinson. The Northrop sank in 400 feet of water and both occupants were killed.

An eye-witness, J.H. MacDonald of Yew Street in Vancouver stated that the aircraft's engine was missing badly and it also appeared to have control problems before it crashed into the sea.

On March 17, the remaining five N-3PBs were relocated to RCAF Station Patricia Bay, near Victoria, to complete the pilot training syllabus. The students and the Northrops remained at the Pat Bay Station for twelve days and then they returned to Jericho Beach where the Northrops were dismantled and shipped by rail to Toronto.

On the second day of the training programme at Patricia Bay, #305 stalled shortly after take-off. The crash killed two of the three occupants of the Northrop. The unfortunate accidents were attributed to the Norwegians inexperience with the power and weight of a larger seaplane.

The Northrop N-3PB had an operational range of 1000 miles. It was powered by a single Wright "Cyclone" GR-1820 radial engine, which rated at 950 hp at sea level. The aircraft was mounted on two EDO single step floats which were attached to the machine by two fully-cantilevered, all-metal pedestals. The N-3PB carried a crew of three and was equipped with four fifty-caliber machine guns: two in each wing which were operated by the pilot, and one fifty caliber, (or thirty) in each of the upper or lower gun positions. It was also capable of carrying up to 2000 pounds of bombs, or a single torpedo.

NORTHROP N-3PB

PERFORMANCE DATA:

Maximum speed	220 mph	Range	1,000 miles
Cruising speed	217 mph	Empty weight	6,190 pounds
Landing speed	72 mph	Loaded weight	10,600 pounds
Ceiling	24,000 feet		

MFG#		Remarks
302	All N-3PB's arrived at Jericho between February 21 and March 5, 1941, then moved to Patricia Bay March 17, 1941.	Moved by rail to Toronto 20-06-41
303		21-02-41 Cat. "A" Point Atkinson - 2 fatalities
304		Moved by rail to Toronto 20-06-41
305		18-03-41 Cat. "A" Pat Bay - 2 fatalities
306		Moved by rail to Toronto 20-06-41
307		Cat. "A" 20-06-41 in collision with Toronto Island Ferry - 3 fatalities

N-3PB in California prior to delivery. CFB Comox Rowe Library

REFERENCES

Air Board: F.H. Hitchens; National Museum of Man, Ottawa

Aleutian Warriors, The: John Haile Cloe; 1990; Anchorage Chapter, Air Force Pictorial Histories Association & Publishing Co.

Arctic Pilot: W.E. Gilbert & Kathleen Shacklston; Thomas Nelson & Sons

Aviation In Canada: Larry Milberry; 1979; McGraw-Hill Ryerson

Barnstorming to Bush Flying: Peter Corley Smith; 1989; Sono Nis Press

Boeing, An Aircraft Album Number 4: Kenneth Munson & Gordon Swanborough; 1972

Bush Pilots, The: J.A. Foster; McClelland & Stewart Inc.

Canada's Aviation Pioneers: Alice Gibson Sutherland; 1978; McGraw-Hill Ryerson

Canada's Flying Heritage: Frank H. Ellis; 1954; University of Toronto Press

Canada's National Aviation Museum: K.M. Molson; 1988; National Museum of Science and Technology

Canada's War In The Air: Leslie Roberts; 1942; Alvah M. Beatty Publications

Canada's Wings Volume 1. The Blackburn Shark: Carl Vincent; 1985; Canada's Wings Inc., Sittsville, Ontario

Canadian Aeronautics: G.A. Fuller/J.A. Griffin/K.M.Molson; 1983; Canadian Aviation Historical Society, Ottawa

Canadian Aircraft Since 1909: K.M. Molson & H.A. Taylor; 1982; Canada's Wings Inc., Sittsville, Ontario

Canadian Airmen Of The First World War: S.F. Wise; 1980; University of Toronto Press

Canadian Civil Aircraft Register (1920 - 1945): John R. Ellis; 1972

Canadian Flying Services Emblems and Insignia 1914-1984: Bill Hampson; published by author

Canadian Military Aircraft Serials and Photographs 1920-1968; J.A. Griffin; 1969; Canadian War Museum

Creation of a National Air Force, The: W.A.B. Douglas; 1986; University of Toronto Press

De Havilland Aircraft since 1909: A.J. Jackson; 1987; Naval Institute Press

December 1941 America's First 25 Days at War: Donald J. Young; 1992; Pictorial Histories Publishing Co. Inc.

Early Flying In British Columbia, In Retrospect: Earl MacLeod; 1972

General Dynamics Aircraft: John Wegg; 1990; Naval Institute Press

In Canadian Skies: Frank H. Ellis; 1959; Ryerson Press

Janes All The World's Aircraft: C.G. Grey; Sampson Low & Marston: 1919

Janes All The World's Aircraft: C.G. Grey; Sampson Low & Marston & Co. Ltd.: 1927

Janes All The World's Aircraft: C.G. Grey & Leonard Bridgman; Sampson Low & Marston & Co. Ltd.: 1938

Janes All The World's Aircraft: Leonard Bridgman; MacMillan Co.: 1935; 1941; 1944

Janes Encyclopedia Of Aviation: Michael Taylor; 1980; Portland House

Japan's World War II Balloon Bomb Attacks On North America: R.C. Mikesh; 1973; Smithsonian Institution Press

Magnificent Distances, The: Dennis Duffy & Carol Crane; 1980; British Columbia Provincial Archives

Marine Atlas Volume 2, Port Hardy to Skagway: Frank Morris & W.R. Heath; 1959; Bayless Enterprises

REFERENCES

Number 120 Bomber Reconnaissance Squadron: A.J.D. Angus (recollections)

Pioneering Aviation In The West: Lloyd Bungey; 1992; Hancock House

Recovery Of A Secret Weapon, The: Ray E. Woolston (recollections)

Royal Canadian Air Force At War, 1939-1945: Larry Milberry and Hugh Halliday; 1990; CANAV Books

Royal Canadian Air Force Station Ucluelet, Recollections: Eric Stofer; 1995; published by Author

Royal Canadian Air Force Squadrons and Aircraft: S. Kostenuk & J. Griffin; 1977; Historical Publication 14, Canadian War Museum, National Museum of Man, Ottawa; Samuel Stevens Hakkert & Co, Toronto & Sarasota

Seaplanes And Flying Boats, An Illustrated History Of: Maurice Allward; Dorset Press

Seaplanes And Flying Boats, The Illustrated History Of: Louis S. Casey & John Batchelor; Phoebus Publishing Co. Ltd.

Sixty Years, The RCAF and CF Air Command 1924-1984: Larry Milberry; 1984; CANAV Books

Snowbird Decades, The: William Paul Ferguson; 1979; Butterworth & Co.

Sunk: Mochitsura Hashimoto; 1954; Avon Publications Inc.

There Shall Be Wings: Leslie Roberts; 1959; Clarke Irwin & Co. Ltd.

Thousand Mile War, The: Brian Garfield; 1969; Bantam Books

Zero, Japans Air War In The Pacific, 1941-1945: Masatake Okumiya, Jiro Horikoshi, Martin Cadin; 1956; Ballantine Books Inc.

PERIODICALS:

Canadian Aviation Historical Society Journal
(Winter 1972): The Canadian Vickers Vedette; K.M Molson
(Spring 1972): The Curtiss HS-2L in RCAF/CAF Service; Ingwald Wikene
(Summer 1965): The Delta Story; E.P. (Paddy) Gardiner
(Summer 1995): "Mawdie"; J.D. "Jack" Hunter

High Flight (Volume 2, Number 4): Canadian Vickers Vedette in the RCAF; Carl Vincent

High Flight (Volume 3, Number 2): Flying Forest-Fire Fighter, The Story of Canadian Vickers Varuna; Carl Vincent

High Flight (Volume 2, Number 4): Canadian Vickers Vedette In The RCAF; Carl Vincent

Roundel: (RCAF Station Bella Bella, First Edition, Volume 1, Number 7): Managing Editor Sgt L.G. Laramee; 1942; published by permission of Wing Commander D.E. Galloway

Roundel: (Second Edition, in existence after World War II) Published by authority of Chief of Air Staff RCAF

NEWSPAPER CLIPPINGS:

All Jericho newspaper clippings courtesy of Canadian Forces Vancouver Detachment CFB Chilliwack, and British Columbia District Headquarters Public Affairs Officer, Captain Dan Thomas, C.D.

LINE DRAWINGS:

Courtesy of Carl Vincent: Blackburn Shark, C.V. Varuna, C.V. Vedette, C.V. Viking.

Courtesy of Paddy Gardner: Northrop C.V. Delta.

FIRST LOVE - "FLIGHT"

Chris Weicht, the son of a serving RAF officer, was born in London, England in 1935. At the outbreak of World War Two and the beginning of Hitler's blitzkrieg against London, five year old Christopher was among the thousands of children evacuated from the city. He was sent to Coventry, a supposedly safe haven which sadly proved to be otherwise. A bomb hit the house where Chris was billeted and several children were killed.

After a series of refugee-like moves to various volunteer care homes in the English countryside, Christopher's father enrolled him in a fundamentalist boarding school founded for the education of the sons of military officers. Located in Monmouthshire, the school was without heat, electricity or running water. This was meant to emphasize fortitude, self-discipline and resourcefulness, and was supported by a curriculum which encouraged personal integrity and a belief in God, King and Country. Indiscretions were not tolerated and were rewarded by the energetic use of the cane.

At the end of the war, and on the return of Christopher's father from a tour of duty in South East Asia, the family emigrated to Canada. They arrived at Vancouver, British Columbia in 1948 and, their fortunes being meagre, stayed for a time in the back of a Robson Street beauty parlour operated by his aunt. His father quickly found employment as an Editor of two Fraser Valley newspapers and moved his family to a small cottage on forty acres of rural land in Port Coquitlam.

In 1949 Chris joined 513 Squadron of the Royal Canadian Air Cadets at New Westminster, where he rose through the ranks to Warrant Officer, and, in 1952, received a flight training scholarship. Chris had a determined plan to establish a career in aviation, which led him to enlist in the RCAF at Jericho Beach in 1953.

In 1956 he accepted a position with Pacific Western Airlines at Vancouver, and later served on DEW line operations in the North West Territories. A vision problem became a temporary setback, but Chris elected to use the opportunity to continue his academic studies. He enrolled in a business administration program in 1960, and four years later the new graduate was given a management position with a Vancouver based oil company. His deep desire to fly never left him - his office desk became the most challenging piece of equipment he had ever flown.

In 1967, following three years of persistent effort, Chris returned to active aviation as a pilot at Fort St. John, B.C., flying forestry contracts. During the 1970s he flew for several west coast airlines and corporate flight departments, gaining valuable experience on an interesting variety of amphibious and wheel aircraft - Super Cub, Grumman Goose, Mitsubishi MU-2, Westwind Jet and many others.

In 1980 Chris became the Chief Pilot for a B.C. based manufacturing company, but over the next few years the economy gradually closed down their aviation department. His flexibility was challenged again, and he remained with the firm in a sales capacity, using his free time

About Christopher Weicht

to instruct Air Cadets of 861 Squadron at Abbotsford, B.C. He became the Commanding Officer of the Squadron in 1982, and was promoted to Captain.

In 1983 he founded a scholarship program that gave young people an opportunity to experience the joy of flying. The Ultra Light Flight Training Scholarship was awarded to 65 teenagers, many of whom are now actively employed in aviation.

In 1985 he took the position of Operations Manager and Chief Pilot for a recently formed First Nations Airline operating out of Vancouver and Bella Bella. In 1987 Chris took on a project to promote and fly charter flights for a lower mainland corporation. He had the pleasure of flying with his son as his co-pilot, and together they flew corporate charter flights all over North America. The '90s brought Chris back in touch with the Air Cadet movement, and he spent three summers flying a tow plane for the Cadet glider program at CFB Penhold, Alberta.

At present he and his wife live in Chemainus on Vancouver Island where Chris flies for a Nanaimo based airline and pursues his interest in recording aviation history. Over the course of a lifetime career in aviation, Chris has flown over 14,000 hours in more than 50 different types of aircraft and has met many of the dynamic personalities who have played a significant role in the evolution of aviation in western Canada.

About Michael Dean, cover artist

Michael Dean was born at Lancashire, England in 1948, emigrating to Vancouver, British Columbia, in 1972. Dean later moved to Cortes Island where he quickly developed an insatiable fascination with British Columbia's coastal history and the workboats, tugs as well as classic vessels, that ply the waterfront.

Now living in Ladysmith on Vancouver Island, Michael has opened a home/studio and, fortunately for the public, many of his original works on display in the studio gallery are available as prints.

More recently Dean has become intrigued with coastal aircraft and the intrepid breed of flyers who have been part of the west coast scene for over eighty years. His sensitive interpretation of the scene at Jericho Beach on the damp winter morning of January 6, 1925 draws us into the preparation for launching the HS-2L out onto the cold, rippled surface of English Bay.

INDEX

INDEX

INDEX

INDEX